Red Guide to WALES

Printed in Great Britain by
Cox & Wyman Limited
London, Fakenham and Reading

RED GUIDE

Edited by Reginald J. W. Hammond

The Complete
ALES

*A survey of the main
holiday areas and
places of interest*

WARD LOCK & CO., LIMITED
London and Melbourne

Maps and Plans

Contents

CONTENTS

CONTENTS

Illustrations

8

THE PEOPLE AND THE LAND OF WALES

by Patrick Macnaghten

It is not an unusual experience to see the stern and sombre countryside of Wales explode into joyous beauty between one corner and the next. And the beauty of Wales is no sudden flash, swiftly fading. It breaks upon you dramatically, and then is sustained for mile after sweeping mile until, abruptly, you come to a place so exquisite that Man has had to render it hideous with nasty little souvenir shops and ice-cream wrappings and cigarette packets.

Then is the time to turn away and, as quickly as you came to it, you leave the "beauty spot" behind and once again you are in solitary, lovely country following a lonely mountain road or edging your way down some forgotten lane beside a secret stream. The fact that after you have opened about fourteen gates (do please shut them after you, or the sheep will soon be half-way across the next county) you end up in a farmyard matters not at all. If you are really in luck the farmer's wife who comes out to give you good-day will be wearing the national costume of shiny witch's hat and cloak and long, wide skirt almost hiding her sensible boots. But this is getting rarer; television, radio and the shiny, if not the glossy, magazines are sweeping Wales into the twentieth century. Not completely, though; at least, if they are, it is strictly a Welsh twentieth century. National pride burns strongly and the Welsh language is not only a living tongue, it is one which is thriving strongly. The Welsh have always been a proud independent race and they have every intention of remaining proud, independent—and, above all, Welsh.

There may be a nuclear power station on the shores of Lake Trawsfynydd, the villages of the Elan valley may have been submerged beneath waters of a string of reservoirs for

9

the sake of the people of Birmingham, but Wales is still very much the country of Gelert and Owen Glendower. The women of Wales are the lineal descendants of those who arose with flailing broomsticks to beat off what they thought was Napoleon's invasion. It was all a muddle, really, but the spirit was fierce and true and it still is today.

They are a well-mannered, hospitable people and they find it quite gratifying that tourists come and rave about the beauties of their country. But they have jobs to do and they want to get on with them. You won't find many Welshmen on the pleasure beaches. But if you want to discover the Welsh way of life get away into the solitude of the mountains or turn from the busy towns into the austere little villages clustered round the pitheads. The choice is yours—that is what this book is for.

Archaeology and History

If the aphorism that "happy is the country which has no history" were true Wales would be one of the unhappiest countries on earth.

When the Ice Age at last began to melt and give way to the Old Stone Age the population of Wales consisted of such forbidding animals as mammoth, hyena, cave-bear and caveman. There have been rich archaeological finds in north Flintshire and at Perthichwareu and Rhos Ddigre near Llanarmon-yr-Iâl in Denbighshire as well as farther south at Coygan Cave in Carmarthenshire, Paviland Cave in Gower and Monkton Cave in Pembrokeshire.

The Middle Stone Age, characterised by the making of small flint implements by coastal dwellers, has yielded finds at Aberystwyth, at Burry Holm in Gower and at Nab Head and other places in Pembrokeshire.

The Neolithic, or New Stone Age was the period when Man first began to domesticate animals and to cultivate grain. Their implements were generally finely ground and polished and often attached to hafts. At Tre'r Ceiri there is a fascinating site dating from this period and one can gain a very good idea of how these people lived by visiting it (*see* p. 136). Some years ago a most important find was made at Craig Lwyd on the slopes of Penmaenmawr. It must have been a sort of factory for the fashioning of implements because implements which were made there have been found in many other parts of the country, indicating that there was quite a trade in them.

The Neolithic Age extended from about 2500 B.C. to about 2000 B.C. and there is still evidence of it for all to see in the

shape of Cromlechs (Welsh, Cromlechau). They are chambered tombs capped with enormous stones some of which are still standing, notably that at Clynnog Fawr in Caernarvonshire. A list of over forty cromlechs is given in a publication issued by the National Museum of Wales, *The Megalithic Monuments of Wales* by W. F. Grimes. Cromlechs are often mistaken for Druid's altars and the issue is further confused by the many masses of stone which were deposited by the glaciers of the Ice Age; years of weathering have often given them the appearance of having been shaped by hand.

The fifteen hundred years of the Bronze Age, up to about 500 B.C. has left many traces in Wales. Bronze shields have been found near Harlech and the Dovey estuary and in a peat bog at Moel Siabod in Caernarvonshire while whole hoards of bronze articles are occasionally brought to light. During the digging of a drain at Guilsfield in Montgomeryshire 10 spear-heads, 12 spear-shaft ferrules and over 30 other objects—or fragments of them—including axes and swords were found. At Corston in Pembrokeshire a dagger was found with part of its wooden handle still intact. But the Bronze Age folk did not only make weapons of war; they applied their knowledge of melting, if not actually of smelting, metal to peaceful purposes and quite a lot of pottery has been found—such things as beakers, food vessels and cinerary urns.

Relics of the Iron Age (from about 500 B.C. to about 50 A.D.) include bronze as well as iron. A tankard of bronze-plated wood was found at Trawsfynydd and the sand dunes of Merthyr Mawr have yielded iron slag, crucibles and a bronze brooch. There are a number of Iron Age forts dotted about and exciting finds are still being made. If you should have the luck to find some relic of pre-history please don't throw it away—any one of the museums would be glad to have it. They are: The National Museum of Wales, The Royal Institution, Swansea, The Town Museum, Tenby, The museum of the Carmarthenshire Antiquarian Society at Carmarthen and that of the Brecknock Society at Brecon.

Wales was conquered by the Romans between 50 and 75 A.D. and they established fortresses from which they controlled this frontier district of the Roman Empire. In the north the most important was Deva (now Chester) but there are Roman sites at Segontium (Caernarvon), Caersws near Newtown and at Tomen-y-Mur near Trawsfynydd. The results of excavation at Segontium are housed in a museum built for them at Caernarvon.

The depot works of the XXth Roman Legion was at Holt, near Wrexham and unused building materials—bricks, drain-pipes and tiles—have been found there. In the south a base fortress was established at Caerleon where an amphitheatre gives a glimpse of what life was like in Roman times. There is also a museum—the Legionary Museum—at Caerleon which houses many things discovered in the vicinity.

The Romans do not seem to have interfered very much with the life of the natives and the two civilisations went on side by side, with the Romans living in their centrally heated barracks and the natives living in clusters of huts. Traces of the hut settlements have been found at Caer Drewyn near Corwen, near Llanaber in Merionethshire and near Llanbrynmair in Montgomeryshire. There is an excellent book on Prehistoric and Roman Wales by R. E. M. Wheeler and the Ordnance Survey map of Roman Britain is a great help when seeking out these sites.

In the twilight of civilisation between the departure of the Romans and the coming of the Normans very little is known of the history of Wales but there is evidence—in the shape of carved stone crosses such as those at Merthyr Mawr, Llantwit-Major and Margam in Glamorgan and at Carew in Pembrokeshire—that Christianity came to Wales during this period.

When the Romans came to Wales they found it occupied by two types of Celt, the stronger and more numerous tribes being "Brythons"—Britons. The Germanic tribes who came to the country after the Romans left gradually drove the Britons westwards into the mountains and referred to them as *Wealhas*, which meant foreigners. To the Anglo-Saxons everybody west of the Marches was a foreigner and so the name Wealhas was applied to the whole country and ultimately became corrupted into "Wales".

William the Conqueror began the systematic subjugation of Wales by settling barons along its frontier but it was not until the victories of Edward I and the death of Llewelyn, Prince of Wales in 1282, that the country was finally annexed to England. A couple of hundred years later the Welsh were satisfied that an ancient prophesy that they should once again rule their own land had come true. For Henry Tudor, King of England and Wales, was a nobleman of Welsh descent.

The destruction or damage which many Welsh castles can be seen to have suffered took place during the Civil War when they were beseiged by the Parliamentary troops. Wales was predominantly on the side of the Royalists.

There is one small part of the Principality whose history branches off in Norman times—that part of southern Pembrokeshire known as "Little England Beyond Wales". This is where the followers of William the Conqueror had some success and they settled their tiny gains with Flemings, refugees from the flooding of the Low Countries. They were reinforced in the time of Henry the Second who brought Flemish soldiers to settle in Wales and interspersed them with Englishmen in order that they should learn to speak English. To this day they have not been entirely assimilated into the country and most true Celts still secretly regard them as Giraldus Cambriensis did—"the plague of Dyved and South Wales on account of their deceit and lies". But they are far too polite to say so.

14

Scenery and Geology

The dramatic scenery of North Wales with its steep mountains, its deep and sudden gorges, its U-shaped valleys and its ripple of sand-dunes is mute evidence of an age-long and complicated process of geological evolution, itself as dramatic as the result.

It is an area of very old rocks squeezed by the compression of the earth's crust and etched by the erosive forces of wind and rain and frost. The highest parts of North Wales, Snowdonia and Cader Idris, consist largely of volcanic rock or of crystalline (igneous) rock which, when it was molten, cooled beneath the earth's surface instead of erupting from it in the form of volcanoes.

In the north of Cardiganshire and Merionethshire, although the mountains rise steeply to nearly 3,000 feet the skyline seen from Cader Idris or the Arans looks astonishingly even. All the higher peaks look uniform, as if they were a hedge clipped by a giant. In fact they were once a plateau, a couple of thousand feet above sea-level, which has been gnawed away by streams and rivers so that now it is a series of highlights divided by gorges with waterfalls and cascades.

In simple terms, this is how it all came about. In early times (geologically speaking, which means very early indeed) the sea covered this part of the earth's surface. Upon its bed collected a sediment of layers of sand and mud interspersed with layers of lava and volcanic ash. The seething gurgling birth-pangs of the world (known to geologists as the Devonian period) caused it to be thrown up as a mountain mass and the first stage of erosion began. But then, aeons later, it sank beneath the sea once more and the pounding of the waves blunted the sharp edges. Then up it came again —it may even be that the process recurred—and finally the second (or maybe the third) stage of erosion delineated the landscape which formed the skeleton of central Wales.

Then came the Ice Age. Great glaciers gouged out valleys in the U-shape of the Cresta Run, like Llanberis and Nant Ffrancon while ice-sheets planed the plateaux—but rather inefficiently because they left scratches and furrows which can still be seen on the rock surfaces of the hills. Over the subsequent ages nature clothed the starkness with soil and plant-life to give us the beauty which we see today. But it all took an awful long time.

Throughout Wales the mineral deposits are rich. There is gold in them thar hills above Dolgellau. Three and four hundred years ago they got a lot of silver and lead out of the country behind Aberystwyth. Then there is the slate; the soft rocks, of the nature of clay, were obligingly compressed into this substance which makes such excellent roofs and it is still quarried, notably at Llanberis, Blaenau Ffestiniog and Nantlle. But slate quarries and slagheaps are hideous. So, of course, are coal mines and iron foundries but the industrial area of Wales is compact and circumscribed and when you are scrambling about under the limestone cliffs of Pembrokeshire you might be a thousand miles from Swansea.

Welsh Place-names

The seeming jumble of letters which go to make up place-names in Wales are often, in reality, vividly descriptive.

ABER, the place where a river discharges into the sea or into another river.

AFON, a river.

ALLT, a cliff, or side of a hill.

BACH (or FACH), little.

BANC, platform, tableland.

BECHAN or (FECHAN), small—the lesser.

BEDD, a grave (beddau, graves).

BLAEN, extremity or beginning: used as a prefix in the name of a place at the head of a valley.

BOD (or FOD), a dwelling-place.

BONT (or PONT), bridge.

BORTH (or PORTH), a port or gate.

BRITH, spotted, mottled.

BRON, the slope of a hill.

BRYN, a mound or hill.

BWLCH (or FWLCH), a pass or gap.

BYCHAN (or FYCHAN), small—the lesser.

CAE, an enclosed field.

CAER (or GAER), a camp or fortress.

CANOL (or GANOL), the middle one.

CARN (or GARN), a prominence.

CAPEL (or GAPEL), a chapel.

CASTELL, a castle or fortress.

CAU (or GAU), fenced or enclosed.

CEFN, a ridge.

CELLI (or GELLI, sometimes GELLY), a grove or copse.

CIL, a recess or retreat.

COCH (or GOCH), red.

COED (or GOED), a wood.

CORS (or GORS), a bog or marshy place.

CRAIG (or GRAIG), a crag.

CRIB (CRIBYN), comb, crest, or summit.

CROES (or GROES), a cross.

CRUG (or GRUG), a heap or mound (e.g. Crickhowell, for Crughywel).

CWM, valley.

16

CYMMER, a junction or confluence.
DIN (or DINAS), a town or hill-fort.
DREF (or DRE), a dwelling-place or village.
DU (or DDU), black.
DWFR (or DWR), water.
DYFFRYN, vale or valley.
EGLWYS, a church.
ESGAIR, a long ridge.
FACH, little.
FAEN, a stone.
FAES, a field.
FAN, a fence.
FAWR, great, large.
FELIN, mill.
FFORDD, way, road.
FFRIDD, a plantation.
FFYNNON, a well or spring.
FOEL, a bare hill.
FYNYDD, a mountain.
GAER, a camp or fortress.
GARN, a prominence.
GARTH, hill or headland.
GELLI, a grove or copse.
GLAN (or LAN), a bank or shore.
GLAS (or LAS), blue (if water), green (if fields).
GLYN, a glen.
GOCH, red.
GOED, a wood.
GOITRE, a home in the wood (from COED and TRE).
GRAIG, a crag.
GROES, a cross.
GWAITH, work.
GWAUN (or WAUN), a common or moor.
GWERN (or WERN), a swamp or bog.
GWYN (or WYN), white.
HAFOD, a summer dwelling: in olden times this signified a hill-residence used during the summer, in contrast to the main homestead, *Hendref* or *Hendre*, in the valley, occupied during the winter months.
HEN, old.
HIR, long.
ISAF, lowest.
LLAN, primarily an enclosure; its secondary meaning is a sacred enclosure or churchyard—hence the present meaning, a church.

LLECH, a flat stone.
LLWYD, grey, sometimes venerable.
LLWYN, a grove.
LLYN, a lake.
LLYS, a court or hall.
MAEN (or FAEN), a stone.
MAES (or FAES), an open field, in contrast to a closed field, CAE.
MAN (or FAN), a place.
MAWR (or FAWR), great, large.
MELIN (or FELIN), a mill.
MERTHYR, a martyr.
MOEL (or FOEL), a bare hill.
MWYN, a mine, ore.
MYNACH, a monk.
MYNYDD (or FYNYDD), a mountain.
NANT, a brook.
NEUADD, a hall.
NEWYDD, new.
OGOF, a cave.
PANDY, a fulling mill (used in wool manufacture).
PANT, a hollow place, a valley.
PEN, head, or top.
PISTYLL, a spouting waterfall.
PONT (or BONT), a bridge.
PORTH (or BORTH), a port or gate.
PWLL, a pool, pit, or hollow.
RHAIADR, waterfall or cataract (in English, often spelt Rhayader).
RHIW, a slope, or ascent.
RHOS, an open moor.
RHUDD, reddish.
RHYD, a ford.
RHYG, rye.
SARN, a causeway.
SYCH, dry.
TAL, a headland, brow of hill.
TIR (or DIR), land-soil.
TRE (or DRE), a dwelling-place or village.
TREF (or DREF), same as TRE.
TŶ (or DŶ), a house.
TYDDYN, tenement or smallholding.
UCHAF, higher, highest.
UWCH, above.
WAUN, a common or moor.
WERN, a swamp or bog.
WYN (WEN), white.
Y, YR, the, of the.
YN, YM, in.
YNYS, island.
YSTRAD, low flat land by a river.
YSTWYTH, winding, flexible.

Routes in Wales

Car journeys in Wales always take you much longer than one thinks they are going to. So often you set off intending to do a set run and find that, by sunset, you are only half-way round your circuit and have to scuttle back by the shortest route. There are several reasons, practical and emotional. The practical reasons are that although Welsh roads are, if they have surfaces at all, astonishingly well-surfaced, they are almost never straight and level. The corners, the switchbacks, the cross-roads crowd so closely on one another that a motorist sometimes has the impression of trying to drive through a maze set in a choppy sea. Accelerating, changing up, braking, changing down, cornering, appear to merge into a continuous process—at least they do if one is trying to keep to a schedule. But nobody in his senses tries to keep to a schedule on a holiday. And the driver who is more interested in putting impressions in an hour than miles is welcomed with open arms by Wales.

Another purely practical reason against attempting to hurry is that so many Welsh roads traverse mountains. They are finely engineered and there are less steep hills than one might think but this is bought at the price of loops and turns and hairpin bends which would make a snake slip a disc. Also mountain roads tend to be on ledges with unresilient outcrops of rock on one side and hundreds of feet of absolutely nothing on the other.

Gates and wandering sheep. Wales is richly endowed with both.

The greater part of the Principality is an enchanting playground. One must expect, therefore, that its roads will be full of motorists out to enjoy themselves and more attentive to the scenery than the traffic. As for the inhabitants, farmers going to market do not drive—and God bless them for it—like commuters in the suburban rush hour. A very small, very compact and very important part of Wales is highly industrialised. The road traffic of commerce behaves differently from the road traffic of pleasure but the driver who deliberately thrusts you out of the way is just as menacing as the ambler who hasn't seen you at all.

So much for the practical reasons for driving slowly with the mental antennae alertly waving. The emotional reasons are simpler but no less cogent. It is a country of such beauty that it is a sin not to stop and drink it all in when you have the chance. I do so agree with W. H. Davies, the Welsh poet.

> "A poor life this if, full of care,
> We have no time to stand and stare"

provided, of course, we are sufficiently full of care to park well off the road while we do it.

Wales is a country which contains a little of everything but not too much of anything. The country can be roughly divided into seven unequal areas, each of which has a somewhat different appeal.

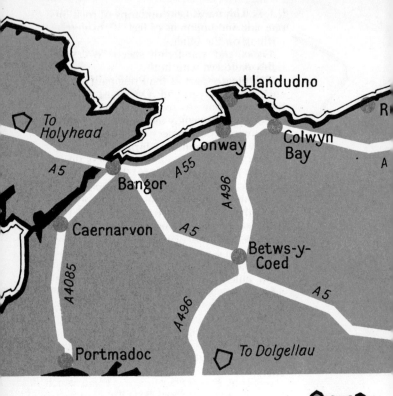

To Holyhead

A5

Bangor

A55

Caernarvon

A5

A4085

A4096

Portmadoc

Llandudno

Conway

Colwyn
Bay

R

A

A496

Betws-y-
Coed

A5

To Dolgellau

**The North Coast
and Anglesey**

20

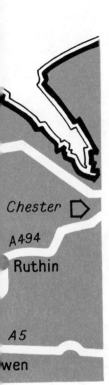

Chester ▷

A494

Ruthin

A5

wen

1. The north coast. The 20-mile stretch of coastline from Prestatyn to Llandudno is virtually one long sandy beach, very popular, very populous—a sort of Costa Brava of Wales. A sharp contrast to this seething gaiety can be found only 5 miles or so from Colwyn Bay, on the eastern side of the Conway estuary. For here lies Bodnant, the exquisite gardens which have been lovingly created by four generations of Lord Aberconway's family. The fifty acres of perfection provide breath-taking distant views and as the gardens sweep down a hillside in a series of magnificent terraces the closer views entail a great deal of breath-taking too. But what splendid exercise after sitting in a car all day!

On up the Conway valley, you can cross the river a dozen miles to the south and make for Betws-y-Coed, Capel Curig and the glory of the Swallow Falls. Or from Capel Curig you can trundle up the busy A5 to Bangor and across the Menai Strait to—

2. Anglesey. A5, the London–Holyhead road, bisects the Isle of Anglesey and as soon as you turn off it, to north or south you enter a network of narrow roads which meander through gently undulating grasslands with hardly a tree in sight.

Anglesey is like a plain self-coloured carpet with a bright and beautiful border. The little bays on the north-east and south-west sides of the island have beaches as good as any on the mainland coast but you have to go and look for them. Not many people bother, so if you like the sand to yourself it is worth taking the trouble.

21

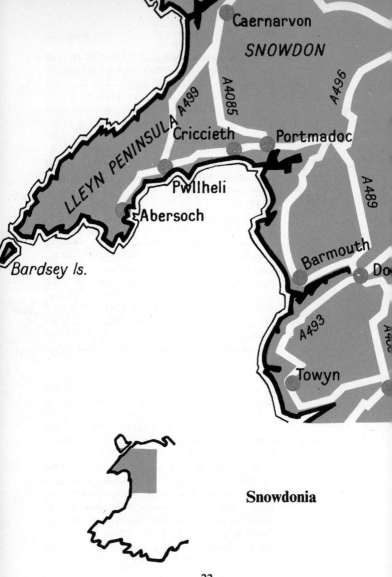

Snowdonia

Llanrwst

Betws-y-Coed
A5

langollen

Bala

A94

L.Vyrnwy

au

458

084

chynlleth

3. Northern Snowdonia. Utterly different from Anglesey is that part of Wales which points like an accusing finger out into the Irish Sea. It contains everything from Snowdon to sand dunes, from Caernarvon Castle to Portmeirion, that fantastic collection of architecture formed over a lifetime by Clough Williams Ellis. There is nothing quite like Portmeirion anywhere in the world but each chunk of building, whether wonderful or whimsical, is reminiscent of a style of somewhere else—anywhere but Wales.

All the little towns in this area are full of bustling life and there isn't a square inch to park a car—and if there is, somebody swoops into it before you can say Penrhyndeudrath. Curiously, though, the great stretch of sand, known as Black Rock, just outside Portmadoc, seems to attract fewer people than its attractions warrant; perhaps they all go to Pwllheli.

Snowdon is circumscribed, at a respectful distance, by a narrow road of great scenic splendour. The Pass of Llanberis is one of the most spectacular mountain roads in Britain and worth—just—driving over although the driver has no eye to spare for the scenery. Almost as lovely and far less crowded is—

4. Southern Snowdonia, on the borders of Merioneth and Montgomeryshire and if you tire of mountains there are two big lakes, Bala and Vyrnwy, with roads running right round them. In this part there are not quite so many walls flanking the roads so it is somewhat easier to find somewhere to pull off and park.

23

The West Coast

To Portmadoc   To L

A496

A487

A494

Barmouth

Dolgellau

A493

A487

A4084

Ma

A4

Towyn

Machynlleth

A487

A487

A44

Llanid

Aberystwyth

A487

To Cardigan

To Bu.
We

Of course, like all mountainous country, southern Snowdonia is subject to sudden changes of weather but it works both ways. You may set out on a sunny morning and find yourself eating your picnic lunch in the car with the rain coursing down the steamed-up windows. But never put off an outing on account of a wet day—by afternoon the clouds are likely to have risen above the peaks and the sun will be blazing. And there are peaks all the way down from Snowdon in the north to Plynlimon Fawr across the Montgomeryshire border in Cardigan.

On the whole the hills tend to be steeper than in most other parts of Wales but this is the area in which one can most easily achieve a judicious mixture of main road and lane driving and still have something really worthwhile to look at all the time. The permutations of trips here are almost endless, and wherever you go there are views of mountains—but sharpened by the little sudden streams and the broad sheets of the still lakes. The only typically Welsh scenery that one cannot enjoy east of Dolgellau is the coast. And those who pine for it should visit area number—

5. West coast. Except for two short stretches where the cliffs run straight into the sea there are golden beaches all the way from Criccieth to Aberystwyth—as the crow flies, well under 40 miles but as the road winds, over 90. If it were not for those anachronistic toll-bridges the drive would be longer still. It is a fascinating journey, though, because for the most part it gives one open views of the sea on the one hand

25

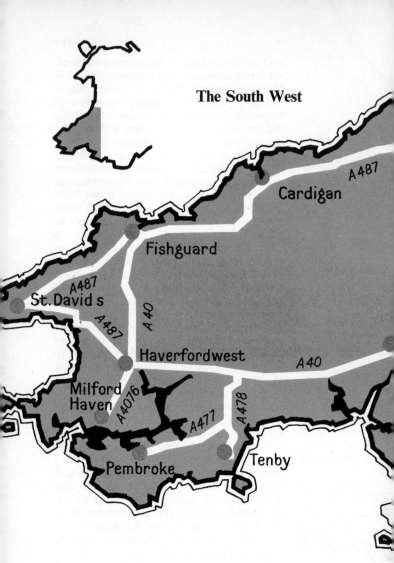

The South West

A487

Cardigan

Fishguard

A487
St. Davids

A40

A487

Haverfordwest

A40

Milford
Haven

A4076

A477

A478

Pembroke

Tenby

Aberayron

A482

Lampeter

Llandovery

Carmarthen

A48

Swansea

and of the Snowdon range on the other. At times the sea is hidden when the road kinks in behind the sand dunes but at others one has the feeling that one is motoring along the beach. At others still, the road squeezes between the shore and the cliffs and yet there is another variation still, when the road clings to the cliff.

The reason why the route is so indirect is that this coastline is indented with wide estuaries. After passing through Penrhyndeudrath you loop up to Maentwrog, then cut across the base of a small peninsula to Harlech where all the men seem to be on the golf course.

The road takes a short cut, so that at places there are a couple of miles of dunes between it and the bulging coastline, until you again run beside the sea at Llanaber and so to Barmouth. Then it is right up the Mawddach estuary to Dolgellau where you turn almost right round and come back down the south side of the estuary. You can cut off a bit by toll-bridging across at Penmaenpool. The next 25 miles down to Aberdovey is probably the most interesting bit of the whole route, particularly near Llwyngwril where the road and railway jostle one another for a foothold on the cliff. After Aberdovey you repeat the process of driving up one side of an estuary and down the other (this time it's the Dovey), with Machynlleth as the pivoting point. For the final 18 miles into Aberystwyth there is the fairly direct main road, A487, but if you want to follow the coast all the way you have the choice of making a detour through Borth.

If you had come down the main road all

27

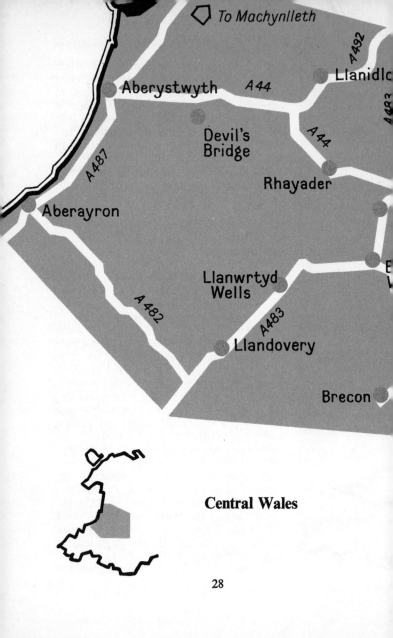

To Machynlleth

Llanidlo

A492

A492

Aberystwyth

A44

A44

Devil's
Bridge

A487

Rhayader

Aberayron

Llanwrtyd
Wells

A482

A483

Llandovery

Brecon

Central Wales

28

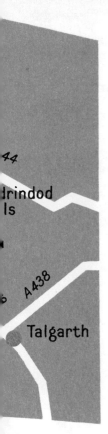

44

Irindod
Is

A438

Talgarth

the way from Penrhyndeudrath, past Lake
Trawsfynydd and through Dolgellau direct
to Machynlleth you would have nearly
halved the distance and seen the same
mountains from the other side. You would
also have saved something on toll fees and
goodness knows what on petrol. But you
would have missed the double event—the
glorious combination of mountain and sea.

6. Central Wales. Again the mood of the
country changes as you strike inland from
Aberystwyth. Heavily wooded at first with
steep—but not high—hills plunging down
to gurgling brown streams it gradually
opens out as you climb the Cambrian
Mountains. Still on the western side of the
range there are lonely wide stretches of
country—great peat bogs and the plantations of the Forestry Commission. The
ruins of the gigantic Strata Florida Abbey
are a mute indication of how the population has, over the centuries, shifted away.

The mountain roads are so smooth that
one hardly notices the gradients and they
are often wider than they are farther north.
However, beware of the sudden narrowing
where ancient bridges dumbly protest about
the volume of traffic for which they were
never designed. Beware, too, of disregard-
ing shabby old signs proclaiming that a
well-surfaced road is unsuitable for cars.
The Forestry Commission has done up
many of these tracks—but for its own purposes, not for the tourist—and they have
a disconcerting habit of just abruptly ending. Turn back unless you like the sound
of rending metal as a jagged rock rips
through your sump. Fully to appreciate

29

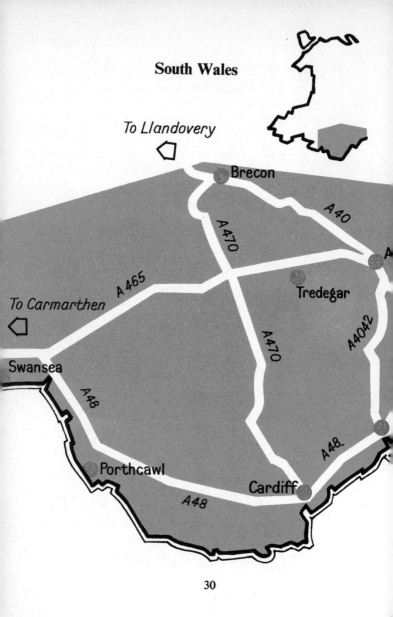

South Wales

To Llandovery

Brecon

A40

A470

A465

Tredegar

To Carmarthen

A4042

A470

Swansea

A48

Porthcawl

A48

Cardiff

A48

30

the loneliness of Wales you need to get your car stuck in some remote ford as dusk is falling.

On the eastern side of the Cambrians the country becomes much gentler, as befits the setting of such spas as Llanwrtyd and Llandrindod Wells. If you seek grandeur in the scenery press on south-eastward from Builth Wells down the Wye valley.

7. South Wales. Just as the engine of a car is sealed off from the passenger accommodation so the heart of industrial Wales is sealed off from the touring areas. Neatly contained by the Usk valley and the Brecon Beacons, the industrial and mining districts in no way intrude upon the peninsula formed by the southern half of Cardiganshire, Carmarthenshire and Pembrokeshire. In this comparatively small area you can find a microcosm of all Wales—sea, mountains, forests, rivers and fat meadowland. But more than any other part of the Principality it gives you the choice between exploring a small area in detail and 'tasting' the whole in a series of long drives. The best thing, of course, is to do both.

The main A40 road from Ross-on-Wye is as good a way of combining getting there quickly with enjoying the journey as any. You run beside the Usk from Abergavenny until you are half-way between Brecon and Llandovery. At Llandovery you pick up another river, the Towy, and follow its broad valley all the way down to Carmarthen.

From Carmarthen the whole peninsula lies open to you—St. David's Head is only about 50 miles away in a more or less

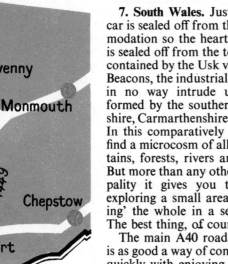

31

straight line and the entire peninsula is criss-crossed with lanes. In fact the whole thing might have been laid out for the benefit of the tourist—but perhaps that is, true of all Wales.

Hotels

Hotels in Wales range from the very lush right down to the "simple but spotlessly clean" and well below. The seaside resorts and some of the spas have fine, large hotels which cater for conferences so that they are likely to be full at almost all seasons of the year. It is, therefore, always wise to book well in advance.

Further down the scale there are plenty of good hotels and boarding houses and there is quite a lot of farmhouse accommodation available.

The Welsh are keenly aware of the value of the tourist industry but they have too much sense to exploit it out of existence. Prices are, consequently, neither very low nor outrageously high but on the whole reasonable for the accommodation and service provided.

Selective lists are given at the appropriate places in this book but more detailed lists may generally be obtained for a specific area from the local authority (County, Borough, or Rural District Council) concerned.

RHYL

Amusements. Bathing, boating, fishing, bowls, tennis, golf; concerts, band and theatrical performances, cinemas, a model yacht lake, paddling pool, large amusement park, coach tours.

Banks. *Barclays; Westminster; Lloyds; Midland; National Provincial; District; Martin's; Trustee Savings.*

Baths. Open-Air Swimming Pool, near the Pier.

Boating. On the Marine Lake.

Bowls. Public crown greens on the Promenade east of pier and in the Botanical Gardens, Grange Road. The Rhyl Bowling Club greens are in Seabank Road.

Churches, etc. *Trinity Parish Church,* Russell Road; *St. Thomas's,* Russell Road; *St. John's,* Wellington Road; *St. Anne's,* Vale Road; *Roman Catholic,* Wellington Road; *Presbyterian,* Princes Street; *Congregational,* Water Street; *Baptist,* Sussex Street; *Methodist,* Bath Street. Several Welsh churches.

Dances in Pavilion Ballroom, Ritz Ballroom, Regent Ballroom, etc.

Distances. Abergele, 6; Bangor, 30; Betws-y-Coed, 27; Bodelwyddan, 6; Cardiff, 169; Cefn Rocks, 9; Chester, 30; Colwyn Bay, 12; Conway, 16; Denbigh, 12; Dyserth Waterfall, 4; Gwrych Castle, 7; Holywell, 14; Llandudno, 20; London, 211; Prestatyn, 3½; Rhuddlan, 3; Ruthin, 18; St. Asaph, 6.

Early Closing Day. Thursday.

Fishing. Good sport is obtained in the Clwyd and the Elwy. In the Clwyd, between the sea and Rhuddlan, fishing is free, except for salmon and trout. A portion of the River Elwy beyond Rhuddlan is preserved by the Rhyl Angling Association. Information, permits, etc., from Fishing Secretary, 31 Sussex Street.

Golf. 9-hole course on shore between Rhyl and Prestatyn.

Hotels. *Crescent,* Crescent Road; *Country Club,* Rhuddlan Road; *Marine Hydro,* East Parade; *Morville,* East Parade; *Sandringham,* West Parade; *Palace,* West Parade; *Queens,* West Parade; *Westminster,* East Parade; *Ye Windsor,* Windsor Street; *Haven,* West Promenade; *Sunholme,* Marine Drive; *Grange,* East Parade; *Panshanger,* West Parade; *Mostyn,* Wellington Road; and many others.

Information Bureau. At the Town Hall.

Population. About 21,000.

Post Office. Chief Office is in Water Street. Branch office in Wellington Road.

Putting Greens on Promenade and in Botanical Gardens.

Roller Skating. Open-air rink on the promenade.

Tennis. Hard courts on Promenade, east of Pier, and in Botanical Gardens, Grange Road.

Theatres, etc. *Pavilion, Gaiety Theatre, Coliseum,* on the Promenade; two cinemas, in High Street.

One of the most popular holiday resorts in Wales is Rhyl. It is near the centre of the level seaboard which extends across the mouth of the Vale of Clwyd. For what it may lack in striking

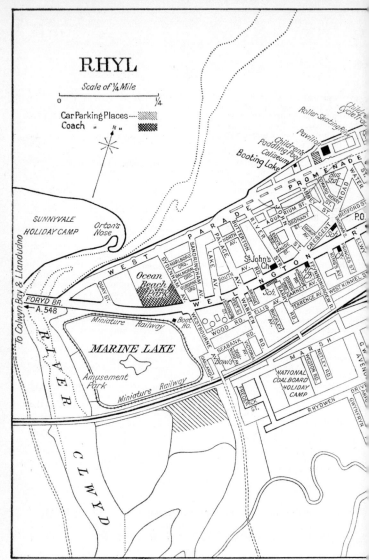

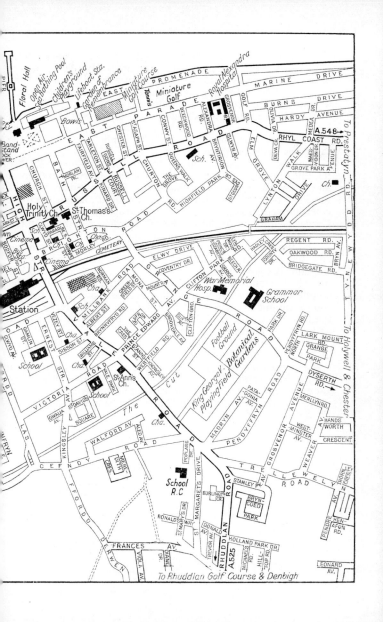

scenic attractions it makes up tenfold in the excellent facilities it provides for a very considerable number of holiday visitors each year. The magnificent beaches of firm golden sand provide safe and pleasant bathing. When the tide is too far out an open-air pool on the Promenade is a fine substitute.

The **Marine Drive and Promenade** extends for 3 miles along the entire front of the town. At the eastern end the road runs behind rock gardens and sandhills, while the Promenade separates the latter from the sea.

The most imposing feature of the Promenade—near the Pier it is unusually wide—is the domed **Pavilion Theatre,** where shows and other forms of entertainment are always popular. West of the Pavilion is a **Paddling Pool** for children and an open-air entertainment arena. East of the Pavilion are the sunken **Pavilion Gardens** with the expanse of **Queen's Gardens** adjoining. In the latter is a Children's Cycling Track.

The **Pier** is a fine viewpoint, not only for the sands and the coastline, but for the distant mountainous area between Conway and Bangor. Dominating the view behind the wooded hill on which stands Gwrych Castle is Carnedd Llewelyn, the second highest mountain in Wales. Notice too Y Foel Fras, a round summit to the right of Llewelyn, Tal-y-Fan to the left of the lime-works at Llandulas, and Penmaenmawr to their right and also the Great and Little Ormes.

Near the **Gaiety Theatre,** and the swimming pool, and protected by glass-walled shelters, are bowling greens and tennis courts and a number of sunshine chalets, while an interesting attraction on the Promenade is the **Royal Floral Hall,** in which many varieties of flowers, shrubs and cacti are displayed.

West of the Pier, the **Foryd Bridge** (Foryd means the *Ford of the Sea*) spans the estuary of the River Clwyd, and carries the main road westward to **Kinmel Bay** and **Towyn,** with a number of holiday camps, and on to Colwyn Bay.

The bridge commands a view of a large portion of the **Vale of Clwyd,** through which the stream flows. This Vale, which has been described as "the Eden of Wales," is very extensive compared with the size of its river, being some 24 miles in length and from 5 to 7 miles in breadth, while the greatest width of the river is usually barely 10 yards. The banks, however, are low, and after heavy rain the swollen stream floods the adjacent lands and rolls onward to the sea with destructive force. In the Vale are the three towns of St. Asaph, Denbigh, and Ruthin. The first-named is the nearest to Rhyl, and the tower of its cathedral can be seen from Foryd Bridge. A more conspicuous object is Rhuddlan Castle, to the left of the Cathedral, while to the right is the lofty spire of Bodelwyddan Church. Then away to the left again, and barely visible, are the scanty remains of Dyserth Castle, over which rises Newmarket Cop, famed for the view it commands, and for the great tumulus on its summit. To the right of the Cop are Moel Hirad-dug, and, farther away, Moel Fammau. The prospect from the bridge is finest at high tide, as then the estuary is full of water.

South of the bridge is the **Marine Lake** for boating and yachting, and there is also a children's boating pool. On the adjoining ground is an amusement park.

In Grange Road, east of Gladstone Bridge and the railway station, is another of Rhyl's recreation grounds, the **Botanical Gardens,** consisting of eight acres of delightfully laid-out grounds with tennis courts, crown bowling green, putting, aviary, aquarium, conservatories and a children's playground. There is, too, a café and a car park.

The **Parish Church** (Holy Trinity) where the services are held in Welsh is in Russell Road, sharing the same churchyard as the large **St. Thomas's Church,** in Early English style with tower surmounted by a 203-foot-high shingled spire.

In the centre of the town are the Town Hall and Public Library, the latter having good lending and reference facilities.

In Wellington Road is **St. John's Church**, of unusual design incorporating a central dome.

Prestatyn

Banks. *Barclays; District; Martins; Midland; National Provincial; Trustee Savings; Westminster; Williams Deacon's*—all situated in the High Street.

Bathing. Royal Lido Open-Air Pool. Sea Bathing at Central, Ffrith and Golf Beaches.

Bowling Greens. Bryn Newydd; Coronation Gardens; Highbury Avenue, and Roundwood, Meliden.

Early Closing Day. Prestatyn, Thursday; Meliden, Wednesday.

Entertainments. *Dancing:* Royal Lido (Saturdays; also Mondays and Thursdays in summer).

Theatre: Ffrith Pavilion (Repertory).

Cinemas: Palladium and Scala, High Street.

Golf. Prestatyn Golf Course (18 holes); St. Melyd Golf Course (9 holes); Ffrith Beach Golf Course (miniature 12 holes).

Hotels. *Royal Victoria; Nant Hall; Grand; Prestatyn Holiday Camp.*

Population. 10,500.

Post Offices. Head Post Office, King's Avenue. Sub Post Offices at Marine Road; Meliden Village; Meliden Road; Victoria Road.

Tennis. Municipal Courts, Gronant Road.

Prestatyn is an attractive resort nearly 4 miles east of Rhyl. Close to the industrial areas of Lancashire and the Midlands, the town has for generations been popular with holiday-makers.

While its natural advantages, including excellent sandy beaches with safe bathing have been maintained in their natural state, both municipal and private enterprise have combined to give the place all that can be asked for by the visitor. At Ffrith Beach there is something for everyone, including a children's playground, boating and canoe lakes and putting greens. There is a miniature golf course, a Repertory Theatre and various other amusements.

A 20-foot promenade with a stepped wall to the beach, links the Ffrith Beach with the Central Beach, where there is a Lido, with modern swimming pool, ballroom restaurant, children's centre and shops. One of the largest holiday camps in Britain is situated close to the shore. Its gay colourful chalets surround modern swimming pools, tennis courts and bowling greens.

The font in the Church of **Gwaenysgor,** rather more than a mile south-east of Prestatyn, resembles that of Lincoln Cathedral, and is one of the best specimens of Norman work in North Wales. The chalice is Elizabethan and is inscribed "The Cuppe of Gwaynisker". The registers date from 1538. They are the oldest in the diocese of St. Asaph.

Excursions from Rhyl and Prestatyn

Standing at the mouth of the Vale of Clwyd, Rhyl presents innumerable opportunities for excursions to interesting spots away from the coast.

Rhuddlan (*Castle, Marsh, New*) is a small town on the Clwyd, less than 3 miles by road from Rhyl or $2\frac{1}{2}$ miles by a path across the fields. Its Bridge appears to have been either built or repaired in 1595 as the abutment of one of the arches bears the arms of the Bishop of St. Asaph at that time. Another ancient building, known as the **Old Parliament House,** is in High Street. Upon it is inscribed:

"This fragment is the remains of the building where King Edward the First held his Parliament, A.D. 1283, in which was passed the Statute of Ruddlan, securing to the Principality of Wales its judicial rights and independence."

Rhuddlan Castle (*Admission 6d.; apply at cottage opposite entrance*). A castle was founded early in the tenth century by the Prince of North Wales, who made it his principal residence. It was taken and burnt in 1063 by Harold, the "Last of the Saxons" and rebuilt by the Welsh, but, before the end of the eleventh century a new one of the motte and bailey type was erected by Robert of Rhuddlan, nephew of the Earl of Chester, by command

of William the Conqueror. More than half a century later it was retaken by the Welsh, and was alternately in the hands of the Welsh and of the English. After the defeat of Llewelyn, Edward I gave instructions for the erection of an entirely new castle a little to the north-west and this began in 1277.

The present castle is constructed of native red and yellow sandstone and is a rectangular building with a tower at each angle and two at the entrance gates. The present entrance, by way of an earthen ramp across the northern end of the moat, is a modern development, there having originally been no break at this point in the moat.

Rhuddlan Marsh, which lies between Rhyl and Rhuddlan, was the scene in 795 of the utter defeat of the Welsh by the Saxon forces under Offa, King of Mercia.

Quite close to Rhuddlan Castle, and believed by many to be connected with it by a subterranean passage, is the **Old Banquet House.** Also near the Castle, and reached by a short walk along the river bank, is **Abbot's Hill** (known locally as *Bonc Hill*), which is a good point to survey the surrounding country. It is said to be the site of an ancient stronghold. A quarter of a mile south-east is **Abbey** or **Plas-Newydd Farm,** on the site of an ancient Priory of Dominican friars. Remains of the Abbey form part of the outbuildings. The inscribed slabs of the Abbey are now preserved in Rhuddlan Church.

There are bus services from Rhyl, St. Asaph or Abergele which pass **Bodelwyddan Marble Church,** described on p. 48.

Dyserth, on the eastern side of the lower part of the Vale of Clwyd, is some 2½ miles from Rhuddlan, 3½ miles from Rhyl, via Gladstone Bridge. Near the centre of the village is a **Waterfall,** formed by a stream from Ffynnon Asaph, or St. Asaph's Well, in the adjoining parish of Cwm.

The **Church,** which is quite old, contains a ninth-century cross, formerly n the churchyard, the pedestal of a cross which apparently belonged to the eleventh century, and a fine fifteenth-century "Jesse" window, one of the many traditional monastic relics found in Welsh churches, it being said to be part of the spoil of Basingwerk Abbey. In the churchyard are curious arched tombstones and old yew-trees.

A **Castle** formerly stood on a rocky promontory about half a mile from the village. From the site there is a wide and delightful prospect. At the foot of the north side of the rock is the **Talargoch Leadmine,** which has been worked almost continuously from the time of the Roman occupation until recent years. The excavations are of enormous extent and numbers of Roman coins have been found in the district.

In a field adjoining the Castle site on the south are the remains of a fifteenth-century **Manor-House** of a shape and size common in many parts of Ireland, but rare in Wales.

St. Asaph

St. Asaph in Flintshire, is some 5½ miles by road from Rhyl. Next to St. Davids, it is the smallest of cities, having a population a little over 2,200. It occupies a slight eminence between the rivers Clwyd and Elwy, and from the church built on the latter gets its Welsh name of Llanelwy, "the church on the Elwy". (Hotels: *Plough, Kinmel Arms, Bryndinas, Talardy.* Early Closing—Thursday.)

The city claims great antiquity in ecclesiastical history, its origin being due to Kentigern, better known as St. Mungo, first Bishop of Glasgow, who, having been driven from his See by persecution, fled for refuge to Wales, and on the pleasant site of St. Asaph built a monastery and a church about the year 560. Being recalled to his charge in his native country at the end of the persecution, he nominated a pious scholar, called Asa or Asaph, as his successor, after whom both the church and the place came to be named. In later days, the monastic church became the cathedral of the diocese.

The **Cathedral** (*Services.—Sundays—8.15, 11 and 6.15. Weekdays—7.40, and 5.30*) is the smallest in England and Wales. Its principal dimensions are: extreme length, 182 feet; breadth of nave and aisles, 68 feet; length of transepts from north to south, 108 feet; height of central tower, 100 feet. It is a plain cruciform building, chiefly in the Decorated style, but with Early-English windows in the chancel. The main feature of the exterior is the low square **Tower.** This is entered from the North Transept, and should be climbed (*charge*) for the sake of the view it affords.

Of the earliest building, or of those by which it was successively replaced during the first seven centuries of the history of the diocese, there are no remains, for, as was customary in those days, the first edifice was of wood, as were probably others which took its place. The oldest portions of the Cathedral are a doorway and other parts of the chancel. They are remnants of the Norman church, which was burnt to the ground by an English force during the invasion of Wales by Edward I. The work of rebuilding was undertaken by Bishop Anian II, who held the See from 1268 to 1293. In 1402 the Cathedral was burnt by Owen Glyndwr. The Chancel lay in ruins until 1482, when it was repaired under Bishop Redman. The next great event in its history was its restoration, 1870–80, from designs by Sir Gilbert Scott, the beautiful reredos, the Bishop's throne and the pulpit being then added. More recently it has had to undergo extensive repair owing to a subsidence in the foundations of the Tower and the ravages of the death-watch beetle. New roof timbers have been placed in the North and South Transepts.

In the interior the **Stalls** in the chancel are specimens of the Perpendicular style, and the oldest portions are the work of Bishop Redman. The **East Window,** an example of the Decorated style shows scenes from the life of our Lord. It is a memorial of Bishop Carey (1830–1846) and Mary, his wife. The reredos is of Derbyshire alabaster. The two eastern windows on either side are in memory of Bishop Short (1846–70) and his wife. The middle window on the north, above the stalls, contains subjects suggested by the songs of Miriam and Deborah, and is a *Memorial of Mrs. Hemans,* the poetess, who is commemorated also by a tablet in the south aisle of the nave. Next to this window, representing Joshua and St. Paul, is a window in memory of Bishop Joshua Hughes (1870–89). On the south side the central window, "the Magdalene and Mary," is a memorial to Susan Maria Sisson, d. 1865, and the three-light window to the west, with scenes in our Lord's life, commemorates Dean Bonnor (1859–86).

The **South Transept** contains the *Lady Chapel* and a chantry chapel recently restored. In various parts of the nave are several objects of interest, including one of the oldest of hornbooks, a copy of the Petition of the Seven Bishops to James II (the Bishop of St. Asaph was one of the signatories), the earliest edition of the New Testament in Welsh (1567), a "Breeches" Bible, a "Vinegar" Bible, three copies of the first Prayer Book of Edward VI, one of which belonged to Roger Ascham, Queen Elizabeth's tutor; a sealed Prayer Book (1662), a letter of Charles I to the Dean and Chapter, a map of Flintshire dated 1610 (Rhyl is not marked upon it), a small bronze figure of a horse taken out of a grave at Gwaenysgor, a manuscript Lexicon in Welsh, Greek and Hebrew, made by the self-taught Dick of Aberdaron.

In front of the Cathedral stands a handsome **Monument,** dating from the tercentenary commemoration of the translation of the Bible into Welsh by Dr. Morgan, who became Bishop of St. Asaph in 1601. It is an "Eleanor Cross", 30 feet high, with eight figures upon it, the chief being that of Bishop Morgan. The others represent scholars who assisted him. Against the west door of the Cathedral is the tomb of *Bishop Barrow*

(d. 1680), with an inscription containing a request for the prayers of passers-by which was used in a lawsuit as evidence of the lawfulness of prayers for the dead.

To the west of the Cathedral is the Bishop's Palace. The new Deanery, formerly the Canonry, is opposite the Cathedral. The Old Deanery, now a hotel, is about a quarter of a mile distant, on the west bank of the Elwy.

The **Parish Church** stands at the bottom of High Street. It is an ancient and beautiful building, mainly in the Perpendicular style and is a good example of the "Clwydian" type of church, consisting of two parallel aisles separated by an arcade.

South-eastward of St. Asaph are the villages of Tremeirchion (bus service) and Caerwys.

Near **Tremeirchion Church** is a house called *Brynbella*, built by Mrs. Piozzi, better known as Mrs. Thrale, the friend of Dr. Johnson. She was buried in a vault on the north side of the nave; there is a wall tablet near by.

On the road leading north along the hillside, at a mile from the village, is **St. Beuno's College,** built in 1848 for theological students of the Jesuit order. On the way will be seen *Capel y Craig*, a tiny chapel of striking beauty, looking out over the valley from the summit of a great rock. It stands on the college estate and was built in 1866 to the plans of a church student who had been an architect. Dedicated to the Virgin Mary, it sustains a tradition expressed by St. Mary's Well at Cefn (*see* below) and other ancient shrines in North Wales. In the entrance court of the college stands a fourteenth-century cross acquired from the churchyard of Tremeirchion.

In the opposite direction, at the south end of the village, is *Ffynnon Beuno*, an ancient well dedicated to the uncle of St. Winefride and patron of the college (*see* under Holywell, p. 49).

Caerwys, 3 miles eastward, though now a very small place, was originally the site of a Roman station, Near it are beautiful woods, through which visitors usually walk when approaching Caerwys by way of the ancient village of **Bodfari,** which stands nearer the river, and also farther south.

Cefn Rocks and Caves. In the bend of the Elwy some 2½ miles south-west of St. Asaph are the **Cefn Rocks,** with caves in which have been found articles left by primitive man, and bones of the bear, bison, reindeer, hyaena and other animals now extinct in the British Isles. The caves are approached by terraced and zigzag paths up the face of the cliffs, and are open to visitors daily from April to September, free of charge. There is nothing to see, and the caves are of interest only on account of what was found in them, but the view from the Rocks is charming.

Trefnant, about 2½ miles south of St. Asaph, is notable for a handsome memorial church in the Decorated style, erected in 1855.

St. Mary's Well. Less than a mile below the Cefn Caves is St. Mary's Well, or Ffynnon Fair, in a field by the side of the Elwy, at a spot about two miles from St. Asaph Cathedral. In olden days the well was thought to be holy, and was used for baptisms. It was also at one time noted for the secret marriages performed in the chapel above. This chapel was very like that of St. Winefride at Holywell. Only the main walls are now standing, but the stonework of the well is still perfect.

Denbigh

Distances. Betws-y-Coed, 24; Mold, 16; Ruthin, 8; St. Asaph, 6; London, 203.

Early Closing Day. Thursday.

Golf. Denbigh Golf Club (9-hole course), one mile from town centre.

Hotels. *The Bull; Crown; Talbot; Hope and Anchor; Hawk and Buckle.*

Market Days. Wednesday. Livestock on second Tuesday of month.

Population. 8,200.

Denbigh is an important and pleasantly situated market town in the centre of the Vale of Clwyd, 12 miles from Rhyl by road and about 30 miles from Chester via Mold. To lovers of historic sites, it is of great interest and it is equally delightful to those who enjoy fine scenery, for the surroundings are of great rural beauty. The town is attractive also to anglers, being in the centre of good fishing in the Clwyd (1½ miles), the Elwy (4½ miles) and their tributaries. Stretches of the rivers are under the control of the Dee and Clwyd Fishery Board.

The ruins of the **Castle** (*charge, open summer 9.30–7*) crown the hill above Denbigh and are a prominent feature. Denbigh was granted by King Edward I to the Earl of Lincoln, who surrounded the town with a wall, and commenced the building of the Castle in 1282, an extensive and superb structure, largely formed by grouting. After the death of the Earl of Lincoln, the Castle passed to a succession of courtiers, including Hugh de Spencer, one of the unworthy favourites of Edward II; Roger Mortimer, Earl of March, the lover of Edward II's consort, Queen Isabella; and Henry Percy—"Hotspur". It was besieged, captured and re-captured by the Lancastrian and Yorkists during the Wars of the Roses. In 1643 the Castle was fortified and garrisoned by Col. William Salusbury at the command of Charles I. Later that year it was besieged by Parliamentarians under General Mytton who starved out the garrison. Denbigh Castle was one of the last Welsh castles to hold out for Charles I. It was deserted in 1660 and the ruins left to decay.

The boundary of the Castle is still marked by high walls and towers, most of them ruined, though the entrance gateway and the adjoining tower are still imposing. The enclosed area is one great lawn. At the foot of the walls on one side is the *Royal Bowling Green*, now used by a private club.

Just inside the entrance to the Castle is a small **Museum** in which is a model of the birthplace of the famous African traveller and friend of David Livingstone, Sir H. M. Stanley (originally John Rowlands).

43

The tower below the castle entrance is all that remains of the old garrison chapel of *St. Hilary*, probably erected before 1334, while nearby is the long wall of the unfinished *Leicester's Church* (1579). The Earl intended the building for a cathedral in place of St. Asaph's, but he died before it was completed.

In the lower part of the town are the ruins of the **Friary** of White Friars founded in the fourteenth century, and damaged by fire in 1898.

The **Parish Church**, dedicated to St. Marcella, is situated a little over a mile eastward of the town centre. Occasionally known as *Eglwys Wen*, meaning Whitchurch, it is in the Perpendicular style with two parallel aisles separated by light octagonal pillars. One interesting monument is a tomb with recumbent figures of Sir John Salusbury of Llewenni (ob. 1578) and his wife. It also contains a monumental brass representing Richard, the father of the famous Sir Hugh Myddelton, with Jane, his wife, kneeling at an altar with their children behind them. It is also the the burial-place of other worthies, including Humphrey Llwyd, the Welsh historian, and Thomas Edwards, the writer of witty dramatic "Interludes."

North of the town is **Plas Clough,** built more than three centuries ago by Sir Richard Clough, who assisted Sir Thomas Gresham to establish the Royal Exchange.

One and a half miles from Denbigh and forming part of the ancient borough is the lovely village of **Henllan.** The tower of the church is separate from the main building probably on account of weakness in the foundations.

About 4 miles due east of Denbigh is **Llangwyfan,** with a large sanatorium erected as part of a Welsh memorial to King Edward VII, the corresponding building being at Talgarth, in mid-Wales.

At a distance of 7 or 8 miles slightly south of east from Denbigh rises **Moel Fammau** (pronounced *Vamma*), distinguished by the ruins of a lofty pyramidal mass of masonry erected to celebrate the Jubilee of George III and overthrown by a storm in 1862. It is the loftiest point of the Clwydian range of hills, extending from Rhyl to Ruthin, its elevation being 1,823 feet.

A short distance south-west of the castle is the white farmhouse, known as **Galch Hill,** notable as the birthplace of Sir Hugh Myddelton, the great engineer who supplied London with water by means of the New River, which he formed, with King James I as financial partner. In the dingle beyond, called *Dolhyfryd* (beautiful meadows), is a cottage having over its doorway lines attributed to Dr. Johnson, who stayed at **Gwaenynog** nearby, and then the seat of the Myddelton's, for a few days. To commemorate his visit, Mr. Myddelton set up a monument in a field beyond the second of the cottages mentioned above, **Johnson's Cottage** as it is called. The memorial consists in part of a Grecian urn with an inscription.

In the corner of the wood, half a mile or more to the left of Gwaenynog, is **Segrwyd Hall,** the birthplace of Dr. Dolben, Bishop of Bangor in the reign of Elizabeth I. In the hollow between more distant hills is the beautifully situated little village of **Nantglyn** (4 miles from Denbigh), the birthplace of the surgeon, Edward Samwell, who went with Captain Cook on his first voyage round the world, and the burial-place of Dr. Owen Pughe, the grammarian.

Denbigh to Pentrefoelas. The mountain road from Denbigh to Pentrefoelas (17 miles) reaches a height of 1,523 feet, and passes over the hills known as **Mynydd Hiraethog,** a featureless group extending across Denbighshire from the Conway to the Clwyd and forming an irregular platform from which there are fine views of Snowdonia. The highest point of the group, $3\frac{1}{2}$ miles north-east of Pentrefoelas, is 1,742 feet above the sea. In the neighbourhood are several large reservoirs.

Denbigh to Ruthin. Two miles or so south of Denbigh is **Llanrhaeadr,** one of several villages bearing a name which appears generic in Wales (the full name of this one being Llanrhaeadr-yn-Cinmerch). The principal objects of interest are the fine fifteenth-century Jesse window and the chancel roof of its church. There is a tradition that it was purchased with the votive offerings of pilgrims to the Holy Well, Ffynnon St. Dyfnog, near the church. Farther up the Vale of Clwyd, in the fairest of all its fair spots, is the ancient and attractive little town of Ruthin.

Ruthin (*Castle, Wynnstay Arms, Eagle, London House*) is situated on the Clwyd, 18 miles from Rhyl. St. Peter's Square has a number of old timbered buildings. That on the south side, and now occupied by the National Provincial Bank, was the former *Courthouse* and prison, having a gallows, a beam of which may still be seen projecting from beneath the eaves. On the west side of the square is Barclays Bank occupying the old Exmewe Hall erected in 1500 by Thomas Exmewe, who later became Lord Mayor of London. It was later the home of Gabriel Goodman who became Dean of Westminster and a great benefactor of the town. Before the building is a block of limestone, *Maen Huail* (Huail's stone) on which King Arthur is said to have beheaded a rival. On the north side the iron gates lead to the churchyard.

The **parish church of St. Peter,** originally a chapel-of-ease to the church at Llanrhydd, was built and endowed in 1310 by John, son of Reginald de Grey. There were two buildings, side by side, one for parishioners and the other for the monastic priests.

The College being dissolved at the Reformation, the collegiate church fell into decay and finally was almost completely demolished. The present **North Aisle** was the nave of the parochial church. The **South Aisle** was added in the early part of the eighteenth century. The most interesting feature of the church is the fine oak roof of its north aisle, presented by Henry VII. It is divided into about 500 panels, bearing carved devices, pious mottoes and sacred figures, no two of the ornaments being alike. In a recess in the north wall of the chancel is a bust of Dr. Gabriel Goodman, Dean of Westminster. On the wall of the north aisle is a portrait brass of his father Edward Goodman (d. 1560), and there is also one of the Dean's father and mother, with their five sons and three daughters. Near the western end of the wall is a curious tablet, prepared by the man it commemorates, a Castle servant who died in 1874. It is of bog oak, inlaid with bone, and exhibits in the latter material a picture of the church. The tower contains eight bells. Upon one the curfew is still rung, with the tolling of the day and month of the year.

North of the church are the old **Cloisters,** and opposite, the residence of the incumbent, styled the Warden, owing to Dr. Goodman reinstituting the Wardenship in connection with **Christ's Hospital,** which he founded. Its buildings consist of twelve cottages on the east side of the churchyard.

The Dean also founded a **Grammar School.** It occupied a site northward of the church. In 1700 it was rebuilt. The building then erected is now the social centre, a more suitable building having been provided in 1891–93 on the Mold Road.

The remains of **Ruthin Castle** are in the grounds of a private nursing home. It was founded in 1281 by Edward I and had an uneventful history. In 1400 Owen Glyndŵr made an unsuccessful assault on it when attacking Ruthin in an old quarrel with Lord de Grey. In the Civil War it was held by Charles I, but after a seige in 1646 by Parliamentarians, was demolished. On part of the site a castellated mansion was erected using local red sandstone in harmony with the ancient work. The castle was the seat of the late Colonel Cornwallis West, a descendant in the female line from Sir Thomas Myddelton, Lord Mayor of London in 1613, who subsidised publication of the first cheap Welsh Bible (*Y Bibl Coron*). He was a brother of Sir Hugh Myddleton of New River fame.

Llanrhydd, about a mile eastward, has an ancient church of British origin, with many interesting features. On the north side is *Plas Llanrhydd*, formerly the residence of the late Mr. Stanley J. Weyman, the novelist. **Pool Park,** a former residence of Lord Bagot and now a hospital, about 2 miles west of Ruthin, contains a stone seat called the **Queen's Chair** (originally near an earthwork called the *Queen's Court*) and a **Celtic Monolith,** bearing Ogham characters on its edges and a Latin inscription on one of its sides.

Llanfair Dyffryn Clwyd, two miles south, has a handsome Parish Church, supposed to have been built in 1403, with a Jesus Chapel built and endowed in 1619 by Rice Williams, a verger of Westminster Abbey.

Five miles westward of Rhyl is—

Abergele

Banks. *Barclays, Midland, National Provincial,* all in Market Street.

Distances. Betws-y-Coed, 22; Chester, 35; Colwyn Bay, 7; London, 214; Rhyl, 5; St. Asaph, 7.

Early Closing Day. Thursday.

Hotels. *Bee,* Market Street; *Bull; Cambrian* (pension), Marine Road; *Gwrych Castle; Gwindy,* Market Street; *Harp,* Market Street; *Castle,* Water Street; *Hesketh Arms,* Bridge Street.

Population. 7,900.

A small market town, Abergele is about a mile from the sea and mid-way between Rhyl and Colwyn Bay. Between the two places there is an extensive stretch of sand providing safe bathing. Its suburb, **Pensarn,** is close to the sea.

The **Church** dates from the reign of Henry VIII, and was restored in 1879. On the screen separating the nave from the chancel the date 1511 is carved. Another screen at the west end cuts off a portion which was used as a school in the sixteenth century. Other objects of interest are a thirteenth-century stone cross in the floor within the Communion rails, "probably the coffin lid of an Abbott"; remnants of early glass in the vestry window; a wooden safe made of a single log of oak; and the Communion plate, which includes a chalice dated 1601.

Less than a mile from Abergele is **Castell Cawr,** a tree-covered hill that was a Roman stronghold. It affords a fine view into the Vale of Clwyd.

Westward of Abergele is **Gwrych Castle** (*charge, Easter to October*), a modern building built in an antique style, and one of the most picturesque residences in the country.

The road skirting Gwrych Castle Park leads to the summit of **Cefn-yr-Ogof,** a hill (668 feet) containing several caverns and providing a widespread view.

Southward is **Moelfre Isaf,** which can be reached by a pleasant walk of 3½ miles through Plas Uchaf Woods. Another way is along the St. Asaph Road for 1½ miles and then to the right. The summit is 1,038 feet above sea-level, and affords a delightful view of Snowdonia.

Abergele to St. George and Bodelwyddan. St. George is a small village, 2½ miles to the south-east of Abergele, and the site, tradition says, of the great conflict between St. George and the Dragon. In bygone days those who told the story sought to convince their hearers of its truth by pointing to the marks of the horse's hoofs on the coping stone of the churchyard wall.

According to another tradition, Oliver Cromwell was once at neighbouring **Kinmel Hall.** The original building was destroyed by fire in 1841, and the present building now serves as a girls' school.

Above the village is a wooded height locally known as **Fort Dinorben.** Upon it are the remains of extensive ancient British fortifications which have been intensively excavated.

Bodelwyddan Marble Church, with its elegant spire, 202 feet high, forming a landmark for miles around, is 2 miles from St. George. It is a magnificent building, erected in 1856–60, at a cost defrayed by the Dowager Lady Willoughby de Broke, as a memorial to her husband.

Abergele to Llanrwst. This is a pretty if in no way remarkable road, running for many miles through pleasant hills and agricultural land and with a surprising scarcity of villages. (*N.B.*—check petrol.)

Llanfair-Talhaiarn is a small, straggling village, 5 miles nearly due south of Abergele, in a picturesque situation on the *Elwy*, a tributary of the Clwyd. The main road to it from Abergele ascends to a height of about 600 feet and then dips down to the bed of the River Elwy, which offers sport to anglers. Welshmen regard Llanfair-Talhaiarn with great interest, as the churchyard contains the grave of the Welsh bard Talhaiarn. In the church are valuable pewter vessels, and a place where people can be baptised by complete immersion.

Permits for fishing in a 1-mile stretch of water can be obtained from the *Black Lion Hotel*, or the Rhyl Anglers' Association.

The **Bryn-y-Pin Pass** forms part of a popular motor tour through this region. The sides of the rugged mountains are beautifully wooded, magnificent views are obtained, and the effects of a great landslip add further interest. The Pass is 7½ miles long. At the northern end is the *Cross Foxes* (once an inn), concerning which much interest has been aroused by coach proprietors and others associating it with Sir H. M. Stanley, but though it was at one time the home of his mother, the great traveller himself never lived in it.

Five miles south-west of Llanfair-Talhaiarn the Llanrwst road reaches the old town of **Llangerniew,** beyond which the road climbs to a point over a thousand feet above sea-level, passing on the way the pleasant residence called **Hafod-yn-Nos** ("built in the night", or "a one night's rest"), now used as a Girls' School, and going through an avenue of *Araucaria imbricata*—"Monkey Puzzle" trees. The summit of the road commands beautiful views of mountain, vale and sea, and is the site of an old-fashioned Welsh inn. The final 2 miles to Llanrwst are of great beauty owing to the fine view over the Conway valley to the distant mountains.

To Holywell and Pantasaph

Holywell is a turning point of a road trip of which the outer run goes along the Flintshire side of the Dee estuary, and the homeward one passes over pleasant hills a few miles inland.

The coast road passes **Mostyn Hall,** the seat of Lord Mostyn. The Hall is famous for the Welsh relics it contains. Elsewhere the route swings abruptly from labour to leisure—there are several busy collieries, and along by **Gronant** and **Talacre** are camping-grounds and bungalow towns.

Holywell

Banks. *Barclays, Midland, National Provincial.*
Distances Chester, 16½; Rhyl, 14.
Early Closing Day. Wednesday.
Golf. *The Holywell Golf Club* has a 9-hole course on Penyball Mountain.
Hotels. *King's Head; Red Lion,* High Street.
Market Day. Monday.
Population. 8,240.

Holywell is an ancient town deriving its name and its importance from the **Well of St. Winefride.**

For 1300 years the well has been a centre of pilgrimage. Several kings of England are said to have visited the well, which was the most famous in Europe during the Middle Ages. Richard I made a pilgrimage in 1189 and Henry V in 1416. The last English king to visit the well was James II in 1687. From all parts of Britain pilgrims have travelled to St. Winefride's Well to seek favours—many sick people claiming to have been cured.

The spring was once the largest in the country, but mining operations have greatly diminished the flow. The water never freezes, but remains at a constant temperature of 50° fah.

According to legend, there lived in the neighbourhood in the seventh century a young girl named Winefride. She was loved by Caradoc, a local chieftain's son, but she had determined to devote her life to the service of the church, and so refused him. One day Caradoc tried to force her hand. She fled from him and he, catching up with her, cut off her head with his sword. Where the head fell a large spring of water burst from the ground, and at the same time the ground opened and engulfed Caradoc. St. Winefride's head was then restored by the intervention of St. Bueno, and the girl lived to become Abbess of Gwytherin.

The basin in which the spring rises is in a crypt under **St. Winefride's Chapel.** This chapel is one of the most perfect examples of late fifteenth-century Perpendicular architecture. It was erected by Margaret, Countess of Richmond and Derby and mother of Henry VII. It took the place of the earlier well chapel which was then falling down. In the ceiling of the well crypt and on the corbels of the chapel above, are carved the arms and emblems of the Lady Margaret and of her husband, the Earl of Derby.

On the steps of the well is a fine reddish moss (*Byssus iolithus*) which appears like splodges of blood.

The principal feast of St. Winefride is on June 22nd, which commemorates her martyrdom, while a second feast each year on November 3rd celebrates the anniversary of her natural death.

Behind St. Winefride's Well is the **Parish Church,** a plain Georgian structure containing an ancient dug-out chest, the "Gloch Bach" (little bell) and other interesting items. **St. Winefride's Church,** the Roman Catholic Church, is in Well Street, while nearby is **St. Winefride's Convent.**

In New Road is St. Winefride's Catholic Primary School, in the grounds of which is a large bronze statue of the Sacred Heart. On the opposite side of the road is a large Hospice for pilgrims run by the Sisters of Charity of St. Paul.

A charming retreat is afforded by the **Strand Woods,** which extend from Strand Walk nearly to the railway station, where remains of **Wat's Dyke** are visible. At the end of the wood a footpath leads to the ruins of **Basingwerk Abbey,** originally built about 1131. The house was Cistercian, and was founded by Ranulph, 2nd Earl of Chester, for a community of monks already settled here, probably attracted to the neighbourhood by the well of St. Winefride.

The Community was dissolved in 1535, and for many years the Abbey lay in utter ruin and neglect. Recently, however, it has been restored by the Ministry of Public Building and Works.

Halkyn Castle, 3 miles south-east of Holywell by the main road, was formerly one of the seats of the Duke of Westminster. Near the entrance lodge is a beautiful church erected by the late Duke.

In a field near Whitford, 3½ miles north-west of Holywell, is the **Maen Achwynfan**—the Stone of Lamentations, one of the finest wheel crosses in the kingdom. It is probably an early Christian monument.

Pantasaph is to the west of Holywell, 2½ miles by road, or 1½ miles through the fields. The small village contains numerous Roman Catholic institutions, which have clustered around a church, built by a former Earl and Countess of Denbigh and opened in 1852. The buildings comprise a Franciscan Monastery, a Convent, and an Orphanage accommodating some 100 children. Francis Thompson, author of *The Hound of Heaven* and other famous poems, at one time lived in this village.

The **Church** contains some fine wood carving and stained glass, and a beautiful canopied tomb with the recumbent effigy of the Earl of Denbigh who died in 1892. At the rear of the monastery is a fir-clad hill, known as **Mount Calvary,** with a winding path containing the Stations of the Cross and leading to the summit, where a gigantic cross and the Chapel of the Sepulchre are to be found. At the foot of the hill a disused quarry has been transformed into a representation of the Grotto of Lourdes.

The car round-trip may be extended to include Flint, the county town, and Hawarden.

Flint is on the coast, 4½ miles south-east of Holywell. It is an ancient borough with the ruins of an historic castle. Flint Castle stands on a slightly elevated rock between the railway and the sea. It is a bare and square ruin consisting of four towers, and appears to have been built by Edward I about 1275. Two unfortunate kings are associated with its history—Edward II and Richard II. The former welcomed his banished favourite, Piers Gaveston, within its walls, and outside them Bolingbroke, if we may believe Shakespeare, offered his mock homage to the latter.

Hawarden

Admission. The main drives of the Park (entrance by village gate) are open to visitors daily from dawn to dusk. Cars and picnics are not allowed.

The Old Castle is open to visitors on Fridays, Saturdays and Sundays (2 p.m.–6 p.m.) from Easter until October. Entrance by Leopold Gate, admission 6d. (1s., with booklet.) Parties wishing to visit the Old Castle at other times are always welcome on written application to Hawarden Castle, or to the Estate Office.

Rather more than 10 miles from Holywell on the Chester road is **Hawarden** (pronounced *Harden*), with a pleasant park, the picturesque remains of an old castle and a church which, though simple, has much of the dignity of a miniature cathedral. The views from the Castle and the churchyard are good and extensive.

Little remains of the Old Castle except part of the Banqueting Hall and the huge circular Keep, which gives an impression of great strength. The Chapel, which is well preserved, can be seen by climbing the steps in the Keep.

Hawarden Church stands north of the village street on an eminence overlooking the Dee estuary. It has a central tower surmounted by a short spire, a nave and two aisles and a chancel which does not geometrically fit in with the nave. The west window, by Sir Edward Burne-Jones is a memorial to W. E. Gladstone, whose name is indissolubly linked with Hawarden. Note also the effigies in white marble of Mr. and Mrs. Gladstone, lying side by side, with guardian angel.

The ecclesiastical status of the Parish, which is the only Peculiar in Wales, and which has enjoyed this distinction since pre-Reformation days, was challenged in 1953 but was confirmed and established by the High Court in 1957.

St. Deiniol's Library and Hostel is a national memorial to the "Grand Old Man." The Library is exceptionally well-equipped and has been visited by students from all over the world. Residence is available for thirty-five. Students with some bona fide object wishing to apply for residence should write to the Warden quoting personal references.

The return route to Rhyl or Prestatyn may include **Newmarket Trelawnyd** near Dyserth. The village is noted for its **Gop** or **Cop**, an artificial mound, or cairn, 350 feet in diameter at the base and 46 feet high. It is the largest tumulus in North Wales. **Offa's Dyke**, which starts near Prestatyn, passes on the east side of Newmarket Trelawnyd.

51

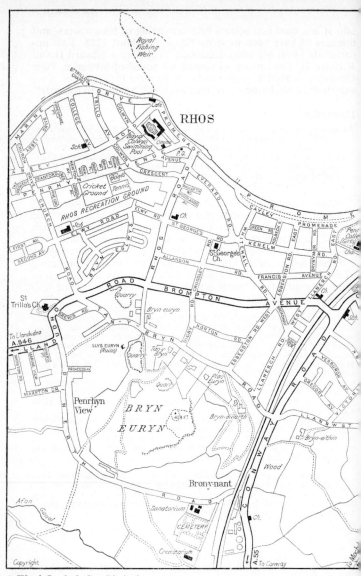

COLWYN BAY

Scale of ¼ Mile

COLWYN BAY

Banks. *Midland,* Conway Road; *National Provincial,* Abergele Road; *Westminster,* Station Road; with branches at Old Colwyn and Rhos. *Lloyds,* Conway Road; *Barclays,* Conway Road; *District,* Conway Road, and at Rhos; *William Deacon's,* Conway Road; *Martin's,* Conway Road; *Trustee Savings,* Penrhyn Road.

Bathing. Safe and pleasant bathing. The beach is of firm, sloping sand. Open-air swimming pool at Rhos.

Buses to and from Llandudno, Old Colwyn and Abergele, Lysfaen, Rhyl, Conway, etc. Runabouts traverse the 3-mile Promenade during summer. Through Rhos-on-Sea to Llandudno every 5 minutes.

Distances. Abergele, 6½; Aber Waterfalls, 15; Betws-y-Coed, 20; Caernarvon, 30; Cardiff, 176; Conway, 6; Llandudno, 5; London, 221; Marble Church, 11; Penmaenmawr, 10; Rhuddlan, 12; Rhyl, 12; Trefriw, 15.

Early Closing Day. Wednesday (except July–August).

Entertainment. Summer shows and municipal orchestra in Pier Pavilion. There are cinemas and a theatre. Dancing at the Pier Pavilion and at other halls and the principal hotels. Miniature railways. Zoo and Botanical Gardens.

Hotels. *Colwyn Bay,* Promenade; *Colbourn,* West Promenade; *Stafford House,* West Promenade; *Edelweiss,* Lawson Road; *Commodore,* Conway Road; *Norfolk,* Princes Drive; *Green Lawns,* Bay View Road; *Queens,* Old Colwyn; and many others.

Information Bureau. Station Square.

Population. Including Rhos and Old Colwyn, 23,090.

Post Office. Prince's Drive.

Sport. Bowls and tennis in Eirias Park and at various clubs. Golf at Old Colwyn and Rhos-on-Sea. Good fishing from Pier Head or boats.

Colwyn Bay is an attractive modern resort situated on a beautiful bay, with gradually sloping sands. On the landward side the town is nearly surrounded by well-wooded hills among which are dells or dingles with brawling streamlets or cascades falling to the shore.

The Bay, after which the town is named, sweeps gracefully round from **Penmaen Head,** on the east, to **Rhos-on-Sea,** on the north-west, from which there is a slighter curve to **Little Orme's Head,** projecting farther north and protecting Colwyn Bay from the gales which occasionally sweep the Irish Sea.

On the **Pier,** near the centre of the Bay, is a Pavilion used for concerts and other forms of entertainment.

Towards the east end of the Promenade is the **Dingle**, a feature reminiscent of the Hampshire chines. The town's principal recreation ground, **Eirias Park**, on the east side, covers about fifty acres and provides facilities for all types of sport. To the back of the town **Pwllycrochan Woods** provide a charming retreat.

Along the lower side of the woods runs the Old Highway, part of the old Chester and Holyhead stage-coach road, running westward past the **Four Crosses** to Mochdre and Conway. The Four Crosses is the meeting-place of four roads at the western end of the woods, and was the sign of an ancient inn which stood there.

For a walk commanding excellent views go uphill from the Four Crosses and bear left, into Pen-y-Bryn Road, which runs high above the town. The road runs eastward for nearly a mile and then swings back, downhill, to the Old Highway not far from **Nant-y-Glyn Valley** of which the Dingle is the northern portion. The Valley is entered from Nant-y-Glyn Road (opposite the Dingle). It is the most sheltered spot in the whole district. Being entirely screened from north and east winds, it has a temperature so genial that sub-tropical plants are cultivated in it, and flourish in the open all the year round. A walk of about two miles up the valley leads to **Bryn-y-Maen**, a pretty upland hamlet with a handsome church, known as the "Cathedral of the Hills," the tower of which commands one of the finest panoramic views in the district.

Llanelian. Two miles south-east from Colwyn Bay, and often visited on the return by those who have explored the Nant-y-Glyn Valley to its end, is **Llanelian** whose church stands 530 feet above sea-level. From it there is a good view, but the building is the main attraction. It is of the fifteenth century, and is said to have replaced one of much earlier date. The church has a spacious rood-loft, almost unique, and contains some very ancient paintings.

The Little Orme is 3½ miles north-west of Colwyn Bay. The road route is along the Conway Road as far as the Council School, and then to the right over the railway bridge, and past Llandrillo Church, 1½ miles from which, near the Little Orme, is the village of **Penrhynside**. A better route for walkers is along the shore or promenade past Rhos-on-Sea. The Little Orme affords magnificent views; but great care should be exercised, the seaward side being quite precipitous.

Between the Little Orme's Head and the village of Llanrhos are the Bodafon and Gloddaeth Hills, *see* p. 65. The route from Colwyn Bay is by way of Llandrillo Church—the parish church of Rhos-on-Sea. Then, at a point where four roads meet, go to the left for a hundred yards, and at the cottage begin to ascend the **Bodafon Hills,** the summit of which will soon be reached.

Descending, and passing two or three cottages, the **Gloddaeth Hills** are reached at the site of an old mill, now someone's home. The beautiful **Gloddaeth Woods** lie to the east of the house. By keeping a wall and the wood on the left, the visitor arrives at a point from which there is a delightful and extensive view.

Rhos-on-Sea (*Rhos Abbey, Silver Howe, Meadowcroft*), a suburb of Colwyn Bay, and under the same local government, is pleasantly situated on the western horn of the inlet from which the town takes its name. The foreshore is rather stony, with good sand farther out, and many bathers prefer to swim in the Swimming Pool on the Promenade.

The hotel and café adjoining the swimming pool were formerly *Rhos Fynach Monastery*. The building is said to date from 1185 and to have been "the home of the monks who guarded the fishing weir". It contains a collection of interesting antiques; a small charge is made to look at them.

Westward, a number of stakes in the foreshore perpetuate the site of an ancient **Fishing Weir,** so designed that the fish which entered could not find their way out again. The water flows into the enclosure at every tide, and can escape only by a grating at one angle. Salmon, herring, mackerel, and other fish were caught, sometimes in large numbers.

The weir was first formed 700 years ago by the monks of the Cistercian Abbey at Conway, and confiscated at the Reformation. Before the weir fell into disuse the Vicar of the parish claimed and received a tithe of the fish caught. Those entrapped every tenth day were his, being hauled out by the sexton. In former times the proprietor insisted on the Vicar reading prayers at the weir three times during the fishing season, "as was customary on all sea-coasts in these parts when tithes of fish were paid."

The tithe paid to the Vicar used to be the due of the monastery.

The monks were accustomed to pray in the **Chapel of St. Trillo** for a good haul. This building covers a spring of water close to the shore, about a quarter of a mile westward of Rhos Abbey Hotel. It is a plain stone-roofed structure, 11 feet long by 8 feet wide, and with walls 2 feet thick. Services are held on the foreshore adjoining the diminutive building: H.C. Fridays, 8 a.m.

In the vicinity is Rhyd-y-Cerrig-Gwynion, where, according to tradition, Prince Madoc, son of Owen Gwynedd, embarked for the "New World" (Mexico) about 300 years before the time of Columbus.

The **Parish Church** (Llandrillo Church, the old name of the village being Llandrillo-yn-Rhos) is about three-quarters of a mile inland. The building is mainly in the Perpendicular style, but its northern portion and the tower contain traces of Early English and Decorated work. The most noteworthy feature is its massive square tower, with double-stepped battlements. The lych-gate is dated 1677.

Westward of the church the 18-hole course of the **Rhos and Penrhyn Bay Golf Club** stretches toward the Little Orme.

A short distance from the church are the ivy-clad ruins of **Llys Euryn,** or **Ednyfed's Castle.** They are probably the remains of a fifteenth-century manor-house, which succeeded a castle inhabited in the thirteenth century by Ednyfed, whose tomb is in the Parish Church.

CHESTER, LLANDUDNO, BETWS-Y-COED

0 1 2 3 4 5 6   12 Miles

WARD, LOCK & CO. LIMITED, LONDON

© John Bartholomew & Son Ltd, Edinburgh

To the south of Llys Euryn is a grassy hill, called **Bryn Euryn,** in great favour with picnic parties. The summit (400 feet) shows traces of an ancient fortification and commands a wide view.

Old Colwyn is at the eastern end of Colwyn Bay, on the high road a little distance from the sea. The main public buildings in the village are **St. Catherine's Church,** a pretty edifice with an ivy-covered steeple, and **St. John's Church** for English services. The shore is notable for its many kinds of marine life, and affords safe and pleasant bathing. Behind the village is the **Fairy Glen,** a picturesque, wooded dingle traversed by a stream.

A variety of pleasant walks may be taken among the neighbouring woods and hills. One of the most popular of these rambles is over the headland of **Penmaen-Rhos** to Lysfaen, a distance of a couple of miles.

Llysfaen Hill, which is 600 feet above the sea, is visited for the sake of the view. It was formerly one of the chain of semaphore stations from Holyhead to Liverpool, by means of which news of incoming vessels was conveyed. Note the grand view of the Great Orme, on which stood the next westward station.

Llysfaen Church (restored) is a good example of the two-aisled churches of this district. The present vestry was the original church. In the eleventh century there was added to it the portion which is now the north aisle. The remainder of the building belongs to the thirteenth century.

Near Llysfaen is the village of **Llandulas,** on the banks of the *Dulas* and sufficiently near to a good beach to attract visitors in summer.

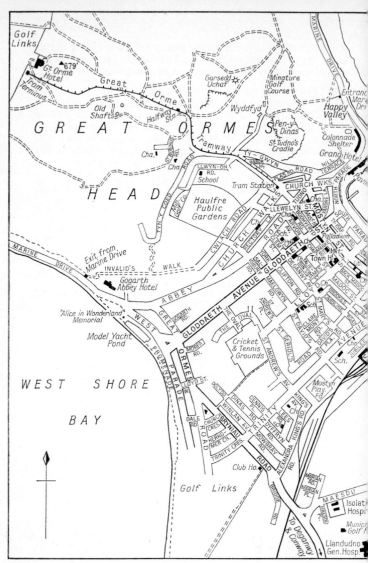

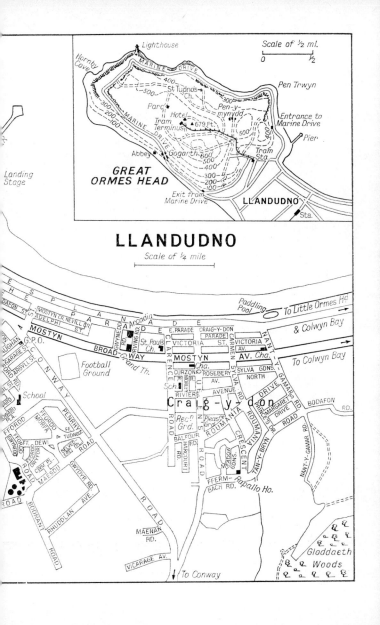

LLANDUDNO

Scale of ¼ mile

GREAT ORMES HEAD

Scale of ½ ml.

Lighthouse
Hornby Cave
MARINE DRIVE
St Tudno's Ch.
Parc
Hotel
Tram Terminus
Pen-y-mynydd
679 Ft.
Pen Trwyn
Entrance to Marine Drive
Pier
Abbey
Gogarth
Tram Sta.
LLANDUDNO
Sta.
Exit from Marine Drive

Landing Stage

Paddling Pool
To Little Ormes Hd
& Colwyn Bay
To Colwyn Bay

ESPLANADE
ADAFON ST
MOSTYN CR. NEVILL DR.
ADELPHI ST
Arcadia
IRVING DR.
E. PARADE
CRAIG-Y-DON PARADE
MOSTYN
G.P.O.
GWYNEDD
St Paul's Ch.
E. PARADE
VICTORIA ST.
VICTORIA AV.
Cha.
NANT-Y-
VAUGHAN
GARAGE ST
ARGYLL ST
BROADWAY
CLARENCE
St Pauls Ch.
MOSTYN
Cha.
SYLVA GDNS.
GAMARD RD.
Football Ground
Grand Th.
CURZON
CHAPEL
ROSEBERY AV.
SYLVA RD.
NORTH
DRIVE
BODAFON RD.
School
CONWAY
Riviere
Sch.
Craig-y-don
ROAD
ROUMANIA
MARGARET DRIVE
BODAFON RD.
FFORDD MORFA
PENRHYN
FF. TUDNO
DEWI
Rec.n Grd.
Please Grd.
BALFOUR RD.
HARCOURT RD.
NANT-Y-BRYN
PRINCES DR.
NANT-Y-GAMAR RD.
COED
DEWI
GWYDYR
CWM
GWYNEDD
MAESCLU
SEVERN
GWYDYR RD.
ROUMANIA CRESCENT
'SNOG'
FFERM-BACH RD.
Rapallo Ho.
RHUDDLAN
BODNANT AV.
ROAD
MAENAN RD.
VICARAGE AV.
To Conway
Gloddaeth Woods

LLANDUDNO

Angling. Excellent from Great Orme Rocks, and boats. Sea Angling Festivals are held in April and September. Salmon and trout in nearby rivers and mountain lakes.

Banks. *National Provincial, Midland, Lloyds, Westminster, Williams Deacon's, Barclays, Martin's* and *District*, all in Mostyn Street.

Bathing. Bathing in the sea is quite safe. Tents can be hired on the beach.

Boating. Rowing and motor boats for hire and trips.

Bowls. Crown greens on the Sports Ground, The Oval, Gloddaeth Avenue, and at Craig-y-don.

Buses. To and from Deganwy, Llandudno Junction, Conway, Llanfairfechan, etc.; and up the Conway valley to Llanrwst and Betws-y-Coed. Eastward to Colwyn Bay, Rhyl, etc. Great Orme bus service from the Town Hall, Lloyd Street, to St. Tudno's Church. Bus station and enquiry office, Clonmel Street.

Cinemas. *Odeon, Palladium* and *Savoy*.

Concerts and Music. Pier orchestra at the Pierhead Pavilion mornings and evenings. Town Band at the Promenade Bandstand each evening. Sunday concerts also at Pier Pavilion and Odeon Theatres. Symphony orchestras, recitals and celebrity concerts.

Cricket. The Oval cricket ground off Gloddaeth Avenue is one of the finest in North Wales. Fixtures are arranged by the *Llandudno Cricket Club*.

Dancing. At the Café Royal and Winter Garden Ballrooms, and at hotels.

Early Closing Day. Wednesday.

Golf. There are three 18-hole courses—*The Maesdu*, the *North Wales Links* and the residential *Rhos and Penrhyn Bay Club.* These are all within easy reach. The links of the *Caernarvonshire Golf Club*, on Conway Morfa, are also available. *See* under Deganwy, p. 67. *Rhos and Penrhyn Golf Club* (*see* p. 56). *Miniature Golf* at Arcadia in centre of bay and at The Happy Valley.

Distances. Aber, 13; Abergele, 13; Bangor, 20; Beaumaris, 25; Bethesda, 23½; Betws-y-Coed, 19; Capel Curig, 24; Caernarvon, 27; Conway, 4; Denbigh, 28½; Dolwyddelen, 24; Gloddaeth, 2; Liverpool, 67; Llanberis, 36; Llandulas, 11; Llandrillo-yn-Rhos, 4; Llanfairfechan, 11; Llangelynin, 8; Llanrhos, 1½; Llanrwst, 14½; London, 227; Mochdre and Pabo, 5½; Menai Bridge, 20; Penmaenmawr, 8½; Penrhynside, 2½; Pen-y-Gwryd, 29; Pontypant, 23; Rhuddlan, 20½; Rhyl, 17; Ruthin, 35; Snowdon, 36; St. Asaph, 19; Trefriw, 15¼.

Hotels. *St. George's*, on Sea Front; *Imperial*, on Sea Front; *Marine* on Sea Front; *Hydro*, Nevill Crescent; *Empire*, Church Walks; *Grand*, North Prom; *Gogarth Abbey*, West Shore; *North-Western*, Vaughan Street; *Queen's*, Promenade; *Royal*, Church Walks; *Clarence*, Gloddaeth Street; *Esplanade*, Promenade; *Warwick* (private), Church Walks; *Dorchester* (private), Promenade; and many others.

Information Bureau. Town Hall. Tel.: Llandudno 76413.

Library. Mostyn Street.

60

Parking Places. The seaward side of the Parade, between South Parade, and Nant-y-Gamar Road, Craig-y-don, in North Parade, overlooking the Pier, in Gloddaeth Street, Lloyd Street, and elsewhere in the town. There is also a public car park outside the football ground.

Police Station. Oxford Road. Tel.: 76149.

Population. About 17,000.

Post Office. Vaughan Street, close to Station. Sub-offices in Gloddaeth Street, Queen's Road, Alexandra Road, and in Great Orme's Road, West Shore and Craig-y-don.

Putting and Miniature Golf. In Happy Valley. Haulfre Gardens, on the Promenade and on the Great Orme.

Sailing. In North Bay; also with *Llandudno Sailing Club*, centred in Mostyn Broadway.

Skating. Open-air rink next to Catlin's Arcadia, on the Promenade.

Steamer Trips to Menai Bridge, etc.; to Isle of Man and to Liverpool. Also from Conway Quay, motor launch up the Conway River to Trefriw.

Tennis. Hard courts at Queen's Road Recreation Ground, hard and grass courts at the Oval.

Theatres. Excellent summer shows at the Pier Pavilion, and at Arcadia. Open-air entertainment in Happy Valley, and stage plays at the Grand Theatre and Palladium.

Youth Centre. There is a thriving centre at the corner of Trinity Avenue and Caroline Road.

Llandudno, the most widely-known resort on the north coast of Wales, is situated on a narrow peninsula projecting into the Irish Sea, and terminating in the bold headland known as the Great Orme. Its principal sea-front borders the beautiful bay which sweeps eastward from the Great Orme to the Little Orme, while a second front commands magnificent views across Conway Bay to the Snowdonian mountains.

The name of the town is formed of two words, *Llan* and *Tudno*, the former signifying a consecrated enclosure, or church, the latter being the name of the saint to whom the old Parish Church was dedicated. St. Tudno was a saint of the Celtic Church and belonged to that period of the British Church famous for missionary zeal. He was the son of a chieftain of considerable power and wealth, who lived early in the sixth century, and was sometimes called *Seithenyn Feddw*—Seithenyn the Drunken—associated with the legendary drowned city of Cardigan Bay. St. Tudno founded his cell where St. Tudno's Church now stands.

The town, of rapid growth, covers the plain between the two bays, and extends up the headlands. Eastward, it has almost joined up with Colwyn Bay. There are no shops or vendors on the Promenade. Llandudno can accommodate 60,000 visitors.

On the left of the town rises the grey and green mass of the Great Orme, its steep sides scaled by roads and dotted with houses. At the foot of the Orme the Pier stands out to sea, and the wide Promenade sweeps round in a splendid curve 1½ miles long to the Little Orme, away to the right. Southward the grey of the Little Orme changes to red-brown at the quarries beyond Craig-y-don, and from there the eye is carried back along the rim of the bay by the long line of hotels and boarding-houses. **The north shore** is composed of firm, smooth sand, fringed with shingle.

Towards the western end of the Promenade stands the fine **War Memorial** and a pleasant tree-shaded green, beyond which is the **Pier,** nearly half a mile long and intensely active with steamer traffic. It is in two portions, one extending from the end of the Promenade and in front of the Pavilion and the Grand Hotel, the other continuing to sea. There are two entrances, one at the Promenade, and one near the entrance to the Marine Drive.

The **Pavilion,** near the upper end of the Parade, is renowned for its concerts and is often used for large national conferences. At the pier head is a further concert hall. The Pier provides a good viewpoint, the most prominent of the mountains seen rising in the distance is Foel Fras, at the head of the Aber Glen. To the left of this is Tal-y-Fan, in the rear of the Conway mountains, and still more to the left is Pen-Llithrig-y-Wrach, some 3 miles short of Capel Curig.

Llandudno is well provided with facilities for indoor amusement. In addition to the Pier Pavilion there is **Arcadia,** where various forms of entertainment run from Easter until the end of October. Close by is the **Grand Theatre,** with resident company. Dancing may be enjoyed at the **Winter Garden** Ballroom, Gloddaeth Street, the Café Royal and at many of the hotels. The Odeon Cinema is next to the Winter Gardens and the Palladium Theatre is also in Gloddaeth Street. The Savoy Cinema is in Mostyn Street.

In Fferm Bach Road, Craig-y-don, is **Rapallo House Museum** (*open weekdays, except Tuesdays,* 10–1, 2–5, *free.*) containing some interesting pictures and a number of articles on loan from the National Museum of Wales (to which Rapallo House is affiliated). In an outhouse is a replica of an old Welsh kitchen and in the armoury are Roman exhibits from Conovium. *See also* Nant-y-Glyn, p. 63.

Mostyn Street is Llandudno's principal thoroughfare. Starting at the Vaughan Street end and following it towards the Great Orme, we come immediately to **Holy Trinity Church,** in the Transition style.

Next, on the right, is **St. John's English Methodist Church.** Then almost immediately on the left is the **English Baptist**

Chapel, a commanding structure with a Greek portico. Next door is the Renaissance building of the **Public Library.**

Passing on, we come to the break caused by **Lloyd Street,** which runs inland from the sea-front toward the cricket and tennis grounds and the bowling-green, and contains various public buildings. A few yards inland from Mostyn Street is the **Town Hall,** an English Renaissance building. Just beyond, and in similar style, is the **Welsh Methodist Chapel.** A little farther along, on the other side, is the **Catholic Church of Our Lady, Star of the Sea.** The **Lifeboat House** is equidistant from Llandudno Bay and the West Shore.

Gloddaeth Street and its continuation, **Gloddaeth Avenue,** together form a thoroughfare which runs in a straight line from the shore of Llandudno Bay to the West Parade, on the shore of Conway Bay. On the eastern side of Gloddaeth Street are the **Odeon Cinema** and **Palladium Theatre** and the **Winter Gardens.** At the corner of Chapel Street is the **English Presbyterian Church,** and on the opposite corner the **Welsh Presbyterian Chapel.** Off Gloddaeth Avenue is the **Sports Ground,** where county cricket and other matches are played. There are tennis courts, hard and grass, and bowling and putting greens, open to the public. In winter a hockey festival attracts teams from all parts.

Mostyn Street goes north-westward of Gloddaeth Street, past the Welsh Baptist Chapel, at the corner of Llewelyn Street, to Church Walks, from which a further climb leads to the terraced **Haulfre Gardens** on the steep side of the Great Orme. There is a tea-room, a small aviary and an aquarium of tropical fish, and in the upper part of the Gardens a miniature golf course. The paths through the Gardens form an attractive approach to the Great Ormes Head.

In Church Walks is **Nant-y-Glyn,** open to the public. A collection of antique musical instruments, all in playing order and dating back to 1680, are on display, as are early manuscripts from the fifteenth century.
Also in Church Walks is the lower station of **The Great Orme Railway.**

Great Orme's Head (679 feet)

The head is a mass of carboniferous limestone rising precipitously to the north-west of the town and round which has been cut the **Marine Drive** (*toll for vehicles*) to a total distance of 6 miles. One entrance is close to the Pier, the other being on the West shore. From the Pier a path leads off left to reach the **Happy Valley,** a pleasure-ground resting in a hollow of the

Great Orme; it was donated by Lord Mostyn and developed by the town with lawns, rockeries, shrubberies and flower beds. In the upper part is an extensive Rock Garden to which many plants have been brought from abroad. Just beyond is **Pen-y-Dinas,** thought to be the site of a British fortress. There are remains of an encircling wall of considerable width and a number of circular cavities, 12 feet in diameter and edged with stones. Near this is the old rocking stone, sometimes called *Tudno's Cradle.* Passing the toll-house we soon reach **Pen Trwyn** at the north-eastern corner of the promontory which is a good viewpoint. A little beyond is a path to *Farm Inn,* and beyond this a road leads to **St. Tudno's Church.**

St. Tudno's was the former parish church of Llandudno, but is now replaced by **St. George's** in Church Walks. The interesting oblong building is said to stand on the site of the cell of St. Tudno, who lived in the sixth century. The west end of the north wall is thought to be part of an eleventh- or twelfth-century building, but the rest of the old work belongs to the fifteenth century. Chief items of interest in the church are a Norman circular font and two thirteenth-century tombstones on the south wall.

About half-way round the Orme is the castellated **Great Ormes Head Lighthouse** (*permits from Mersey Docks and Harbour Board, Liverpool*) a solidly built structure crowning a steep precipice at a height of over 300 feet. The beacon is situated at the point of the Head, and in the cliff below is the **Llech,** or **Hiding Cave,** one of several caverns in the face of the promontory. From the western side of the Great Orme the view is magnificent.

From this point the Drive runs down to the Conway shore toll-gate, shortly before reaching which the scanty ruins of **Gogarth Abbey** are passed. They are situated in the grounds of the *Old Abbey Hotel,* and consist chiefly of the remains of a chimney stack, fragments of walls, and some traces of foundations. Enough, however, is left to show that the edifice was of considerable note.

Outside the west gate of the Drive stands the *Gogarth Abbey Hotel,* on the site of what was the residence of Dean Liddell. It is said that here "Lewis Carroll" wrote *Alice in Wonderland*; and we can readily believe that the Walrus and the Carpenter in *Alice Through the Looking Glass* "wept like anything to see such quantities of sand" where are now the Golf Links.

Between the ends of Abbey Road and Gloddaeth Avenue is a Model Yacht pond. Southward of the Pond extends the **West Shore** promenade and the gorse-covered warren that stretches to Deganwy and the fine links of the **North Wales Golf Club** and also those of the **Maesdu Club.**

eat Orme, Llandudno

Deganwy, from Conway Harbour

Dinas Gynfor, Anglesey

The Sychnant Pass (*Woolverto*

Little Ormes Head

The Little Orme, at the eastern extremity of Llandudno Bay, although less imposing than the larger headland, has features of much interest. It is about 200 feet lower than the Great Orme, being only 463 feet above the level of the sea, but the views from the summit are extensive and delightful, and the cliffs are much finer than those of the loftier headland, some having a sheer height of 300 feet. Like its more famous neighbour across the bay, the Little Orme is composed of limestone, in which a number of caverns have been formed by the waves. The best known are the **Eglwys Wen** (Whitechurch), **Porth Diniweid** (the Innocents' Gate), and **Ogof Cythreuliaid** (the Devil's Cave).

The walk round the headland is easy and pleasant, and can be accomplished in a couple of hours or less. Follow the road along the shore until it ascends between the Little Orme and Mynydd Pentre (pentre = village), and there take the path leading to the headland. For the sake of the view the complete circuit should be made, but the greatest care should be exercised, because the cliffs are precipitous and fatal accidents have occurred.

For an easy means of ascent the road that goes eastward from the Parade to the Craigside Hydro should be followed. Just after passing the Hydro, take a path that will be seen leading up the slope. By following it and keeping to the left, the summit is soon reached, and then the beautiful view of mountain and sea more than compensates for the hard work of the climb.

The view from the cairn on the summit includes Moel Fammau, the highest point of the Clwydian range, with the tower of St. Asaph Cathedral and the lofty white spire of Bodelwyddan Church in front of it. Then to the right are Penmaenmawr and the Isle of Anglesey. Nearer are the Gloddaeth Woods, with Conway Castle behind them; and in the rear of that are Penllithrig-y-Wrach to the left, and Foel Fras and Carnedd Llewelyn to the right. On a clear day there may be seen far away in the south the peak of Arenig-fawr, near Bala.

About 90 feet from the summit is a small cave called *Ty-yn-y-craig*—"the house in the rock"—which, tradition says, was used as a priests' hiding place at the time of the Reformation. Overlooking the sea, the cave provided a safe retreat. When discovered in 1587 the cave contained weapons and food, an altar and a printing press. The occupants are said to have escaped. These probably included William Davies, a missionary priest later martyred at Beaumaris, and his friend and companion Robert Pugh of Penrhyn.

Walks from Llandudno

1. **To Gloddaeth,** about 2½ miles. Of the many pleasant walks in the immediate neighbourhood of Llandudno that which lies through the woods of Gloddaeth is one of the most delightful. Although there is no timber of unusual size, the trees generally have a remarkable aspect of antiquity.

Either on foot or by bus follow the Conway Road (on the left of the Post Office) as far as the Church of Llanrhos (1½ miles), and then turn to the left by a footpath across the fields. Parts of the **Church of Llanrhos** (Eglwys Rhos) belong to the thirteenth century, but it is reputed that there was a church on this site in the time of Maelgwyn, King of Gwynedd, in the sixth century. Note the stone porch, and the steps of the church by the lychgate. The churchyard is the burial place of the Mostyn family. Inside the church is an inscribed stone dating from the sixth century. It was removed to the church in 1906, from Tyddyn Holland.

Gloddaeth Hall (now a girls' school) is one of the old residences of the Mostyns. Part dates from before 1550.

2. **"My Grandmother's Chair."** A seat formed of two flat stones a few hundred yards to the north of Gloddaeth Woods. Follow the shore road until Nant-y-Gamar Road is reached. Continue along this road to a gate at the end. Beyond the gate approach a wall bordering the wood and keeping the wall and wood on your left a farmhouse is seen below. Turn right past farmhouse and the stones will be found on the slope of the hill. On a clear day, the view from this point is very beautiful.

To reach the seat from Gloddaeth Woods, make for an old mill house, on the hill, bear left, around the wood until the farmhouse is seen below. Then turn right as above.

3. **To Bodysgallen,** one of the residences of the Mostyn family. It is pleasantly situated on a hill near Llanrhos. The first builder is said to have been Caswallon, Prince of North Wales, in the fifth century. Permission to view is very rarely given. The shortest route from Llandudno (2½ miles) is along the Conway Road as far as the second turning on the left past Eglwys Rhos. Southward of Bodysgallen is **Marl Hall,** the scene of Wilkie Collins's *Haunted House.*

4. **To Ffridd,** or Quarry Hill. This is easily accessible, and though only 350 feet in height commands one of the finest views in the neighbourhood. Proceed through the wood at Bodysgallen, pass through the upper gate, and turn to the right for a short distance. Then take the first turn to the left (by a lane leading to the village of Pydew). From here a gate gives access to the green slope by which, in about three minutes, the top of the hill is gained.

5. **To Penrhyn Old Hall.** This was for several centuries the seat of the family of Pugh. It is now used as a private hotel and café and is open to the public. It stands to the right of the bus route between the Little Orme and Llandrillo, and is reached from the road along an avenue of poplars.

6. A charming **Circular Walk** is along Conway Road to **Llanrhos,** thence past the lane leading to Bodysgallen (referred to already), up Tywyn Hill to Marl Lane on the left. Follow the lane, bearing always to the left, through the village of **Glanwydden** to the foot of Penrhyn Hill, and thence back along the main road running at the foot of the Little Orme. Distance, about 6 miles.

DEGANWY

Amusements Bathing, boating, yachting, sea and river fishing, golfing, mountaineering; excursions by rail, steamer, or coach.

Banks. *National Provincial, Midland, District.*

Bathing. On a sandy beach.

Boating and Yachting. These are among the principal attractions of the place. Various craft are available for hire.

Bus Services. To Llandudno, Colwyn Bay, Llanrhos, Conway, Llandudno Junction, Llanrwst, Trefriw, etc.

Fishing. Salmon, sea-trout, and brown trout, in the *Conway*. Other waters for fly-fishing are within easy reach of Deganwy. There is good fishing for bass within the river, and outside the harbour and round Gt. Orme's Head there is good fishing for plaice, skate and codling. From July to October mackerel visit the bay. There is an unlimited supply of mussels and soft crabs for bait.

Hotels. *Bryn Cregin, Castle.*

Sunny Deganwy, though within the borough of Conway, stands on the east side of the Conway estuary. It faces south and provides some good bathing from a sandy shore.

Deganwy Castle. The scanty remains of the castle stand on the *Vardre*, a small hill 353 feet high behind the village. From the site of the keep there is an extensive view. The first Castle is said to have been built by Maelgwn Gwynedd, King of Britain and the Outer Isles, early in the sixth century. It was destroyed by lightning in 810. The castle was rebuilt by a Norman, Hugh Lupus, Earl of Chester, and was demolished by Llewelyn the Great. Once more it was restored by an Earl of Chester, and was finally destroyed by Llewelyn ap Gruffydd in the year 1262.

Walks from Deganwy

Along the Warren to the Black Rocks, a group of seaweed-covered boulders in the direction of the Orme.

To the hill-tops of **Pydew and Pabo,** starting by the footpath below the Church, going through the Marl Park Estate, or across the fields to Marl Old Hall, and thence by the Nun's Steps.

To **Little Orme's Head,** across the Vardre to the village and ancient Church of Llanrhos, then through the Gloddaeth Woods to Penrhynside, and so to the Head.

To **Conway Mountain,** a mile across the Morfa (bus to Conway).

Visitors to Deganwy can join the excursions arranged by several of the Llandudno coach companies, whose vehicles pick up people in the village.

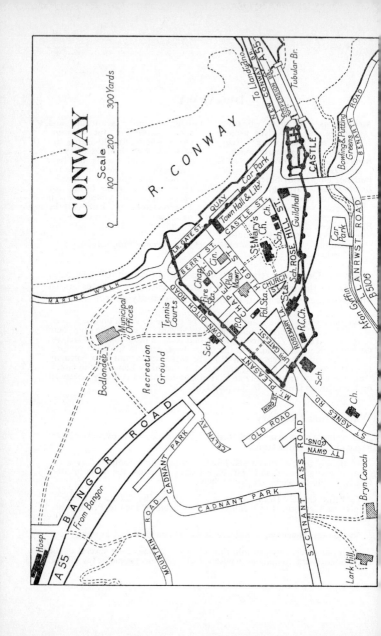

CONWAY

Amusements. Boating, yachting, fishing, bathing, mountain-walking, golfing (*see* below), tennis, bowls, cricket.

Banks. *Barclays*, High Street; *Midland*, Lancaster Square; *National Provincial*, Castle Street; *Williams Deacon's*, Lancaster Square.

Bathing on Conway Morfa; good sandy beach.

Boating. At the quay are rowing and sailing boats as well as motor-launches, while the bay is a favourite anchorage for yachts, which have good berths on the west side of the river. The holding ground is good, and the site is sheltered from the prevailing westerly winds. A hard, shingly beach, running steep down to dead low-water springs, makes landing particularly clean. Ample fishing facilities.

Bowling Green on south side of Castle.

Bus Services. Conway is well served by buses running east and west and also up the Conway Valley.

Camping and Caravanning. There is a municipally owned and controlled caravan and camping site at Morfa Conway. All facilities laid on, including shop and store. Open from 1st April to 30th September. There are several private sites both seasonal and residential.

Cinema *Palace* in High Street.

Early Closing Day. Wednesday.

Golf. The Caernarvonshire Golf Course is on Conway Morfa, 1 mile on Bangor road. Visitors are welcome. This championship course is one of 18-holes of typical seaside character. Sunday play. Fully licensed clubhouse with catering.

Hotels. *Castle*, High Street; *Park Hall*, coastal road; *White House*, coastal road; *Erskine*, Rosehill Street; *Bridge*, Rosehill Street; see also Deganwy.

Library. In old Town Hall.

Markets and Fairs Two fairs are held in the course of the year. The September fair is noted for the sale of honey and beeswax in High Street, opposite the Castle Hotel. Seed Fair in March.

Parking Places. Castle Square, Porth Bach, Mount Pleasant, Morfa Bach.

Population. 11,392.

Post Office. Bangor Road, near North Gate.

River Trips. During the season motor-launches ply to and from Trefriw, according to tide. The round trip takes about 3½ hours. *See* announcements and the description of the journey on pp. 74–5.

Tennis. Public courts at Civic Centre Bodlondeb.

Conway is a popular tourist centre, situated on the west bank of the Conway estuary. It is seen to advantage when approached by road from **Llandudno Junction,** less than a mile to the east. The road passes over a modern bridge (1958) which replaced the adjoining Telford suspension bridge. The town has retained its magnificent medieval walls in almost perfect condition.

The **Castle** (*open throughout the year, Ministry of Public Building and Works standard hours; charge*) was begun in 1283 for Edward I. It is of oblong form, and extends along the verge of a precipitous rock, washed on two sides by the river. The other sides front the town. The walls are at least 15 feet thick, and are flanked by eight vast circular embattled towers, each surmounted by a turret, but only four of the latter now remain. There were two ways of entering the Castle. One, by a narrow flight of steps cut out of the rock, formed a communication between the fortress and the river. This is now destroyed, but the position may be seen from the eastern terrace, close to the Tubular Bridges. The main entrance was at the north-west end by way of a ramp and over a drawbridge. The entrance is now by a zigzag path, but the drawbridge remains.

The interior of the fortress consists of two wards. On the south side (i.e. to the right) of that which the visitor first enters is the **Great Hall**. Its length is 125 feet, breadth 38 feet and height about 30 feet. It has lost its roof, which was supported by eight arches, of which the one rebuilt serves to indicate the former beauty. Gone, too, is the floor, under which were extensive cellars. At one end and on two sides are the fireplaces. Beyond the well is the entrance to the Inner Ward, originally defended by a drawbridge. The rooms on the south side are known as the **King's Hall** and the **King's Chamber** and the south-east tower as the **King's Tower.** On the first floor of the north-east tower is a beautiful little oratory of the thirteenth century.

Beautiful views of the town and of the surrounding country are obtained from a small grassy platform known as the **East Barbican,** beyond the eastern towers, and from the battlements, reached by steps leading from the main courtyard and near the entrance to the Great Hall and cellars. The north-western tower should be climbed for the remarkable views.

On the final destruction of Deganwy Castle by Llewelyn in 1262 preparations were made by England for the complete subjugation of Wales. Snowdonia was Llewelyn's stronghold, and Conway the key to the eastern portion. Edward I made Conway his headquarters, and ordered the erection of the Castle in 1283 after the defeat of Llewelyn. In 1290, Edward, having pushed ahead of his army with only a small following, was shut up within the castle by a large Welsh force from the hills, who had observed the swollen state of the river. It subsided however, and enabled the English to rescue him from a position of great peril and privation.

In 1399 Richard II took refuge in Conway, then considered impregnable, but finding it unprovisioned was compelled to treat with his foes. Travelling under a safe-conduct to meet Bolingbroke, he was led into an ambush a few miles from the Castle, and delivered as a prisoner.

The fortress played a prominent part in all the disturbances of subsequent years. In 1646 it was garrisoned for the King, but was taken, after a siege of three months, by the Parliamentary army. Charles II granted it to the Earl of Conway, by whom it was dismantled. Under the pretence of the requirements of His Majesty's service, the Earl ordered all the iron, timber and lead to be taken down and shipped to Ireland for sale. The Earl, however, did not profit by his vandalism, for the vessel conveying the material to Ireland was wrecked at sea.

Plas Mawr (*open daily except Sundays*), with entrance in High Street, was built by Robert Wynne, of Gwydyr, in the reign of Elizabeth I, and is a typical example of the domestic architecture of that period. It is now the headquarters of the **Royal Cambrian Academy of Art,** which has restored to Plas Mawr something of the appearance it presented in its early days. The Academy Exhibition is held annually from Whitsun to September in the **Victoria Room.** The building is in two parts. One faces High Street and is entered through a portico decorated with the royal arms and Greek and Latin inscriptions signifying "bear and forbear". On the house also were the initials "I.H.S.; X.P.S.", with the date 1585. Particular points of interest are the fine Banqueting Hall, fretwork ceiling, curious mouldings and crests over the fireplace, an original oak fender, and in the Small Kitchen an old-fashioned bread safe suspended from the ceiling. It is a curious fact that there are 365 windows and 52 doors in the house, and 52 steps from the bottom to the top of the tower.

St. Mary's Church, Conway's Parish Church, is mainly of the Decorated period, and was originally part of a Cistercian Abbey, founded in 1186, of which few remains exist. The original Cistercian church seems to have comprised the present chancel, nave, and aisles. The transept is fourteenth-century. The tower, built in stages in the fourteenth, fifteenth and sixteenth centuries, was restored in 1953. In the north porch is a nameless *cross fleuris* found with skeletons and believed to date from the Wars of the Roses or earlier. There are some finely carved stalls, a beautiful rood-screen of the fifteenth century, and an interesting font in which Archbishop John Williams was baptized. Near the south door is a fine marble bust to the memory of the sculptor, John Gibson, R.A. (1790–1866), a native of Conway. In a recess in the south wall is a stone figure of the mother of John Williams, Archbishop of York in the reign of Charles I.

The **Walls** (*open daily in summer, charge*) surrounding Conway measure a mile and a quarter in length and resemble the form of a Welsh harp. Believed to be contemporary with the castle (1282–83) they are in some places 12 feet thick and are fortified by battlements and twenty-one semicircular towers. There were three principal gates, the Upper Gate (Porth Uchaf) at the entry of the Trefriw and Sychnant Pass roads, the Mill Gate, in Rosehill Street, and the Lower Gate (Porth Isaf) sometimes called Water Gate. The Castle Gate and Wing Gate are of later date. From the top of the walls there are some fine views.

The saltwater Mill (Felin Heli) was situated near where the Conway is joined by the Afon Gyffin. Close to the Lower Gate is **Aberconway** (National Trust) built in 1300. Just outside the gate is the *Smallest House in Great Britain*.

Walks from Conway

Among the walks which should on no account be missed is the climb to the summit of **Conway Mountain**. It starts from the Penmaenmawr road, crossing the railway by a foot-bridge opposite the old gasworks, then following a green track to the summit, about 800 feet above the sea, on which is *Castell caer Lleon*, the remains of an ancient British fortress. The walk can be continued to the Sychnant Pass and Penmaenmawr. An alternative route is by the Upper Gate (reached from the Square by Rosemary Lane) and the Sychnant Pass road, from which the mountain may be reached by obvious pathways across the fields.

Another is the **Marine Walk**, which extends round the fir-clad knoll of Bonc Hill and the mansion of Bodlondeb. It can easily be accomplished in half an hour, and is especially delightful when the tide is up. It affords the best view of the Castle.

Other recommended walks are :

By Benarth Wood. A walk of 2½ miles. Turn down the Trefriw and Betws-y-Coed road, by the castle. With the castle on the left, cross the *Gyffin* stream, and the bowling green on the left. A public path across the fields to the left leads past a farmhouse, and along the fringe of **Benarth Woods** (*private*). For the return turn right through Gyffin or continue for three-quarters of a mile to Baclaw Farm, and there turn to the right for Conway.

To Llangelynin Old Church (3 miles). Leaving Conway by the Upper Gate (reached from the Square by Rosemary Lane or Uppergate Street), take the left-hand road and in about half a mile disregard the turn (the Betws-y-Coed road) which dips down to the left. Pass through the hamlet of Hendre (*Hendre* = winter quarters) and in half a mile go behind the hill-side hamlet of Groesffordd. Disregard lanes right and left and with a chapel on your right make towards Pen-y-Dinas, the lower shoulder of Tal-y-Fan. As the road rounds this small hill the old church comes into view. It is of great age, and most impressive in its simplicity and environment.

Return routes, eastward by a descent to the valley, northward by footpath to Roe Wen.

To the Sychnant Pass and Dwygyfylchi. Leave by the Upper Gate and follow the right-hand road to the romantic Sychnant Pass (2 miles), from which there is a descent into the village of Dwygyfylchi (2½ miles), and the approach to the Fairy Glen described in the Penmaenmawr section. The return can be made *via* Penmaenbach, making a circular excursion of 5 miles; over Conway Mountain, making a walk of 4½ miles, or cross the hill from the top of Fairy Glen.

Penmaenbach is the prominent headland cutting Conway off from Penmaenmawr. It is a fine view-point, easily ascended from Conway mountain.

Roe Wen is the turning-point of a pleasant little walk which leaves Conway by the Upper Gate. Take the left-hand road and in about half a mile turn steeply down to left to Gyffin. Cross the bridge and immediately turn right. The road then meanders happily through pretty country to the hamlet of Roe Wen. From Roe Wen a Roman road runs westward to Aber and Llanfairfechan.

A mile east of Roe Wen, a few hundred yards east of the Conway-Betws-y-Coed road, is the old church of **Caerhun**, which stands in the corner of the Roman fort of *Conovium*. The church is usually locked, however.

To Penmaenmawr. A good upland walk. As described above to Sychnant Pass, at top of which take a path southward over hills to the *top* of the Fairy Glen, beyond which a gate with signpost will be seen on the western skyline. From the gate are paths to the Jubilee Walk, Green Gorge, etc. (*see* pp. 92–4).

CONWAY TO LLANRWST AND BETWS-Y-COED

There is a road on either side of the Conway Valley. The one on the east passes through Llanrwst and is 17 miles in length, a mile of which can be cut off by crossing the river at Llanrwst and joining the road on the west side.

The **Conway River** (*launches in season between Conway and Trefriw—3½ hours round trip*) has its source in Llyn Conway, a small lake in the mountainous district where the counties of Merioneth, Denbigh and Caernarvon meet. It receives the waters of the rivers Machno, Cletwr, Lledr, and Llugwy, and some other smaller mountain streams. Through nearly the whole of its course the Conway forms the boundary between the counties of Denbigh and Caernarvon. Its extreme length is about 30 miles. It is navigable for roughly 14 miles, and is tidal for about 12. Midway in its beautiful valley is the town of Llanrwst. From the village of Trefriw, a little below Llanrwst, to its outlet, one mile below the town of Conway, it is a large river navigable by small vessels.

By Boat. As the boat proceeds, you get a fine view of Conway Castle and the bridges, while the wood-covered rock of Bodlondeb, on the right, also adds to the beauty of the scene. Having passed under the bridges, there is on the right the well-wooded hill of **Benarth;** beyond which comes **Cymrhyd Point** on the right, and **Glan Conway** on the left. Rounding the point is a magnificent panorama of distant mountains, and the boat quickly comes abreast of **Tyddyn Cynal Farm** on the right. Running up from the opposite bank of the stream may be seen a **Cromlech,** consisting of five upright stones supporting a block 12 feet long, 8 feet broad, and 4 feet thick, and weighing about 20 tons. Behind are two upright stones, each about 9 feet high, and some 6 feet apart. Immediately afterwards the boat passes the old house of *Hendrewaelod*, also on the left. Four miles south of Conway is *Bodnant Hall* standing in its beautiful grounds. The Gardens (*National Trust*) of 50 acres are open to the public in summer on Tuesday, Wednesday, Thursday and Saturday, 1.30 p.m.–4.45 p.m. (*charge*).

Beyond the bridge at **Tal-y-Cafn** some rocks called the *Arrows* are passed, and then on the right in the midst of gigantic yew-trees can be seen the old church of **Caerhun,** erected in one corner of the Roman fortress known as Conovium.

Two miles farther, and some little distance from the river, are, on the right, the villages of **Tal-y-Bont** and **Llanbedr,** the summer quarters of many artists. Then comes an extensive plain, on which some say Llewelyn encamped in 1282 on the eve of a battle with Edward I, the site of the conflict being between this spot and Cymryd Point. On the hills to the right are the **Falls of Porthlwyd** and **Dolgarrog,** and at this point on the river the entrance to the Canal leading to the hydro-electric generating station; the machinery is run by turbines actuated by water coming down to the works in the pipe line which can be seen on the face of the hill.

On the opposite side, a wooded hill called **Porth Hywel Goch** (the gate of Red Howel) rises almost from the river bank. According to tradition, a giant who lived in this locality was accustomed to stand with one foot on the summit of this hill, and the other on the hills above Dolgarrog whilst he washed himself in the stream flowing between.

The river narrows very rapidly as we get near **Trefriw**, nestling at the foot of wooded hills (*see* p. 78).

Llanrwst

Banks. *Midland, National Provincial, Barclays.*

Buses to Trefriw, Conway and Llandudno, starting from Ancaster Square. Also frequent services to Abergele and to Betws, Penmachno and Cwm.

Distances. Capel Curig (via Betws-y-Coed), 10; Trefriw, 1 from Station by new road, 3½ by old road; Conway, 12; Llandudno, 16.

Early Closing Day. Thursday.

Fishing. Excellent trout and salmon fishing in the water of the Conway Fishing Association and Crafnant Lake. For particulars apply Mr. T. G. Roberts, 36 Station Road, Llanrwst.

Hotels. *Eagles; Pen-y-Bont; King's Head; Victoria.* Furnished chalets are available at Glan-y-Borth. Apply Information Centre.

Information Centre. Snowdonia National Park Centre, "Glan-y-Borth", Llanrwst.

Population. 2,550.

Market Day, Tuesday

Post Office. Station Road.

Recreation. Tennis courts, putting and bowling greens, and other games are played in the Recreation Ground in Gwydyr Park. Cinema. Concerts and other forms of entertainment are given in the Church House.

Llanrwst is a market-town in a rich agricultural district situated near the centre of the Conway Valley, amidst lofty hill, rich meadows and lovely woods.

Near the station is the remnant of *Plas Isaf*, the residence of William Salisbury, the first translator of the New Testament into Welsh. Half a mile away is **Ancaster Square**, used as a market

75

place. In the centre is the **Town Hall.** From a corner of the Square, by the Eagles Hotel, a short thoroughfare leads to the **Parish Church** dedicated to the sixth-century saint, St. Grwst.

A church was probably built here in the twelfth century and tradition has it that Rhun, a son of Nefydd Hardd, founder of the fifteen tribes of North Wales gave land for it to expiate the murder of Prince Idwal, son of Owain Gwynedd, by order of his foster father Nefydd to whom he had been entrusted. This building was burned by the armies of the Earl of Pembroke during the Wars of the Roses. Most of the present building dates from 1670. There is a magnificent carved rood-loft probably brought from Maenan Abbey (which formerly stood some two miles north of the town) at the Dissolution.

Adjoining the church is the **Gwydyr Chapel** (*key from verger at the churchyard entrance*) a mausoleum erected by Sir Richard Wynn of Gwydyr in 1634, on the instructions left in the will of his famous father, Sir John Wynn. It is an elaborate Gothic building and retains many of its original fittings. Tradition associates the name of Inigo Jones with the design. The ceiling is of heavy, finely carved oak, probably from Maenan Abbey. Some of the Wynns are commemorated by marble monuments, and others by portrait brasses.

The Jesus Hospital almshouses at the churchyard entrance were founded in 1610.

Llanrwst Bridge bears date 1636 and is said to have been designed partly, if not entirely, by Inigo Jones. It rises to a sharp point in the centre.

Adjoining the west side of the bridge is **Tu Hwnt I'r Bont,** a fifteenth-century stone cottage (*teas*), once used as a court house. It is now National Trust property, the Pilgrim Trust having subscribed toward its restoration.

From the bridge a straight road leads to the highway between Conway and Betws-y-Coed. Along this, some 200 yards to the left, is the entrance to **Gwydyr Castle,** formerly the seat of the Wynn family, restored after fire damage. The castle and gardens (note the peacocks) are open to the public from 10–5, from Easter until October (*admission charge, children half-price*).

Opposite the Castle entrance a steep path leads through the woods to *Gwydir Uchaf,* where the Gwydir family once had a summer residence; it is now the head office of the Forestry Commission. Here is a remarkable little **Episcopal Chapel,** which has inscribed over its door "1673 S.R.W.B."

Llanrwst to Betws-y-Coed via Llyn-y-Parc

(About 6 miles.) This is an exceedingly beautiful walk, and for a considerable distance lies through a wood. Though the wood ends fairly soon it is replaced by a wonderful view of distant Snowdonia. Cross the old bridge and on reaching the Betws-y-Coed–Trefriw road carry on over it, taking the lane straight ahead.

(*a*) The road on the right runs along the side of the valley, above the main road, which it joins near the quarries south of Trefriw village.

(*b*) The well-made road ahead leads up over the hills to Ty Hyll Bridge, a mile above the Swallow Falls on the Capel Curig road.

(*c*) The track on the left is that which works up through plantations to Lyln-y-Parc, and then continues to Betws-y-Coed. As an alternative route to Betws-y-Coed, however, the path by Pen-yr-Allt is strongly to be recommended, though rather longer than the one which comes down from the dam.

For **Betws-y-Coed,** *see* page 80.

Llanrwst to Trefriw

1. **By the High Road** (2¼ miles) This passes over the old bridge, and half a mile beyond turns to the right and continues straight into Trefriw. A more agreeable alternative, scarcely any longer, is by the road (*a*), passing Nant Cottage mentioned below, keeping to the right at the fork.

2. **Past Llanrhychwyn Church** (About 5 miles) Proceed as above, and at Nant Cottage take road (*a*) to the right. It at once crosses a stream just above a small fall, called the *Grey Mare's Tail*. Proceed along this road for

about three quarters of a mile until a small hamlet of four or five houses is reached, then take the road to the left, passing through a farm gate, and the church can then be seen on the right-hand slope partly obscured by yew-trees.

Llewelyn's Old Church, as it is called, is one of the oldest churches in the Principality, and is a unique specimen of primitive ecclesiastical architecture. It is about 40 feet long internally, and consists of two aisles, of which the northern is the older, and a bell turret. The font is said to belong to the eighth century. On the lych-gate is the puzzling inscription: IT. ID. OT. 1462. WO.

On resuming the journey to Trefriw, pass into the lane at the west end of the church, and follow that to the right for about a quarter of a mile, and then take a track on the left. This goes to the left of a hill called *Clunllom*, the summit of which (slightly off the track) is 938 feet high, and commands a grand view. Thence a path leads first round the southern extremity of a wood and then through the wood into a road which soon enters Trefriw.

Trefriw

Early Closing Day. Thursday.
Fishing in Lakes Crafnant (apply Ll. Phillips at Cynllwyd) and Cowlyd and several rivers

(Licences from Gwynedd River Board).
Hotels. *Belle Vue, Ye Olde Shippe Inn, Fairy Falls.*

Trefriw (pronounced *Trev-rewe*) is a large village, pleasantly situated under the tree-clad hills on the western side of the Conway River. Through it runs the high road between Conway and Betws-y-Coed, 11 miles from the former, 4¾ from the latter. It is in the midst of romantic scenery and is a favourite resort of those requiring quiet quarters within easy reach of upland walks and yet in touch with busier centres such as Llandudno.

The pretty little **Fairy Falls** are on the stream coming down from Llyn Crafnant, 2½ miles distant. The **Chalybeate Wells,** about a mile from the village, yield the richest sulphur-iron waters in the world.

One of the most enjoyable walks in the neighbourhood is that to Llyn Crafnant which lies to the south-west of Trefriw, in a most beautiful spot in the midst of the mountains. The route leaves Trefriw village by the lane beside the Glanrafon flats and is unmistakable if one remembers to keep right at the fork about half a mile above the village (*i.e.* to follow the north side of the stream). The lake is about a mile long, nearly half a mile wide, and 600 feet above sea-level. To increase its utility to the village the level of the water has been artificially raised. Towards the far end is a cottage where refreshments may be obtained, boats are on hire and fishing facilities are available. Cars can be taken to this point.

The continuation to **Llyn Geirionydd,** however, is for walkers only. There are two routes, one starting behind the tea-house just mentioned, the other beginning at a gate below the falls at the lower end of the lake. The path first leads to the left of a slate quarry, then across another track, and finally over the slopes. Geirionydd Lake is not so lovely as Llyn Crafnant.

It is said to have been the ornamental water in front of the reputed home of Taliesin, the first and greatest of Welsh poets who lived in the sixth century. At the foot of the lake is a monument to the bard.

Porthlwyd Falls are three miles north of Trefriw. There are important hydro-electric undertakings near the foot.

Trefriw to Capel Curig by Llyn Cowlyd

(*About 10 miles, 3–4 hours.*)

Leaving Trefriw, cross the bridge over the Crafnant stream, and turn up at once to the left, keeping straight on till the road forks. Take the right-hand branch, skirting a cemetery on the left. When you have passed through a gate, the road sweeps round to the right. Go through another gate on the left, and pass a farm-house. There are good views of Llyn Crafnant and Llyn Geirionydd on the left during the climb. After passing the long and almost level ridge of Careadwydd (1,407 feet), a tiresomely boggy one, you see two farms, *Brwynog-isaf* and *Brwynog-uchaf*, "Lower and Upper Brwynog," by which the path goes, crossing the stream by a bridge at the bottom of the valley. During the descent a corner of Llyn Cowlyd comes into view, with Pen Llithrig towering beyond it. From the stream the path leads past two cottages, *Carregwen* and *Cwm Cowlyd*, about three quarters of a mile apart, and then bears down to the lake with which it runs parallel, about 100 feet above the water.

From Cwm Cowlyd the ascent of **Pen Llithrig-y-Wrach** ("The top of the Hog's Slide," 2,621 feet) may be made. Turn up west for the ridge, which is rather boggy, and follow it to the top. Descend by a steep grass slope—quite easy going *down*—to about the middle of the lake.

Llyn Cowlyd is over 1½ miles long by quarter of a mile wide and 1,165 feet above the sea. Its east side is a steep green slope, with a crest of dark rock, *Creigiau Gleision*. The west side is not so steep, and the path is distinct. It supplies water to Conway, Deganwy, Rhos, Colwyn Bay, Old Colwyn, and Llysfaen, the surplus water going to the Dolgarrog works.

At the south end of the lake the path leads over a spur on Pen Llithrig, and high up along the side of the corrie. It then skirts a patch of boggy ground, turns left to the cairn on the top of the *col* (1,366 feet; Tryfan's three humps and Glyders in view) at an angle of a wire fence, which **it** skirts for ten minutes, after which, for another ten, it passes over a bog to a gate, beyond which the descent to *Tal-y-Waen* farmhouse takes four minutes. The Bangor road is soon afterwards entered three quarters of a mile from Capel Curig.

BETWS-Y-COED

Bank. *Midland.*

Buses to Penmachno and Cwm and to Llanrwst and Abergele; also to Cerrig-y-Drudion and Ruthin; and to Capel Curig, Bethesda, and Bangor.

Distances. Beddgelert, 18; Bethesda, 14; Capel Curig, 5½; Caernarvon, 24; Conway Falls, 3; Dolwyddelen Castle, 7; Fairy Glen, 1½; Llanberis, 16; Miners' Bridge, 1; Nant Ffrancon, 10; Pandy Mill, 3½; Penmachno, 4½; Pen-y-Gwryd, 10; Pontypant Bridge, 4; Swallow Waterfalls, 2½.

Early Closing Day. Thursday.

Entertainment. Concerts, and other entertainments.

Fishing. Excellent fishing for trout and salmon in the waters of the Conway Fishing Association and the Betws-y-Coed Anglers' Club.

Hotels. *Gwydyr; Royal Oak; Swallow Falls*, facing Falls; *Glan Aber; Craig-y-Dderwen* (private).

Population. 750.

Road Routes. The Holyhead road comes down from Capel Curig and past the Swallow Falls, forms the main street of Betws-y-Coed, crosses the Conway by the iron Waterloo Bridge and at once begins to climb towards the moors in the direction of Cerrig-y-Drudion.

At the top of the village, the old stone Pont-y-Pair bears the road running down the *west* side of the Conway Valley to Trefriw and Conway.

Beyond the Waterloo Bridge the road to the left leads down the *east* side of the Conway Valley to Llanrwst, Llandudno Junction, Colwyn Bay, etc.

The road forking to the right as the Cerrig-y-Drudion road begins to climb after crossing the Waterloo Bridge, leads to Beaver Pool, Dolwyddelen, the Lledr Valley and Ffestiniog.

One other road is worth noting: the by-road which branches from the main road just short of the elbow leading to the Waterloo Bridge, and runs round to Beaver Pool and the Ffestiniog road. It is more hilly than the more usual route, but affords good views of the surrounding hills and some charming peeps of the river and the Beaver Pool.

Betws-y-Coed is charmingly situated among tree-clad hills at the point where the Llugwy valley meets the wider, softer valley of the Conway. It claims with justification to be "the Beauty-spot of Wales". During the season it is besieged by visitors, for although the village consists almost entirely of hotels and apartment houses, "Betws-y-Coed" to the world at large includes also the far-famed Swallow Falls and the romantic glen of the Conway.

The name means "the Chapel (or Sanctuary) in the Wood",

n Gwynant (*G. D. Bolton*)

Moel Siabod and Lledr Valley (*G. D. Bolton*)

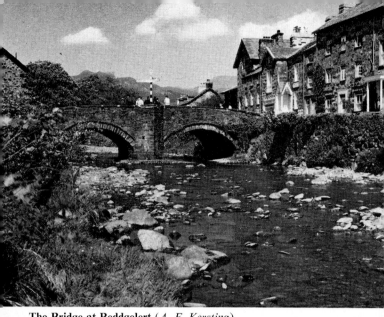

The Bridge at Beddgelert (*A. F. Kersting*)

Pont-y-Pair, Betws-y-Coed (*Woolverto*

and woods and water are its characteristics. The site is low, 80 feet above sea-level but it is healthy. The rainfall is somewhat heavy, but as the soil is light and porous, the water is quickly carried off.

The village has long been a favourite haunt of anglers and artists. David Cox visited it for many years, and in the entrance hall of the Royal Oak Hotel is the signboard he painted in 1847.

The Old Church, one of the oldest in Wales, is now used only for weddings and funerals. It contains the recumbent effigy of Gryffydd ap Dafydd Goch, a grandson of the last Llewelyn's brother David. He lived in the Lledr Valley, in the fourteenth century. For the old building, which is dedicated to St. Michael, there has been substituted **St. Mary's Church,** on the main road.

Towards the northern end of the village is the picturesque **Pont-y-Pair,** "the Bridge of the Cauldron". It is sometimes attributed to Inigo Jones but tradition says it was designed and partly built by a native mason named Howel, who died about 1470, before the work was finished. Jagged rocks here form the bed of the river, causing a miniature cataract. Just above the bridge is **Fir Island** and above the island is the **Still Pool,** alongside which is a path that may be followed to the Miners' Bridge and the Swallow Falls.

At the opposite end of the village is the graceful **Waterloo Bridge,** built in the year of the great battle. *Y Bont Haiarn* ("the Iron Bridge"), the Welsh have always called it.

Short Walks and Excursions

The Miners' Bridge and Swallow Falls lie respectively 1 and 2½ miles north-west of the village along the Capel Curig road. The **Miners' Bridge** is a wooden structure, placed like a ladder, the lower end resting on one bank of the stream, the upper end on the rocks on the opposite side. It was originally erected to enable the miners of Pentre Du, the village on the left, to pass to and from the mines on the opposite hills, where formerly about 500 hands were employed.

The main road continues to climb beside the Llugwy for another mile, with beautiful glimpses of the stream dashing over its rocky bed.

Two and a half miles from Betws-y-Coed are the **Swallow Falls** (*admission 6d.; Hotel and tea rooms face the Falls*). Here the Llugwy, hurrying down from the mountains beyond Capel Curig to mingle its waters with those of the Conway, and reinforced by countless torrents, hurls itself into a chasm some 60 feet wide. Jagged rocks break the stream into three large falls, and these again are subdivided and broken by jutting crags, which disperse the waters and dash them in all directions.

The Fairy Glen can be reached directly from Betws-y-Coed by crossing the Waterloo Bridge and taking the river-side road immediately beyond it on the right, or (a prettier route) by turning up a narrow lane on the right a

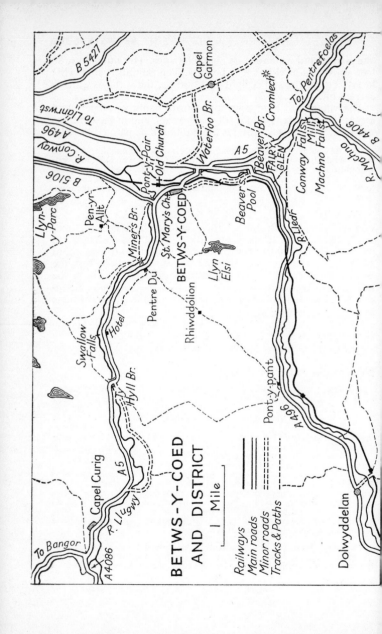

BETWS-Y-COED
AND DISTRICT
1 Mile

Railways
Main roads
Minor roads
Tracks & Paths

little short of the railway bridge. The two roads are of about the same length. They reunite on the east side of **Beaver Bridge,** at the Beaver's Pool, about a mile from the village. From the east end of the bridge a lane leads to the Glen, a truly enchanting spot. Rocks and trees tower high above the stream, which in some places rushes tumultuously over the rocks and forms a placid pool reflecting and heightening the beauties of the lovely scene in others.

Pandy Mill and Falls are reached by turning off the main Corwen highway by the Penmachno road, about 2 miles from the Waterloo Bridge. This runs high above the Conway River, and at the end of half mile leads to a lane on the right, beside a mill. Just below the point where this lane crosses the Machno is an ancient semicircular bridge, probably of Roman origin. A few hundred yards beyond the bridge, the lane arrives at the farm where the key is kept (*charge*) of the path leading to the **Falls of the Machno.** In a neighbourhood famed for falls, Pandy is one of those most worthy of a visit. It is small but perfect, and the glen below is equally charming. **Penmachno,** a small village two miles farther south-west, contains the gravestone of Carausius (a relic of ancient British Christianity), and in the Church is a memorial window to Bishop Morgan the translator of the Bible into Welsh, his birthplace being *Ty Mawr,* in this parish.

The **Conway Falls** (*admission 6d. Hotel*). The entrance is close to the junction of the Corwen and Penmachno roads. Here the Conway, rushing wildly down to the sea after receiving the waters of the Machno, is turned in its course by the unyielding cliffs and split into two streams by an immense boulder. Between the two falls is the old salmon ladder. The actual falls have not the grace of the little fall at Pandy, but the setting of greenery and rocks is beautiful.

Capel Carmon Cromlech (3 miles). The road crosses the Waterloo Bridge, goes to the left for about 300 yards and then branches up on the right. Walkers can cut off a corner by going a few yards to the right after crossing the Bridge and ascending some steps to a footpath which leads into the above road. At the junction turn to the right. Three-quarters of a mile farther turn to the right for **Capel Garmon.** Two-thirds of a mile beyond the village, pass through a gate on the right to a cart-track that leads past Tyny-Coed Farm to the *Cromlech.* Although locally referred to as "the Cromlech" the monument is more correctly described as burial chambers of the long barrow type in use at the beginning of the Bronze Age.

From the Cromlech there is a path to the Corwen and Pentrefoelas road, by which the return can be made. The circular walk will be about 5 miles.

Llyn Elsi, a small lake up among the hills, two miles to the south-west of Betws-y-Coed, is a pleasant spot for a picnic. The lake is the main source of water supply of Betws. The best route is by the "Jubilee" Path starting from the Capel Curig road about half a mile from the Post Office next to a house known as Mount View. The way is clear, and there are seats along it. At the fork beyond the fourth seat bear left, cross a wall by steps and from these make for a cairn and flagstaff and so to the monument erected in 1914 by the Earl of Ancaster.

Another route starts by the lane running up beside the (modern) Parish Church. The way is unmistakable, but steep in places.

Llyn-y-Parc, or Park Lake, lies up in the hills to the north of Betws-y-Coed, about 40 minutes easy walk from the village. One can return the same way, go back by Pen-yr-Allt, or continue alongside the lake to the main road beside Gwydyr Castle, Llanrwst.

From Betws-y-Coed cross Pont-y-Pair and turn sharp to the left. At the top of the first rise turn up the lane between two houses and where this becomes a footpath keep straight ahead. Disregard the path to right in a few hundred yards. The path hugs the hillside and eventually comes to a ravine where it then goes steeply up to the left and at the top a short strip of green path brings you to the end of the lake.

The Valley of the Lledr

This valley is extremely picturesque, particularly the portion between Betws-y-Coed and beautiful **Pont-y-Pant.** Beyond that point the scenery becomes more open, and at the Roman Bridge takes on an aspect of moorland which is only lost when the slag heaps of Blaenau Ffestiniog are reached. The Lledr Valley is highly interesting both to the geologist and the botanist.

Dolwyddelan, a village about $1\frac{1}{2}$ miles beyond Pont-y-Pant, was once a centre in the now defunct slate-quarrying industry. It has a curious ancient **church** as well as a modern one. The former was founded early in the sixteenth century by Meredydd ap Ifan, the ancestor of the Wynns of Gwydyr and of the Wynns of Wynnstay; he is commemorated by a brass inside the church.

A mile beyond the village, overlooking the road to Ffestiniog, are the remains of a **Castle** (*charge, apply farmhouse below castle*) in which Llewelyn the Great is said to have been born. He reigned from 1194 to 1240. The last Prince Llewelyn was his grandson.

A short way beyond the Castle, where the road crosses the river, there is a good distant view of Snowdon over the lower parts of Moel Siabod.

CAPEL CURIG

and Excursions Therefrom

Bus from Betws-y-Coed (5½ miles) or from Bangor (15 miles).

Fishing. All the neighbouring lakes provide excellent fishing, though some are private or held by clubs.

See local announcements. Cobden's Hotel has 1½ miles of Lugwy fishing.

Hotels. *Cobden's; Bryn-Tyrch; Tyn-y-Coed.*

Capel Curig, beautifully situated on the Shrewsbury and Holyhead road, is one of the oldest tourist resorts in the Principality. The village is about 600 feet above sea-level, and has a bracing air. It is a capital resort for anglers, for, besides the lakes close at hand, there are other good fishing waters not far away. It is also much frequented by climbers and walkers, since it is one of the handiest centres for Tryfan, the Glyders and Snowdon. The church is dedicated to St. Curig, a British recluse—hence the name of the village.

There are first-class hotels, several good boarding houses, and accommodation can also usually be found in one or other of the cottages. The village is strung along the Holyhead road for nearly two miles at the point where the Beddgelert and Llanberis road strikes off westward. Buses pass through it on their way to or from Betws-y-Coed or Bangor.

From Capel Curig the Holyhead road rises steadily until it reaches an altitude of 1,000 feet as it passes between the mighty **Tryfan** (3,010 feet) and **Llyn Ogwen,** the latter famed for trout and eels. From the western end, at Benglog, the road begins the long gradual descent of **Nant Ffrancon,** "the Vale of Beavers". But to be properly appreciated the pass should be *ascended* (*see* p. 107).

Tryfan (3,010 feet) is a really noble mountain and one highly popular with climbers. It is no place for the inexpert, however. In shape it resembles a pyramid, and, bristling as it does with fantastic and pinnacled rockwork, it affords unlimited scope for the hardy cragsman. The Eastern Traverse is the goal of many parties of expert climbers. On the summit are two stones known to climbers as *Adam and Eve;* they are clearly visible from the high-road and look like a couple of statues.

To climb Tryfan from Ogwen Lake, take the path to *Llyn Idwal* (*see* below). Where this bends sharply to the right, leave it and strike across boggy ground to the stream which flows from *Llyn Bochlwyd*. Follow a steep narrow track by its side to the lake above, from there make for *Bwlch Tryfan* (the narrow pass between Tryfan and Glyder Fach), and just before reaching its top, bear up the steep, rugged slopes to the left (there is a slight track) and the rocky summit will be gained after a stiff scramble.

To Llyn Idwal and the Devil's Kitchen

To Benglog, at the head of Nant Ffrancon, as described on p. 85 (*bus service*).

It should be understood that walking in this neighbourhood is often terribly rough, and frequently would be more accurately referred to as "climbing." It is inadvisable for an inexperienced person to set out without a companion, particularly in bad or doubtful weather.

Take the path striking up beside Ogwen Cottage and its neighbouring *Youth Hostel*, and in about a quarter of a mile turn sharp to the right, over swampy ground. The point to make for is a gate in a fence which is at the foot of **Llyn Idwal**, 1,200 feet high, in a hollow ground out by a glacier. On the western side are four moraines, arranged in long symmetrical mounds, one within another. Few scenes of the same dimensions in Wales are more stern and wild than those around this lake. In some places the rocks are perpendicular, and stand like a defiant wall around the pool. It is one of the many spots in the Principality with which a dark tradition is linked. A young prince whose name was Idwal (whence the name of the tarn) was here drowned by his foster-father, and it was long believed that, in consequence of the cruel deed, no bird would fly over the lake.

Beyond Llyn Idwal the rocky heights of Y Garn on the right and Glyder Fawr on the left descend so steeply as apparently to bar further progress. Looking up the Cwm, however, we may note, a little to the right of its far corner (W. side), a narrow rift in the rocky wall—a small "V" on the cliff-top. This is Twll-du (literally the "black hole"), and to reach it from the end of the lake the climb is a very steep and rough one, first up the ridge of a moraine, and then over rough debris, which descends almost to the water's edge. The height of Llyn Idwal above sea-level is about 1,200 feet; of the "Kitchen" (the bottom of the chasm) 1,700 feet, and the top of the chasm, 2,000 feet.

Twll-du (the **Devil's Kitchen**) is only a few yards wide, and the perpendicular rocks which form its walls are from 200 to

300 feet high. It is quite impassable, the small stream which threads it leaping from rock to rock in the wildest fashion.

Most tourists will be content to admire the chasm from below, but for stout walkers a very steep and somewhat loose path strikes up across the face of the rock to the left of the Kitchen. The path is indistinct in places—therefore keep close to the precipitous cliffs. The path becomes less steep, and near the summit bends to the right. When the ridge is reached, a walk of three minutes takes you to the top of the chasm, a little beyond which is the small lake, *Llyn-y-Cŵn*. Shortly beyond this the view opens out westward over Snowdon and Llanberis. To the left the ground rises steeply to the summit of **Glyder Fawr** (3,279 feet). For the *descent* to Pen-y-Gwryd, *see* below.

The Glyders

The tongue of land enclosed by the Holyhead and Beddgelert roads, and upon the tip of which Capel Curig may be said to stand, rises steeply westward to Glyder Fach (3,262 feet) and Glyder Fawr (3,279 feet). The word Glyder has a significance similar to the "clitter" of Dartmoor, and the aptness of the name will not be disputed by any who have passed from the Fach to the Fawr. The twin summits of the Glyders provide the roughest going in Wales.

From Capel Curig direct to Glyder Fach (2–2½ *hours*). For this ascent you may either follow the ridge (Cefn-y-Capel) all the way, striking up it directly from the Post Office, or (shorter and better) you may take the Pen-y-Gwryd road for about 1½ miles, passing the two lakes, and then turn up the fell by the farmhouse of *Dyffryn Mymbyr*; whence, after crossing a wall, you will come to a long smooth ascent over grass to the part of the ridge which overlooks **Gallt yr Ogof**. Hence Tryfan comes into prominent view. A stretch of level swampy ground, containing a few tarns, is crossed, beyond which, passing another northward spur, you look down into the desolate **Cwm Tryfan**. Glyder Fach is now directly in front. A series of cairns marks the way from the edge of the swampy ground nearly to the summit.

Pen-y-Gwryd (or Gorphwysfa) to Glyder Fawr (1½–2 *hours*). Go for a good 200 yards along the Capel Curig road from Pen-y-Gwryd; then pass through an opening near a shed and go north-westwards with the little height of *Moel-Berfedd* between you and the road on your left and the stream issuing from *Llyn-cwm-Ffynnon* some distance on the right. Cross this stream as it issues from the north-east end of the lake, and make straight ahead for the ridge which leads up to the Glyder Fawr. Hereabouts the ground is thickly strewn with moraine debris. The way to the ridge is steep but easily found, and when once you are on the ridge you have only to bear away slightly to the right till you reach the top of the mountain.

From Ogwen Lake. This has already been described in connection with the Devil's Kitchen excursion.

To **Glyder Fach** the way lies along the summit plateau of Glyder Fawr in an east-north–easterly direction till it narrows at the slight depression between the two mountains. Hence the direction is almost due east, over an extraordinary jumble of rocks and stones, and negotiating them requires care. The summit of *Glyder Fach* itself is composed of huge blocks of rock which are not easy to climb.

Descent to Pen-y-Gwryd presents no difficulty. Those making their way down from Glyder Fawr to Pen-y-Gwrd should proceed cautiously on account of the numerous masses of rock over and between which it is necessary to pass. In clear weather these are merely awkward; but in mist or darkness they are *dangerous*, especially to strangers, since a fall from one of these boulders might easily result in a broken leg, or worse. The hotel is seen below, but the point to aim at is a little way down the road on the Capel Curig side of the hotel.

It should be born in mind that the Glyders are extremely precipitous on their northern sides and that almost everywhere the going is hard.

Descent by Devil's Kitchen. Except to those who know the way, this is emphatically a dangerous route, owing to the difficulty of getting off the top of the path down the face of the rocks to the Kitchen Door.

Y Garn and the Elidyrs

A capital expedition may be taken over these heights from the head of Nant Ffrancon to Llanberis. The first part of the route is that to the top of the *Devil's Kitchen* (*see* p. 86). From this point strike up the side of **Y Garn** (3,104 feet) in a north-westerly direction till the summit is reached. Thence the way lies due north to **Foel Goch**, fine views being obtained on the way of the wild scenery at the head of Nant Ffrancon. From Foel Goch a steep descent along the ridge takes us to the head of a little green valley on our left, and bending round this till we face due west, a track will be struck which leads along the narrow rocky ridge of **Bwlch-y-Brecan**. No mistake can be made now, for the fine, craggy summit of **Elidyr Fawr** (3,029 feet) rises straight in front of us. The descent to Llanberis takes us in a westerly direction over the summit of **Elidyr Fach** (2,564 feet), and then on between quarries to a road. Follow this till the main road is gained, by which the Llanberis Lakes are reached.

Moel Siabod

(2,860 feet) is easily ascended from Capel Curig by crossing Pont Cyfyng at the lower end of the village. Take the second by-road right, beyond the bridge, and go up a stony farm track that rises above the woods. Pass two small farmhouses, and leave the track for a straight grassy road. Half-a-mile on, go through a wire fence, and along a shallow grassy hollow to the skyline. At the top, turn left for about a mile of ridge walking, then for a last few hundred yards over grass to the summit.

Standing a little apart from the group, this peak gives a grand view of the mountains of Snowdonia, with their lakes and hollows, and of the Irish Sea, with the bays of Caernarvon and Cardigan. Guides can be engaged at local hotels.

The Carnedds

These lie north-west of Capel Curig, in the angle made by the Bangor road. Compared with Tryfan and the Glyders, they do not make a tremendous climb, but those who appreciate tramping over good turf will enjoy them, and the views are very good.

Carnedd Dafydd (3,426 feet) is the nearer to Llyn Ogwen and can be reached by an obvious route leaving the main road near the 36th milestone from Holyhead. Follow the farm track at first, but just before reaching the house bear off to left and climb Craig Llugwy. From Carnedd Dafydd to Carnedd Llewellyn (3,484 feet) the way is rough and those who diverge from the direct path miss the best views.

A better way up leaves the main road 2½ miles from Capel Curig Post Office, strikes up to Tal-y-Braich cottages and then climbs the ridge called "Braich." From the top of Pen Helig (2,731 feet) follow a path winding down among the rocks and out on to a narrow grassy ridge reminiscent of Striding Edge on Helvellyn. Onward the way to the summit of Llewellyn is undeniably rough, but the scenery is fine.

To Llyn Crafnant and Trefriw. Take the path from the north side of the Church at Capel Curig. After crossing a small stream follow the right-hand fork, which leads across boggy ground between two craggy bluffs. After winding round the base of the crags on the left, the path turns left across a bog, and a stream is crossed by a wooden bridge. The path is now unmistakable up to the top of the col. From this point alternative routes are available. (a) Take a narrow track on the right, which runs along a little ridge, from which the views are very lovely. Soon a descent is made by a little hollow and a wall is reached on the left, which must be crossed in a short distance, and the track followed through the wood along the side of the steep slope, till another wall is reached. Cross this and a good path is gained which leads down to the road by the head of the lake. (b) An unmistakable path winds down to the valley, and after passing through two iron gates, joins the road which begins there.

By Llyn Cowlyd to Trefriw. From *Plas-y-Brenin* follow the Bangor road for a mile and just beyond a brook go up by a footpath to *Tal-y-waen Farmhouse*, behind and above which is a cart-track that leads to Llyn Cowlyd. Cross a brook, climb to a gate, turn right (*i.e.* N.) over the bog to a wire fence, which is skirted, as far as a cairn, at an angle to the fence on top of the *col* before the lake. From there follow the path over spurs of Pen Llithrig, above a corrie and the end of the lake, continuing along (about 100 feet) above the lake. For the rest of the way *see* the description of the reverse route, p. 79.

Other routes to Trefriw and Llanrwst begin at Ty Hyll Cottage (*see* p. 81).

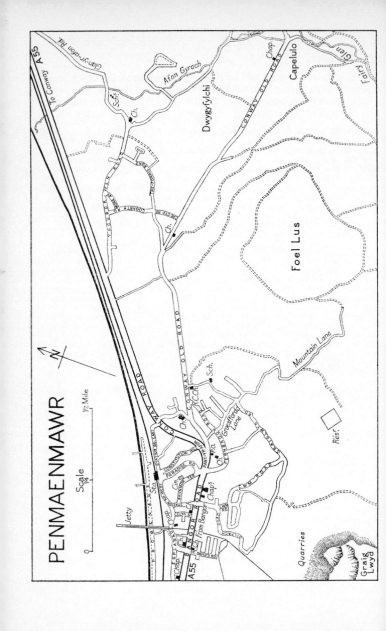

PENMAENMAWR

Scale
0   ¼   ½ Mile

N

To Conway A 55

Glan-yr-afon Rd.

Afon Gyrach

Sch⁵
Ch.

Dwygyfylchi

Chap.

Capelulo

Fairy Glen

CONWAY OLD ROAD

Ch.

Foel Lus

Mountain Lane

Rés.

Quarries

Graig Lwyd

Jetty

CONWAY ROAD

BANGOR RD

A 55

Sta.

ESPLANADE

Chap.

KN. & R RD

OLD RD

MELYN TER.

Chap.

From Bangor

DRUID'S RD

FERN RD

FERN

FFRIDD RD

CWM ROAD

Sch.

Ch.

P.O.

Groesffordd Lane

Ch.

BRYNIAU RD

PANT-YR-AFON

Chap⁵

Ch.

CONWAY OLD ROAD

Cio.

CONSTITUTION HILL

PARADISE RD

DENVENUM HILL

TY GWYN RD

COGARTH RD

MEYRICK RD

CEFN BR

Ch.

PENMAENMAWR

Amusements. Boating, bathing, and mountain-walking. Golf, tennis, bowls. Cinema. The Young Men's Institute, containing four billiard tables, is open to visitors. Dances are also held. . .

Banks. *National Provincial, Midland* and *Lloyds.*

Bathing. Perfectly safe. The beach is of firm sand and slopes gradually. Chalets have been built near the railway subway, and at the west end of the beach. The chalets are fitted with electric radiators, etc.

Beach. A fringe of shingle, succeeded by a good stretch of fine sand.

Bowls. Green near Railway Station. Also at Dwygyfylchi.

Buses *via* Conway and Deganwy to Llandudno, also to Llanfairfechan, Aber, Bangor and Caernarvon. There is also a good service to Dwygyfylchi, Golf Links, Fairy Glen and Sychnant Pass. At Conway connection is made with the Llandudno-Llanrwst buses, and there are also buses to Colwyn Bay, etc.

Distances. Bangor, 11; Betws-y-Coed, 21; Birmingham, 125; Caernarvon, 18; Chester, 51; Colwyn Bay, 8; Conway, 5; Llanfairfechan, 2; Llandudno, 9; Liverpool 65; London, 231; Manchester, 90.

Early Closing Day Wednesday.

Golf. A 9-hole course in a valley at the back of the town, below the road to Dwygyfylchi, 10 minutes' walk from the centre of the town. Buses run to and from the links. It is well drained and is dry all the year round. The hazards are natural and varied. There is a well-equipped club-house.

Hotels. *Ardre* (private), Fernbrook Road; *Plas Arvon* (private); *Bryn Helig Guest House*, Fernbrook Road.

Population. 3,770.

Post Office. Close to junction of Conway and Dwygyfylchi roads, Penmaenan and Capelulo.

Road Routes. The Chester-Caernarvon road forms the main thoroughfare of Penmaenmawr and leads eastward to Conway, etc.; westward to Llanfairfechan, Bangor, etc. For motorists almost the only deviation worth noting in the village is the old Conway road, cutting up between the Mountain View Hotel and the Post Office, and running *via* Dwygyfylchi (for the Fairy Glen) and the Sychnant Pass (1 in 7½ ascent) to Conway.

Tennis. Hard Courts on Club ground in Mountain Lane. Teas and refreshments at Pavilion.

Penmaenmawr is a quiet seaside resort standing at the mouth of a beautiful valley and bounded by lofty hills terminating in headlands known respectively as Penmaenmawr and Penmaenbach—the great and little headlands. From the larger and nearer of the two the town takes its name. It is a majestic rock

1,300 feet high, rising almost perpendicularly from the sea, and forming the northern termination of the Snowdonian range. Unfortunately this headland is composed of stone which has a commercial value, and consequently its sides are scarred by quarries.

Penmaenmawr offers an almost unique combination of sea, woodland and mountain and is a favourite spot for campers.

As in the case of most of the resorts along this part of the Welsh coast, the railway runs between the sea and the village, but by reason of the elevation of the site of Penmaenmawr the line does not block the view, which is charmingly varied and extensive. On the north is the sea, with Puffin Island and the north of Anglesey to the west; on the north-east the rugged rocks of Penmaenbach and Great Orme's Head; on the south-east the hill of Y Foel Llys with its many paths and its carpet of heather and bilberry plants; on the east the Fairy Glen and the Sychnant Pass, while between the two hills is a beautiful valley.

Its sheltered position gives the spot a genial climate, yet the air in summer is bracing and invigorating.

The centre of the town is linked with the sea-front by Paradise Road, at the head of which a bronze bust of W. E. Gladstone recalls that statesman's association with "dear old Penmaenmawr", as he called it.

The beach is an expanse of clean, firm sand, with a fringe of pebbles. It is bordered by an asphalted **Promenade** near the centre of which are rows of attractive chalets for bathing, etc. As the tide never recedes very far, safe bathing may be enjoyed at all hours of the day, and the bay is equally favourable for boating. There is also a paddling pool.

Walks from Penmaenmawr

The Fairy Glen (*charge. Refreshments at lower entrance*). The Glen is reached by the road leaving the village near the Post Office and passing through the hamlet of **Dwygyfylchi,** a name signifying "the place of the twin semicircles"; it gives an accurate description of the shape of the parish which corresponds exactly to two semicircles side by side. Cars should be left here since the remainder of the lane is very narrow; after passing between two hotels it runs in among hills for about half a mile to the entrance to the glen.

The lower part of the glen, with its solemn pines and quietly murmuring stream, will remind many Southern visitors of a Hampshire chine; but the upper portion is more characteristic of Welsh scenery and has a pretty display of rocks, pools and falls. It is a delightful retreat on a hot day.

From the upper gate we step out on to grass- and bracken-covered moorland surrounded by mountain peaks. A short way ahead (westward) will be seen a gate with a sign-post indicating the Green Gorge, the Jubilee Walk, etc.; the path following the wall leading down from the gate descends to the lane close to the lower entrance of the Fairy Glen. From the upper end of the glen there is an excellent walk towards Conway, through bracken and heather. The Sychnant Pass will be reached in a short distance.

The Sychnant Pass. The steep ascent of the Pass begins just beyond the lane leading to the Fairy Glen at Dwygyfylchi. The road rises about 300 feet in a mile, and the *descent* (1 in 7½) requires caution from motorists, as there are sharp elbows where the narrow road runs between unyielding cliffs of rock and a steep open precipice.

The scenery is impressive, the bareness of the rocky flanks of the pass contrasting vividly with the luxurious green slopes above the Fairy Glen. On the right, near the top, is a cliff near which a fine echo can be produced. Almost opposite this rock is the beginning of a path which crosses the head of the valley and leads over Conway Mountain into the town of Conway; walkers bound for Conway should take this in preference to the high road.

The Jubilee Walk. This is a promenade cut across the breast of **Y Foel Llys** (the Bilberry Hill), rising 1,181 feet high, at the back of the village, from which the view is grand and extensive. Of the several routes to it the most direct is by the lane leading to the Green Gorge. Two stone pillars mark the beginning of the path from this direction, and will be a sufficient guide as soon as they are in sight.

The Green Gorge. Pass at the back of the Mountain View Hotel, and almost immediately turn up Groesffordd Lane (the first on the right). It is very long and in parts steep. At the upper end is a gate; go through it and the Green Gorge is straight before you.

The Druids' Circle. This is on the moorland at the back of the village. It is about 1,200 feet above sea-level, and consists of a dozen stones, some 6 feet high, intermixed with smaller stones. The nearest way (1½ miles) is by Gilfach Road and Mountain Lane; from the lane turn to the left by Cwm Road. In a hundred yards or so a path crosses the field on the right to Graiglwyd Road, and here turn to the right for about 100 yards to a road leading to Graiglwyd Farm. Pass through the farm, and the way is then clearly sign-posted.

A short distance west of the Circle is a smaller collection of stones. In 1921 a large number of flint weapons and tools were unearthed in Graiglwyd Quarry, giving rise to the belief that in the Stone Age the place was an important site for the manufacture of those articles.

To Bwlch-y-Ddeufaen and Llanfairfechan. Walk up the Green Gorge and past the Druids' Circle, and continue half a mile farther along a green track winding westwards, where a sign-post directs to the Bwlch, about 2½ miles distant. The walk may be continued to Tal-y-Cafn, in the Conway Valley or the Roman Road (now but a track) followed towards Aber or Llanfairfechan (*see* p. 99).

Llangelynin Old Church (3 miles) **and the Conway Valley.** The route is through the Green Gorge, and then to the left and over a stile from which the path runs across the Fairy Glen stream to a derelict cottage a short distance beyond which the Church will become visible. It is said to have been built in the year 1350, stands 927 feet above sea-level, and is used only for a Sunday service at 5 p.m. during the summer. The keys are kept at a cottage near the church. (The last cottage on the right—"Garnedd Wenn" provides *refreshments*). The return may be varied by either of the routes described under Walks from Conway.

Ascent of Tal-y-Fan. The summit is 2,000 feet above the sea. It may be reached by striking across the tableland from the Druids' Circle, the time required for the walk between the two points being about three-quarters of an hour. But a better route will be found by making for the ruined cottage mentioned in the last route, and then climbing the hill (Cefn Maen Amor) on the slopes of which the cottage stands; thence keeping along the ridge until the final ascent begins. To the right is an upright stone, called for some unknown reason the *Stone of Games*. The summit of Tal-y-Fan is marked by two cairns, and by this route is about 4 miles from Penmaenmawr.

LLANFAIRFECHAN

Amusements. Mountain-walking, boating, bathing and fishing; tennis, crazy golf and bowls. Football and cricket fields in the Bryn-y-Neuadd Park. Concerts, dancing, etc.

Banks. *Lloyds, Midland, National Provincial.*

Bathing. Perfectly safe on a firm, sandy beach.

Beach. A belt of shingle succeeded by a stretch of firm, flat sands which the tide uncovers to a distance of half a mile. Ideal for children.

Boating. A popular trip by motor-boat is across the Strait to Puffin Island. Local sailing club.

Bowls At the Recreation Ground, adjoining model Yacht Pond.

Buses to Aber, Bangor and Caernarvon, and to Penmaenmawr, Conway, etc. Service between the Promenade and Three Streams during summer months.

Distances. Aber Village, 2; Aber Falls, 4½; Bangor, 8; Betws-y-Coed (*via* Glan Conway), 23; Caernarvon, 15½; Colwyn Bay, 12½; Conway, 7; Liverpool, 68; Llandudno, 12; London, 234; Manchester, 93; Penmaenmawr, 2½.

Early Closing Day. Wednesday.

Fishing Freshwater fishing in the Three Streams, Llyn Dulyn and the Aber Lake (licences required). Sea-fishing is very good, especially at the "Swash," a mile out.

Hotels. *Llanfairfechan; Bryn Onnen; Min-y-Don; Myrtlewood; Bryn Celyn; Rhiwlas Guest House.*

Model Yacht Pond. At western end of Promenade.

Population. 2,950.

Post Office. Village Road; branch offices in Shore Road, Station Road and towards eastern end of Penmaenmawr Road.

Road Routes. The Chester-Bangor road passes at the back of modern Llanfairfechan and leads eastward to Penmaenmawr, etc., and westward to Aber, Bangor, etc.

Tennis. Hard courts at Victoria Gardens, towards eastern end of the Promenade, and hard courts at the Recreation Ground, near the Model Yacht Pond. Tennis tournaments are arranged during the season.

In its brief but merry course to the sea the little Afon Llanfairfechan dashes first through rocky, fern-clad gorges; then through the gradually widening valley in which the original village of Llanfairfechan stands, and finally, passing under the coast road, it rattles past the modern resort called into being by visitors who appreciated this airy, healthy site, on the verge of the sea yet within a stone's-throw of the mountains. This charming combination of interests is well illustrated by the stream which bubbles beside the main street of the village, for although its source is some 2,000 feet above the spot where it runs into the sea, its length is scarcely three miles. The eastern side of its valley terminates abruptly in the prominent headland known as Penmaenmawr Mountain; its western side falls away gradually in green, wooded hills above which the giants of Snowdonia raise their heads to the sky.

The hills stand sufficiently far inland for their majestic proportions to be seen and admired without the observer being oppressed with their too immediate proximity. Yet they are near enough for the ascent to begin at the door of the village post-office, and from any of them views of great beauty and variety may be had.

The front at Llanfairfechan is unpretentious, but bathing is safe and there is a wide expanse of firm sand at low tide. There is a **Green** on which games may be played and at either end of the Parade public tennis courts, bowling and putting greens. A feature of even greater interest to juvenile navigators is the Model Yacht Pond.

The path between the Yacht Pond and the Recreation Ground leads (walkers only) to the **Embankment Walk,** a sea-wall which is continued by a grassy path through fields, across the railway and back to the main road. The circuit (about three miles) forms a favourite short evening walk, the sunset effects over the mountains, the Strait and distant Anglesey being often indescribably beautiful.

This walk encircles the beautiful grounds of **Bryn-y-Neuadd,** laid out by the late Colonel Platt, who also built the charming mansion, now in use as a convalescent home. The farmlands surrounding **Gorddinog** are the subject of many comments. Gorddinog is noted for its sheep and cattle.

Of the buildings in the village calling for notice, the chief are the two churches. **St. Mary's,** the "little church of St. Mary", stands on a knoll above the village and has all its services conducted in Welsh. **Christ Church** (English services), situated near the entrance to the village from the west, is a striking building with a spire that stands up from among the trees and is prominent from many a neighbouring mountain-side. The church has a good screen and one of the finest organs in North Wales. (Recitals Sunday evenings during the season.)

Excursions from Llanfairfechan

1. An excellent introductory ramble is by the **Terrace Walk,** along the western side of the valley in which "old" Llanfairfechan lies. Turn up the lane between the Midland Bank and the School, opposite the Post Office. Cross bridge, turn left, and at the end of the path go up Bryn-y-Mor Terrace, opposite. Where these houses end turn right for a few yards and then immediately left, through a council housing estate which leads to the bottom of an incline that is the commencement of the **Terrace Walk.** Climb this short incline and carry on for a mile or more to some charming paths alongside the stream. As an alternative, return by the other side of the valley.

2. The **Meeting of the Three Streams.** The lane leading to this delightful spot is the southern continuation of Valley Road and the Terrace Walk. The "Meeting" is a place of rock and tree and fern at the foot of the bare, black rounded hill known as **Dinas.** Part of the east side of the stream near Dinas has been appropriately labelled **The Happy Valley.**

3. **Carreg Fawr** (the "big rock"), (1,167 feet). Proceed as in walk 1 as far as the incline at the beginning of Terrace Walk, which is then followed to a point about 300 yards beyond the open space on left, with iron seats. Here are two iron gates: one leading to a sand pit, the other crossing our path; the path goes up for 200 yards to where, just short of iron swing gate, a narrow lane on right leads up past a small hamlet and farm buildings and between walls to an iron swing gate; beyond it the way, with a wall on the *right,* is as obvious as it is steep. Bracken, foxgloves, gorse and countless wild flowers make it a beautiful climb. The path passes through a second iron gate on to a grassy track contouring easily up to the left, round the hill. This may be followed for a short distance higher, or an attack on the summit can be made at once. The way is steep and although nailed boots are not a necessity they ease the climb over the slippery grass. An alternative route turns out of the Aber main road by Cae Ffynon road, about 300 yards west of the bridge. Disregard all left-hand turnings and follow the lane for about half-a-mile, until a pair of cottages are reached on the left (with the sign, Llanerch Road). Turn up lane beside these cottages and on the farther side of the farm, 200 yards on, turn up right. From now on "upward" is the only direction required.

4. **The Roman Milestone.** Take the road up from the Post Office bearing right up the Penybryn Hill and on along Llanerch Road to where the road branches down to Gwyllt. From here turn up in the direction of the old golf course and on to Llys-y-Gwynt Farm on the right. Passing the farm on its upper side by a grassy path and out on to a stony road, go up some yards to a field on the right. The milestone (a replica of the original in the British Museum) is set up on the site on which the original was found. Entry to the field is by the small swing gate set in the wall. Llanfairfechan can be regained by continuing on and circling left.

5. **Bwlch-y-Ddeufaen,** a pass some 3¼ miles south-east of Llanfair-fechan, owes its name to the presence of two stones near the highest point (1,403 feet). They are about 9 feet high and 16 feet in circumference.

The shortest and easiest route is to follow the road to the Three Streams. When this place is reached, the cart-road up the hill to the left of the central stream should be followed. After passing through several gates open ground

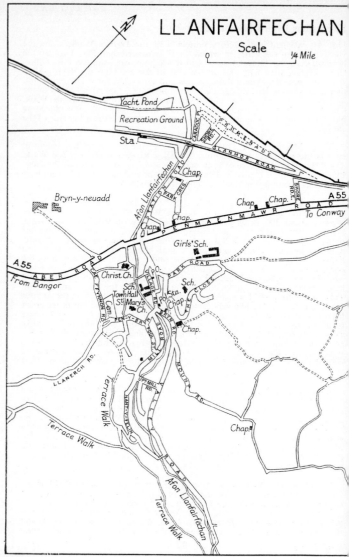

LLANFAIRFECHAN

Scale

0   ¼ Mile

Yacht Pond

Recreation Ground

Sta.

PARADE PL.

SHORE RD.

PROMENADE

GLANMOR ROAD

Afon Llanfairfechan

STATION ROAD

Chap.

PARK CRES.

Chap.

Chap.

Chap.

Chap.

Chap.

SHORE RD. E.

A55

To Conway

PENMAENMAWR ROAD

Bryn-y-neuadd

Girls' Sch.

A55

ABER ROAD

From Bangor

PARK ROAD

Christ Ch.

FFYNNON RD.

Cwm

Sch.

Town Hall

St. Mary's Ch.

P.O.

P.O.

Sch.

Sta.

PARK CLOSE

PEN-Y-CAE

MILL ROAD

Chap.

LLANERCH RD.

Terrace Walk

UP. MILL RD.

NANT-Y-FELIN

MILL ROAD

MOUNT RD.

Chap.

Afon Llanfairfechan

Terrace Walk

Terrace Walk

is reached, and a slight track, very wet in places, leads straight to the Pass, which lies in the gap between the heights of *Y Drosgl* on the right and *Foel Llwyd* on the left. You are now on the old Roman Road that ran from Aber to Conovium. The walk can be continued along this road, and the descent made to the Conway Valley. There are fine views eastward and to the south during the descent.

6. To Aber Lake (*Llyn-yr-afon*). It is a most interesting and not very difficult walk to Aber Lake (from which Llanfairfechan's water supply is obtained). Pass round Carreg Fawr and on by the path worn in the shoulder between Drum and Yr Orsedd, almost due south of Carreg Fawr. The lake comes into view down on the right as Orsedd is rounded, the sheer sides of Foel and Llwydmor guarding it to the south and west. Aber village may be reached by following the public path running parallel to the stream to the point where it joins the old Roman Road at a gate— an easy walk of perhaps four miles; or a return made over the hills to Llanfairfechan by following the track round the flank of Foel Dduarth at the point where the route to Aber takes to a grassy lane between two walls, down on the left.

Note. The Aber Falls are on the farther side of Llwydmor, and are not seen on this excursion. The ridge walk around and high above the Lake is exhilarating and worth while, but exploration of the vicinity of the Falls from this side has led to several nasty accidents and is not recommended.

7. Aber Falls. One of the finest walks from Llanfairfechan. Cross the bridge on the Bangor Road and turn up beside Christ Church grounds by the Caeffynon Road. Follow this and its continuation, Llanerch Road, to the fork with Gwyllt Road. Here keep to the left, and where the lane goes up left to old golf course, take the track on the *right*, which leads round the breast of the hill to a stony lane near the Kennels. Just above the house a gate in the lane wall opens on to a path descending across fields to stepping stones over a stream in the Gorddinog woods. Fork sharp left up a bank and over the wall by some steps, thence up across the open to Bodsilin House, over the wall, and then to the top of the rise. From here continue down a steep grassy track to the old Roman Road through an iron swing-gate, and on down to Bont Newydd, at the commencement of the field track to Aber Falls, and about half a mile from Aber village. For Aber, see p. 100.

The walk of at least half an hour from Bont Newydd to the Falls is by an extremely beautiful path across fields fringed with graceful trees and watered by the burbling stream which springs from the Falls. On either hand rise high hills, glorious with heather and bracken and the shimmering green of closely-packed trees. There is no café or car park at the falls, but motorists can leave their cars at Bont Newydd.

There are two falls, of which the finer is reached first. It is some 120 feet in height, projecting rocks breaking its waters into lesser falls of extreme beauty. The second fall is reached by turning to the right, in a south-westerly direction, and walking along the foot of the hill for about five minutes.

8. To the Druids' Circle, Fairy Glen, Dwygyfylchi, Green Gorge, Jubilee Walk, and Llangelynin Old Church. Take the Village Road past the Post Office. Turn up Mount Road, on the left, and continue along it, skirting Penmaenmawr Mountain, until the highest point of the road is gained. The **Druids' Circle** is on a small hill two hundred yards ahead, and slightly to the right. After viewing the Circle, join the road, and continue a short distance until sign-posts direct you to the places mentioned. (*See* pp. 92—4)

9. **Llyn Dulyn** (The Black Lake). This is the objective of a delightful mountain expedition, but it is suitable only for good walkers in clear weather. From *Carreg Fawr*, a green track will be seen winding up and round the shoulder of *Yr Orsedd* (*the Thrones*) in a south-easterly direction. Make for this and follow it till it ceases on *Drum*. On the right the steep slopes of Llwydmor descend to Aber Lake, or *Llyn-yr-afon*, and we get a glimpse down the Aber Valley. From the end of the path the best guide is the wire fence running up to the right. Cross the depression between *Drum* and *Y Foel Fras* and climb a short distance up the latter mountain. About a third of the way up, cross the wire fence on the left, and descend the mountain-side diagonally in a southerly direction, passing below a steep rocky slope, until the lake is reached. It is backed by a fine precipice which descends sheer into the water, the edge of which can be reached at the exit of the lake.

Aber

Buses to and from Llanfairfechan. Penmaenmawr, Conway, Bangor, etc.

Hotels. *Aber; Aber Falls.*

Teas, etc. can be obtained in the village or at Bont Newydd, though it is well to go prepared to save disappointment. There is no accommodation of any kind at the Falls themselves, 1½ miles from the Bridge. It is an ideal spot for picnics.

"Aber" signifies river-mouth, and it is at the entrance to a deep and romantic glen that we find the village of Aber. The erection of a footbridge over the river mouth has opened up a very pleasant walk along the shore to or from Llanfairfechan. Aber has not become a seaside resort, though there is safe bathing. Its full name is Aber-gwyngregin, said to signify the Mouth of the Stream of the White Shells.

In the village is an artificial mound, called the **Mŵd,** on which once stood a castle built by Llewelyn the Great, Prince of Wales, who married Joan, daughter of King John. It was in this castle that the last native Prince of Wales, Llewelyn ap Gruffydd, received and declined the summons of Edward I to attend the English Parliament at Westminster. Attendance meant the voluntary surrender of the independence of Wales. The Prince's refusal was soon followed by the conquest of the Principality.

For the **Aber Falls,** *see* p. 99.

100

BANGOR

Banks. *National Provincial, Lloyds, Midland, Barclays, District,* all in High Street. *Midland* and *National Provincial* in Upper Bangor. *Martins* and *Trustee Savings.*

Bathing. Sea bathing safe at all times of the day.

Bowls. Public crown greens near Town Hall, in Glynne Road, Heol Dewi and Glanadda. The Conservative Club and Upper Bangor Bowling Club greens are both open to visitors.

Buses run all the year round between the Town Clock and Beaumaris and Llangoed. There are also services from Bangor to Menai Bridge and the whole of Anglesey; to Caernarvon, Snowdonia; to Bethesda, Capel Curig, and Betws-y-Coed; Conway, Llandudno and other coastal resorts.

Car Park. Dean Street.

Distances. Bethesda, 5; Betws-y-Coed, 20; Caernarvon, 9; Chester, 61; Conway, 15; Holyhead, 24; Llanberis, 17½; Llandudno, 18½; Llanfairfechan, 8; Llanrwst, 26½; London, 235; Menai Bridge, 1½; Penmaenmawr, 10; Rhyl, 30.

Early Closing Day. Wednesday.

Ferry across the Strait. Half-hourly from the pier head to Llandegfan. Service to Beaumaris.

Fishing. Ogwen and Idwal Lakes and the upper reaches of the Ogwen river are let to the *Ogwen Valley Angling Association;* the lower reaches are let to the *Penrhyn Fishing Club.* The Aber and scores of other streams and lakes are within easy reach. The deep-sea fisher finds excellent sport in the Menai Strait with bass, bream, conger-eel, pollock, etc. There is also good sea-fishing from the pier, where codling, plaice and whiting are taken.

Golf. Excellent 18-hole course on the hill bordering the city on the south-east, facing the Snowdonian range and overlooking the sea.

Hotels. *Castle,* High Street; *Belle Vue,* Upper Bangor; *Albion,* High Street; *British,* High Street; *Garth,* Garth Road; *Glanrafon,* Deiniol Road; *Gwynedd,* High Street; *Waverley, Nantlys, Greystones.*

Library. In Ffordd Gwynedd, adjoining the Post Office.

Market Day. Friday.

Newspaper. *North Wales Chronicle,* published Friday.

Population. 13,750.

Post Office. Ffordd Deiniol; branches in High Street, at Upper Bangor, etc.

Road Routes. Bangor High Street is for one-way traffic only (west to east) and those bound for Holyhead or Caernarvon must turn off to the right along Beach Road, left into Garth Road and its continuation, Deiniol Road. Running up the valley this joins the main Holyhead road opposite the station, as it climbs to Upper Bangor. Thence it bears left for the run to the Menai Suspension Bridge.

For Garth, the Pier and the Ferries turn right at the junction of Beach Road and Deiniol Road.

Steamers. During the season steamers run to and from Menai Bridge (reached by bus in about 10 minutes) to Llandudno and Liverpool.

Tennis. Garth and Heol Dewi Municipal Hard Courts; Glanadda; Glyndyl, Upper Bangor.

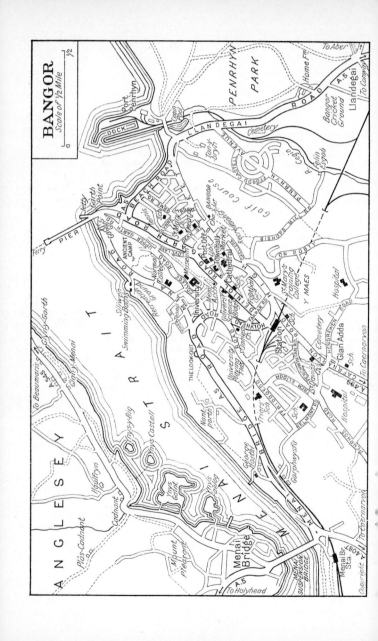

Bangor, situated on the southern coast of the Menai Strait, is one of the most ancient cities in Wales. Its authentic history begins with the erection of a monastery about A.D. 525, by Deiniol, who became the first bishop of the diocese. The name is by modern authorities derived from the "bangor" or wattle fence which protected the first monastic settlement.

It is a busy little town, and a good centre for the exploration of north-west Wales. From it there is easy access to the heart of the Snowdonian range, and to the popular spots in Anglesey. It commands delightful marine and mountain views; is handy for the Liverpool and Llandudno steamers, and is well served by railway and roads; it offers a large choice of hotels and good apartment houses; and facilities for various sports.

Old Bangor, the commercial part of the city and site of the cathedral, lies along the valley through which runs the road to Caernarvon. On the opposite slopes are the buildings of the University College and beyond them lies Upper Bangor, the favourite residential quarter, commanding splendid views across the wooded Menai Strait.

The **Cathedral** consists of an aisleless choir, transepts, and nave with aisles, and in appearance resembles an ordinary large parish church. It was founded in A.D. 548 by Deiniol, son of the Abbot of Bangor Iscoed (Bangor-under-the-wood) in Flintshire. He became its first bishop and to him the church is dedicated. Of his building there are no remains. The Cathedral that was standing in 1071 was destroyed by the Normans. In 1102 its rebuilding was begun. The structure then erected was destroyed about a century later by order of King John, who is said to have repented immediately and to have contributed liberally towards its restoration. The Cathedral was, however, almost a total ruin, when in the closing years of the thirteenth century Bishop Anian undertook its reconstruction. Being liberally aided by Edward I, he produced a building more magnificent than any that had preceded it. In 1402 this fine Cathedral was destroyed by Owen Glendower, when in rebellion against Henry IV. It remained in ruins until its restoration was begun by Bishop Deane in 1496. Further restoration was undertaken in 1532, by Bishop Skeffington, who, according to an inscription over the west door, rebuilt the west tower and the nave. After that, with the exception of much disfigurement due to repairers, the edifice remained practically unaltered until its restoration was begun in 1866, under the care of Sir Gilbert G. Scott.

At that time a central tower was commenced but left unfinished owing to the difficult nature of the sub-soil. The tombstones in the churchyard were laid flat, and the railings facing the High Street were put back and lowered—indeed everything that could be devised was done to lessen the effect of its lack of height.

Internally many improvements were made. In the core of the fifteenth-century walls, where it had been embedded as mere rubble, Sir Gilbert Scott found much of the beautiful work of earlier date. It was thereby possible to reproduce in the transepts and the great arches of the central

103

tower the structure of Edward's time, and some of the ancient stones were used again for the purpose for which they had been originally carved.

The choir was beautified without disturbing its main lines. The Perpendicular windows remained unchanged, but the roof was beautifully transformed. It is of open woodwork, richly decorated with gold and colour. A new pavement was designed following the style of ancient tiles found *in situ*. Other features of interest in this part of the church are the reredos and the east window which was transposed to the west end.

The restoration of the nave was not completed till 1880. The roof, which was too substantial to be removed, was skilfully covered with a richly panelled oak ceiling, but no new works of importance were undertaken.

The monuments in the Cathedral are not numerous. Behind the stalls in the choir are two tombs of the Decorated period, that on the right belonging to one of the Tudors, while the other is probably the tomb of the second Bishop Anian (d. 1328). Under a pointed arch in the south transept (which forms a War Memorial Chapel) is the stone coffin, with a cross upon the lid, containing the remains of *Owain Gwynedd*, a valiant Prince of North Wales (d. 1169), whose father, Gryffydd ap Cynan, was the last to bear the title King of Wales. Owain's brother Cadwaladr was also buried in this church. On the west wall of the north aisle is the effigy of a lady, apparently dating from the fourteenth or fifteenth century, and discovered in 1897, under the floor of the chapter-house. A mural tablet bears the epitaph of Goronwy Owen, the eighteenth-century poet. On the south wall at the western end of the north aisle is a pair of tongs for removing dogs from the church.

Laid out in part of the Deanery Grounds, is the well-known **Biblical Garden** (Handbook from City Library).

Bangor Mountain is leased from Lord Penrhyn by the Corporation as a Recreation Ground. There are several approaches, the principal being close to Horeb Chapel, near the upper end of Dean Street. The highest part commands views of great beauty and considerable extent. Walks have been laid out, paths made, trees planted, and seats placed in convenient positions.

From this retreat there is a pleasant walk southward to **Felin Esgob** ("The Bishop's Mill"), half a mile distant, on the River Cegin, but the mill from which the spot obtained its name is not now standing. Thence one can go across the fields to Llandegai, or may return to the city by a pleasant path, passed on the left just before reaching the mill.

The University College of North Wales dominates the city. The College buildings were formally opened by King George V on July 14, 1911, immediately after the Investiture of the then Prince of Wales at Caernarvon. The College "campus" of about 15 acres, consists of two comparatively flat building sites separated from each other by a long and fairly steep slope. The Arts Departments, Administrative Section, Great Hall and Library are next to one another, and are placed on the upper plateau, the first three forming a regular, closed quadrangle.

The College was first established in 1884, in a building long known as the Penrhyn Arms Hotel (now destroyed), to which physical, chemical

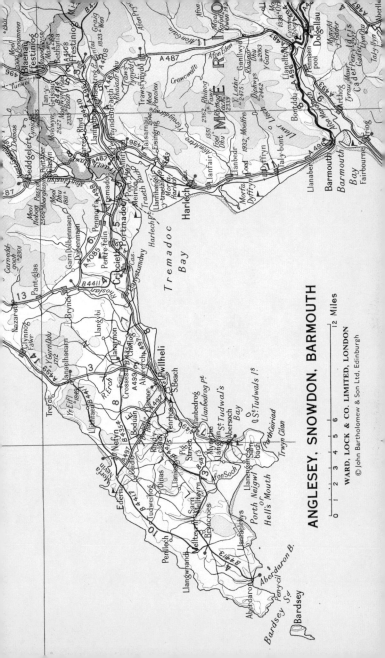

ANGLESEY, SNOWDON, BARMOUTH

WARD, LOCK & CO. LIMITED, LONDON

© John Bartholomew & Son Ltd, Edinburgh

and biological laboratories were added. The staff now consists of about thirty Professors and Independent Lecturers and a large number of other lecturers and teachers. In addition to the ordinary Arts, Science, Theology and Music courses, there are technical departments—the Agricultural Department, which not only provides a training in scientific and practical agriculture at the College and on the College Farm at Aber, but also conducts evening lectures, field experiments and dairy classes throughout North Wales, the Department of Electronic Engineering, the School of Forestry and Departments for the professional training of those who wish to teach in elementary schools, secondary schools and kindergartens. The College buildings include a beautiful Library, and there is also an interesting Museum of Welsh antiquities housed in a separate building near the College. Open free, 10–1, 2–5 in summer; 2–5 in winter.

In Deiniol Road stands the **North Wales Heroes' Memorial Archway,** a Memorial to the men from North Wales who fell in the 1914–18 War. The names (they number 8,500) are inscribed on panels in the room above this beautiful Tudor archway. It is one of the most impressive War Memorials anywhere and the panelled room, with its bronze doors, is particularly worth a visit.

The Pier at Bangor runs out two-thirds of the way across the Strait, being 1,550 feet in length. At several points there are landing steps for small boats, and from these rod and line fishing may be enjoyed. The Pier is much used as a lounge and promenade, and dancing and other forms of entertainment take place here in summer.

The prospect which the Pier commands is delightful. Across the Strait are beautifully wooded slopes and charming houses; westward, backed by the densely wooded shores of the Straits is the Suspension Bridge; eastward the neck of land on which Llandudno stands is almost lost below the horizon, so that the Great Orme rises from the sea like a huge island; southward are the Carnedds Dafydd and Llewelyn, divided by the great Cwm Llafar, and the connecting ridge between the two mountains sharply outlined against the sky. Near at hand is **Port Penrhyn,** from which the slates quarried at Bethesda are shipped, and just behind, **Penrhyn Castle** rears it tower above the surrounding greenery.

Llandegai

Between two to three miles east of Bangor on the Conway road, is Llandegai, amid grand scenery comprising on one side a fine amphitheatre of mountains and on the other a fine view of the Menai Strait. Lord Penrhyn's "model village" was built for workmen employed on the estate and consists of church, schools, and twenty-nine cottages.

The **Church** (*always open*) is supposed to have been erected in the reign of Edward III, and to stand on the site of one built by St. Tegai (to whom the present edifice is dedicated) at the close of the fifth century. It is approached through a fine avenue of yews, said to be at least 700 years old. Under a great yew-tree on the east side of the church is displayed a slate coffin in a good state of preservation. Among objects of interest in the interior are a mural monument of Archbishop Williams, Lord Keeper of the Great Seal in the reign of James I ("hasty, hot Welsh Williams" as Carlyle calls him), his spurs and helmet which are displayed near the monument, a monument by Westmacott to the memory of the first Lord and Lady Penrhyn and a curious monument removed from the religious house of Llanfaes at the Dissolution.

Penrhyn Castle. A splendid battlemented gateway gives entrance to the Park surrounding Penrhyn Castle, built 1827–40 for the first Lord Penrhyn. Now National Trust property it is open June–September. Weekdays including Bank Holidays, 10.30–12.30, 2–5. Also on Sundays during August only, 2–5; April, May and October, Mondays, including Bank Holidays, Wednesdays and Thursdays, 2–5. Admission, Castle 3s., grounds 1s. The structure, in the Norman style, is said to occupy the site of a palace of a Welsh prince, who began his reign A.D. 720. The five-storied Keep is almost the only portion of the Castle visible to the outside world, the remaining portions being swallowed in the surrounding groves. A feature of the Park, and indeed of the road between Bangor and Llandegai is the large surrounding wall, 13 feet high and seven miles long.

The Penrhyn Slate Quarries

Admission. Visitors are freely admitted, under the conduct of a guide, between 8 a.m. and 5 p.m. from April to September, and between 9 and 4 during the winter.

Routes. By road to Bethesda. Visitors who walk from Bethesda should take the first turn on the right beyond the town, and then first left along the river.

Motorists should turn out of the Bangor–Conway road at Llandegai, and take the road alongside the Ogwen river, running down from the top of Nant Ffrancon. Mountains loom grandly ahead and the road is prettily wooded for part of the way to the town of **Bethesda,** inhabited almost entirely by workmen in the adjacent quarries. Slates were obtained from the Penrhyn Quarry in the reign of Elizabeth, but it was not systematically worked until about 1782, when the Lord Penrhyn of that time undertook the development of the quarries instead of continuing the practice of allowing the quarrymen to work on their own account. The quarries are among the largest in the world, and in good times over 2,000 men and boys have been employed at them. Seen from a distance the succession of terraces on the mountainside is striking.

The Nant Ffrancon Pass and Ogwen Lake

Route *via* Bethesda (*see* p. 106), which lies at the foot of the Pass. *Buses* run *via* Nant Ffrancon and Capel Curig to Betws-y-Coed and Llanrwst.

The roads of Wales contribute to many a notable scene, but Nant Ffrancon is a supreme example of grandeur. As the road leaves Bethesda and runs through the birch woods above the Ogwen there is little indication of the wildness ahead. Then woods are left behind and the road begins to elbow its way along the inhospitable stony flanks of Carnedd Dafydd and there comes into view the wonderful amphitheatre of craggy precipices forming the northern flank of the Glyders. This rocky corner can be visited again and again, and every time with rich reward; but best of all is it seen after heavy rain when mists are swirling about the Devil's Kitchen and a defiant sun lights up from the west the jagged rock-pinnacles that top the gloomy and mysterious cliffs. Ages ago the valley was the bed of a glacier, as the marks of the ice upon the rocks testify. In the hills as well there are hollows due to the action of the ice; they are the beds of smaller glaciers which remained longer than the main one lower down in the valley. Cwm Craninog, the most remarkable of these hollows, or cwms as they are called, is on the western side of the valley, $2\frac{1}{2}$ miles from Bethesda.

At the head of the Pass is **Llyn Ogwen** (984 feet above sealevel), famed for trout and eels. The Ogwen river issues from it in a series of **falls** which are best seen from a path which doubles back just below the *Youth Hostel*. Note also the old bridge under Ogwen Bridge and the old road—a wonderful piece of engineering.

For description of the walks in the Llyn Ogwen district *see* pp. 85–9.

The Menai Bridges

The **Menai Suspension Bridge** is some 2 miles from Bangor by way of Upper Bangor and thence along the beautifully wooded shore of the Strait. Buses run to Menai Bridge, and there is a railway station close to the Caernarvonshire end of the bridge itself. The best view of the bridge, with its lovely setting of woods and water and mountain background, is from a point about a mile along the Holyhead road on the Anglesey side, near the monument referred to on p. 109.

The bridge, which spans the Strait at a point 1½ miles from Bangor station, carries the road. Telford's plans for the bridge having been approved by Parliament, work was begun in 1818, and on January 30, 1826, it was opened. The roadway is 100 feet above the surface of the water at the highest tides; the distance between the points of suspension is 560 feet, and the total length of the roadway is said to be 1,000 feet. The roadway was widened and the whole structure strengthened in 1939.

The **Britannia Tubular Bridge** is exactly a mile west of the Suspension Bridge and carries the railway across the Strait through long hollow tubes, of which the floor and roof are formed of small cubes firmly connected.

The name is derived from a rock in the middle of the Strait, on which rests the central tower, 230 feet high. The bridge was constructed by Robert Stephenson with the co-operation of Sir William Fairbairn, between 1846 and 1850. The tubes are 104 feet above the water. Their total length is 1,513 feet, but the bridge is 328 feet longer. On the central tower the ends of the tubes are immovable, but on the shore towers and abutments they rest on roller beds to allow for the contraction and expansion of the metal due to variation of temperature. At each entrance is a pair of colossal lions made of limestone, 25 feet 6 inches in length, and 12 feet 8 inches in height.

ANGLESEY

Ferries. Bangor Pier and Beaumaris (*summer only*); Bangor (Garth) and
Llandegfan (*half-hourly*); Port Dinorwic and Mael-y-don (*as required*).

The Isle of Anglesey (Ynys Môn—Isle of Môn), forming a
county of Wales, has an extreme length of 21 miles and at its
broadest part is 19 miles wide. The Menai Strait which separates
it from the mainland of Wales is about ¾-mile wide. North,
west and south-west of the island is open sea.

The general aspect of the island is slightly undulating, and it
is almost bare of wood. The county contains five market towns,
namely Amlwch, Beaumaris, Holyhead, Llangefni, and Llanerchymedd. The seaside resorts are small and mostly originated
in small fishing hamlets. Trearddur Bay, near Holyhead, has
probably developed most rapidly, though Rhosneigr is a close
rival. The island, as a whole, is thinly populated. Outside the
towns, the people dwell in sleepy little hamlets, formed of old-
fashioned cottages and connected with one another by a network of winding lanes.

Anglesey is connected with the mainland by two famous
bridges—the Britannia Tubular Bridge carrying the railway and
the Menai Suspension Bridge carrying the road (*see* pp. 107–8).

From the Holyhead road beyond the Suspension Bridge is seen the
Anglesey Column erected in 1816 in memory of the first Marquis of Anglesey, second in command at Waterloo. The column stands on a knoll 250
feet above the sea, and is surmounted by a statue of the Marquis. The top,
which is 91 feet above the base, is reached by 115 steps, and commands a
magnificent view. (*Small admission charge. Car park.*)

Beyond the statue is **Llanfairpwllgwyngyllgogerychwyrndro-
bwllllandysiliogogogoch** which literally means "Church of St.
Mary in a hollow of white hazel, near to a rapid whirlpool and
to St. Tysilio's Church, near to a red cave". The name in its
entirety, however, is seldom used, but "P.G." is added to
"Llanfair" to distinguish the place from other Llanfairs. It is
also contracted to "Llanfairpwll". Except for the name the
village is quite unremarkable. Beyond it the main road runs
westward to Holyhead, one of the straightest and fastest roads
in North Wales.

Plas Newydd the seat of the Marquis of Anglesey, is a mile south of the village. It is built of marble from the Moelfre quarries. George IV was entertained at Plas Newydd on his way to Ireland in 1821, and Queen Victoria was visitor for several weeks in the summer of 1832, before her accession.

On the water's edge, near the Tubular Bridge, stands a colossal **Statue of Nelson,** sculptured by Admiral Lord Clarence Paget, a son of the Marquis commemorated by the lofty roadside monument referred to on p. 109.

At the Anglesey end of the Suspension Bridge are several pleasant tea gardens, and a gate gives access to a lane that leads through a fir plantation and across a causeway to **Llandysilio Church,** on a small rocky peninsula. It is about 15 yards long and half as wide. The nave is of very early date—possibly sixth century. During summer, English service is held in the Church on Sundays, at 6 p.m.

The little cattle market near the bridge is a great sight on Mondays, when all kinds of beasts arrive from all parts of the island, shepherded by farmers and prodded and inspected by dealers who are at least as interesting to the onlooker from far away cities as the animals themselves.

Eastward from the bridge is the village of **Menai Bridge** (*Anglesey Arms*) with facilities for boating, and for sea-fishing, which is remarkably good. Ten minutes' walk along the road to Beaumaris is **Cadnant Dingle,** a romantic spot containing an old

watermill and a woollen factory. The Beaumaris road is delightfully shaded by trees, except near its northern end, and through
openings in the woods are many glimpses of the Strait and the
coast of the mainland.

Beaumaris

Banks *Lloyds, National Provincial, Midland.*

Boating. Town beach, ideal for children—Fryars Beach also very popular.

Bowls. In Happy Valley.

Buses run from Bangor several times daily all the year round *via* Garth Ferry and Menai Bridge. The buses also run between Beaumaris, Llangoed and Penmon.

Early Closing Day. Wednesday.

Fishing. Plenty of flat fish and small codlings along the Straits opposite the town (baits: black bait, soft crabs and mussels). Between Menai Bridge and Tubular Bridge good for bass. Puffin Island for pollack, cod and lobsters. Sand eels obtainable from Dutchman's Bank.

Golf. A capital 9-hole course about half a mile from the town.

Hotels. *Bulkeley Arms; Liverpool Arms; White Lion; Bull's Head.*

Population. 1,910.

Tennis in the Castle Pleasure Grounds. Also three good grass courts in the Happy Valley.

Yachting and Boating. Annual Regatta Week held at beginning of August. Yacht racing every week during season. Boats—rowing, motor and sailing, may be hired in the town.

Beaumaris, though rather small, ranks as a borough, and is
the capital of Anglesey. Except for the Church and the Castle
it has few buildings of architectural merit, but the place has an
"air" that is very attractive to those from bustling cities. The
Green overlooking the Menai Strait is a broad expanse of turf,
and at all times the views across the water to the mountainous
mainland are a sheer delight. There is a Pier, and at the east
end of the Green is an open-air Swimming Bath.

Beaumaris Castle (*admission charge; open, March, April, Oct., Weekdays:*
9.30–5.30, *Sundays:* 2–5.30, *May–Sept.* 9.30–7, daily, *Nov.–Feb.:* 9.30–4,
2–4), restored by the Ministry of Public Building and Works, covers a lot
of ground, but is not very high. There is an outer octagonal wall, and an
advanced work called the Gunners' Walk. On the outside of its walls are
rings for mooring the vessels that came up to it by a marine canal. The main
structure is nearly quadrangular in form, with a large round tower at each
angle and two striking gate-houses north and south. The most beautiful
room in the Castle is the Chapel, reached by a wooden stair near the site
of the old racquet court.

The Castle was built by Edward I in 1295, who then changed the name
of the place from Bonover to Beaumaris, a French word descriptive of its
pleasant situation on low ground. The only event of importance in the history of the Castle was its surrender to the Parliament in 1646.

111

In the grounds are tennis courts. Bowling greens in the Happy Valley close by.

The **Church** (Sunday services, 8, 11, and 6.30; daily service, 11) was erected in the early part of the fourteenth century. It contains some ancient stalls, with finely carved misericords brought from Llanfaes Friary at the time of the dissolution of the monasteries, monuments to members of the Bulkeley family (the best is in the vestry), a stone, on the south side of the communion table, in memory of the father of Sir Philip Sydney (d. 1563), and a tablet in memory of David Hughes, a native of the island, through whose beneficence the town possesses a Grammar School, erected in 1603, and Almshouses. The north door is secured by a stout wooden bar drawn from a cavity in the wall. In the south porch is the sculptured sarcophagus of the *Princess Joan*, consort of Llewelyn the Great, and daughter of King John. She was buried at Llanfaes, two miles distant, in a monastery erected by Llewelyn. In the beginning of the nineteenth century her coffin was rescued from use as a watering-trough and her effigy was discovered in a ditch.

Also of interest in Beaumaris is the ancient **County Hall** dating from 1614, in which the Anglesey Assizes are held.

Baron Hill is delightfully situated in the vicinity of the town. The house was built in the time of James I, for the reception of Henry, the eldest son of that monarch, when on his way to Ireland, but the death of the prince so much affected Sir Richard Bulkeley, the then owner, that he gave up his original and magnificent plan, and used only the part that was then completed for his family seat.

Beyond the grounds of Baron Hill is the **Bulkeley Monument.**

The Baron Hill estate is connected with the Arthurian legend, for on it is a hill called **Bwrdd Arthur** (Arthur's Round Table), whereon are the remains of British fortifications. In the Church of Llaniestyn, some three miles north of Beaumaris, is a tomb said to be that of "Iestyn, son of Geraint, a noble knight of Arthur's Round Table, slain by Saxons at the Siege of London".

North of Beaumaris and overlooking the expansive Red Wharf Bay is **Wern,** a small but attractive settlement of modern buildings.

Penmon Priory at the north-eastern extremity of Anglesey, is 4 miles from Beaumaris by road. The road, which winds considerably and becomes narrow, passes the Penmon Transmitting Station of the B.B.C.

The **Priory** was founded in the sixth century. There are remains of Saxon work, but the most striking parts are the nave and south transept of the Norman church, the latter containing a tenth-century cross. The finely moulded arches and arcades are very impressive, though this (the Norman) end of the church is very dark. The vicarage was originally the Prior's Lodging and the ruined building on the seaward site of the little garden was the Refectory, above which was the Dormitory. A hundred yards east of the church is a very fine stone Dovecot.

The wishing well has been identified as being the original shrine used by Seiriol to baptize his converts. Close by are the remains of the hut where Seiriol lived.

A mile or so beyond the Priory is Anglesey's most easterly point. It is occupied by the residences of the coastguard men, and is a very popular picnic ground. Teas and light refreshments are obtainable.

The light is automatic and becomes operative when daylight falls below a certain level of intensity. In view of the possibility of sudden fogs, the fog-bell tolls day and night, fair weather or foul. It has a melancholy note which, however, harmonises with the remoteness of the spot.

The lighthouse guards the passage between Anglesey and—

Puffin Island also known as **Priestholm** and by the Welsh as *Ynys Seirio* (Seiriol's Island), because Seiriol, a holy recluse in the sixth century, had a cell upon it. It was called Priestholm by the Danes who destroyed the monastic buildings in the year 853. And, lastly, it is known as Puffin Island through being the resort of immense numbers of the puffin auk. About half a mile in length, it is separated from Anglesey by a strait about half a mile wide. Near the centre is an old square tower, the remains of a religious house or a church. The island is the objective of boating excursions from many of the mainland resorts.

Menai Bridge to Holyhead

The road from Menai Bridge to Holyhead strikes directly across the island, and is broad and straight for nearly the whole of its 20 miles. It passes through rather flat and uninteresting country. There are, however, a number of turnings to the left which will lead to more interesting places on the south-west shore. One or two little settlements around **Malldraeth Bay** have distinct possibilities for a quiet and enjoyable holiday; and the sandy heaths onward to **Aberffraw** come close to being a natural and perfect golf course. Aberffraw itself is a small village near the head of an estuary, but Aberffraw sands are glorious. Farther west are rock-bound coves, with sandy floors, such as Porth Tre-Castell; and then comes **Rhosneigr** (*Bay, Glan Neigr, Maelog Lake*), a small village with a station on the Holyhead line. It lies some 4½ miles from the main road and commands fine views. The shore is broken by rocks, but there are firm sands which provide excellent bathing. Golfing, fishing and boating on sea and lake can be had in abundance. The air is bracing. There is a fine tramp northward along the sands to **Cymyran Strait,** and the trip can be extended by ferrying across to Holyhead Island, the nearest village being Rhoscolyn (*see* later).

Southward from Rhosneigr is **Llangwyfan Old Church,** which can be approached on foot only at low water, as at other times its site is an island. Five miles south-east of Rhosneigr is **Llyn Coron** where excellent trout fishing is free.

Holyhead Island

The island, 8 miles long by 3½ miles wide, lies off the west coast of Anglesey, from which it is separated by a sandy strait, and is crossed by a causeway that carries the high road and the railway; it has an arch in its centre for the tide to pass through; it is also connected to Anglesey by another causeway a mile or so more to the southward, and by the Cymyran ferry.

Long known principally as the terminus of the steamer route to and from Dublin, Holyhead Island is gaining fame as a holiday resort.

Holyhead Town has an interesting harbour popular for sailing. There is a promenade and various open spaces for picnics and games. There is a good range of shops, cinemas and facilities for tennis and bowls in the local park (*Trearddur Bay Hotel*).

The Parish Church dedicated to St. Cybi, who lived in the early years of the sixth century, is in the Perpendicular style and consists of a nave with north and south aisles, shallow transepts, a long and narrow choir, a western tower, and a fine south porch. The wall which bounds three sides of the churchyard is considered by some antiquaries to have been built soon after the departure of the Romans. The oldest part of the Church is the chancel. mostly rebuilt in the fifteenth century on thirteenth-century foundations, The battlemented parapets of sixteenth-century work with their interesting carvings, should be noted.

The **Harbour of Refuge,** constructed about half a century ago, is one of the most complete works of the kind in Britain. Its **Breakwater,** the result of twenty-five years' incessant labour, is about 1½ miles in length, and consists of a solid masonry wall, rising nearly 40 feet above low-water mark and backed by a strong rubble mound. It is used as a promenade, and affords a fine view of the rugged coast. Looking northwards across the Harbour, one sees on the horizon, about 8 miles away, the island which the English call the **Skerries,** and the Welsh, *Ynys y Moelrhoniaid,* the Island of Seals.

The **Salt Island,** on the east side of the Harbour, is another promenade. In spite of its name it is a promontory, an artificial one. It owes its name to having been the site of works for extracting salt from the sea-water. The manufacture was established in the reign of Queen Anne, and continued until Holyhead began to acquire its present importance, about a century ago. The Stanley Sailor's Hospital occupies a site on Salt Island.

114

Holyhead Mountain is a mass of rock, 710 feet high, on the western side of the island. Its summit unfolds a lovely panorama, including the heights of the Isle of Man, the Cumberland hills, the mountains of County Down, and the Snowdonian range from end to end. Around the mountain, 60 or 80 feet from the top, is a massive wall traditionally ascribed to Caswallon, a Celtic chieftain of the sixth century. On the seaward side of the mountain is a deep chasm. At the top of it are the slight remains of a tiny *Chapel*, one of the six or seven sacred edifices that led to the isle being called Holy. Although the mountain is steep on the side nearest the town, it can quite easily be ascended by paths starting near the South Stack lighthouse. On the S.E. slopes of the mountain are found the **Cytiau'r Gwyddelod,** remains of the stone huts where the Gaidelic inhabitants of the district lived in pre-Christian days. They are circular in shape and are of great historic interest.

At the foot of the mountain is **Gigorth Bay.** Off its northern horn is the tiny islet of North Stack, and off the southern horn is the islet called **South Stack,** famous for its lighthouse, its storm signals, and its bird sanctuary. The **Lighthouse** (*open to visitors*) was erected in 1809. A chain suspension bridge, 110 feet long, spans the Sound between the rock and Holyhead Island. The bridge is attained by descending Holyhead Mountain by a flight of 380 steps.

Buses run between Holyhead town and the Stack, where there are refreshment rooms.

Overlooking the South Stack is **Ellin's Tower,** perched upon the edge of the cliff. It was erected by a former lord of Penrhos. Preserved in it are stone implements discovered on the site of prehistoric huts, near the foot of the mountain. The tower is in a dilapidated condition and care should be taken if entering.

On **Trefignath** farm, less than a mile south-east of the town, is a Bronze Age *souterrain*, of great interest to antiquaries, as is also a prehistoric grave mound, called *Gorsedd Gwlwm*.

The sands of **Rhoscolyn,** at the south end of Holyhead Island, are reached by a series of lanes that wind and twist in a most extraordinary manner. The bay is semicircular, about half a mile across, with low, grass-covered rocky headlands on either hand, which fall away to lower ground at the head of the bay.

Trearddur Bay is directly south of Holyhead town. The wide inlet faces south-west and is broken into numerous smaller bays by low ridges and piles of rock, between which are sands and pools. There is magnificent bathing, fishing, boating and tennis as well as two golf links. Above all there is the atmosphere of a modern resort that is being developed on attractive lines. The Church, dedicated to St. Ffraid (St. Bridget), stands in the centre of Trearddur Bay (services in English).

Anglesey's Northern Coast

A good road leads northward from Valley and passes through a number of pleasant villages. **Llanfachraeth, Llanfaethlu, Llanrhyddlad** and **Rhydwen,** are typical in their own way of the rural scene in Anglesey. Within a short distance of these villages are several charming coves and bays with miles of golden sands safe for bathing and other sports. The principal bays are **Church Bay, Borthwen** and **Silver Bay.**

Amlwch (*Dinorber Arms, Grenville, Maesllwyn*) is a seaport and market-town. Once it was of considerable commercial importance through the great development of the Mona and Parys copper mines in the Parys Mountain, $1\frac{1}{2}$ miles south. The harbour from which the ore was shipped is tightly wedged between great rocks. Of interest is the Roman Catholic Church, a concrete building in an original treatment of the Romanesque style.

Bull Bay (*Trecastell, Bull Bay*) takes its name from a neighbouring inlet in the rock-bound coast. During summer, when south and west winds prevail, the Bay is usually smooth, though northerly winds lash its surface into great roaring waves. The village of Bull Bay is small, the two hotels and thirty or so houses complete the whole picture.

Shipping makes Bull Bay lively, for liners between Liverpool and America pass at a short distance, picking up or dropping pilots, and small vessels often come in for shelter. The Bay is safe for boating, except in stormy weather, and the numerous creeks are safe bathing-places, being quite free from dangerous currents. Good sea-fishing may be enjoyed from the rocks or from boats, whilst fresh-water fishing and rough shooting are close to hand. The *Bull Bay Golf Club* have an admirable 18-hole course on the Amlwch road.

Westward from Bull Bay, the cliffs become higher and more precipitous. At the end of $1\frac{1}{2}$ miles we reach **Porthwen Bay,** a small inlet with a heather-covered hill at its western point. Close to it is a natural arch projecting into the sea.

Westward again, and connected with Amlwch by bus, is **Cemaes Bay** (*Park Lodge, Gadly's*), another interesting rock-bound bay, divided, as it were, into three "compartments". Two of these have firm sandy beaches; the shore of the third is composed of small pebbles. Boating and fishing may be enjoyed without danger within the Bay. Cemaes village is rather reminiscent of some of the Cornish porths, but the resemblance of the coast is even stronger. Eastward between Cemaes Bay and Porthwen, the coast is indented with rocky creeks, of which that known as **Hell's Mouth** is the finest as regards scenery. In the opposite direction, from Cemaes Bay to **Carmel Point,** the north-western extremity of the island, the coast is very wild.

Fresh-water fishing and shooting can be had by arrangement with the landowners or tenants.

Cemaes contains the only ancient Church in Wales dedicated to St. Patrick. It was restored a few years ago by the late Lord Stanley of Alderley. An Ichthus stone may be seen at the west end, but the chief treasure of the venerable building is an Eliza-bethan communion cup.

Four miles from Cemaes Bay is the **Garn,** the highest point in the island, commanding a view of the whole of Anglesey, the Snowdonian Range, the Isle of Man, and parts of England and Ireland.

Eilian Bay, 2 miles eastward of Amlwch, is a well-sheltered inlet with excellent sands and facilities for bathing, boating and fishing. **Lynas Point** is the eastward termination of the coast of Eilian Bay, and is a great resort of picnic parties. Besides the pilot station, it is the site of a modern **Lighthouse,** a Semaphore Signal Station and a Coastguard's Station. The light—bright 8 seconds, eclipsed 2 seconds—is visible 16 miles, and in clear weather the white-washed buildings can be seen from almost as great a distance. Near the Point is *Ogof y Saint*, or **Saint's Cave,** which penetrates the land for some distance. Near it, too, is the sandy gravel beach of a cove called **Porth-y-Cwrwgl,** a secluded spot for bathing where boats can be hired for picnic or shooting parties on **Dulas Island.** Another secluded gravel beach suitable for bathing is that of **Porth Ysgo,** a little farther from the Point. Still farther westward, but yet within Eilian Bay, is a third cove, *Porth yr Ychain*, or **Oxen's Cove.**

About 500 yards southward of Porth yr Ychain is **Llaneilian Parish Church,** a notable building. It is in two unequal parts, connected by stone steps. The smaller portion was originally built in the fifth century; the larger in the twelfth. The rood loft, with its screen, is in its original position. It is entered from a spiral staircase that also leads to the roof.

About half a mile to the west of Porth yr Ychain is the cursing well, called **Ffynnon Eilian,** where, no more than a hundred years ago, corks were often seen which contained rows of pins standing for the name of a person who had been cursed; the legend has it that this person would suffer physically as long as the cork with his name remained in the well.

Southward of the village is **Llaneilian Mountain,** 600 feet high, commanding fine views over land and sea. On its north-eastern side, near the summit, was the court of Caswallon, a Welsh prince of the last half of the fourteenth century, famous for his gallantry in the wars of his country.

Close to **Ceint** (keint) is a farmhouse which in George Borrow's day was an inn, and was the scene of that pleasant time described in Chapter xxxvii of *Wild Wales.* The road from Ceint to Penmynydd (meaning the "top of the hill") and on to Pentraeth, about 3½ miles, was travelled by Borrow, and his experiences there are related in Chapter xxxvi of the book just named. The view from the high ground of Penmynydd is extensive and very fine indeed.

About half a mile from Ceint is **Plas Pen Mynydd** (munnith), the birth-place of Owen Tudor, who married the Dowager Queen Catherine, widow of Henry V. Their son, Edmund Tudor, married Margaret Beaufort, and their son became Henry VII.

Benllech (*Glanrafon, Carreg Lwyd, Breeze Hill*) is a develop-ing little resort with sands and good sea views. There is a good caravan site here. It stands above a lovely bay, 4 miles in width, with firm sands on which there is safe bathing at all states of the tide and where children can paddle and play in perfect safety. There are facilities for tennis and bowls. The village consists of quaint rustic cottages and modern residences, and forms part of the parish of Llanfairmathafarneithaf. In another portion, locally known as *Rhosfawr*, is a small cottage called *Dafarn Goch*, notable as the birthplace in 1722, of the celebrated Welsh bard Goronwy Owen, whose pathetic history George Borrow graphically narrates.

The area teems with carboniferous fossils. The Geological Survey collection contains over a hundred specimens, mostly corals, collected from Benllech cliffs. Northwards the coastline is chiefly formed of lofty rugged cliffs, and the narrow coast path that follows it is not for everyone, particularly in a high wind. The cliffs are, however, indented by some delightful coves, some of which can be reached by car, and these are very popular with local visitors. **Traeth Bychan,** a couple of miles north of Benllech, is one such cove. There is a good caravan site here and sailing is popular in the bay. A mile or so farther north is the tiny village of **Moelfre,** built around a small cove and inhabited for the most part by fishermen and seafaring folk.

About half-way between Benllech and Moelfre is **Marian Glas,** a pretty hamlet with good accommodation for visitors. Also easily accessible from Benllech and Red Wharf Bay are the old-world market-town of **Llanerchymedd, Bodafon Mountain** (4 or 5 miles), the resort of picnic parties, **Llangefni** (about 6 miles), the principal market-town of Anglesey, **Lligwy,** where there are remains of a Romano–British village enclosed with a low wall and covering half an acre, and the ruins of an ancient chapel and **Arthur's Quoit,** one of the finest specimens of the Anglesey cromlechs, supposed to date from 1200 B.C.

Red Wharf Bay is a wide inlet girdled by low hills and pleasant sandy beaches. Low tide leaves a waste of sand and small pools. Sailing is very popular and there is a flourishing club. Sea fishing is also good.

The village is situated on the north side of the Bay, where there is a pretty little cove, which forms (or used to form) a natural landing-place for the cargoes of small coasting vessels. Here stand the Hotel and a few cottages. The Camping Club of Great Britain and Ireland have a site for canvas campers at Red Wharf Bay. There is also a good caravan site. The rock pools along the shore northward are extremely interesting and display fine specimens of anemones and other marine creatures. Overlooking the bay on the south side is the small village of **Landdona** with its modern neighbour **Wern,** already mentioned on page 112.

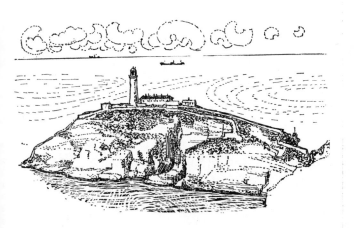

CAERNARVON

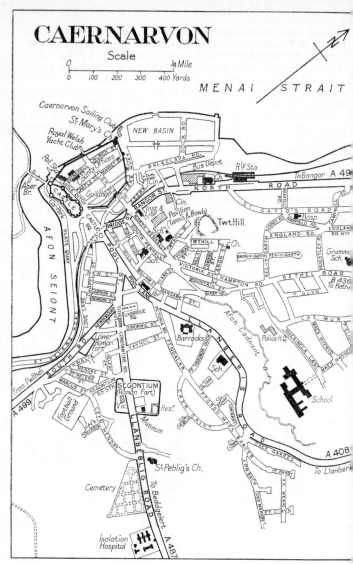

Scale

MENAI STRAIT

CAERNARVON

Banks. *Lloyds, Midland, National Provincial, Barclays.*

Bathing. Open-air sea-water baths, reached by crossing the Swing Bridge and walking along the shore path below Coed Helen. Hot and cold baths in Library building, Bangor Street.

Bowls. Crown green in the Pavilion Field at the foot of Twt Hill.

Bus Services. To Bangor, etc.; to Llanberis; to Beddgelert; to Pwllheli, and several local services to outlying villages.

Car Park. On the Quay between the Castle and the river.

Distances. Bangor, 9; Beddgelert, 13; Betws-y-Coed, 24; Capel Curig, 18; Chester, 70; Llanberis, 7½; Llandudno, 28; Pen-y-Gwryd, 14½; Snowdon Ranger, 7.

Early Closing Day. Thursday.

Fishing. Good sport, chiefly with trout and salmon, in the Rivers Seiont (¼ mile from the station), Gwyrfai and Llyfni, also in Lakes Cwellyn, Gadar, Nantlle and Llanberis Lake (excellent char). Permits and tickets for salmon and trout must be obtained.

Boats and tackle may be hired for fishing in the Strait—cod, conger, flat-fish, bass, mackerel, whiting.

Golf Course (9 holes), reached by crossing Swing Bridge. The club-house overlooks the Menai Strait.

Hotels. *Prince of Wales*, Bangor Street; *Royal*, Bangor Street; *Eagles*, South Road; *Black Boy Inn*, Northgate Street.

Library, Bangor Street; County Library Llanberis Road.

Road Routes. The Castle Square is the meeting-place of the roads at Caernarvon, and just below the Square and the Castle is the Car Park. The Bangor road comes to the Square *via* Bridge Street and the Railway Station. Pool Street serves the road to Llanberis, to Beddgelert, and to Pwllheli; the Llanberis road turning off on the left at the first fork: the Beddgelert road on the left at the second fork, while Newborough Street, the right-hand road at that fork, is the road to Nevin and Pwllheli.

Population. 9,200.

Post Office. Castle Square.

Tennis. Hard courts in the Pavilion Field (also one grass court).

Caernarvon (*Caer-yn-Arfon*, "the fortress in Arvon") stands just inside the western entrance to the Menai Strait, at the mouth of the River Seiont. It is the ancient "metropolis of the hills"—the chief town in that mountainous stronghold known as *Eryri*. Caernarvon, created a royal borough in 1963, is the modern representative of the British fortress, *Caer Seiont*, and of the Roman military station, *Segontium*. In position, beauty and historic associations there are few towns, if any, in Wales to compare with it.

121

Caernarvon Castle

Open. Daily 9.30–7. Closes Sunday mornings and at 5.50 in March, April, October; and at 4 during November to February. Admission charge.

The erection of the fortress was begun by Edward I in 1283, and completed by his son. It was twice unsuccessfully besieged by Owen Glendower. During the Civil War it was garrisoned for the King, after changing hands more than once, was finally captured by the forces of the Parliament in 1646. In 1660 a warrant was issued for its demolition, but the order was never executed.

Among the prisoners immured in the Castle was William Prynne, one of the most notorious of the Roundheads. For an attack upon Archbishop Laud the Star Chamber fined him £5,000 and sentenced him to lose the *remainder* of his ears, to be branded on the cheeks and to be imprisoned in Caernarvon Castle for life.

Caernarvon Castle is one of the finest in Great Britain. The walls enclose an area of about 3 acres and are from 7 to 9 feet thick. The entrance is at the **King's Gate,** beneath a beautiful and lofty archway, over which is a statue of Edward II. In front of the gateway are two Spanish guns. On each side of the archway are portcullis grooves. In the towers flanking the gateway were the guard-rooms and other apartments, and over the archway an oratory and a small room used in raising and lowering the drawbridge. The interior of the Castle is separated into the Inner and Outer Bailies, on right and left respectively of the entrance. Beautifully kept lawns are now spread where formerly there were halls and other apartments.

On the right are remains of the **Kitchen.** The adjacent steps lead to the interior of the **Well Tower,** and the **Eagle Tower,** at the western corner of the Castle, may be reached from the ground or a path along a curtain-wall, from the Well Tower. Its name is reputed to have been derived from the figure of an eagle, said by some to have been brought from the ruins of the neighbouring Roman station of Segontium; but an eagle was one of Edward's crests, and one of the weather-worn stone ornaments crowning the battlements is said to have represented an eagle: the others portrayed the helmeted heads of warriors. This majestic tower rises to the height of 124 feet, and has three fine turrets. Access to the summit is gained by 158 stone steps. By following the narrow passage running round the tower wall at the first-floor level the dark recess known as the **Queen's Oratory** is reached, and, along the corridor, a small dark room, measuring 12 feet by 8 feet, in which Edward II is said to have been born, although as archaeologists state, the tower was not built until long afterwards. The window has been filled with coloured glass in the design of the Prince of Wales's feathers.

The **Queen's Tower,** on the right, beyond the Eagle Tower, is nearly opposite the Well Tower and houses the regimental Museum of the Royal Welsh Fusiliers. A door close to the curtain-wall gives access to a passage that leads to a corridor in the thickness of the wall. The windows opened into the **Banqueting Hall,** which was 100 feet long, 45 feet broad, and about 50 feet high. Nothing remains but the foundations of the outer walls. The corridor leads to the **Chamberlain's Tower,** and thence to the **Black Tower,** which contains the smallest rooms in the Castle; it was probably the prison. Beyond this tower is the entrance on the east side, called **Queen Eleanor's Gate,** because that Queen is said to have entered the Castle by it.

The **Walls,** which are still almost intact, formerly enclosed the whole town, but are now around only a small portion of it. They had originally two principal gates, but others were added as they became needed. A tour of the walls can conveniently be started by turning to the right on leaving the Castle and again to the right at the extremity of the Castle. This way leads past the river-front of the fortress, and beyond the Eagle Tower comes to a promenade running at the foot of the western wall, along which are towers that house various institutions.

The **Town Church**, or St. Mary's, at the north-western angle, was formerly the garrison chapel. The windows which face outward are, of course, modern, being in the town wall.

From the Church the wall begins its eastward course. Its northern portion crosses High Street, at the top of which is the **East Gate.**

Visitors to Caernarvon should on no account miss **Segontium,** half a mile from the town on the Beddgelert road. This Roman site has been partially excavated so that the ground plan is clear, while the very interesting finds are housed in a small museum. Admission charge. Open 9.30–7, Sundays 2–7. Closes 5.30 March, April, October; 4 November–February. The whole place is under the control of the Ministry of Public Building and Works.

Further along the Beddgelert road is Caernarvon's ancient parish church which gets its name of **Llanbeblig** (*Peblig's Church*) from the uncle of Constantine the Great who is said to have been born at nearby Segontium. Much of the building is older than the fourteenth century. It has a beautiful oak roof, and a fine altar-tomb of the sixteenth century which commemorates a son of Sir William Griffith, who was with Henry VIII at the siege of Boulogne. The tower is remarkable for its stepped battlements, a feature rarely seen except in Ireland. During the partial restoration of the Church a few years ago a grave was discovered which was supposed to be that of Constantine Chlorus, father of Constantine, the Great. Here, too, it is said, that Emperor was buried, and by order of Edward I his remains were removed to the "new church" which the English monarch was building within the walls of the town.

The Aber Swing Bridge gives access over the River Seiont to the swimming pool and some pleasant walks. To the right after the bridge a path leads along the shore of the Menai Strait. A little more than a mile on is the disused Llanfaglan church, a tiny ancient building, with Roman bricks in its walls.

A pleasant drive is to **Dinas Dinlle,** on the Caernarvon Bay shore. Take the Pwllheli main road as far as the fifth milestone, and shortly after that the road bearing to the right. The sands are excellent and the Nevin Rivals are seen rising very finely from the shore.

The land between the main road and the sea is flat and uninteresting; but for this, the site would doubtless develop rapidly. As it is, Dinas Dinlle has the inevitable cafés, a boarding house or two and a small colony of bungalows. Historically it is of great interest. Here Watling Street ended; its remains form the stony track ending opposite the Coastguard look-out. Dinas Hill is an old Roman encampment.

123

Caernarvon to Beddgelert (12½ miles)

Leave Caernarvon by way of Pool Street. After a steady climb the road passes the historic church of Llanbeblig and gives a foretaste of the scenery ahead.

Shortly, **Betws-Garmon,** with a picturesque three-arched bridge, is reached, with Nant Mills falls a mile farther on. Then the road begins to run in among the mountains, Moel Eilio on the left and Mynydd Mawr on the right leaving only just enough room for the river and the road, until the rocks on the left fall back at Llyn Cwellyn to give one of the best views of Snowdon.

On the western side of the lake is **Mynydd Mawr** (the Great Mountain). One of the cliffs, **Carn Cwm Bychan,** rises perpendicularly from the water for several hundred feet, looking almost like a fortification.

A mile beyond the lake is the wayside village of **Rhyd-ddu,** consisting almost entirely of quarrymen's cottages, an inn, and a hotel. It is within 3½ miles of the summit of Snowdon, and almost the entire path up the mountain can be seen.

From Rhyd-ddu a secondary road runs westward beneath the frowning crags of Y Garn on the left, and Craig-y-Beri (Mynydd Mawr) on the right. It leads in about 6 miles to **Nantlle,** a village devoted entirely to slate-quarrying, but well worth seeing for the huge open quarries dropping sheer from the roadside for some 400 feet.

The highest point on the Beddgelert road (651 ft.) is reached about a mile beyond Rhyd-ddu, close to an isolated mass of rock on the right, which has received the name of **Pitt's Head;** its resemblance to a human profile—Pitt's or otherwise—is striking. From near here the so-called "Beddgelert path" strikes up towards Snowdon.

The remaining three miles are nearly all descent, with good views of Snowdon on the left and on the right of Moel Hebog.

For Beddgelert, *see* p. 125.

SNOWDONIA

Snowdonia National Park

Snowdonia became a National Park in 1951. Its 845 square miles extend into Caernarvonshire, Denbighshire and Merioneth, stretching from below Conway to as far south as the Dovey estuary. By its designation as a National Park, the area has been marked out as standing in special need of preservation for public enjoyment. Here landscape beauty is safeguarded as a national asset against threats of spoilation. Here that same beauty is enhanced by measures such as the removal of all kinds of eyesores. Measures are also taken to improve facilities for open-air recreation. But land in the park is still privately owned, so visitors must respect the Countryman's things, taking care to do no damage—by following the maxims of the Country Code.

Beddgelert

Distances. Rhyd Ddu, 4 miles; Betws-y-Coed, 17½; Portmadoc, 8; Caernarvon, 13.

Fishing. Permits for fishing above Beddgelert Village and in Dinas Lake obtainable from Beddgelert Post Office. Permits for Glaslyn River obtainable locally. Price of permits, etc., from the Secretary, Glaslyn Angling Association, Portmadoc.

Hotels. *Royal Goat; Saracen's Head; Plas Colwyn; Tanronen; Bryn Eglwys.*

Road Routes. The road to Aberglaslyn Pass and Portmadoc *crosses* the Bridge in the village; that to Caernarvon and Capel Curig keeps on the north side of the stream as it flows through the village.

The picturesque village of Beddgelert stands at the junction of three vales, near the confluence of the Glaslyn and the Colwyn, amid lofty mountains, woods and murmuring streams. It is a favourite resort of anglers, artists, and climbers, and is a good centre for those wishing to explore the district by road. Of interest is the railed enclosure in the meadows south of the church—the **Tomb of Gelert,** Llewelyn's faithful dog, from which the place is said to have received its name (*bedd* = a grave). To reach the grave take the path running between the end of the Old Bridge and "Llewelyn's Cottage" and follow it alongside the Colwyn stream (here about to unite with the Glaslyn) as far as the footbridge; here take the footpath on the right. The grave is beneath a rail-surrounded tree in the large field on the right. There is no historical foundation for the story.

Beddgelert Church is on the site of an early Celtic monastery which was refounded later as a house of Augustinian canons.

Walks from Beddgelert

Pont Aberglaslyn. Follow the riverside path past Gelert's Grave to the main road; cross the river by the Aberglaslyn bridge and then follow the path as it winds along beside the rushing water through the **Pass of Aberglaslyn.** The final part of the walk is very beautiful, and looking back from the romantic **Pont Aberglaslyn** there is an uninterrupted view of naked brown precipices rising to the sky beyond the fir trees and the dashing stream.

Moel Hebog (the Hill of the Hawk) where Owen Glendower hid himself when pursued by the English, guards Beddgelert on the west. The ascent (2,566 feet) and the summit can be reached from Beddgelert in 1½ to 2 hours, by taking a track on the north side of the Goat Hotel, and striking up the mountain to a conspicuous gap in a wall. Beyond this, bear to the right up a steep slope.

Those who have come to Beddgelert to climb Snowdon, and find themselves cheated by mists, might take one of the following three walks in the neighbourhood:

(1) Take the path which leads along the river past Gelert's Grave and follow it till the Portmadoc road is reached. At Aberglaslyn, cross the bridge and follow the main road for ¼ mile to a narrow turning on the left leading up past Nantmor (Post Office). The lane continues between walls and through woods, descending to cross a considerable stream beyond which is a white cottage (Bwlch-gwernog). Here turn left into a lane leading upstream and go past Cae Ddafydd. As the road descends steeply glorious views across to Snowdon and wooded Nant Gwynant open up. The main road is gained near a phone kiosk and the foot of the Watkin Path up Snowdon; turn left for Beddgelert, which is reached in about 3 miles.

(2) Follow the same route to Bwlch-gwernog; or, alternatively, go along the old railway track which leads through a long tunnel and out to the Nantmor road on the farther side of Pont Aberglaslyn. At Bwlch-gwernog strike up right along a steep path, past some pylons; at the top it turns to the left and winds among rocks, heather and bracken, the general direction being eastward. Exquisite views open up to the west, and on reaching the eminence above Croesor there is a grand view southward across Cardigan Bay. To the left the steep peak of Cnicht rises majestically —one of the most beautiful mountain-forms in Wales. **Croesor** is reached by a steep descent. Go straight ahead, across the tramway, and the way is then unmistakable across beautiful moorland and through wooded dells until **Tan-y-Bwlch** station, on the Ffestiniog Railway is reached. From here a bus from the foot of the hill may be taken to Portmadoc.

(3) An easier walk may be had by going up the Gwynant valley to the Power House below Cwm Dyli, about a mile short of Pen-y-Gwryd, and returning along the northern side of the stream, and through the woods clothing the lower slopes of the Snowdon mass as they descend to Llyn Gwynant. The path is easy to trace and leads through a region which has an air of remoteness that will remind many of the pastoral uplands of Switzerland.

126

The road is regained at the lower end of the "Watkin Path," from Snowdon, close to the bridge (telephone box).

Moelwyn (2,527 ft.) and Cnicht (2,265 ft.)

These mountains rise abruptly at the head of Traeth Mawr, and about midway between Beddgelert and Ffestiniog village. Cnicht from the neighbourhood of Portmadoc appears as a sharp and steep peak, and has, not inappropriately, been styled the Welsh Matterhorn. The summits of the two mountains are, as the crow flies, about 1½ miles apart, and those who do not object to a steep down-and-up course can proceed pretty direct from one to the other—a stiff hour's work. If, however, the intervening dip of Cwm Croesor is passed at its head, the additional mile or so in distance will involve no extra time, and save a good deal of fatigue. The walk from Beddgelert to Ffestiniog village, or vice versa, over both summits is about 13 or 14 miles, and the time required not less than 6 to 7 hours.

Moelwyn

From Tan-y-Bwlch Station cross the wall by the wooden steps, close to the down platform. The old mountain-road from Maentwrog—at best but a mule-track the greater part of the way—is then joined, and has to be followed for about 2½ miles. Moel Hebog is soon prominent in front, Moelwyn-bach is on our right, and on the left we get a wide view over Traeth Mawr to the sea around Portmadoc. Then, about two miles from the station, we cross the mouth of the great combe that runs between Moelwyn-bach and Braich-y-Parc (the western ridge of Moelwyn) and get a full view of Moelwyn. Still following our mountain-road, after the next steep, we turn to the right along the road that ascends the southern flank of Cwm Croesor to the Moelwyn slate-quarry. **Cwm Croesor** is a fine glen, but has lost much of its original wildness. A considerable collection of quarrymen's houses occupies its mouth, and a tramway runs up it. Cnicht rises almost precipitously on its north side, and is scarred by a quarry on its southern flank. After reaching the Moelwyn quarry the course bends sharply round to the right, and a steep but not difficult climb ends at the cairn on the top of the mountain.

From Tan-y-Grisiau about 1½ hours. This is an easy climb that, without much effort, can be accomplished in an hour, and the route is almost wholly in sight from the station. Looking down the line—*i.e.* towards Portmadoc—high up on the left of the mountainside is seen an inclined plain, with the usual erection across its top. To the right of this, and somewhat below, a water-wheel and the white streak of a small cascade can be seen. The way lies just to the right of this cascade. Start down the line, about 250 yards below the station, where the second tramline on the right joins company, climb over a gate on that side and turn at once to the left, following a wall past a cottage. Then there is a rough path, which is possibly more trouble to follow than one's own choice. The ascent is over rock-broken grassy ground, more or less close to the burn from Llyn Trwstyllon. When the

127

cascade, mentioned above, is close by on the left, a wall must be scaled, and the water-wheel and disused quarry-works are then seen. In a minute or two the desolate **Llyn Trwstyllon** is reached. (Before reaching the Llyn, a green slope on the right offers a tempting way up, but this must not be taken.)

From the shore of the lake the rounded summit of Moelwyn is on the right front, and the best way up is to attack the easy ridge from the foot of the lake and then to turn to the left along it. The cairn on the top of the mountain is not seen from below.

From Moelwyn to Cnicht. The most direct way is to descend to the head of Cwm Croesor and climb the steep screes that rise from the combe just east of the summit of Cnicht. There is no danger, though it is a stiff ascent to the ridge, which is gained a few hundred yards east of the top of the mountain. A longer, but easier route, is to descend Moelwyn by its northern flank—Moel-y-Rhudd—to *Bwlch-cwm-Orthin*, the pass at the top of the combe running up from Tan-y-Grisiau. Then, by climbing gradually to the somewhat boggy watershed, sprinkled with lakelets, that divides Cwm Croesor from the Lledr valley and is about 1¼ miles due north of the pass, the northern ridge of Cnicht is gained with the uninteresting Llyn-yr-Adar just below. The summit of Cnicht is a few hundred yards farther along the ridge to the left and above Llyn-y-Biswail.

Cnicht (2,265 ft.)

From Beddgelert. By far the most interesting ascent is by the south-west ridge of the mountain. Leave Beddgelert by one of the two routes mentioned on p. 126, cross the Dylif stream into Merionethshire, and then climb on the end of the ridge, just short of **Cwm Croesor,** and by it you can make the whole ascent. This ridge commands a fine view of that combe and of Moelwyn and on our left Snowdon rises to a noble peak. It is best, however, to bear to the right of the ridge and go over a wall which crosses the ridge in a hollow. The track then continues along the summit of the next long ridge, affording fine views on either side. The final climb to the summit is easiest made on the right of the rock face. When this has been covered a stone-strewn turf-slope is reached. The summit is only a few minutes farther.

Beddgelert to Llanberis (14 miles)

The first part of this route is notable for the beauty of its woods contrasting with the rocky heights of Moel-y-Dyniewyd across the valley. In about a mile and a half the road passes below a wooded hill called **Dinas Emrys,** to which, legend says, Vortigern retired and where Merlin came to his aid. Then it continues through a miniature pass to the beautiful **Llyn Dinas,** fringed with trees and ferns and fed here and there by dashing falls of water which has hurried down from the heights beyond. The craggy ridge of Cnicht forms the background. Woods canopy the road as far as the bridge over the Gwynant stream,

Llanberis Pass from Crib Goch (*A. F. Kersting*)

Y Garn behind Llyn Ogwen (*A. F. Kersting*)

Aberglaslyn Pass

from which the Watkin Path ascends Snowdon. Between the trees there are good views across the flat meadows and up Cwm-y-Llan to Snowdon peak, and then the eye is caught by beautiful **Llyn Gwynant**, 4 miles from Beddgelert. Rising out of the water, its lower slopes beautifully wooded, is *Gallt-y-Wenallt*, a rocky shoulder of Snowdon.

As the road climbs up from Llyn Gwynant there comes into view the little hydro-electric power-house at the foot of **Cwm Dyli.**

The rainfall in this neighbourhood is considerable, averaging 150 inches per annum with probable total falls at higher elevations of 200 inches in a wet year. Economic use is made of this heavy rainfall in the hydro-electric power station situated in Cwm Dyli, which was laid down in 1906. The power station is fed by pipe lines from Llynoedd Llydaw and Glaslyn; water from about 1,000 acres drains off the eastern face of the Snowdon massif into these lakes.

From the roadway to the east side of the valley at Cwm Dyli a magnificent full-length view of Snowdon, gloriously set between the crags of Crib Goch, on the right, and Lliwedd, on the left, is obtained. The lakes feeding the pipe-line lie in the hollow at the foot of these cliffs. At **Pen-y-Gwryd** (907 ft. above sea-level) is the junction of the Gwynant road with the Pass of Llanberis and the road to Capel Curig and Betws-y-Coed. The hotel is a noted headquarters for climbers—among them the famous Everest men—and anglers.

Behind it tower the cliffs of the **Glyders,** and their ascent may be begun by a path leaving the Llanberis road about 200 yards from the hotel. With little Moel Berfedd on the left, keep the stream on the right, then cross it as it issues from Llyn Cwm Ffynnon. *The way is now up the ridge ahead.* Strangers should note that this side of the Glyders is dangerous to descend in mist or darkness, owing to the number of large boulders which have to be negotiated. **Glyder Fawr** is 3,279 feet high; **Glyder Fach,** 3,262 feet, lies about a mile eastward along one of the roughest tracks in Britain. The views from the Glyders are magnificent, particularly towards Snowdon and down into Nant Ffrancon; but *only experienced walkers* should tackle the descent down the precipitous northern flanks overlooking Llyn Idwal and Ogwen Lake.

At Pen-y-Gwryd the road, still climbing, turns sharply to the left along the breasts of the Glyders, until at **Pen-y-Pass,** or **Gorphwysfa** ("the resting-place"), it is 1,169 feet above sea-level. Here is the starting-point of several aspects of Snowdon (*see* pp. 131–32).

Pass of Llanberis

From Gorphwysfa begins the descent of the celebrated Pass, the finest mountain road in Wales. Shattered masses of every form, which have fallen from the heights, lie in strange confusion, and amid them the *Seiont*, rushing and roaring, hastens its descent to the head of Llyn Peris.

Beyond the foot of the Pass is the village of **Nant Peris** (with an interesting old church), formerly known as **Old Llanberis,** and then comes **Llyn Peris,** on the opposite shore of which are the Dinorwic slate-quarries. Quarrying has been going on here for two centuries, and the workings now extend some two thousand feet up the mountain. Modern Llanberis lies beyond the remains of **Dolbadarn Castle** (recently restored). They consist only of a round tower, which probably does not date back many centuries, but the site is said to have been held by the Prince of North Wales in the sixth century.

Llanberis

Angling. The Llanberis lakes contain salmon, trout and char.
Church. *St. Padarn's Parish*, services in Welsh and English.
Distances. Betws-y-Coed, 16 miles; Beddgelert, 14½ Capel Curig, 10½; Caernarvon, 7; Pen-y-Gwryd, 6½; Port Madoc, 22; Pwllheli *via* Pen-y-Gwryd, 35.
Early Closing Day. Wednesday.
Hotels. *Royal Victoria, Padarn Lake, Dalbadaran, Castle.*

Llanberis is situated on the western side of **Llyn Padarn,** a lake 2 miles in length. This lake is connected with **Llyn Peris** by the River Seiont. Boating is available on both lakes, and lakes and river alike afford sport for the angler.

Near the start of the Snowdon path is the **Fall of Ceunant Mawr,** the height of which exceeds 60 feet. It is effective only after heavy rain and is reached by following the lane on the right from the bus turning point.

At the southern end of Lanberis is the lower terminal of the Snowdon Mountain Railway, *see* p. 131.

THE ASCENT OF SNOWDON

Access. Motor-coaches run to and from Llanberis for the railway ascent of Snowdon. Some firms also provide lunch at Llanberis.

The western walking routes up Snowdon are served by the buses between Caernarvon and Beddgelert and buses run to Gorphwysfa and Pen-y-Gwryd and past the foot of the Watkin Path.

Refreshments. At the summit is a large modern licensed restaurant, with windows commanding grand views.

Mountain Railway. Trains run several times daily (week days only) in season. Journey up or down (1 hour). The length of the line is 4¾ miles, the gauge being 2 feet 7½ inches.

Snowdon, the highest and finest mountain in the southern portion of Great Britain, has five distinct peaks, viz., *Yr Aran*, *Lliwedd*, *Crib-y-Ddysgyl*, *Crib-goch*, and *Y Wyddfa*. But the name Snowdon is popularly reserved for the Wyddfa, the central and loftiest point, 3,560 feet above sea-level.

It may be well to summarise the five principal ascents. With the possible exception of the zigzags at the top of the Watkin Path, all these routes are free from danger and within the scope of the ordinary good walker.

1. That *from Llanberis* is the most popular, on account of its easy access by rail and road. It is rough and very wet in places, but is an easy walk considering that it climbs 3,000 feet in 5 miles.

2. Next in point of ease is the *Snowdon Ranger Path* from Llyn Cwellyn. It is inclined to be wet and the track is rather hard to find but it has the advantage of good views. The Caernarvon-Beddgelert buses pass its foot.

3. The *South Snowdon Route* (which incorporates the Beddgelert Path) is less easy than the others, but throughout commands grand views. There is a little ridge-walking towards the top, but nothing to disturb ordinary folk. The foot of this path is served by bus.

4. The *Watkin Path* presents one of Snowdon's most noble sides to the climber, and for two-thirds of the way the path is good and comparatively easy. The last part, however, zigzags across the precipitous face of Wyddfa by a path loose and narrow and the route should be left severely alone by all but the sure-footed and steady-headed, and even those should not attempt it in mist or when snow is lying. These same zigzags are a very disturbing factor to those using the route as a *descent*. This way is rather dull because it is shut in by the cup of the mountains.

5. The *Cwm Dyli* routes from Gorphwysfa or Pen-y-Gwryd. These converge above Llyn Glaslyn and then for more than a thousand feet zigzag steeply up loose stony paths that are not always easily traced in the climb up. This is perhaps the most arduous of the ascents, but the best rewarded with views of mountain majesty. It is more frequently used as a descent, but the looseness of the path leaves few opportunities for looking at the view, and

131

is apt to play havoc with optimistic time-tables and appointments for tea at Pen-y-Pass.

For those who require something more ambitious there is the famous **Horseshoe**, "the finest ridge walk in Europe"—though "walk" is hardly the term to describe this exhilarating scramble up the steep south-eastern end of Crib Goch, along the ridge by the Pinnacles to the summit of Snowdon and then down the Watkin zigzags to the magnificent ridge of Lliwed (pronounced "Looeth") from which one descends eventually to the lower end of Llyn Llydaw (or to the southward from Lliwedd over Wenallt and so to Nant Gwynant). Throughout, the views are magnificent. It must be repeated that this walk is *not* for the new-comer to mountains and should in *no* case be taken without a companion.

1. The Path from Llanberis

This, although somewhat wet, is the easiest route for walkers and on that account the most generally chosen. It is, indeed, so comparatively easy and gradual that motor-cycles and land-rovers have been driven all the way. Unfortunately, it is the least interesting. Its length is just under 5 miles, and may be accomplished in about 3 hours. To get to the path from the station, follow the main road to the Victoria Hotel and then take a road on the right to a small square. Go through the gate at the end of the road, and follow the winding road up the hill-side. At the first fork turn sharply to the left; thence the track is plain. At a height of 1,525 feet, about 2¼ miles from Llanberis, the path passes under the railroad. About a mile farther is a refreshment hut, generally called the *Halfway House*. Afterwards the track is steeper. At the height of 2,521 feet the path again passes under the railroad, and a fine view is afforded of the Llanberis Pass and Cwm Glas Bach, which lie immediately below. Some distance farther on the path meets the Snowdon Ranger route on the right and the Pen-y-Gwryd route on the left. The elevation of this spot is about 3,260 feet, and a steep climb for about a quarter of an hour completes the ascent.

2. The Snowdon Ranger (Cwellyn Lake) Route

The distance by this route is about 4 miles, and will occupy a couple of hours. The path commands fine views, but is very soft after rain. The ascent begins close to the Snowdon Ranger Youth Hostel (Caernarvon-Beddgelert bus route). Near the lower end of the path is a farmhouse; soon after passing it the path has a zigzag course, and leads through a gate. At the end of half an hour's walk there is another gate, and, the path becoming indistinct, the left shoulder of Snowdon must be taken as a guide until the track again appears. It leads along the crest of the ridge of Clogwyn du'r Arddu and finally joins the Llanberis path near the junction of that route with the path from Pen-y-Gwryd.

Those making the *descent* by this path should make for the Youth Hostel, situated in a clump of trees about the middle of the eastern side of the lake, and visible from the top of Snowdon. The path leaves the Llanberis route half a mile from the summit.

132

3. From Beddgelert or Rhyd-ddu

The distance to the summit from Beddgelert is 6½ miles (3 of which are along the road); from Rhyd-ddu it is 3½ miles. Some three-quarters of a mile from the high road the paths unite. The ascent from the road at Rhyd-ddu will occupy a good three hours. From Beddgelert follow the Caernarvon road for about 2¾ miles and there, just short of the *Pitt's Head Rock*, pass from the road to the right through a farm (Ffridduchaf).

From beside the Post Office of Rhyd-ddu a path crosses the old line at the site of the disused South Snowdon Station. At the fork in about 250 yards go right, past ruined buildings and slag heaps. In about 20 minutes the Beddgelert path comes in on the right. Look out for a narrow iron gate on the left. Take the path beyond and strike across a depression. Near this point small cairns lead up to a gate in a wall, past a sheepfold and a large cairn to a piece of "staircase"; from the top of it make for an iron gate in wall ahead. About here there are fine views westward to Nantlle. From the gate the path makes a wide sweep right, rejoining the wall above the grim precipices around the head of Cwm Clogwyn, which is skirted until the narrow path (known as the Saddle) on Bwlch Main passes to the other side of the ridge and we have a magnificent view of Lliwedd and the peaks and ridges eastward. The path now works round to the left, and then a final sharp ascent brings us to the summit.

For the *descent* pass the end of the restaurant farthest from the station. The track is unmistakable. In three-quarters of a mile it swerves to the right, and runs along the ridge of Llechog, near the end of which it passes through a wall and presently goes through the wall again. After a steep descent to the large cairn it crosses open ground to some sheep-pens, and through a wall, beyond which small cairns point the way to a small gate beside a big rock. For Beddgelert keep straight ahead, but for Rhyd-ddu follow the road to the right.

4. The Watkin Path

By this route the summit is 7½ miles from Beddgelert and 4½ miles from the high road, which is left by passing through a white gate a few yards short of the bridge over the river and close to a telephone box at Nant Gwynant. The route continues on past the late Sir Edward Watkin's house, the Gladstone Rock, and then some distance farther on the ruins of some quarry buildings. Here the path turns abruptly up to the right (an arrow in the ground indicates the route). This is the Watkin Path, and leads up to *Bwlch-y-Saethau* (Pass of the Arrows), the dip between Lliwedd and Y Wyddfa. From there it runs along the ridge and then zigzags steeply up the final peak. The zigzags are narrow and loose and should not be attempted when covered with snow. In case of doubt, once the final zigzags have been entered, do not take apparent branches of the path leading downward. The real path leads steeply up all the way. At a cairn the Rhyd-ddu path is met near the summit.

The *descent* doubles back by these zigzags from the South Snowdon track a few minutes' walk below the restaurant. The actual point of departure is marked by two cairns on the left where the South Snowdon path makes a turn to the right.

Mist is frequently encountered soon after leaving the quarry buildings, and only those thoroughly acquainted with the route, or accustomed to mountains, should proceed with the ascent. The return to Beddgelert can be varied, and a dignified retreat carried out, by striking westward from the quarry to the gap between Aran and Llechwedd (the wall is a guide). Beyond the gap are two tarns and a slate quarry. When these have been skirted (the left-hand side is easier, though sometimes wet), a track will be seen descending to Rhydd-ddu, by Llyn-y-Gader. This track, lower down, crosses the Beddgelert route up Snowdon, and by turning leftward along that the road will be reached near Pitt's Head; or one can descend to Rhydd-ddu and get refreshments while awaiting a bus.

5. From Pen-y-Pass

From this side is the wildest and grandest (and most arduous) of the approaches to Snowdon open to the non-climbing walker.

The "Pyg" Track (P.Y.G. = Pen-y-Gwryd, and is presumably a memento of the part borne in its construction by climbers from that headquarters). From the gate opposite the Gorphwysfa Hotel, at the top of Llanberis Pass, take the track running half right and climbing by the Bwlch Moch over the lower ridge at the foot of mighty Crib Goch. Llyn Llydaw comes into view as you cross the Bwlch and the track begins to hug the precipitous southern face of Crib Goch. Soon **Llyn Glaslyn** comes into view, and then the path suddenly becomes very steep on the zig-zags and not too easy to find, notwithstanding an occasional cairn. Keep well to the right at the copper mine, to find the path and avoid the worst of the scree. Patient plodding eventually brings the walker out on comparatively level ground where the Llanberis route and the railway are joined, and then ten minutes' comparatively easy walking leads to the summit. In a mist it would be a dangerous place for an inexperienced walker, as the scree is very loose in many places. From the top the path looks clear and simple; from the bottom and on the way up, it is by no means clear. The windings of the path as seen from above are simply lost owing to the vastness of the mountain-side.

Note. The old route, starting by the bridle-path from the Pen-y-Pass Hotel Car Park, and crossing Llyn Llydaw by the causeway, is not always available owing to the rise of the lake-water and the consequent submersion of the causeway. This is frequently exposed, however, and in case of need one can remove boots and stockings and paddle across. Those who ascend Snowdon by this route skirt the lakes and at the upper end of Llyn Glaslyn strike steeply up the scree. Afterwards it is a hard and uninteresting "slog" for an hour or so; and on the whole the P.Y.G. Track is to be preferred since the final scramble is not so difficult.

Llanberis to the P.Y.G. Track. Follow the Pass up past Dinas Mot, below which the road crosses the river. Some way above the bridge—which is about 4 miles from Llanberis station—look out for cairns indicating the path up to the Bwlch at the foot of Crib Goch. This is quite a good pull-up, and generally speaking it is best to follow the road to Gorphwysfa and thence come back as already described.

To *descend* by the P.Y.G. Track, follow the Llanberis path alongside the railway for $\frac{1}{4}$ of a mile. Do not be in a hurry to get off the main ridge; the beginning of the track is marked by a cairn, and for the first few yards at any rate the way is quite a good path. The P.Y.G. Track keeps well up on the slopes and throughout is at a good height above the lakes. The Capel Curig path descends more steeply to the head of Llyn Glaslyn. In this case follow the cairned route carefully or you may come to grief in a disused mine. The greater part of the route is visible from the summit in clear weather.

THE LLEYN PROMONTORY

Caernarvon to Nevin and Pwllheli

The road from Caernarvon to Clynnog ($9\frac{1}{2}$ miles) crosses the Seiont and at Pontnewydd (2 miles) the Gwrfai stream which drains Llyn Cwellyn on the Beddgelert road. There is little of note except the beautiful church at **Llandwrog,** off the road on the right.

In 10 miles is **Clynnog** (or Clynnog Fawr), a small village close to the coast. It has a magnificent old church, standing on a site which has been hallowed ground since A.D. 630. The present church dates from 1530 and is cruciform in plan and late Perpendicular in style. It has a good rood screen (restored), carved miserere seats, some "dog-tongs", and an ancient oak chest once used for the proceeds from the sale of calves and lambs, on Trinity Sunday, and with the special earmark *Nod Beuno.* On the south side of the church and connected with it by a dark cloister is the old *Chapel of St. Beuno* where, at the saints' tomb, many cures are said to have been made.

About $\frac{1}{4}$ mile south of the church is **St. Beuno's Well.** Within sight of the highroad and between it and the sea is a fine **Cromlech,** 6 feet high, 8 feet long and 5 feet wide. The way to it is along the lane on the south side of the church for $\frac{1}{2}$ mile and then across to the field in which the relic stands. This lane lies through private property, and motorists must obtain permission to use it at the house beside the gate.

Llanaelhaearn, where the Nevin and Pwllheli roads part company, is over 300 feet above sea-level. Its church was originally built in the sixth century. The building was restored in 1892 and the chancel enlarged. During the restoration there were discovered on its walls certain curious inscriptions attributed to British pilgrims. The church possesses a fifteenth-century wooden screen and in the wall of the north transept is an inscribed stone which has attracted the attention of eminent antiquaries.

On the Nevin road, about 300 yards from the church, is **St. Aelhaearn's Well,** which formerly supplied the village.

The Rivals

Llanaelhaearn is at the foot of the Rivals, as the English call the triple peak situated between the main road and the coast. To the Welsh they are *Yr Eifl* or *Geifl*, the plural of *gafl*, a fork.

The best point from which to ascend the Rivals is on the Nevin road, about midway between Llanaelhearn and Llithfaen. Do not be tempted into making direct cuts from the outskirts of the former village, as the upper part of what appears a very attractive route suddenly becomes quite dangerous, at least half the climb being over loose and easily dislodged boulders. The best way is to proceed farther along the Nevin road and then to strike up a green track which makes for the depression between the eastern Rival and the tallest one.

On the eastern peak is Tre'r Ceiri, "the Giants' Town," the most important of the prehistoric towns in North Wales. It covers 5 acres and was originally enclosed by three walls. Parts of the walls are 15 feet high. Within the enclosures are numerous cells or dwellings of various forms and sizes. The diameter of some of the circular dwellings is 15 or 16 feet, and considering their great age and the fact that the spot was some years ago rumoured to harbour a hoard of gold, the present condition of the walls is wonderful.

The View from the summit point just above the camp is glorious, embracing the coast of Wales from St. David's Head to beyond Bangor. Snowdon is slightly north of east, and on a clear day the train may be seen puffing up the mountain slope. Anglesey is laid out as flat as a map, with Holyhead Island to the north-west, and under very favourable conditions the Isle of Man may be sighted across the sea beyond. Westward the coast can be followed from Pwllheli to Bardsey. But the best view of the Lleyn Peninsula as a whole—and possibly of the Wicklow Hills in the distant west—is obtained from the highest Rival, reached by crossing the prehistoric town and going straight ahead.

Between this peak and the sea is Nant Gwytheyrn (Vortigern's Valley), a gloomy glen owing its name to the tradition that Vortigern fled hither after betraying his country to the Saxons. Remains said to be those of the chieftain were discovered in a large mound on the east side of the valley.

From the tallest peak of Yr Eifl will be seen the cliff route which forms the best way for walkers bound for Nevin. Having descended the mountain, enjoying, while doing so a fine view down Vortigern's Valley, follow obvious paths along the cliff-top as far as Pistyll, there leaving the path for the road. A mile out of Nevin there is a fine (backward) view of the cliffs and headlands. There is no doubt which is the successful Rival when viewed from this side.

Llanaelhaearn to Nevin (6 miles). The road rises to the pass (823 feet) between the Rivals and Moel Carnguwch, then keeps high up to **Llithfaen** (2 miles). The name Llithfaen means "loadstone", and preserves the tradition that the neighbouring heights possessed the fatal power of driving vessels from their course. It is then 2 miles to Pistyll whose tiny church is seen on the right, and 2 more to Nevin.

Nevin

Banks. *Barclays, Midland, National Provincial.*

Buses. Services connect Nevin with Pwllheli, Morfa Nevin, Edern, Tydweiliog, Penygraig and Aberdaron. Also to Caernarvon.

Early Closing Day. Wednesday.

Golf. 18-hole course at Morfa Nevin. Sunday play.

Hotels. *Nanhoron Arms; Caeau Capel; Plas Pistyll; Cliff Castle; Manora.*

Population. 2,000.

Post Office. Well Street.

Nevin (Nefyn) is a healthy and pleasant fishing town of some 2,000 inhabitants, perched on the cliffs of the west coast of the Lleyn promontory. The beach is of firm, clean sand, and affords good and safe bathing at all states of the tide. There is boating and canoeing in the little bay fronting the town, and some excellent sea-fishing. The scenery is magnificent. In the immediate neighbourhood there are pleasant cliff walks, and the surrounding district affords a wide range of excursions.

Nevin is historically interesting as the spot where, in 1284, Edward I held a grand triumphal festival, at which tournaments were the principal amusement. The site of the lists can still be traced. The old **Church** (*St. Mary's*) has a singularly narrow tower, surmounted by a disproportionately large ship which does duty for a weathercock.

Bodvean Woods, 2 miles from Nevin on the Pwllheli road, are very extensive. A public road passes through and joins the Four Crosses road.

Morfa Nevin (*Cecil*) is on the coast about a mile west of Nevin, near the golf links. **Edern** is a short distance farther on, and beyond it are **Tydweiliog** and **Penygraig,** strung out along the road leading to the end of the promontory. Fronting Morfa Nevin and part of Edern is **Porth Dinlleyn Bay,** an inlet divided from Nevin by a sharp promontory and forming a fine natural harbour. Its beach, about 2 miles long, is safe for bathing at all states of the tide.

Llanaelhaearn to Pwllheli. An almost straight road of 6½ miles leads directly south from Llanaelhaearn to Pwllheli. At 2 miles the road to *Llangybi* village leads off to the left. Another mile brings you to *Pont-y-Rhyd-goch* where the bridge over the Erch stream is picturesque. **Four Crosses** is a small hamlet at cross roads. That to the left for Chwilog and Llanystumdwy, that to the right for Nevin and Edern. From this point the road follows for 2 miles the ridge, west of the Erch valley, and then drops quickly to Pwllheli (*see* p. 139).

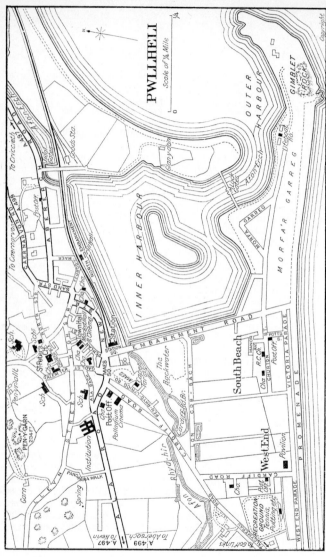

PWLLHELI

Scale of ¼ Mile

PWLLHELI

The name Pwllheli means "the salt-water pool", but there is some evidence, including the inscription on the corporate seal of the borough, that the name is a corruption of Porth Heli, the port of one Heli, who was lord of the district. The railway station is the north-western terminus of the Cambrian Coast section of British Railways. Pwllheli is the market town of a large agricultural district. It is situated on Cardigan Bay, its climate is health-giving, its sands are delightful, and the surrounding scenery is varied and beautiful. The town was made a free borough by the Black Prince in 1355, and is still governed by its own mayor and corporation. It consists of an **Old Town**, a compact mass of houses, north of the station, and two seaside suburbs a quarter of a mile apart.

The **Harbour** at full tide forms a splendid lake of saltwater about 100 acres in extent, while in the Outer Harbour many yachts and pleasure craft find accommodation.

The **Parish Church,** consecrated in 1887, and dedicated to St. Peter is in the Early Decorated style, and exhibits some of the leading features of the ancient Welsh churches.

The seaside portion of Pwllheli consists of two distinct districts, known respectively as **South Beach** and the **West End.** The former is about half a mile from the Old Town by way of the straight and level **Embankment Road,** forming the western boundary of the Harbour. A wide asphalted promenade extends in an unbroken line along the sea front of the two districts, each of which has a number of attractive residences and hotels, and first-class boarding houses.

The **Beach** extends westward in crescent form from the Gimlet Rock, at the mouth of the Harbour, to a wooded headland near Llanbedrog, a distance of 5 miles. It is composed of sand and small shingle, has a southerly aspect, and is of gradual and uniform slope. As the water never recedes more than a few yards safe bathing may be enjoyed at all states of the tide. On the shore rare shells can be found.

A very pleasant walk is that from South Beach to the **Gimlet Rock** by way of the sand-hills.

East of the harbour are the extensive sands of **Abererch Beach** extending in a curve of 3 miles to Penychain with its large holiday camp.

Pen-y-Garn is a hill immediately above the town, from which it may be reached direct by way of Salem Terrace, up the hill to which that leads, and then through the second gateway on the left. The summit commands an extensive view of the Snowdonian range, the Rivals and the coast of Merionethshire.

Excursions from Pwllheli

Llanbedrog is a pretty village near the coast 4 miles southwest of Pwllheli. The rocky and partly wooded headland **Mynydd Tir-y-Cwmwd,** rises to a height of some 400 feet above sea-level, and can be climbed by a public footpath which commences at a point near Glan-y-Mor boathouse on the beach—

the climb, although rocky, is a reasonably practical one to undertake, and affords wide views over Pwllheli, Abersoch and St. Tudwal's Islands.

In the shelter of the head is a delightful little sandy cove that forms an ideal picnic spot. The bay is sheltered from the south-westerly winds, and often when other bays are gale-swept Llanbedrog is in complete calm. For those who desire a picnic on a rough day this is worth remembering.

Tucked in on the shore at the base of the headland are *Glan-y-Mor Cottages* and *Foxhole Cottage.* Foxhole, a seventeenth-century cottage—now modernised— is so prettily situated that it is the regular subject of painting and photography by a great number of visitors.

There is an attractively situated car park, public tennis courts, a miniature golf course, and a café adjoining Llanbedrog Beach, and boats, canoes, floats, bathing huts, fishing trips and horses for riding are available. The fine flat sands and clear calm water make bathing ideal, particularly for children, and the bay affords good yachting facilities.

South-west of Llanbedrog is the village of **Mynytho.** From the hill behind the school is obtained one of the finest panoramic views in the peninsula. Near Voelgron Schools is **Ffynnon Arian** (Silver Well), an ancient wishing well. Another ancient well which was accounted holy is **Ffynnon Fyw** (Well of Life). Tradition credits it with having restored sight to the blind and health to the sick. It is reached by turning to the left at the post office and bearing towards a chapel; a few yards beyond it is the wall surrounding the well.

Abersoch (*St. Tudwal's, Vaynol, Lluesta*) is situated on the coast 3 miles beyond Llanbedrog and 7 miles from Pwllheli. It stands on the shore of a pretty little bay with an extensive, gently sloping sandy shore, affording good bathing. From full to half-tide, swimmers will find deep water under Benar Head. Those who care to spend a day fishing for mackerel may make arrangements for accompanying one of the roomy boats belonging to the little port. The bay is ideal for sailing. During August there are various races daily. A 9-hole golf course stretches parallel with the coast.

In the stream from which the village takes its name there is good trout-fishing. About a mile from the shore are the **St. Tudwal's Islands** and **Lighthouse.**

About 2 miles south of Abersoch is **Porth Ceiriad,** or Caered, a weird, romantic cove shut in by perpendicular cliffs rising to a great height. On the ledges innumerable seabirds nest.

141

One and a half miles south-west of Abersoch is the quaint village of **Llanengan,** containing one of the oldest churches in the peninsula. It has a double nave and a richly carved screen, considered by some the finest in Wales. It has also the holy vessels from Bardsey, and a coffer of solid oak, in which tradition says the inhabitants deposited their Peter's Pence. The miserere stalls and the pointed arch below the tower are also worthy of note.

About a mile from Llanengan is **Porth Neigwl** (Hell's Mouth), a fine stretch of 4 miles of sandy beach. It owes its name to the danger it is to shipping—a danger partly due to currents. As the place is fully exposed to the Atlantic gales, the surf and breakers present a magnificent spectacle during a storm. At the western end is a steep rise to **Rhiw,** the loftiest village in Lleyn.

About 1½ miles west of Abersoch is the quaint hamlet of **Llangian,** nestling at the foot of a hill. The parish Church, dedicated to St. Gian, was founded in the sixth century.

Some five miles north-west of Llangian is **Bottwnog** (Botwnnog). The Grammar School was founded by Bishop Henry Rowlands in 1616. There is a memorial tablet in the school to John Owen, Bishop of St. David's from 1897 to 1926, who received his early education here.

From Bottwnog the road leads on to Sarn and **Aberdaron** or a return may be made in the other direction to **Nanhoron** and through the wooded Nanhoron valley (past Inkerman Bridge) to Pwllheli. A diversion may be made by keeping straight on at Nanhoron Bridge for **Mynytho** and **Llanbedrog.** In about half a mile a lane leads off this road to the right for Capel Newydd (New Chapel) one of the oldest meeting-houses of the Congregationalists. It stands in a field and is only used for an occasional harvest thanksgiving service.

Those returning to Pwllheli by the main road up the Nanhoron valley would be well advised to take a by-road which leads off to the right, 2½ miles from Nanhoron Bridge, to **Llanfihangel Bachellaeth** church. From this spot, which is described as "the quietest in all Lleyn" there is a magnificent view extending from Holyhead Mountain on the left to Cader Idris on the right and including the whole extent of the Snowdon range. On rejoining the main road, go through **Rhyd-y-clafdy** to join the Nevin-Pwllheli road at **Efailnewydd.**

The Nanhoron Valley, south-west of Pwllheli, is 3 miles long. Its woods and rich meadow-lands form a fine foreground to **Carn Fadryn,** or **Madryn Mountain** (1,217 feet), about 6 miles from the town. Next to the Rivals, Carn Fadryn is the highest point of the peninsula. On the summit is a large prehistoric fortress with a stone called **Arthur's Table,** which some antiquaries connect with the Stone of Destiny in the Coronation Chair in Westminster Abbey. Nestling under the north side of the hill is **Madryn Castle,** once the seat of Sir Love-Jones Parry, Bart., and in days more remote the home of Tudor knights. The old gatehouse remains untouched, and one of the old-fashioned rooms still displays the arms of the noble family that lived in the castle for generations.

Aberdaron (bus service) is the most remote and charming village on the Lleyn promontory, 16½ miles from Pwllheli by the shortest route (via Sarn). It has acquired a modest fame as a quiet and peaceful holiday resort. (Hotels: *Ty Newydd*, *The Ship*.) Here was born in 1788 an eccentric person named Richard Robert Jones, better known as Dick of Aberdaron. He spoke thirteen or fourteen languages, but could make little profitable use of them. He died at St. Asaph in 1845.

The church of Aberdaron has a Norman doorway and two naves, one dating from the twelfth century and the other from the fifteenth century. The morning services are in English.

Bodwrdda, rather over a mile from Aberdaron on the Pwllheli road, is an interesting fifteen-century farmhouse.

At **Carreg**, about 2 miles north of Aberdaron, are quarries from which jasper and pink marble have been obtained. The stone has been used in numerous public buildings in London and elsewhere, but is no longer worked. Some of the roads near here are paved with blood-red jasper. On the coast near Carreg, at Porth Orion, is a beach of "whistling sand".

About 2½ miles south-west of Aberdaron is the cape known as **Braich-y-Pwll,** the Land's End of Wales, where the rock scenery is magnificent. On the shore to the east of the extreme point is **Ffynnon Fair**, "St. Mary's Well", which always yields fresh water, although it is often covered by the sea. The approach to the well is extremely dangerous. At a spot called **Parwyd** (the wall) are precipitous rocks rising from the sea to a great height.

Bardsey Island

Motor-boat service from Aberdaron.

Bardsey Island lies 2 miles off the cape, the intervening channel, Bardsey Sound, being more picturesquely and significantly known as the "Race of Bardsey". From the harbour the one and only road takes the visitor across the island to the little cemetery. Here the principal monuments are a tall Celtic cross of white Anglesey marble, marking the grave of the third Baron Newborough (died 1888), and another smaller cross, erected to the memory of the 20,000 saints. But the most conspicuous object is a ruined tower, a relic of the Abbey of St. Mary, founded in the fifth or sixth century.

According to old chronicles, those of the monks of Bangor Iscoed who escaped the general massacre by the Saxons fled to Bardsey. The island gained a reputation as a place of sanctity, and was the goal of countless pilgrims, who, it is supposed, built the church of St. Mary at Braich-y-Pwll, and refreshed themselves at the Ffynnon Fair before trying to cross the Sound. Under the denomination of *Insula Sanctorum*, Bardsey is referred to by early poets as the burial place of 20,000 of these holy men or "saints." Colour to this tale is given by the fact that human bones and remains in great numbers have from time to time been unearthed.

Some interest has been taken recently in the so-called **"King of Bardsey."** The history of this dynasty of peasant monarchs is quaint. Bardsey, it should be explained, with much of the neighbouring mainland, belongs to the Wynn family, descendants of the first Lord Newborough, a member of one of the most ancient families in Wales. When communication with Pwllheli was infrequent and uncertain, the islanders were scarcely amenable to the laws of the country, and, while not deliberately setting these aside, drew up their own code of rules and ordinances by which the little community was governed. The third Baron and fifth Baronet, perceiving the need of some directing influence, selected from among his tenants one of superior parts, and, appointing him head man, bade the islanders obey his ruling. By way of jest, Lord Newborough declared that his vice-regent should indeed be "king," and in pursuance of his whim presented the peasant monarch with a "crown" of brass, a "treasure" in the shape of a silver casket, and an "army" to guard the treasure, in the guise of a wooden effigy painted to represent a soldier. For many years the "king" ruled with tolerance in Bardsey, the office passing at his death to his son, who, however, after hiding his crown, fled from his responsibilities, and settled on the mainland as a farmer. To the vacant office was elected a weather-beaten old salt, a member of another family, and modern democratic ideas have changed the title from King to President.

...d-y-Llyn (*Woolverton*)

The Afon Mawddach, Llanelltyd (*Woolverton*)

Bwlch-y-Groes

Valley of the Mawddach, near Dolgell

CRICCIETH

Angling. Trout, sewin and salmon. Local rivers: Dwyfawr and Dwyfach. Most of the waters of these streams are under the control of the Criccieth, Llanystumdwy and District Angling Association. The authority for the area is the Gwynedd Rivers Board. Information from Mr. Pritchard, Ironmonger, High Street, Criccieth.

Banks *National Provincial, Barclays,* and *Midland,* in High Street.

Bathing. Safe at all states of the tide.

Boating. Rowing, small sailing and motor boats for hire. Canoeing is popular in the sheltered bays.

Bowls. Green near station.

Buses to all parts of North Wales. Regular services to Caernarvon, to Pwllheli and Portmadoc. Coach tours in summer to all beauty-spots.

Distances. Barmouth, 25 miles; Beddgelert, 11; Caernarvon, 17; Ffestiniog, 15; Harlech, 15; Pont Aberglaslyn, 10; Portmadoc, 4; Pwllheli, 9.

Early Closing Day. Wednesday.

Entertainments. Cinema in Memorial Hall, where are also held Concerts and Dances.

Golf. A 9-hole course. Annual tournament in August. Sunday play. Registered club. There is a miniature course (approach and putt) in the centre of the town.

Hotels. *George IV, Lion, Henfaes, Marine, Prince of Wales, Plas Isa, Bodlondeb, Caerwylan, Bron Eifion, Glyn-y-Coed,* and many boarding houses.

Parking Places. On Esplanade, and in centre of town.

Population. 1,650.

Post Office. High Street. Sub-Post Office, 1, Marine Terrace.

Sea-Fishing. Boats with boatmen who supply bait and tackle may be hired. Mackerel, herring, gurnet, whiting and flat fish can be caught in the sea, and good baskets of prawns can be obtained from the rocks.

Tennis. The Lawn Tennis Club at the west end of the town has both grass and hard courts in excellent condition.

Criccieth is an ideal resort for a quiet seaside holiday. Its mild climate makes it specially attractive for an out-of-season visit. Standing on the north-east of Cardigan Bay, it commands a delightful panorama of mountains and sea. The town is well-laid out; there is a good shopping centre, and the numerous hotels and boarding-houses are all situated in open surroundings with good views.

Running through the town from east to west is the Main Road, or **High Street.** Along this thoroughfare, or near it, are the shops, the principal Post Office, the railway station, the bus centre, and most of the places of worship. In the centre is an open recreation ground known as the **Maes** (i.e. village green).

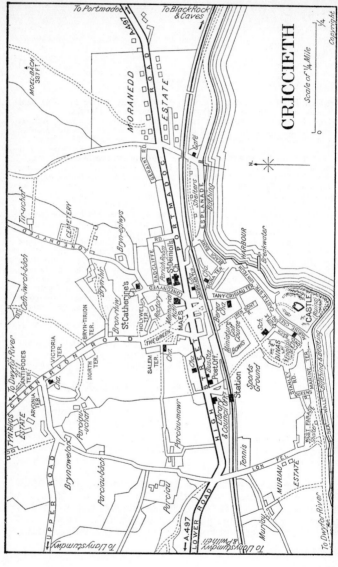

CRICCIETH

Scale of ¼ Mile

¼

Copyright.

© Ward Lock & Co., Limited

Dividing the shore in two is a rock on which are the remains of—

Criccieth Castle stands on a rock in the centre of the shore (*charge to castle and grounds*). The founder of the present Castle is unknown. Edward I is said to have strengthened and cased the towers in 1286, and portions of two still stand. They are of rough, unhewn stone. The Castle was occupied down to the time of Elizabeth I. It is now in the care of the Ministry of Public Buildings and Works who have carried out restoration work.

There are two beaches bordering each side of the Castle, each having a sheltering wall. West of the Castle the **Marine Terrace** stands above the shore; to the east is an **Esplanade** where there is free parking. Behind these are shelters and a green for games.

The **Parish Church,** dedicated to St. Catherine, on the by-road to the golf course, is a low building, consisting of a small nave and aisle.

On the main road through the town stands the much larger **Church of St. Deiniol,** in the Early Decorated style. The services are in English.

On the Maes near St. Deiniol's is the **Memorial Hall,** the civic centre of the town. Regular cinema shows are given, concerts, dances and plays are held from time to time, and in August the local Garden club holds its colourful annual show.

Brynawelon, the Criccieth residence of the late David Lloyd George, stands well above the town. Its beautiful gardens, with unrivalled view of sea and mountain, are open to the public at specified times during the season.

Walks from Criccieth

The **Black Rock,** so called from its appearance, projects into the sea about a mile eastward of the Castle Hill, and is very popular with boating and picnic parties. By land it can be reached by walking along the beach, a rough part of which can be avoided by taking the path along the railway line to Black Rock Halt. The entrance to this is at the level-crossing, at the east end of the esplanade; a signpost indicates the way.

The caves in the cliffs immediately beyond the Black Rock are best seen at low water. They can be reached by boat, or by a path leading over the hill. Refreshments are obtainable at the cliff-top and on the sands behind the caves.

Instead of returning by the beach, the steep cart-track to the left of the Black Rock can be taken. This leads towards **Treflys Church,** seen on a hill. The Church has an inscribed stone bearing the XP (Chi Rho) monogram of Christ. There is only one other in Wales, and only seven in Great Britain It is assigned to the sixth century.

From the village of Pentrefelin a by-road leads to the lonely church o Ynyscynhaiarn. In the churchyard is a locally noted grave, the resting place of David Owen, a young harpist, whose bardic name was *Dafydd Garreg Wen* (David of the White Rock). He has been immortalised by Si Walter Scott. A return to Criccieth can be made along a footpath betwee the old manor house of Ystumllyn and the sea.

Ednyfed Hill is a mile north of Criccieth. The summit, thoug only 443 feet above sea-level, commands an extensive view including Snowdon and Cardigan Bay. One route to it runs pas the Parish Church (the old church), along a road which lead through two gates and almost to the summit. The golf links ar here.

Another route is as follows: go up the Caernarvon road to Arvoni Terrace, there turn to the right and follow a by-road approached throug an iron gate. From this road take a path which leads through some field into a carriage drive. Cross the drive and go through a gate at the gabl end of the coach-house and stables. Then a second gate will be reached there turn to the left for the summit of the hill, keeping as close to the wa as possible.

Llanystumdwy (the church-at-the-bend-of-the-Dwy-river), i a village about 1½ miles west of Criccieth, on the Pwllheli road It is a picturesque little place, in a wooded hollow on the bank of the Dwyfawr, here crossed by a bridge.

In the wood near the bridge is the grave of the late David Lloyd George It is enclosed in local stone and covered with the boulder on which he use to sit to watch his beloved stream. It is now a place of pilgrimage.

At the entrance to the village by the main road from Criccieth is th *Feathers Inn*, and nearly opposite the public house are two cottages at th roadside. The westward one was David Lloyd George's home during hi early years, and in the small lean-to building at the side of the cottage hi uncle, Mr. Richard Lloyd, by whom he was brought up, followed his trad of shoemaker. Between the Village Institute and his early home is th *Lloyd George Memorial Museum*, which contains many interesting relics o the statesman. (*Open weekdays in summer, 9 till dusk, charge.*)

Rhydycroesau Bridge, across the *Dwyfach* river, is a mile beyond Llanys tumdwy amid even lovelier surroundings.

Rhydybenllig Bridge crosses the *Dwyfawr* river about a mile north-wes of Llanystumdwy.

The **Ystumcegid Cromlech**, the largest cromlech in the district, stands about 2 miles from Criccieth. Go along the Caernarvon road for about a mile. Then take the road to the right, opposite a gabled farmhouse called *Gell*, which stands on the left-hand side of the road, a few yards from the turning at the top of the hill. Follow the road until a farmhouse is reached on the left. There follow a car-road leading past the house and through two fields (taking care to close all gates which have had to be opened). Beyond the second field farm buildings are reached. These are left on the right, and another field is entered over stone steps. The cromlech will then be found just within the next field ahead. The capstone is nearly 5 yards long.

Cwm Pennant (The Pennant Valley), through which the river Dwyfawr runs, is in its upper reaches singularly secluded and beautiful. It is the subject of a well-known modern Welsh lyric by Eifion Wyn (Eliseus Williams, a clerk at Portmadoc), and is known to botanists as a habitat of rare ferns.

It is best reached by turning right at Dolbenmaen church and following the narrow road upstream, past the ruins of Plas Brynkir and Llanfihangel-y-pennant church. From the head of the valley a track leads over to Rhyd-ddu, past Bwlch-y-ddwy-elor, through the Forestry plantation.

Moelygest (861 feet). This is a popular excursion from Criccieth, the easily accessible summit providing some splendid views. For walkers, one way is *via* Black Rock and Treflys on the Wern road to Bron-y-foel farm. For others the bus may be taken to Wern Bridge. The second gate on the right gives on to a mossy road leading up to the farm. From there the way is through bracken and heather to a stone wall over which one must cross and then work left for the summit. A return can be made from the end of the ridge to the Morfa Bychan road a mile from Portmadoc.

149

PORTMADOC AND VALE OF FFESTINIOG

Angling. Salmon, trout and sea-trout can be taken from the Traeth. Good centre for Glaslyn River for trout and salmon.

Bathing. On a firm sandy beach stretching from Borth-y-Gest to Criccieth.

Boating. In the Glaslyn estuary. Rowing and sailing-boats are on hire at Borth-y-Gest.

Bus Services. To Criccieth and Pwllheli, to Caernarvon *via* Dolbenmaen (or *via* Beddgelert), to Betws-y-Coed and Llanrwst in summer, to Maentwrog and Ffestiniog, to Harlech and Barmouth, as well as a local service to Borth-y-Gest and Morfa Bychan.

Distances. Ffestiniog, 10; Cardiff, 149; London, 224.

Early Closing Day. Wednesday.

Golf. A sporting course of 18 holes, at Morfa Bychan. Licensed Residential Club-House.

Hotels. *Royal Sportsman, Queen's, Commercial, Madoc* (Tremadoc).

Population. 3,890.

Post Office. Head Office opposite the Town Hall, Portmadoc.

Railway Station. Station with connections to Paddington and Euston.

An added attraction for visitors is the narrow-gauge Ffestiniog Railway (*see* p. 151) now re-opened as far as Tan-y-bwlch.

Sea-fishing. Mackerel, whiting, pollack, and gurnet are plentiful from July to September. Large bass and plaice are caught with rod and line off the rocks at Borth-y-Gest.

Tennis, Bowls and Putting in the Park.

Portmadoc stands at the entrance to the Vale of Madoc, which opens into Cardigan Bay. It is mainly a business centre, with well-built houses and churches, wide streets, good hotels and a little harbour. Southward it commands a fine view of Cardigan Bay and the Merioneth mountains.

Slightly north is **Tremadoc** named after Madog ap Owen Gwynedd who, according to tradition, set sail from nearby Ynys Fadog for America long before Columbus. Much later, in 1821, Parliament consented to the construction of a harbour, and Portmadoc may be said to have come into existence at that date.

During 1812–13 Shelley lived at **Tan-yr-allt,** a long, white verandahed house, about three-quarters of a mile from Portmadoc, above the Beddgelert road, sheltering under lofty rocks and surrounded by magnificent woods. Some of *Queen Mab* was probably written here.

An interesting association also is with Lawrence of Arabia, who was born (1888) in a house now called Woodlands, in Tremadoc.

At **Penmorfa,** 3 miles from Portmadoc, on the road to Caernarvon, is an ancient church approached by a lane on the left, containing beautiful recent wood-carvings by a local lady. There are memorial tablets to Sir John Owen, sentenced to death for his valiant support of Charles I, but pardoned and allowed to end his days at Clenennan, his old home; and to the Huddart family, of Brynkir.

Borth-y-Gest, or Borth Bay, about half a mile south of Portmadoc, lies in a picturesque cove in the Glaslyn estuary. The pretty village is well sheltered. Innumerable sand-dunes, cliffs and open, breezy downs are among natural advantages here, while boating, bathing at Carreg Goch, trout and salmon fishing, sea-fishing and golf (at Morfa Bychan, $1\frac{1}{2}$ miles away) are recreations for which there are excellent facilities. Bathing is best when the tide is coming in, owing to estuary currents. Four miles of firm sand skirted by sand-dunes stretch from Borth-y-Gest to Criccieth. There is a bus service between Portmadoc, Borth-y-Gest and Morfa Bychan.

Morfa Bychan has become a popular centre for campers and caravanners, several sites being available.

For **Moel-y-Gest** which lies between the road and shore west of Portmadoc, *see* p. 149.

Portmeirion is situated on a long tongue of land between the estuaries of the Glaslyn and Dwyryd rivers. It was built by Mr. Clough Williams-Ellis in the Italian style, and while certainly not Welsh in type makes a delightful and entirely congruous picture, whether seen at a distance from the Barmouth road, or examined in detail on the spot.

The Vale of Ffestiniog, steep-sided, and beautifully wooded, winds its way eastward from Penrhyndeudraeth into the Migneint range.

High along the western edge of the Valley winds the track of the *Festiniog Railway,* 1 foot $11\frac{1}{2}$ inches, which extended from Portmadoc to the slate-quarries at Blaenau Ffestiniog. It was originally built to carry slates from the quarries to Portmadoc for shipment to home and foreign ports. In 1865 a passenger service was inaugurated after the introduction of steam traction two years previously, but passenger services ceased in 1939, and most other services in 1946. Control of the company changed hands in 1954, and with the aid of much voluntary help the line has been steadily re-opened, services now running to Tan-y-Bwlch.

About midway through the Vale is **Tan-y-Bwlch** (*Oakley Arms*), where a road climbs through the woods to the station on the Festiniog Railway, 400 feet above sea-level, and a mile or so by road from the hotel.

From Tan-y-Bwlch station a road leads via Rhyd to **Beddgelert**

(8¼ miles). Tan-y-Bwlch is also a starting point for the ascent of **Moelwyn** (2,527 feet) (*see* p. 127). It is, however, from Tan-y-Grisiau that the best ascent of **Moelwyn** can be made (*see* p. 127). There is an easy route to the summit past **Llyn Cwmorthin** and the Rhosydd Quarry.

Maentwrog is a village in the most romantic part of the Vale. It is situated at the important junction of the Betws and Dol-gellau roads. Swiss-like in setting and appearance, it derives its name from a large stone in the churchyard, Maen Twrog, "the Stone of Twrog". Twrog is said to have been a British giant who died about the year 610. He is supposed to have thrown the stone down from the height above to the church.

The Rev. Edmund Prys, one of the most eminent Welsh poets of his time, was rector of this parish and Archdeacon of Merioneth. He was the author of the metrical psalms used in Welsh churches, and assisted Bishop Morgan in translating the Bible into Welsh. He died in 1623, and was buried in Maentwrog Church.

In the hills above Maentwrog is a large artificial reservoir—**Trawsfynyd Lake**—constructed in recent years for the generation of electric power. The lake is some 3 miles long by a mile wide, and the fishing rights are held by the Prysor Angling Association. Visitors tickets and boat permits may be obtained from "Beehive", Trawsfynydd.

On the western side of the lake is the new 500 megawatt Nuclear Power Station, the first of its type to be built in Wales.

Ffestiniog

Buses. There are services daily between Ffestiniog and Portmadoc, *via* Penrhyndeudraeth and Maentwrog; to and from Harlech and Barmouth *via* Maentwrog; to and from Dolgellau *via* Trawsfynydd, and to and from Llanrwst *via* Betws-y-Coed. Buses run to all these parts from Blaenau Ffestiniog.

Fishing. Trout in the Rhaiadr. Trout and sewin in the Dwyryd. Good trout fishing in Lakes Morynion and Gamallt, 3½ miles. Good facilities at Trawsfynydd Lake.

Hotels. *Abbey Arms, Pengwern Arms.*

This delightfully situated village should not be confused with the slate-quarrying town of Blaenau Ffestiniog, which is 3 miles or so to the north. The scenery in and about Ffestiniog has been the subject of enthusiastic admiration by philosophers, poets and painters. Lord Lyttleton wrote, "with the woman one loves, with the friend of one's heart, and a study of books, one might pass an age in this vale, and think it a day." Glorious mountain walks can be enjoyed in all directions, and there are notable waterfalls in the locality. The small mount behind the churchyard near the *Pengwern Arms* is a magnificent viewpoint.

Walks from Ffestiniog

The **Cynfal** (*cunval*) **Falls** are in a romantic glen about half a mile south of the old station. One fall is 300 yards above, the other as far below, a small bridge. Cars should be left at a Congregational chapel just before the railway bridge and, turning right, you find a footpath marked Cynfal.

In the bed of the river, between the lower cataract and the bridge, is a tall columnar rock, called **Hugh Lloyd's Pulpit.** Tradition declares that Hugh Lloyd, a sage and bard of the time of James I, used it as a rostrum from which to deliver his incantations.

High on the other side of the stream is the view-point called the **Goat's Bridge,** a slab connecting the bank with a boulder in the bed of the stream.

Beddau Gwyr Ardudwy. Follow the Bala road for about 2 miles, and then turn to the left up **Sarn Helen,** a part of the great Roman road through Wales and now a green cart-track. The site of the "graves of the Men of Ardudwy" is about half a mile from the main road. All trace of them has disappeared.

Rhaeadr-y-Cwm. The Rhaeadr-y-Cwm cataracts are 3½ miles from Ffestiniog, along the Bala road, from which they are visible. They can also be reached by footpath *via* Bont Newydd, which is 1¼ miles from Ffestiniog, on the Dolgellau road.

After crossing the bridge and turning to the left, the path follows the stream, and in about 1¼ miles passes *Cwm Farm*, near which is the Rhaeadr-y-Cwm.

Tomen-y-Mur. This great attraction for antiquaries is 3¼ miles from Ffestiniog. Proceed as far as the old *Maentwrog Road* station. Follow the road for about a quarter of a mile to a schoolhouse, turn left, and then take the second cart-road on the left (about 350 yards from the previous turning). In a few minutes you reach **Tomen-y-Mur,** site of an important Roman station and fort, dating possibly from the first century A.D. Near Tomen-y-Mur two Roman roads meet. Within the fort is a great mound of earth from which the station takes its present name. The tomen is a medieval castle-mound, and is considered to have been built by William Rufus during his inroad into Wales in 1095. In 1114 Henry I used it as a rendezvous on his way to meet Gruffydd ap Cynan.

It can be reached from Maentwrog village by the Dolgellau road, which meets the one from Ffestiniog mentioned above at the school-house.

Rhaiadr-Du and The Raven Fall. The Rhaiadr-Du and the Raven Fall are on the River *Prysor*. The former (the Cataract Fall) is 6¼ miles and the latter 6½ miles south-west from Ffestiniog.

From the schoolhouse mentioned above, take the road towards Maentwrog Uchaf (or Gelli-lydan), turning to the left after a quarter of a mile, and to the right half a mile farther on, then, after a quarter of a mile or so, to the left again. There is a cottage half a mile from this last turning, and then a steep descent to the glen in which the falls are situated. After descending for a short distance, pass over a stile in a wall on the left, and go a few steps down through a wood; then follow a track to the left, to **Rhaiadr-Du.**

The **Raven Fall** is a short distance lower down the glen.

153

Blaenau Ffestiniog (*Wynne's Arms, North-Western, Queen's*), 3 miles from Ffestiniog, is the largest town in Merioneth. It is situated at the head of the Vale of Ffestiniog, in the horse-shoe bend formed by the Moelwyn and Manod ranges, which rise to over 2,500 feet above sea-level. It is completely dominated by its bluish slate, which is largely used for paving, roofing and fencing. There are facilities for outdoor sports and indoor entertainments, while the nearby quarries are worth visiting.

A Hydro-electric Pumped Storage Scheme is in course of construction at Tanygrisiau, about a mile from Blaenau Ffestiniog. This scheme is believed to be the second largest in the world, the largest being planned for Loch Awe. Llyn Stwlan will be enlarged to form the upper reservoir while there will be a lower reservoir 1,000 feet below.

Ffestiniog to Bala

Eastward from Ffestiniog a class B road climbs up to over 1,400 feet above sea-level and passes between the Arenigs to Bala (18 miles). A detour southward from Ffestiniog takes one to **Trawsfynydd,** a small village from which an interesting road leads across the moorland to Dolgellau. Trawsfynydd is well known in Wales as the home of Hedd Wyn, a shepherd-poet who was killed in the First World War, and whose memorial may be seen in the village street. More recently it has been in the news in connection with the Nuclear Power Station on the west side of the lake. Of the two Arenigs, that to the south of the road—Arenig Fawr, 2,800 feet—is the more interesting both to look at and to look from.

For Bala, *see* p. 184.

BARMOUTH

Banks. *Midland, Barclays,* and *National Provincial,* High Street.

Bathing. Good at or near high tide on clean firm sand from bathing station.

Boating. Rowing - boats, motor - boats, and sailing-boats for hire. Terms should be arranged beforehand. The trip up the estuary to Penmaenpool should not be attempted without some local guidance as to shallows, and the tide must be carefully watched.

Bowls. In the Memorial Park.

Bus connections with Dolgellau, Harlech, Maentwrog, and intermediate villages.

Car Parks. On sea front and at Quay.

Distances. Aberdovey (*via* Dolgellau), 35; (*via* the Bridge), 16; Aberystwyth (*via* the Bridge), 42; (*via* Dolgellau), 44; Bala, 28; Beddgelert, 24; Betws-y-Coed, 36; Blaenau Ffestiniog, 26; Caernarvon, 38; Criccieth, 25; Dolgellau, 10; Harlech, 11; Llandudno, 57; Llangollen, 50; Machynlleth (*via* Dolgellau and Corris), 27; Pwllheli, 32; Towyn (by the Bridge), 12; (by Dolgellau), 31.

Early Closing Day. Wednesday.

Entertainments. Barmouth Male Voice Choir—open-air sacred concerts on Sunday evenings. Cinema. Dances at the Church Hall.

Fishing. There is excellent sea-fishing, free of charge, at the bridge. Bass, from the latter part of May to September, and plaice can be caught anywhere. Pollock, all around the bridge and the rocks from the latter part of May to August. Mackerel, from June to September.

Hotels. *Cors-y-Gedol,* High Street; *Royal,* High Street; *Plas Mynach*; *Marine,* Seafront; *Hendre Mynach Hall,* Llanaber Road; *Ty'r Craig Castle*; *Min-y-Mor,* Seafront; *St. David's*; *Victoria,* Marine Parade; *Wave Crest,* Marine Parade; *Marine Mansion*; *Endeavour House,* Marine Parade; *Gallt Hyfryd*; *Last Inn*; and many others.

Population. 3,000.

Post Office. King Edward Street.

Recreation Ground. The Memorial Park.

Tennis. Visitors may become daily, weekly or monthly members of the Tennis Club. Hard courts and putting greens in the Memorial Park.

Barmouth is situated at the point where the long billowy Llawr Llech range of hills sinks abruptly to the water in the angle formed by the open sea and the Mawddach estuary. The original name was Abermawddach, corrupted into Abermo, thence into Bermo, which, in its turn, has been anglicised as the familiar Barmouth. There is little in the town itself that is

155

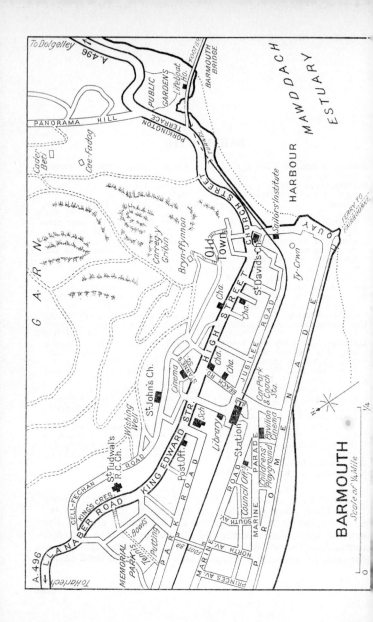

BARMOUTH

Scale of ½ Mile

To Dolgelley

A.496

PANORAMA HILL

PUBLIC GARDENS

Lifeboat Ho.

BARMOUTH BRIDGE

PORKINGTON TERRACE

MAWDDACH ESTUARY

Cader Seit

Cae-Fadog

CHURCH STREET

HARBOUR

Carreg-y-Gribin

Bryn-ffynon

Old Town

Sailor's Institute

QUAY

FERRY TO FAIRBOURNE

G A R N

St David's Ch.

Ty-Crwn

St. John's Ch.

Cha.

Cha.

HIGH STREET

Cha.

Cha.

Cha.

JUBILEE ROAD

Wishing Well

Cinema

BEACH RD

Library

Car Park & Coach Sta.

Sch.

King Edward S.T.R.

St Tudwal's R.C.Ch.

King's Cres.

Post Off.

PARK ROAD

Station

ROAD

Pavilion Cinema

Children's Playground

P R O M E N A D E

Council Off.

MARINE PARADE

CELL-FECHAN

Llanaber Road

Memorial Park

Bowls

Tennis

Putting

Foot Br.

MARINE AV.

NORTH AV.

SOUTH AV.

PRINCES AV.

A.496

To Harlech

N

0   ¼

remarkable, but few other places in England or Wales so effectually combine the charms of the sea and of the countryside.

Ruskin visited Barmouth in 1876, and no doubt many of his pen pictures of sea and sky and mountain were inspired by the glorious scenery. Richard Wilson, R.A., J. M. W. Turner, R.A., and other famous artists have painted it.

The climate is mild and bracing, and the best months to visit are May and June.

The beach consists of firm, smooth sand extending along the shore for a distance of 3 or 4 miles. It is inadvisable to bathe at the south end, opposite the car park, as currents are sometimes strong.

The **Promenade** extends for nearly 2 miles, from the Harbour to Llanaber, now part of Barmouth. It is not only a delightful walk but forms a sea defence work.

The **Barmouth Library and News Room** was built to house Miss Frances Power Cobbe's bequest of her valuable library of some 3,000 volumes, comprising rare editions and the autographed works of famous authors.

St. John's Church is one of the finest ecclesiastical structures in Wales (open 7.30 a.m. until nightfall, with H.C. daily). The original tower fell in 1893, causing much damage to the fabric and was replaced by the present one, which contains very musical bells. The principal feature of the interior is the beautiful font, which has the form of an angel holding a large shell.

The **Roman Catholic Church** is in Llanaber Road.

There are many quaint by-ways and alleys in the old town, climbing up to the hill and lending it a charming continental air with their narrow twists and turns.

Barmouth Bridge (*pedestrians and cyclists only, toll*) spans the wide estuary of the *Mawddach*. It is half a mile in length, and is of wood, except over the channel of the river. There, for over four hundred feet, it is carried by means of huge girders, supported by steel cylinders driven deep into the river-bed. A part can be swung aside to allow the passage of ships. One side of the bridge carries the railway, while the other forms a promenade pier and is provided with sheltered seats.

At the Barmouth end of the Bridge is the little harbour of **Aberamffra,** and here, near the toll-house, is the lifeboat house. At the mouth of the estuary is **Friar's Island,** said to have been the residence of a hermit.

In the vicinity of the bridge is another good view-point. It is the knoll called **Figle** (or Fegla) **Fawr,** passed on the way to Barmouth Junction, which is half a mile south of the Bridge.

Excursions from Barmouth

On and around **Craig Abermaw** (Barmouth Hill) a number of delightful walks can be taken. The rock that overhangs the town and has Old Barmouth upon its seaward slope is the **Garn Rock.** Several paths lead up to it. One goes past St. John's Church, another by the side of the Cors-y-Gedol Hotel, and a third begins by a lane opposite St. David's Church. From the summit (870 feet) one path runs in a northerly direction; another leads eastward to a road that is on one of the routes to the Panorama Walk.

Above the *Last Inn* is **Carreg-y-Gribin,** a stony slope upon which visitors may wander. It commands a charming view of the estuary and bay. Part of **Dinas Oleu** has been acquired by the National Trust.

The **Panorama Walk** provides one of the most popular rambles close to the town. A convenient approach is by a steep lane, indicated by a signpost on the left of the Barmouth-Dolgellau road just beyond Porkington Terrace. At the top of the lane bear to the right; the road continues along a depression in the hills. After about half a mile, turn sharply to the right, through a gap in the hills, then, turning right through a gate, you soon reach terraced paths from which the whole estuary of the Mawddach is overlooked. The highest point (500 ft.) lies a little to the right. Seats are placed at intervals.

Llanaber Church is on the Harlech road, 1¾ miles north of Barmouth, of which it is the parish church.

Dating from the early years of the thirteenth century, it is dedicated to St. Bodfan, with a later dedication to the Virgin Mary. The building has been described as "one of the greatest triumphs, for its size, of architectural genius and judgment," and as "the most beautiful church in Merionethshire." In 1860 it was carefully restored. Externally it is very plain, the grey stone and slate roof looking almost modern, but the interior is of great interest. The chancel has a finely decorated roof, and the east window consists of a single lancet, a very uncommon feature.

Carneddau Hengwm is a group of gigantic tumuli or burial mounds and megalithic monuments, probably of Neolithic Age, and situated about 2½ miles from Llanaber. The largest is about 150 feet long. The tumuli are formed of stones, and contained several cists or chambers surmounted by huge capstones. One of the chambers is approached by a passage several feet in length.

Overlooking Egryn, which is nearly midway between Barmouth and Dyffryn, are the remains of an immense camp known as *Pen-y-Dinas.* Two miles north-east is another ancient camp, *Craig-y-Dinas,* 1,164 feet above sea-level.

Dyffryn Cromlechs, Llanddwywe Church and Cors-y-Gedol Lakes

Dyffryn is a village with a station 5 miles north of Barmouth; it consists of numerous scattered houses, pleasantly placed behind a dune-fringed beach, and appeals especially to visitors who enjoy a quiet seaside place. There is a village hall, while on the Morfa, or plain, are some pleasant little bungalows (let furnished), camping sites and tennis courts.

There is a very fine cromlech at the back of the Dyffryn Primary School. To reach it, leave the main road, through a small gate on north side of the main entrance to the school (sign "Public Footpath"). Follow the path for a hundred yards and the cromlech will be seen on the right.

About ¼-mile southward of Dyffryn the Harlech–Barmouth road passes **Llanddwywe Church.** This is mainly of Perpendicular date; it retains the original east window and medieval roof-timbers. The wooden screen dividing the Cors-y-Gedol chapel (which contains many interesting monuments) from the chancel is dated 1620.

Opposite the Church is the entrance lodge of **Cors-y-Gedol,** but the house itself is not visible from the main road. The mansion (*private*) was for centuries the seat of the Fychans (*anglicé*, Vaughans), the descendants of Osborn Wyddel, or Fitzgerald, the son of an Irish nobleman.

On the way to Lakes Bodlyn and Irddyn a visit can be paid to a large cromlech named **Coetan Arthur** (Arthur's Quoit). It is said to have been thrown by King Arthur from the top of Moelfre, a neighbouring hill, certain marks upon it being the impress of his fingers. The best walking route to it and the lakes is from **Tal-y-Bont,** a picturesque hamlet on the River Ysgethin, about ½ mile south of Cors-y-Gedol lodge. For the Quoit turn inland by the side of the post office and follow first a field road and then a footpath, both running through a pretty valley. In about 1½ miles **Llety-lloegr,** a cottage in a wood, is reached. Thence a turn to the left leads to the stone in about five minutes.

Coetan Arthur may be reached by car from the Cors-y-Gedol drive by turning to the right at the second lodge, skirting a farmyard, going through the second of two iron gates about 200 yards past the farm and following a cart-track for about another 200 yards.

The stone is a little off the track to the lakes. After returning to Llety-lloegr, cross a bridge (Pont Fadog), and then turn to the left and keep eastward for the first of the lakes, **Llyn Irddyn,** about 2 miles away, at a height of over 1,000 feet. The path past Llety-lloegr is part of a Roman road across the mountains from Dolgellau.

The isolated hill to the north of Llyn Irddyn is **Moelfre** (1,932 ft.). It is 4 miles from Dyffryn station to the summit, which can be reached with ease and which commands one of the best views in the district. The prospect includes the Rhinog Mountains, Drws Ardudwy Pass, the valley of the Nantcol, and Snowdon. On the slopes of Moelfre are two cromlechs, and the summit is crowned by a cairn.

159

Passing to the left of Llyn Irddyn a track, near a bridge, is reached. Continuing up-stream, a half-hour's walk leads to **Llyn Bodlyn** (Barmouth waterworks) at a height of 1,245 feet. Having passed to the right of it, another half-hour's walk is needed to reach **Llyn Dulyn,** dominated by **Crib-y-Rhiw** ("the Crest of the Ridge"), 2,219 feet high. This lake is much smaller than the other two, but commands finer scenery.

From Llyn Bodlyn a half-hour's stiff climb leads to the summit of **Diphwys** (2,462 feet), which can be descended on the other side, and the return made by way of Bont-ddu and the main road from Llanelltyd.

Cwm Bychan Lake, the Roman Steps and Drws Ardudwy

The road route from Barmouth is along the Harlech road, passing Llanddwywe Church (p. 159), running through the village of **Dyffryn Ardudwy,** and between 2 and 3 miles farther north reaching **Llanbedr** (*Victoria; Plas Newydd*), one of the best fishing villages in North Wales. The neighbourhood is rich in stone circles and cromlechs, and the village is a centre for many pleasant walks. The fishing for trout, sewin and salmon in the Artro is controlled by the Artro Angling Association.

Llanbedr Church possesses a stone with ancient spiral ornamentation, which dates back to the Bronze Age, and therefore is probably several thousand years old. There are very few of such stones with spiral ornament in the kingdom, and this is the only example found in North Wales. Llanbedr Church was originally the Chapel of Ease of Llandanwg, but many years ago encroachments of the sea destroyed much of the flat land so that the old Chapel of Ease is now the Parish Church. Services are held both in English and Welsh.

The ancient **Church of Llandanwg** is three-quarters of a mile away on the coast. It may be reached by field paths or by car along a narrow lane from Llanfair, a mile north of Llanbedr. This was formerly the parish church of Harlech. It belongs to the early fifteenth century, but in recent years has been re-roofed and repaired. There are several ancient inscribed stones, supposed to date back to the sixth century. The ancient font has been removed to the modern parish church at Harlech. The old building lies right on the sand-dunes, near the water's edge, and blown sand is piled high up against its walls. The key may be obtained from Mr. J. Lloyd, Tyddyn Llwyn, Llandanwg.

There is some good bathing to be had from the beach here, and camping and caravan sites are available.

From Llanbedr the road route lies along the north bank of the Artro, up and down steep hills and through wild scenery. A mile past Gwynfryn, Aberartro, the junction of the Artro and the Nantcol is reached, close to the spot where the former is crossed by a picturesque ivy-mantled bridge. There is a road up Cwm Nantcol over the bridge to the right, but the Cwm Bychan road (signposts) goes straight on up the right bank of the Artro, past a bridge over the river at Pen-y-Bont to Cwm

Bychan Farm, at the head of the lake (refreshments, car park, camping). The road is narrow and runs at the edge of the lake, whose deep blue water, fringed with green grass and rushes, enhances the royal purple and gold of the mountains which encircle it. The fishing is good here. Rising precipitously from its southern side is **Craig-y-Saeth** ("the Rock of the Arrow"), famed for its echo. In the background, separated from Craig-y-Saeth by a ravine, is the cairn-crowned summit of **Rhinog Fawr** (2,362 feet).

For **Rhinog Fawr** follow the path to the Roman Steps for about half a mile, and then strike off towards the right. In about twenty minutes the track passes a little lake called Gloyw Lyn, and about another hour is needed to complete the ascent. The topmost point has two cairns. The summit of the mountain is a grand view-point.

Or follow the Cwm Bychan road for about 2 miles from Llanbedr and there turn to the right over the bridge at Pen-y-Bont. A mountain track leads under Foel-Ddu standing in front of Rhinog.

Both the above routes entail rough going and the paths are difficult to follow. An easier ascent is from Maes-y-Garnedd (see p. 162) which can be reached by car via Nanteol. From here the crest rises over much more open country to the north-east of the last farm.

The Roman Steps, so-called, are reached by continuing along the lake to *Cwm Bychan Farm*, just beyond its eastern end, where cars must be left. Then cross the stream by a rough bridge opposite the house and bear to the left through a wood. There are occasional flights of steps, but the longest stretch is far up the hill, near a wall, some distance beyond the little coppice. On reaching this wall, do not take what seems to be the obvious path straight ahead, but follow the wall to the right for a few yards. The time required to reach this spot on foot from Dolwreiddiog Farm is about forty-five minutes.

The steps are commonly said to have been constructed by the Romans to facilitate the ascent and descent of their sentries to and from the pass, **Bwlch Tyddiad** (1,294 ft. high and 7½ miles from Llanbedr), but the name is quite modern, and the steps are ascribed to medieval times by competent modern authorities. At the top of the pass is a paved way, supposed to have been formed for the sentry who kept watch from this elevated spot. The steps are said to number 2,000. Many are as sound, apparently, as on the day they were first made. There is a tradition of a tunnel from the Steps to Harlech Castle.

Bwlch Drws Ardudwy, (The Pass of the Door of Ardudwy), is a wild pass between Rhinog Fawr and Rhinog Fach. (Ardudwy is the district between Trawsfynydd and Barmouth.) Good walkers, however, often include it in a round from the Roman Steps. To reach the pass leave the path (which goes on to Trawsfynydd) at the top of the Roman Steps, where Cader comes into view, and bear downwards and slightly to the right, over roughish ground to a stream. After crossing it, the way lies due south for about a mile, over very broken ground, interspersed with rocks and boulders. Drws Ardudwy is at right angles to this course, and the opening of the pass is about 2 miles from the top of the Roman Steps. The head of the pass gives fine views over the Maentwrog plain. A rocky path leads through the Drws, which is in parts paved, like the Roman Steps, but it is not in such good condition. However, it is quite passable though difficult in very wet weather.

From the entrance into Drws Ardudwy it is nearly 2 miles to **Maes-y-Garnedd** (the "Field of Stones"), the birthplace of Colonel John Jones, a brother-in-law of Cromwell and one of the judges who condemned Charles I.

From Maes-y-Garnedd there is a road, rough at first, but practicable for cars to **Llanbedr** (*see* below for details). The total distance from Llanbedr and back *via* Cwm Bychan Lake and Drws Ardudwy is 17½ miles, but many people arrange for cars to take them to Cwm Bychan and meet them at Maes-y-Garnedd, which reduces the walking distance to just over 5 miles.

Maes-y-Garnedd itself, where refreshments may be obtained, is an isolated farm with only one other house beyond. Delightful days can be spent exploring the lakes and mountains round it, or fishing in the Nantcol. The right fork over the bridge at Aberartro should be followed, turning immediately to the left through a gate at some cottages. The road is rough and narrow, there are several gates to be opened and closed, and much low-gear driving is necessary, but the scenery is magnificent. In places are valleys lined with fine beeches, while higher up into the mountains are broad views of bare hills above, with the silvery ribbon of the Nantcol winding through its fertile plain below. The rough stone walls that twist over the sides of the hills, and seem a proper part of them, can usually be climbed, and the hills are not difficult, but are boggy in places, while care must be taken, especially in misty weather, to avoid the precipitous manganese workings that stud their sides. From Foel Ddu (1,359 ft.), north of Maes-y-Garnedd, fine views are obtained over the Nantcol and the Artro valleys, while from Moelfre (1,932 ft.) a magnificent picture is spread out to north, south and west.

Mochras or Shell Island

By Road. The route leaves the main road at Llanbedr, and follows the Artro to Talwrn Bach Halt. On the other side of the level crossing the road enters an R.A.F. station, and in rather less than half a mile it bears right and almost immediately right again (signpost Mochras Beach), passing through a gate and leading to the sands. Cars may be left here, or driven, with care, at low tide, to the island.

Mochras is a tongue of land on the coast two miles west of Llanbedr. It is crossed by the River Artro, which practically converts it into an island. At high tide a large lake is formed. On the sandy beach of the island many beautiful shells may be collected, especially after stormy weather. About eighty varieties have been found. An interesting collection may be seen, on request, at the boat station. The island is also noted for its lobster and bass fishing. The best time to visit it is when the tide is in. There is excellent bathing, except near the Bar, where currents are treacherous.

In the vicinity of the island is **Sarn Badrig** (often, but inappropriately, called St. Patrick's Causeway), a ridge of rocks that stretches into the sea for about 14 miles, of which some 9 are bare at low water.

HARLECH

Harlech was in olden times the county town of Merionethshire. It is built on the slopes and summit of a hill, 200 feet high. The seaward side of the hill is crowned by the famous Castle, so widely known by name at least. Perfect combination of sea and mountain air makes the spot exceptionally healthy, and the climate in winter is very mild. A sandy beach, about half a mile from the town, affords safe and pleasant bathing with excellent surfing. On the intervening Morfa or Flat is the course of the Royal St. David's Golf Club. Above the Morfa the town rises sharply giving wide views of the mountains over Tremadoc Bay.

The main road through the village is narrow and tortuous, and in the summer season is best avoided by through traffic. An alternative route goes down past the St. David's Hotel and the station, rejoining the main road after re-crossing the railway at Tŷ-Gwyn Halt.

Harlech Castle (Ministry of Public Building and Works; *charge*) is one of the most finely situated ruins in Wales. The ruins are extensive. Before its destruction the Castle was a massive square building measuring 70 yards along each side, with a round tower at each angle and one on either side of the entrance. In the principal chamber, on the first floor over the left-hand room, are well-preserved Edwardian fireplaces. In the south-eastern angle is a staircase by which the battlements can be reached.

While the place itself is mentioned in the *Mabinogion,* there is no historical evidence that the Castle Rock was occupied before the thirteenth century. The building seems to have been begun in 1285 and completed in 1290, at a cost of some £8,100. In 1464 it surrendered to Owain Glyndŵr, who held a Parliament there; and from 1461 to 1468 was in the possession

163

of Dafydd ap Ifan ap Einion. He was firmly attached to the House of Lancaster, and the Earl of Pembroke was dispatched to reduce the fortress. When called on to surrender, Dafydd replied to the messengers who brought the summons: "Tell your leader that some years ago I held a castle in France for the king so long that all the old women in Wales talked of it; and now I intend to hold this Welsh castle until all the old women in France shall talk of it." He was at last compelled by famine to yield. It is said that the hardships suffered by the garrison inspired the composition of that stirring Welsh air, the *March of the Men of Harlech*. The active history of the castle comes to an end with its surrender to Major-General Mytton in 1647.

The terrace is an excellent viewpoint, while another is **Moel Senigl** a low hill 2 miles from Harlech.

A very pleasant walk may be taken on the road northward to **Talsarnau** (4 miles). About a mile north of Harlech this road passes to the right of a hillock called **Glas Ynys** (the Green Isle). On the eastern side is the old farmhouse, *Lasynys Fawr*, in which was born the famous priest and writer, Ellis Wynne, the author of a Welsh classic, the anglicised title of which is *The Vision of the Sleeping Bard*. A folding bedstead fastened to the wall is said to have belonged to him. He died in 1734, and was buried under the communion table in Llanfair Church, about 1½ miles south of Harlech.

YOUR HELP IS REQUESTED

A GREAT part of the success of this series is due, as we gratefully acknowledge, to the enthusiastic co-operation of readers. Changes take place, both in town and country, with such rapidity that it is difficult, even for the most alert and painstaking staff, to keep pace with them all, and the correspondents who so kindly take the trouble to inform us of alterations that come under their notice in using the books, render a real service not only to us but to their fellow-readers. We confidently appeal for further help of this kind. All such communications will be duly acknowledged.

THE EDITOR

WARD, LOCK & CO., LIMITED,
    Warwick House,
        116 Baker Street,
            London, W.1.

DOLGELLAU

Dolgellau is nearly in the centre of Merionethshire, of which it is the assize and principal market town. It is situated in a wide and fertile valley, on the River Wnion, over which is a handsome stone **Bridge** of seven arches, erected in 1638. The town is an old one: three Roman roads met here and Roman coins have been found. In 1404, Owain Glyndŵr assembled the last Welsh Parliament here, and from it was dated the celebrated treaty with Charles VI of France.

The **Church,** St. Mary's, dates from 1716. The masonry is worthy of note, as are the timber supports to the roof. The main object of interest is the mid-fourteenth century effigy of Meuric ap Ynyr Fychan of Nannau. A small alabaster font on a sill on the south side bears the date 1651. Another monument honours Chief Baron Richards, a native of Dolgellau, and in the churchyard is a monument to an eminent Welsh poet, Dafydd Ionawr. The curfew is rung nightly at nine o'clock.

The **County Hall** contains some good portraits of county celebrities.

In Eldon Square is a **Market Hall,** having above it a large Assembly Room, now the community centre.

Above the road leading to the Torrent Walk is the **Dolgellau Grammar School for Boys,** and on the Barmouth road is **Dr. William's Endowed School for Girls,** a well-known boarding-school. By the side of the school is a footbridge over the river, connecting the Barmouth and Penmaenpool roads.

Near the bridge over the Wnion is the **Marian,** or Green, used as a public recreation ground.

The **Torrent Walk** is in the grounds of *Caerynwch,* a residence at the head of the glen of the Clywedog, about 2 miles eastward from Dolgellau. It may be approached from the lower or the upper end.

The Precipice Walk

This famous Walk makes the circuit of **Moel Cynwch,** the total walking distance being 7 miles from Dolgellau and back. The views are magnificent. The way is clearly indicated by fingerposts. Leave Dolgellau by the Bala road on the north side of the river; after about a quarter of a mile take the uphill left-hand road (for Llanfachreth) at a fork, and follow this up to a road junction on the left, by a telephone kiosk. Turn left here and continue for about a quarter of a mile, and the way to the Walk is signposted on the right. Leaving **Llyn Cynwch** on the right follow the path on the north-west bank to about 300 yards beyond the north-east end of the lake. Turn half-left uphill through a wood, keeping left of and close to a stone wall, in a corner of which there is a stile leading to the Precipice Walk proper.

Visitors are particularly requested to keep to the path and not to climb over or displace stones on walls. There are five separate sheep flocks on the estate and it is essential for gates to be kept closed. Dogs are not allowed.

The **Precipice Walk** has been cut like a ledge completely round the hill and in places reaches a considerable height—about 800 feet above the river. Care is needed in one or two places, but the track is quite safe.

Soon the Arans are seen on the right and the Snowdonian mountains far ahead. On the opposite side of Llyn Cynwch is the mansion of Nannau, with **Moel Offrwm** (the mount of Sacrifice), 1,328 feet, rising above it.

Nannau, the seat of the Vaughan family, is 700 feet above the sea, and is believed to occupy a higher site than any other mansion in Great Britain. The Georgian mansion is open to the public by appointment on Tuesdays and Fridays from April to September. It has been the home of the direct descendants of Cadwgan, son of Bleddyn, Prince of Powis since 1100 A.D. It contains pictures, furniture and ornaments of Welsh historic interest. The Deer Park is also open by appointment. The original mansion was the residence of Howel Sele, the cousin, but inveterate enemy, of Owain Glyndŵr.

166

The walk continues into alignment with the delightful **Ganllwyd Valley,** up which Snowdon may be seen. Beyond the refreshment pavilion the path turns southward, making the circuit of the hill, finally arriving again at Llyn Cynwch.

For those who wish to visit Cymmer Abbey or Llanelltyd, on reaching Efail Fach cottage there is a direct gated-lane, serviceable for cars, leading westward to the main Dolgellau-Llanelltyd road, about ¼-mile south of Llanelltyd Bridge.

The Ascent of Diphwys

(5 miles). From the junction of the Dolgellau and Barmouth road with that from Penmaenpool bridge a rough road leads up through **Cwm-mynach Glen,** the stream being at first on the left. After about three-quarters of a mile a tributary stream comes down on the right. A mile farther up the main stream, the track crosses to the opposite side, and, continuing, leads to the shallow reed-covered sheet of water called **Llyn Cwm-mynach,** nearly a thousand feet above sea-level. At this little lake the track goes off westward over rough, rather boggy and heathery ground. Make towards an old mining tramway, and climb up this, over the rocky slopes of **Diphwys,** to the ridge to the right of the summit.

By following a wall which runs northward along the ridge from Diphwys, the walk can be extended to the summit of **Llethr** (2,475 ft.), 1½ miles distant. Below the precipices of Llethr lie two lakes, *Llyn-y-Bi* and *Llyn Hywel*, only ¼ mile apart, very finely situated under the crags of Rhinog Fach.

A mile west of the beginning of the Cwmmynach valley on the Llanelltyd–Barmouth road is **Bont-ddu** (*Halfway House Hotel*), a quiet village providing numerous holiday pursuits in lovely surroundings. At **Caerdeon,** 2 miles farther west, the church was built in 1862 in imitation of a Pyrennean hillside chapel.

Llanelltyd, Cymmer Abbey, Tyn-y-Groes, Mawddach Falls

North of Dolgellau on the Trawsfynydd road is the village of **Llanelltydd,** its old church and yew-trees making a pleasant picture. From the old bridge a trackway runs close to the river to the ruins of **Cymmer Abbey,** a Cistercian house founded in 1198. Its remains show that it was a fine structure of thirteenth-century work. In the east-end wall are three lancet windows, and the large old refectory of the abbey, together with some parts of the Abbot's Lodge, form the Vaner farmhouse.

Close by is **Hengwrt,** one-time home of the Vaughans, an ancient family, and the birthplace of Robert Vaughan, the well-known antiquary of the seventeenth century. Here he collected one of the most interesting and remarkable private collections of manuscripts in Europe, known as the Hengwrt MSS. Some of these, after passing into the possession of the

Wynnes of Peniarth, were purchased for the nation, and are now in the National Library of Wales at Aberystwyth. During the later years of her life Hengwrt was the home of Frances Power Cobbe, who was buried at Llanelltyd.

Across the river the Trawsfynydd road goes northward for *Tyn-y-Groes Hotel*, about half a mile beyond which is a National Trust car park. On the other side of the road are the fine **Rhaiadr-Du** falls of the Afon Gamlyn. Several small falls and cataracts are seen before the large fall is reached.

Pistyll-y-Cain (the "Spout of the Cain") is about 3 miles from the hotel. Continue along the main road for about half a mile beyond the Gamlan stream, then, forking right, cross the Eden, pass on into the wooded glen of the Afon Mawddach, and follow the road along the stream. Keep the river on the right hand, cross the Mawddach by the bailey bridge, then follow the road keeping the stream on the left throughout. The waterfall will soon be heard on the left. It is about 150 feet high and is surrounded by oak, birch and elm trees, making a delightful picture.

Rhaiadr-y-Mawddach ("the Fall of the Mawddach") tumbles over a rock between 50 and 60 feet in height. It may first be seen on the right hand a short distance before reaching Pistyll-y-Cain, and to reach it continue on upstream for a quarter of a mile, cross by a stone bridge and proceed downstream to the falls. The glen is delightful, but except in times of flood the fall itself, owing to the utilisation of the water by the miners, is not worth the walk to it.

CADER IDRIS

There are at least eight routes up Cader, one from each end of the main ridge (from the Dysynni Valley near the Bird Rock, and from Cross Foxes); three on the south side (from Llanfihangel or Abergynolwyn, from Tal-y-Llyn, and from Minffordd or Dolycae); and three on the northern side (from Arthog, and from Dolgellau by the Pony Track or by the Foxes' Path).

The easiest ascent is from Dolgellau by the Pony Track, and the shortest that from Minfford; the Foxes' Path is better for descent than for ascent.

Of the mountains in Wales, Cader Idris is second only to Snowdon in popularity, while its views are generally considered to be even finer.

Cader Idris is a long mountain ridge, consisting in the main of very old volcanic rocks, that extends from near Arthog to Cross Foxes. It is highest (2,927 feet) near the middle, that is, about 4 miles SSW of Dolgellau. It presents a steep and often precipitous face to the north, and also to the south at its eastern end, while west of the summit (Pen-y-Gader), it slopes more gently down to the Dysynni (or Tal-y-Llyn) valley.

On the north between the main ridge and the valley of the Wnion there are ranges of foothills that have to be crossed by climbers from Dolgellau. One of these ridges—the longer—begins near Arthog and continues along by the Dolgellau road,

WELSHPOOL, BARMOUTH, ABERYSTWYTH

0 1 2 3 4 5 6   12 Miles

WARD, LOCK & CO. LIMITED, LONDON

© John Bartholomew & Son Ltd, Edinburgh

while another (Mynydd-y-Gader) closer to the main ridge is almost due south of Dolgellau.

These ridges are separated by the valley in which runs the old Dolgellau–Towyn road, that is consequently a means of access to the heart of the mountain mass.

Pen-y-Gader, the summit, is a relatively narrow ridge overlooking deep "cwms", one to the north and one to the south. In the former, a semi-circular hollow surrounded by steep slopes of loose stones above which rise precipitous rocks, is a small lake, **Llyn-y-Gader,** while on the other is another lake, **Llyn-y-Cau,** almost completely surrounded by formidable cliffs, and constituting one of the most striking of the natural features of Wales.

The Ascent of Cader Idris from Dolgellau

(*a*) **By the Pony Track** (6 miles). This is the easiest route. From Dolgellau Square take the upper road, the old Towyn hill-road, which goes to the left just outside Dolgellau, opposite the old Grammar School. Continue along this road for about $2\frac{1}{2}$ miles, passing Llyn Gwernan, where there is an hotel, and crossing a bridge beyond it to a farmhouse on the left, "Dyffrydan." Take the lane to the *right* of the house, *not* crossing the stream where the track branches off on the right.

Follow the path for two or three hundred yards and then cross the stream. Climb left, and then bear rather to the right. The track to the ridge can be seen on the flank of the mountain. Coming to a wall on the right and following it for some distance, cross towards the shoulder of the mountain, and climb the stony path on to the ridge (here a small tableland), thence to the spot, marked by upright stones, where the paths from Arthog and Towyn (Llanfihangel) join. These stones are 1,838 feet above sea-level, and $4\frac{1}{2}$ miles from Dolgellau. From them the route is identical with that from Barmouth.

(*b*) **By the Foxes' Path** ($4\frac{1}{2}$ miles). The Foxes' Path is the name given to a track up the stony scree which lies above Llyn-y-Gader to the east. There is no defined path up this immense wreck of stones, as they are always slipping. The best way is near the deep ruts worn by water among the stones. From the lake to the ridge is about 900 feet, and the angle of slope is 35 degrees. It serves better for descent than for ascent. At the top of the ascent before the ridge is gained, by a short path which branches off to the right, there is a spring of delicious cold water.

To reach the Foxes' Path from Dolgellau, follow the old Towyn road as far as Llyn Gwernan, and there take a plain footpath on the left. Keeping rather to the left above the lake, descend and pass through a gate, turning to the right, and keeping left of a stream. Shortly after, turn to the right near a sheepfold, and keep straight on the path going to the left of a wall. Leaving some rocks in front to the left, continue to a wall where the path is clearly marked by white arrows pointing towards Dolgellau. Thence, after crossing a stream, and passing **Llyn Gafr** (The Goats' Lake) on the right, carry on up by a steep and rough path to **Llyn-y-Gader,** (1,837 feet) grandly placed under the crags of Pen-y-Gader and Cyfrwy. On the escarpment of the latter magnificent outlier of Cader, the Table Rock is noticeable; from it crag-climbers make the almost vertical ascent to the ridge.

Descent by the Foxes' Path. Note that Dolgellau cannot be seen from the cairn but the Foxes' Path begins about 250 yards nearly due east of the cairn. (In the direction of Barmouth Junction, the bold peak of Tyrau Mawr [2,167 ft.] is nearly due west.) Turn down from the cairn towards the comparatively smooth plateau beyond the stony slope under the cairn. Then the Foxes' Path leads down from the ridge sharply on the left, and by a rough, steep but short path to the scree of loose stones. Not far below the ridge, a level path branches off left to the spring of water mentioned above. The track to Llyn Gafr and Dolgellau leaves the lake near its western end, and a little to the right.

The Ascent of Cader Idris from Arthog (or from Barmouth)

Visitors from Barmouth proceed first to Arthog, from which the summit is about 6 miles distant. **Arthog** is a hamlet on a spur of Cader Idris, about $2\frac{1}{2}$ miles from Barmouth. It is reached by boat or by the bridge across the Mawddach.

From Arthog proceed to the stream near Llys Bradwen. Do not cross the stream, but keep on to a farmhouse, *Pant-y-Llan.* Then cross some fields by a footpath, and turn to the left along the Old Towyn Road, *Ffordd Ddu.* Go as far as a house on the left, *Hafoty-fach;* pass through a gate on the opposite side of the road, and follow a path across boggy ground beyond which two routes are available. One way leads to the left after crossing the field opposite Hafoty-fach, and takes a path that climbs gradually beneath the face of **Tyrau Mawr** (pronounced *tirry mawr*) or Great Towers, until it passes over the ridge, but a better way is to cross the first two fields opposite Hafoty-fach, keeping a wall on the left and then, climbing a grassy slope that, although steep, is not difficult to negotiate, make for the *lowest point* *in the ridge in front.* This is an easily recognised landmark, and having reached it cross a wire fence, and turn to the left on the south-eastern side of the ridge, following a path that is more or less well defined at first, and becomes less conspicuous after a time. It leads round the shoulder of Tyrau Mawr, with the steep slopes of the summit (Pen-y-Gader) in front about two miles away. Care should be taken to keep at approximately the same level, until *two upright stones* (gate-posts) are seen near the crest of the ridge, half-way between Tyrau Mawr and the summit. These stand at the junction of the routes from Arthog, Dolgellau and Llanfihangel, and are *very import-ant landmarks* to seek in the event of being caught in a mist, as a path to Dolgellau leads directly from them to the left (if going from Arthog). They are incorporated in a fence, with a stile beside.

The **Summit of Tyrau Mawr** is 2,167 feet above sea-level. It lies a little to the north of the direct route to Cader, and can be reached in about 1½ hours from Arthog. The mountain has a steepish slope to the south, and tremendous precipices below the summit to the north. The view is considered by some to excel that from Cader itself.

While traversing the slopes behind the ridge of Tyrau Mawr on the way to the summit of Cader, fine views are obtained (on the right) of the valley leading to Llanfihangel and of the valley in which lies Tal-y-Llyn Lake.

A little beyond the two stone posts the last part of the ascent of Cader (Cyfryw, or the Saddle) begins. It is over ground thickly strewn with large stones and is the most trying part of the route. For the sake of having a path somewhat less rough than the direct route, take the track on the right. In about half a mile it passes a spring of water, a short distance below the topmost point.

Walks from Arthog

To the Arthog Falls, by the grounds of *Arthog Hall,* a castellated house, charmingly situated on the hillside, half a mile from Arthog station, or about 1¼ miles from Barmouth Junction. The grounds command lovely views. Except in times of drought, the falls are worth a visit. Tickets of admission can be obtained at the Hall (*tea-garden*). Alternatively a public footpath from opposite the church leads up to the falls. A third alternative is through the grounds of Tyn-y-Coed (*charge*), the home of Viscountess Chetwynde. Near the falls a path through Arthog Hall grounds leads to an old fort, the view from which is good, though it involves a rather steep climb.

To Penmaenpool (*George*), at the head of the estuary of the Mawddach, 4¼ miles by the delightful highroad.

Penmaenpool can also be reached by boat from Barmouth—a lovely trip.

To the Crogenen Lakes (Llynau Crogenen), about 800 feet above the sea. Opposite Arthog Church a short steep path leads into the road behind the mansion of Tyn-y-Coed. On turning to the right a gate on the left is shortly seen. The road itself leads straight on to Arthog Falls, but passing through the gate just mentioned the way leads up past a small farmhouse on the left, bears round towards the right, past a second farmhouse on the left, and winds upwards to Crogenen Lakes, 1¼ miles from Arthog station.

DOLGELLAU TO TOWYN, ABERDOVEY AND MACHYNLLETH

Westward from Dolgellau the main road runs through Penmaenpool and along the wooded south side of the Mawddach estuary and strikes the coast proper at—

Fairbourne

Angling in the Llyn Cyri.

Amusements. Bathing, boating, fishing.

Early Closing Day. Thursday.

Ferry. Between Penrhyn Point and Barmouth.

Hotel. *Fairbourne Hall*.

Miniature Railway from Fairbourne station to Bathing Beach, Golf House, Penrhyn Point (Barmouth Ferry). Trains run in summer at short intervals, but services may be suspended in extremely severe weather. A mobile canteen at Penrhyn Point supplies tea and light refreshments. When the trains are running a flag is kept flying at Penrhyn Point.

Fairbourne is a small but growing resort on the low-lying land on the southern side of the Mawddach estuary, with the mountains rising to the east and north. Its sandy beach, one of the finest on Cardigan Bay, extends for a mile and a half along the coast. The bathing is excellent, surfing especially proving very popular. Beach huts may be hired and there are camping sites.

From Fairbourne the coast road rounds the headland at a considerable height, and the run to Llwyngwril provides some splendid views.

Llwyngwril is a pretty village on an elbow of the coast midway between Barmouth and Towyn.

It is pleasantly situated on one of the foothills of the Cader range, and is increasingly finding favour with holiday-makers in search of a quiet seaside place with easy access to a town. The accommodation comprises a small inn (*Garthangharad Arms*), bungalows, and several apartment houses. Inquiries may be addressed to the stationmaster.

The beach, about five minutes' walk from the village, is rather stony, but there are several patches of firm sand which make good and safe bathing-places. There is also a good little trout stream running through the parish.

Near the village (by a pillar-box in the wall on the Dolgellau road, with a path leading down to the sea), is a burial ground in which a colony of Quakers interred their dead, until the survivors left the district with Penn to seek a home and religious freedom in the New World. The most notable grave is that of "Gwen," the daughter of the then local squire, and the first love of John Bright. On the entrance gate to the burial ground is inscribed the date 1646.

To the south of the village, turning up by the church, is an interesting hill-fort, **Castell-y-Gaer,** stationed on an eminence, whence it commands a fine prospect over Cardigan Bay.

From the village a mountain-road turns up north-east and leads into Y Ffordd Ddu (the Black or Gloomy Road). Yy Fford Ddu was the usual road between Dolgellau and Towyn, on this side of Cader Idris, until the present comparatively modern coast road was made.

A further 2 miles along the coast the road passes the village of **Llangelynin.** The west end of the church here is of twelfth-century date, and its windows are notable. About a mile south along the beach is **Owain Glyndŵr's Cave.**

Beyond Llangelynin the road strikes inland to the pretty village of **Llanegryn** where there is a monument to Hugh Owen, one of the first Congregational ministers in North Wales. The church possesses a Norman font, a beautiful rood screen, and there are some monuments of the Owens and the Wynnes of *Peniarth* in a mansion near by.

Towyn

Banks. *National Provincial, Midland* and *Barclays.*

Bathing. At all times of the day. Sand at low tide.

Buses run to Aberdovey, Machynlleth, Dolgellau, Abergynolwyn, Llanfihangel-y-pennant and Tal-y-Llyn Lake, Rhiw Ogo (for Cader Idris), Castell-y-Bere, and Dolgoch Waterfalls.

Distances. Aberdovey, 5; Abergynolwyn, 7; Aberystwyth, 27; Barmouth, 12; Machynlleth, 14; London, 220;

Early Closing Day. Wednesday.

Entertainments and Cinema. In the Assembly Rooms and Band Concerts on the Promenade.

Fishing. Good sea fishing. Free fishing in Rhydyronen, Brynglas and Dolgoch brooks. Salmon and trout in the Dysynni.

Hotels. *Corbett Arms, Sandiland Hall, White Hall, Garmedd, Bryntirion,* etc.

Miniature Golf. Course behind the Promenade. Putting.

Post Office. Cambrian Square, in centre of town.

Tennis. Courts in the Pier Road, on the way to the beach, and adjoining the Promenade.

Towyn stands on an extensive plain which is nearly surrounded by mountains, except on the west, which has the sea. The older portion of the town lies to the east of the railway, midway between the sea and the hills, which are about $1\frac{1}{2}$ miles from the shore; the holiday quarter lies nearer the sea.

173

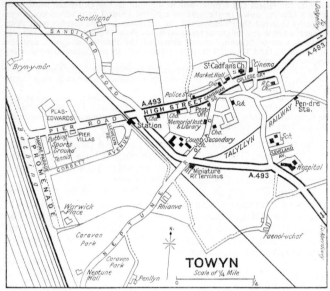

© Ward, Lock & Co., Limited

The beach, extending for some half-dozen miles, is formed largely of pebbles with some patches of sand, and has a gradual slope. Sand-dunes border the beach north and south of the town. Southward a walk can be taken on firm, smooth sand to Aberdovey (4 miles), and northward it is possible to walk by the beach to the mouth of the River Dysynni (a little over 2 miles).

The **Parish Church** is dedicated to St. Cadvan, one of the "Three Blessed Visitors (from Brittany) to the Isle of Britain." It is cruciform in plan, and has a massive central tower. The nave, aisles, clerestory and north transept are Norman work; the north wall of the chancel is Early English; the rest of the chancel, the south transept and the tower are reproductions of the original work.

The most famous monument is the Cadfan Stone. This is just over seven feet long, with inscribed letters on all four sides. It has been explained by Sir Ifor Williams as follows: CENGRUI CIMALTED GU(REIC) ADGAN ANT ERUNC DU BUT MARCIAU. CUN BEN CELEN: TRICET NITANAM. The suggested meaning is: "Ceinrwy wife of Addian (lies here) close to Bud (and) Meir-

174

chiaw. Cun, wife of Celyn: grief and loss remain." At the base of the pillar are two footnotes, MC ER TRI ("a memorial of the three") and MOIC CIC PETUAR ("a memorial of the four"). Other monuments in the church are the recumbent stone effigies of an armoured knight, one Gruffydd ap Adda of Dolgoch and Ynysmaengwyn, who lived in the reign of Edward III, and of a priest of the same period, remarkable on account of the *amice* being worn on the head as a hood instead of being folded about the neck.

To the south of the town is **Escuan Hill** from the top of which there is an extensive and beautiful view.

The Dysynni Walk

This walk is one of the most beautiful in the neighbourhood, and, indeed, in Wales. The river *Dysynni*, from which the walk takes its name, rises in Tal-y-Llyn lake and is fed by many rivulets from Cader Idris and the adjoining mountains. It contains salmon, sewin and trout and its estuary is a feeding-place for bass. In the winter months the stream is the haunt of large flocks of ducks and other wild fowl. Walkers and cyclists may use the bridge over the river. The approach to it is along Sandilands Road, close to the railway station. This leads to **Tonfanau** on the northern side of the Dysynni, 2½ miles north-west of Towyn. There is a large military camp here. From the station follow the road to the Granite Quarries. Pass them on the left and follow the lane through a farmyard to the foot of **Beacon Hill** (500 ft.). From the farmyard follow the lane for nearly a mile and then take the branch to the right. Follow the road to Bryncrug, passing a large, square, modern house called *Pant*. About a hundred yards beyond it is a gate, from which is a remarkably fine view.

Northward is the picturesque village of Llanegryn. About a mile and a half in front is **Moel Cocyn** (1,013 ft.), "haycock hill," so called from its shape. To the left is the **Bird Rock,** and in the same direction but in the far distance is Cader Idris. At the foot of Moel Cocyn is the small village of **Bryncrug.** Nearer still to the spectator, and between the hill and the river, is a cluster of pines on a slight mound known as **Tomen Ddreiniog,** "bramble mound." It is the Keep of the old Manor House of the Welsh Princes.

Follow the road from Pant down hill to the main road, turn right for **Bryncrug,** where, in the burial ground of the Calvinistic Methodist Chapel, is the grave of Mary Jones, whose efforts to obtain a Bible led (*see* p. 185) to the formation of the British and Foreign Bible Society. In the centre of the village turn to the right for Towyn, 2 miles distant, or a quarter of a mile from Bryncrug take a lane on the left, which, in a good half-mile, leads to **Rhydyronen** station on the narrow-gauge railway. The total length of the excursion is about 8 miles.

TOWYN TO TAL-Y-LLYN

There are at least three ways of visiting Tal-y-Llyn Lake from Towyn—by rail to Abergynolwyn, following the road for about 3 miles farther to the north-east; by the road that follows the valley of the Fathew River, or the longer but more interesting route which follows the valley of the Dysynni River.

By the Fathew Valley

Towyn is the terminus of a short railway having a gauge of 2 feet 3 inches and running up the valley of the *Afon Fathew* to Abergynolwyn, a village from which one of the ascents of Cader Idris may be begun and about 3 miles short of the village and lake of Tal-y-Llyn. The line was constructed for the slate traffic. Though only 7 miles long, it has three intermediate stations, each affording access to places which well repay a halt and a walk of greater or less extent. The terminus at Towyn is the Wharf station, a quarter mile from the Western Region station.

Two miles from Towyn is **Rhydyronen** (or Ashford). In the neighbourhood are a slate quarry, the source of Towyn's excellent water supply and, near the station, one of the most powerful chalybeate springs in Great Britain.

A track to the right leads over the hills to the **Happy Valley** passing **Trum Gelli** (1,743 feet) on the left, and **Corlan Fraith** (1,332 feet) on the right.

The next station is **Brynglas** (green hill), in the midst of very beautiful scenery, and quite near a trout stream. From the station there is an extremely pretty walk (by crossing the river towards the Towyn road) to **Dolau Gwyn**, an Elizabethan mansion. The walk may be continued to Bronyffynon, and by Penypark Farm, whence, by taking a turn to the left, Rhydyronen station may be reached in about ten minutes.

A short distance beyond the viaduct at **Dolgoch** (red meadow or dale) are the **Dolgoch Waterfalls**, three in number. To reach them, go down the road from the station and turn up the stream. The falls can be approached by means of a number of protected footpaths, all of which afford interesting view-points. The glen is carefully preserved and is an ideal spot for a picnic.

The **Bird Rock** can also be easily visited from Dolgoch, from which it is only 2 miles distant. The path leaves the main road by a stile at the sharp bend a few hundred yards west of the station; if followed upwards and to the right, where it forks, it will lead through a farmyard to a short lane by which the top of a hill is reached. From there a path runs to a gate in a wall, beyond which is an ascent over stony ground to the summit of the famous rock.

The inland terminus of the line is a half-mile short of—

Abergynolwyn, a village composed mainly of the cottages of the men who worked at the Bryneglwys Quarries, some distance up the hillside (now closed). Trout fishing in the Dysynni requires permit from the Ystumaner Fishing Association, from Cedris Bridge to Caerberllan Bridge. **Tal-y-Llyn Lake** (p. 182) is 3 miles along the main road on the farther side of Abergynolwyn.

Near the Bryneglwys ("Church hill") Quarries are the remains of a Roman road and of a so-called Roman bridge commonly known as **Pont Llaeron.**

Among the excursions that can be made from Abergynolwyn is a charming walk through the **Ceunant Gwyllt** ("wild ravine"). Turn to the right towards the bottom of the incline seen from the centre of the village.

der Idris across Bont Ddu

Bird Rock, near Towyn (*Woolverton*)

The Dee at Llangollen (*G. D. Bolton*)

Rheidol Va

Then take the road to the left, and at the top of the first hill take a path along the bank of a stream which flows through the Wild Ravine.

The ravine is on the direct route to the **Quarries**. At the top of the ravine, cross the stream by the little bridge and follow the path to the right of the incline, and the summit, a good view-point, will be reached. It is only a few minutes' walk farther to the quarries.

Abergynolwyn to Llanfihangel-y-pennant. A pleasant walk of 2½ miles. Take the second road to the left in Abergynolwyn. Follow the path on the right to the Towyn road, and in that turn to the right. The distance, however, can be shortened by bearing to the right along a path that cuts across the bottom of the hill over which the main road climbs. The path rejoins the main road opposite a small hill upon which stands the ruins of **Castell-y-Bere**, or Bere Castle. It was one of the largest and most richly ornamented castles in Wales. In it Dafydd, the brother of Llewelyn, the last of the Welsh princes, established himself against Edward I. The Castle was surrendered to the English king, but Dafydd escaped to Snowdon, and was there a fugitive until he was betrayed by some of his countrymen and went to a cruel death. It is now in the care of the Ministry of Public Building and Works. **Llanfihangel** was the birthplace of Mary Jones, of Bible Society fame. She is commemorated by a monument erected near the bridge and unveiled on June 1, 1907. It stands within the ruins of the house in which she was born (*see* p. 185).

Llanfihangel to Tal-y-Llyn. There is a direct walking route, 3 miles in length, over a pass called **Bwlch Cedris**, about 1½ miles east of Llanfihangel.

Abergynolwyn to Machynlleth. Seven miles. In Abergynolwyn take the road which leads up to the quarries. Keep the stream on the right for most of the way, and later cross it near a small pool or reservoir and climb to the ridge of Foel-y-Geifr, 1,398 feet. After crossing the ridge, the track bears slightly to the left for about a mile, then a little to the right, and eventually leads into the main road half a mile from Machynlleth station.

To Tal-y-Llyn by the Dysynni Valley

About a mile from the town the grounds of Ynys-y-maengwyn are passed and then after rather more than half a mile a turn left for the village of Bryncrug is taken.

The road now bears north-west, and crosses the Dysynni to **Tal-y-Bont**, less than a mile beyond which is **Llanegryn**, 4 miles from Towyn.

Then after skirting Peniarth Park it bends to the right. In less than half a mile it turns left and runs along the valley for a couple of miles to **Pont-y-garth**, where it crosses the Dysynni again. The **Bird Rock** (Craig Aderyn) rises above, and the Cader range is close on the left. Between 2 and 3 miles farther it once more crosses the stream, with the ruins of **Castell-y-Bere** on a hill to the left.

At Pont Ystumanner the road turns towards the south-east, still following the valley of the Dysynni, to Abergynolwyn; this part of the journey— rather less than 9 miles—is especially interesting.

The Happy Valley

The Valley (a very popular walk) lies to the south of Towyn, and is reached by way of the Aberdovey road.

Beyond a path on the right running into the Caethle woods, the road lies above a small ravine, and on the left is **Corlan Fraith**, a hill about 1,300 feet in height. After passing the lead mines of Melin-llyn-pair, said to have been worked from the time of the Romans until recent years, and a sign marked "Route to the Panorama Walk and Aberdovey," a public road to the Towyn and Aberdovey road is reached, and then the little church and graveyard of **Maethlon**. Beyond this is a sign marked "Track to Aberdovey," 2½ miles, A little farther is a gate on which is the name "Bryn Dinas." Here those who wish to visit the Ancient Graves—**Goidel Graves** is their description in *Archaeologia Cambrensis* for April, 1910— turn to the left. It takes about half an hour to reach them and a local guide is a help. Continuing for half a mile farther, a track on the right is reached leading up the hills to **Llyn Barfog**, or the Bearded Lake.

The lake is small, and the surroundings are rather melancholy. From the rim, however, is obtained a magnificent view of range beyond range of mountains and the water of the bay beyond the entrance to the valley.

Returning from the lake, taking a sign-marked path on the left and then one on the right, a stone called **Carn March Arthur** (the Hoof of Arthur's Horse) is reached. On it are marks said to have been made by the hoof of King Arthur's horse when he jumped across the estuary of the Dovey.

Once more following the road there is a very steep ascent to **Pant-yr-On** (591 ft.), which commands a magnificent view of the valley. **Cwrt Pennal**, about 8 miles from Towyn, is rather more than a mile from Pant-yr-On.

About a mile farther east is the village of **Pennal**, described on p. 180.

At Cwrt Pennal the road through the valley meets the main road that comes up from Towyn and Aberdovey. Two miles south-west of Cwrt this road meets the railway, and road, railway and the river continue together to **Aberdovey**. Thence road and railway are close companions for another 3 miles. Then the entrance to the Happy Valley is once more reached, and Towyn after another mile.

Ascent of Cader Idris from Towyn

Cader Idris is described more fully on pp. 168–171, but the following notes may be helpful to those proposing to visit the mountain from Towyn.

There is a choice of the following routes:

(1) The most gradual ascent, but perhaps the least interesting is by Abergynolwyn to Llanfihangel-y-Pennant, as already described. In **Llanfihangel** follow a lane which passes to the right of the church, and at the end of half a mile crosses a stream. Then turn to the right, and follow a tree-shaded cart-track to **Gwastadfryn Farm**, about 1¼ miles from Llanfihangel and 4¼ from the summit of Cader. At the farm refreshments can be obtained. From the farm the route lies at a short distance to the left of the stream, until just past a cow-house it crosses the water, follows a stone wall towards the east, and then goes northward to the stone posts mentioned in the ascent from Barmouth.

(2) **The Maesypandy Route.** From Abergynolwyn follow the road which leads to the Tal-y-Llyn Lake. It passes *Maesypandy Farm*. At the top of a hill, half a mile short of the lake, take a path on the left up the mountain-side. The summit can be reached in 2½ hours.

(3) **The Minffordd or Dolycae Ascent.** This is the shortest and finest, but the steepest ascent of Cader on its southern side. From Abergynolwyn proceed to the lake and follow the road on the right-hand side to the far end of the water. Thence up past the mansion of *Dolycae*, as described on p. 182. The path leaves the main road about half a mile from the Dolgellau end of Tal-y-Llyn Lake, near to a chapel.

Aberdovey

Banks. *National Provincial, Barclays* and *Midland*.

Bathing. From huts which can be hired for a period.

Boating. Good facilities for boating, in the estuary. Motor-launches, etc.

Distances. Aberystwyth, 28; Barmouth, 34; Machynlleth, 11; Towyn, 5; Arthur's Horse's Hoof, 3; Happy Valley, 2½; Panorama Walk, 1; Bearded Lake Echo, 3½; Llyfnant Valley and Falls, 3; Clettwr Valley, 3.

Early Closing Day. Wednesday.

Fishing. Good bass fishing. A large crimson and white fly should be used. Cod are taken by line from boats in that part of the river known as the Train, from March to October. Pollock and bass are caught off the pier from April to September Bass are also fished from a boat anchored in the river. Mullet, plaice, sole, turbot, bass, brill and other fish are caught in draught nets from May to November. Mackerel and gurnard provide good sport in the bay from July to September.

Golf. 18-hole course near station.

Hotels. *Britannia; Trefeddian; Dovey; Limes; Penrhyn; Bryn-y-mor* (boarding)*; Penhelig Arms;* Penrhos Camping Site.

Population. About 1,300.

Post Office. Bodfer Terrace.

Tennis, Bowls, Cinema, etc.

Aberdovey is a small resort situated, as its name indicates, at the mouth of the Dovey. It is on the north or Merionethshire bank and follows the curve of the shore. The houses are for the most part built in terraces on a hill overlooking the estuary. The village faces south, and high hills behind completely screen it from north-east, north, and north-west winds, so that it enjoys a mild temperature even in winter.

There is a long beach of firm sand and in the estuary visitors can enjoy as much boating and free fishing as they please. The golf links, pleasantly situated behind the low sandhills, extend for a distance of 2 miles along the coast.

In the extensive Recreation Ground there are bowls and putting greens, grass tennis courts, and spaces for other games.

The **Church** is a neat, modern building above the line of houses on the front. An interesting peal of bells has been installed in the tower.

The *Outward Bound Sea School* is located here.

The hills above Aberdovey are known as the **Cefn Rhos.** They command extensive and charming views.

Pennal (*Riverside Hotel*) is a charming little village, 6 miles east of Aberdovey on the Machynlleth road. It is set in a beautiful valley with hills around for climbing and streams at hand for fishing. A little south of the village is **Cefn Caer,** said to have been the site of a Roman fortress.

Machynlleth

Banks. *Barclays, Midland,* and *National Provincial.*

Distances. Aberystwyth, 18 miles; Aberdovey, 11; Towyn, 16; Barmouth, 27; Dolgellau, 16.

Early Closing Day. Thursday.

Entertainment. Concerts, dances, etc., in Town Hall. Cinema in Powys Street. Sheep dog trials and annual show.

Fishing. The Dovey Fishery Association strictly preserves about 14 miles of the Dovey, mainly a sea-trout river, but a few salmon run all the time from May to October.

Hotels. *Lion, Wynnstay, Glyndwr.*

Population. Approx, 1,900.

Post Office. Near the Clock Tower in Maengwyn Street.

Machynlleth is a flourishing market town with comfortable hotel and other accommodation and good fishing. It is pleasantly situated at the base of a group of rounded hills that rise in increasing undulations to Plynlimon, and since it is at the junction of several road routes it is a good centre for excursions. The inhabitants mainly depend on agriculture and slate-quarrying.

Between the station and the centre of the town is the **Old Church,** a Perpendicular building, with a tower, and beyond the Clock Tower is the **New Church. Plas Machynlleth,** at the southern end of the town, was presented by the Marquess of Londonderry to the town, and the park is open to the public.

Machynlleth is a place of some historical interest. The name is derived from *ma,* meaning a plain, and *Cynllaith,* the name of a river and district at the other end of Montgomeryshire. There are no grounds for supposing that there was a Roman station (Maglona) here; but there is a record of a grant in 1291 of a weekly market and two yearly fairs. One of Owain Glyndŵr's parliaments was held here, in 1404, when he was at the height of his power.

An ancient building in Maengwyn Street, opposite the entrance to Plas Machynlleth, is the traditional meeting-place of Glyndŵr's Parliament: but it does not appear to be older than about 1500. It is now the Owain Glydŵr Institute. Among notable objects in the Entrance Hall are an open fireplace and a table of ancient tolls and other dues payable to the Lord of the Manor. There are reading, billiard and refreshment-rooms, baths and lawns.

180

On the eastern outskirts of the town is a modern stone circle erected for the National Eisteddfod in 1937.

A mile or two south of the town is the Llyfnant Valley (*see* p. 207).

Machynlleth to Tal-y-Llyn, Cader Idris and Dolgellau

The ascent of the rugged and picturesque mountain of Cader Idris (described on pp. 168–171) is easier from the direction of Aberystwyth, Borth and Machynlleth than from Barmouth or Dolgellau, though the latter are many miles nearer its summit as the crow flies. During the season motor-coaches frequently run from Aberystwyth through Machynlleth and Corris to Tal-y-Llyn, leaving climbers at the very foot of the mountain and within 2½ miles of the summit. The journey from Aberystwyth to Tal-y-Llyn is through magnificent scenery.

From Machynlleth the first portion of the route is up the Corris Valley to Corris, by a tree-shaded highway, about 6 miles in length, along which every few yards new vistas of loveliness are opened up, with the road following faithfully every turn of the river as it flows through its narrow gorge; from Tal-y-Llyn a road goes eastward to Dolgellau and westward to Towyn. The continuation of the Dolgellau road also, after making the circuit of Cader, arrives at Towyn, whence the return is via Machynlleth. The Dolgellau route is strongly to be recommended on account of the scenery—on the one hand the massive mountain-side, and on the other the beautifully wooded estuary of the Mawddach, with a glimpse of Barmouth as the road turns southward along the coast. The routes are described on pp. 176–7.

Leaving Machynlleth, cross the river, turn right, and ¼ mile farther bear left. Here, from **Ffridd Gate** a road goes along the north side of the Dovey Valley past **Llanwrin**, about 2½ miles distant, where there is an early English church with an ancient stained-glass window and a fine oak rood screen. The main road, however, goes northward.

After passing through the beautiful **Ffridd Wood**, **Llwyngwern** is reached, in the vicinity of which are the **Chamber of Hwmffra Goch** and the **Gelligen Stone Chests.** The chamber is a cave behind a waterfall which long served as a highwayman's hide. The "chests" are excavations formed by falling water.

Beyond Llwyngwern the view includes an old mill and a stretch of the river fringed with trees. A little farther there is another delightful reach, and then what looks like a canal, but is in reality a passage cut through the rock by the river. Across the valley are slate-enamelling works.

At **Esgairgeiliog** ("cock's-comb") are other slate-enamelling works and a slate quarry. **Evan's Bridge,** which here spans the Dulas, affords a charming view.

Corris (*Braichgoch, Slater's Arms*) is a quiet village interested in neighbouring slate quarries and afforestation work. Its scenic beauty is constantly breathtaking.

From Corris the road to Tal-y-Llyn Lake and Dolgellau goes off on the left (*see* below), passing through Upper Corris.

Walkers can cut off a corner by taking the footpath opposite the site of the station. It opens up beautiful views behind and on the right. On entering the highroad, keep to the right. After the central point of the route is passed the scenery greatly improves. Just after the lake comes in sight, take a lane on the left steeply descending between high banks. On striking the highroad again, the lower end of Tal-y-Llyn, the site of the hotels, is to the left. (A few yards along the road to the right is a spring of drinking water.) Far up the head of the valley, on the right, may be seen the road to Dolgellau. The eastern end of the lake is 2½ miles from Corris, and the Tyn-y-Cornel and Penybont Hotels are at the lower end, 1 mile further.

Tal-y-Llyn

is beautifully placed in the valley, with the rugged spurs of **Cader Idris** rising on its northern side and the romantic **Pass of Llyn Bach** opening out to the east. It is a shallow sheet, little more than a mile long by about a quarter of a mile wide, and is well stocked with trout. The surface reflects the heights on either side, and the lake is so shut in by them that only a narrow road is left by which the hamlet of **Tal-y-Llyn** can be reached at the lower end.

At the spot where the hamlet stands, the river rushes through a stone arch, on one side of which is the ancient **Church.** At the east-end is an old painting representing the twelve Apostles.

Near the bridge also are the hotels at which cars may park. (*Penybont, Tyn-y-Groes, Tyn-y-Cornel Royal, Royal.*)

The Ascent of Cader Idris from Tal-y-Llyn

Tal-y-Llyn is one of the points from which the ascent of Cader Idris is commonly made. A general description of the mountain is given on pp. 168–171. There are two routes to the summit from Tal-y-Llyn. That usually chosen has its starting-point on the road to Abergynolwyn, about a quarter of a mile from the outlet of the lake. There take a mountain path through a wood to Rhiwvogof Farm. Pass through the farmyard, and take a path which for a short distance follows a wall, then turns to the left and leads through a gap in the wall. Thence the route bears to the right to a ridge; from here go to the right around the head of Cwmammarch, so reaching the summit of **Mynydd Pencoed** (2,494 ft.), which overlooks **Llyn-y-Cau** lying at the foot of **Craig-y-Cau**, a fine precipice of some 700 or 800 feet. Continue along the ridge, descending and ascending again a depression of about 100 feet, then bear to the left to join the Dolgellau track at the foot of the last steep ascent to the summit.

The alternative route is the shortest and finest ascent. The summit is under 3 miles from the starting-point, at *Dolycae* (Minffordd, about a mile from the Dolgellau end of Tal-y-Llyn lake,) from which there is a well-defined path alongside the torrent issuing from Llyn-y-Cau; but before reaching that lake the climber should bear to the left along the ridge with the lake on the right, and beyond the lake follow the path that leads up to that coming from Mynydd Pencoed.

A Fine Round Trip. One of the finest road tours from Machynlleth is as follows: Leave Machynlleth eastwards for Newton along A489, but about ½ mile from the centre of the town turn right on to the road for Staylittle and Llanidloes; the warning which reads "mountain road after 6 miles" need not deter, save possibly during bad weather. The road to Llanidloes rises to 1,671 feet giving fine views of Cader Idris, the Severn Valley and the eastern face of Plynlimon. In Llanidloes turn right on to A 492 for Llangurig, there take A44 for Aberystwyth (described on page 198) and there A487 back to Machynlleth.

Dinas Mawddwy

From Machynlleth the Dovey Valley runs north-eastward for about a dozen miles to **Dinas Mawddwy** (*Buckley Arms*), a slate-quarriers' village picturesquely set in a deep valley amid mountain, forest and river scenery. It is the resort of anglers, who as guests at the hotels may fish the Dovey and Clerifion for salmon, sewin and trout. It is a good centre for mountain climbing, and there is a 9-hole golf course.

A mile short of Dinas is **Mallwyd**, with an ancient church. Half an hour's walk from Dinas Mawddwy is **Seven Valleys**, at a height of 1,000 feet. It affords a glorious view of the Merionethshire mountains, and is an admirable spot for picnics. Refreshments are obtainable at the farmhouses.

Bwlch Oerddrws, on the road to Dolgellau attains an elevation of 1,065 feet at 4½ miles from Dinas Mawddwy. From its head there is a magnificent view towards Dolgellau and Barmouth. The road passes *Cross Foxes* 7 miles from Dinas Mawddwy, and 3½ miles farther on enters **Dolgellau** (*see* p. 165).

Bwlch-y-Groes. The road from Dinas Mawddwy to Bala over **Bwlch-y-Groes**, the summit of which is 8 miles from the quarry village, reveals even grander scenery than the pass on the road to Dolgellau, but it is more suitable for walkers than motorists or cyclists, as it rises from 634 feet to 1,790 feet in just over a mile. The steepest part, 1 in 4½ for 200 yards, is near the summit. The pass of Bwlch-y-Groes is the highest road in North Wales, and is used for motor association rally trials. At its summit (Foel-y-Groes) a track leads to **Llyn Vyrnwy** (p. 187), Liverpool's water supply, in about 3 miles.

THE VALLEY OF THE DEE

Bala—Corwen—Llangollen

The Dee (Dyfrdwy) is one of the best-known rivers of Wales, and the scenery through which it passes is among the most beautiful in the country. It rises in the hills south-west of Llanuwchllyn and is joined by a number of tributaries before, during, and after its course through Bala Lake. The district surrounding the lake still keeps its old name of Penllyn, with its five parishes (Llanuwchllyn, Llancyil, Llangower (*Llangy-wair*), Llanfor, and Llandderfel) and its cultural and musical life retains the vigour which has characterised it for generations.

The river is a good trout stream and it also yields salmon. The fishing is preserved, but tickets are issued at moderate charges.

In April and May, when the river is still high after winter rain, fishing in the Dee between Corwen and Llangollen is carried on by men in coracles, the primitive craft of the ancient Britons. A coracle is constructed by tightly stretching tarpaulin or leather over a wooden frame. Originally hides were the covering. The size is about 4 feet by 3 feet. The sides bulge slightly outward and the bottom is almost flat, so that the vessel rides high upon the water and is swayed and tossed by every wave. A coracle is so light that a man can easily carry it on his back.

Bala

Banks. *Midland, National Provincial* and *Barclays.*

Cinema. *Victoria Cinema*; also Concerts.

Distances. Betws-y-Coed, 23; Cardiff, 138; Chester, 40; Dolgellau, 18; Ffestiniog, 17; Llangollen, 22; London, 197; Ruthin, 22.

Early Closing Day. Wednesdays.

Fishing. On the Tryweryn. Bala Lake contains pike, perch, salmon, roach and trout. Fishing from a boat or from the shore. Bala and District Angling Association supply permits.

Hotels. *White Lion Royal*, *Plas Coch*, *Ship*, *Goat*, *Bull.*

Post Office. In High Street.

Public Library and Reading-Room.

British Legion Social Centre.

Bala is pleasantly situated about a quarter of a mile from the lake of the same name. It is a small, regularly built market town, consisting of a long principal street, crossed at right-angles by a few others.

Close to the River Tryweryn, an important tributary of the Dee, the Calvinistic Methodist College is seen. In front of it is a statue of *Dr. Lewis Edwards*, for many years Principal of the College. A good view of the building and its surroundings is obtained from the railway bridge, and no one should miss the view up and down the Tryweryn afforded by the neighbouring bridge. A few yards down the first street on the left, behind the Grammar School, is a small mound known as **Tomen-y-Bala,** of Norman origin, the site of Bala Castle, captured by Llewelyn-ap-Iorwerth in 1202. On the main thoroughfare there is a fine bronze statue of *Thomas E. Ellis* (1859–99). Born at Cynlas, a small farm 3 miles distant, he became M.P. for Merioneth in 1886, and in 1894 Chief Liberal Whip.

Opposite the *White Lion Royal Hotel* is Tegid Street, leading to Tegid Chapel, near which is a statue of the *Rev. Thomas Charles* (1755–1814), one of the founders of the Bible Society.

Mr. Charles was a clergyman who was led to throw in his lot with the Calvinistic Methodists. Grieved at the ignorance of the people, he established a system of circulating schools, and prepared spelling and reading books and catechisms in the vernacular, for the use of teachers. He also did much towards the foundation of the Sunday schools now so plentiful in the Principality. One day a little girl named Mary Jones walked from Llanfihangel to Bala, a distance of about 25 miles, over the mountains, to buy a Bible from Mr. Charles. His stock had run out, but moved by her distress he gave her one of his own Bibles. The incident moved Mr. Charles to undertake a journey to London to consult with friends as to the practicability of forming a society to print Welsh Bibles on the plan of the Society for Promoting Christian Knowledge, which had printed 2,000 copies, but the edition was exhausted, and was not to be re-issued. The journey resulted in the formation of the great British and Foreign Bible Society.

Bala Lake is the largest natural sheet of water in Wales. Formerly the property of the late Sir Watkin Williams Wynn it passed to the State in lieu of death duty payment. The lake is about $4\frac{1}{3}$ miles in length and two-thirds of a mile wide. In some places near the shore it is very shallow; in others it suddenly becomes very deep. Its greatest depth is about fifty yards. The water lies in a beautiful valley with mountains on all sides. The best view is obtained from the road which runs along the east side. The lake abounds with trout, salmon, roach, pike, perch, eels, etc., and is one of the two places in Great Britain in which is found the gwyniad, an Alpine fish, so called on account of the extremely white colour of its scales. Trout of from 3 to 5 pounds are taken, and pike up to 24 pounds. The lake is popular for sailing and boating and regattas are held by the Bala Sailing Club. Boats may be hired. The British Long Distance Swimming Association hold their Welsh championship race here each August.

The circuit of the lake affords a delightful excursion, with splendid views of the mountains. There is a bus service between Bala and Llanuwchllyn. Leaving by Pensarn Road, the highway keeps close to the lake, and in a little over a mile reaches **Llanycil**, the old parish church of Bala. In the churchyard, with its fine yews, are the graves of Thomas Charles and Lewis Edwards. Two miles farther on we pass on the left Glanllyn, formerly a seat of Sir W. W. Wynn (*see* above) and now a summer holiday centre of Urdd Gobaith Cymru (The Welsh League of Youth). Half a mile farther on a lane through a gate on the right leads up to the farmhouse of Caer Gai. The building dates back to the sixteenth century, and was the home of Rowland Vaughan, a Cavalier man of letters and "gentleman of Merioneth-shire." He is buried in Llanuwchllyn Church. Rejoin the main road, and in another half-mile a road on the right leads up past *Yr Hen Gapel* (The Old Chapel of the Congregationalists, founded in 1746) to **Dolhendre** (a distance of 1½ miles). Here a number of farms were renovated and modernized as part of the 1951 Festival of Britain. The main road leads on towards Dolgellau, but a turning on the left opposite a garage brings us to the village of **Llanuwchllyn** The church, dedicated to St. Deiniol, was built about eighty years ago, taking the place of a much older building; but there remains, on the north side of the chancel, a recumbent effigy of Ienan ap Gruffydd, dated 1370. Farther on, in the village, a wrought-iron revolving gate on the left hand side leads to *Mynwent y Pandy*, a little grave-yard where is buried Sir Owen Morgan Edwards (1858–1920). His work as author, editor, and educationist has been one of the chief factors in the renewed interest of the present time in Welsh language and literature.

At a fork a few hundred yards farther on, the road from Dinas Mawddwy and Bwlch-y-Groes (*see* p. 183) comes in on the right. In about three miles the hamlet of **Llangower** (Llangywair), with its small church, is reached. The building is undistinguished, but the history of the church dates back to the thirteenth century. In the churchyard is the largest yew-tree in Merioneth. From Llangower in about two miles **Pont-Mwnwgl-y-Llyn** is reached, where turn left to reach Bala by Tegid Street. The whole round (including Dolhendre) amounts to some fifteen miles.

There are other smaller lakes in the vicinity of Bala :

Llyn Arenig, some 6 miles distant (about 2 miles off the road) supplies the town with water.

Llyn Tryweryn, where the river of the same name rises, can be reached by a rough road which turns off to the left of the Bala-Ffestiniog road just short of the ninth milestone. It lies 1,267 feet above sea-level.

Llyn Mynyllod, about 9 miles from Bala, lies to the north of Llandrillo, and is best approached by crossing the river near Llandrillo and following the path which leads up through Coedyad Branas.

A fourth lake, **Llyn Caereini,** lies in a delightful hollow between hills just off the upper Bala–Corwen road. It may be reached by following the lane which turns up left at Sarnau, rather less than four miles from Bala. Where the tarred lane stops, a path through a field leads down to the lake. The road may be regained by bearing left, on returning, instead of right for the tarred lane, and following a path over the heather-covered moorland which soon leads down to a lane that emerges by Bethel Chapel and the *Boot Inn*.

Excursions from Bala

Llanfor is a small village about a mile from Bala, on the Corwen road. The Church, like Llanuwchllyn, is dedicated to St. Deniol. The building is modern (1874–5), but part of the tower is old.

Arenig Fawr, which has a height of 2,800 feet, can be approached by the minor road forking left from the main Ffestiniog road a mile north-west of Bala.

Lake Vyrnwy, the principal reservoir of the Liverpool water supply, is 10 miles from Bala at its nearest point; from Bala to the Vyrnwy Hotel is 15 miles. The route is along a mountainous road, now passable for cars, via Rhos-y-gwaliau through a picturesque but solitary district; an alternative for motorists is by the road which begins on the Bala side of Llandderfel, and leads over the Berwyn to Llangynog.
Walkers cross the bridge at the foot of Bala Lake, turn to the left and climb steadily to the hamlet of **Rhos-y-gwaliau,** near which is an old manor, *Rhiwaedog* (*Youth Hostel*).
The road traverses a well-wooded valley, alongside which a small stream tumbles; and after crossing the stream it follows another valley known as the Horseshoe. An uninteresting valley follows; and, still rising, the way crosses the pass, dropping steeply down to the headwater of the **Vyrnwy,** and thence to the road (one-way traffic) which runs round the Reservoir. This road is 11¾ miles long.

Llyn Trywergn Mawr is an artificial lake, 830 acres in extent; some four miles up the Trywergn Valley from Bala. This lake along with Lake Vyrney supplies water for Liverpool.

Pistyll Rhaiadr ("the spout of the Waterfall River") is one of the best waterfalls in Wales. The total length of the fall is about 300 feet. It is possible to reach the waterfall by walking over the Berwyn from Llandrillo, between Bala and Corwen, but the best way is to go from Oswestry by road (there is a bus service) to Llanrhaiadr-ym-Mochnant, whence a road up the valley reaches the waterfall in some four miles.

Aran Mawddwy and Aran Benllyn. The ascent of Aran Mawddwy and Aran Benllyn can be made either from Bala or Dolgellau, and provides some of the finest views in the country. The route is up the left bank of the Afon Harnog starting at Drws-y-nant Halt. Cars may be left on open ground near a row of cottages by the level crossing. Continue along the road to Esgair-gawr Farm where a track runs up the valley through a conifer plantation of the Forestry Commission. Beyond the plantation a gate gives access to a boggy plateau which must be crossed before striking across the bare shoulder of Aran Mawddwy with the final scramble over rocks to the summit cairn. Mawddwy is 2,970 feet high and being somewhat higher than Cader Idris is the peak of the range of mountains next highest to the Snowdon group.
Aran Benllyn is reached along the undulating ridge. From its 2,901-foot peak there is a fine view along the entire length of Bala Lake to Bala.

187

Corwen

Banks. *Midland, National Provincial.*

Bus every weekday between Corwen, Bala, Betws-y-Coed, Llanrwst, Ruthin, Rhyl and Llangollen.

Cinema.

Distances. Bala (north road), 12; (south road), 13; Betws-y-Coed, 23; Llangollen, 10; Ruthin, 12.

Early Closing Day. Wednesday.

Fishing. There are many salmon pools in the district; and besides the Dee there are several other capital trout streams. Season tickets obtainable from the Corwen and District Angling Club, Council Offices, Corwen.

Fair Day. Third Tuesday of every month.

Hotels. *Owain Glyndwr, Crown, Central, Harp, Royal Oak.*

Corwen, a market town of Merioneth, is pleasantly situated at the base of the Berwyn Mountains. The scenery round about is charming, and the town is an excellent fishing centre.

There is a fine Eisteddfod Pavilion, said to be one of the largest in North Wales, seating over 3,000 people, and a modern cinema. There is a fine market at which the annual Special Ewe Sale in September is a notable occasion. Some 5,000 hardy Welsh mountain sheep directly off the Berwyn Mountains are offered for sale.

The **Parish Church** was founded in the sixth century and dedicated to two Celtic saints, Mael and Sulien, two of the missionaries who accompanied St. Cadvan from Brittany to Wales. It contains objects of antiquarian interest. The Norman font, with its cable pattern, dates from about 1100. On the north side of the sanctuary is an incised effigy of a former vicar.

Excursions from Corwen

Pen-y-Pigin, or Glyndŵr's Seat, is a conical hill, a spur of the Berwyn Mountain, approached past the Welsh Congregational Chapel. It is crowned by a cairn out of which rises a flagstaff. The summit affords a fine view of the Vale of Edeyrnion, and the Clwydian hills.

Caer Drewyn, 1 mile distant, on the opposite side of the river, is a bare hill crowned with an excellent example of an ancient fort. The fortress is regarded by antiquaries as the most precious prehistoric monument in Wales. It is about half a mile in circumference, the wall is about four yards thick, and on its north-eastern boundary are the remains of circular apartments. The mountain is also celebrated in history as the camping ground of the great Welsh Prince, Owen Gwynedd, when he was heading a revolt in 1165 against the English King, Henry II, who encamped on the Berwyns where his force was helpless. Owing to stormy weather it had to beat a hasty retreat.

Rhûg, on the north side of the river also, and about as much to the west of Corwen as Caer Drewyn is to the east, is a stately mansion, first a seat of the Salesburys—a family of great note in Welsh history—then of the Vaughans and, later, of the Wynns.

Derwen is a small village, 5 miles to the north. Its church has the only rood loft in the Vale of Clwyd, and in the churchyard is the most perfect and elaborate Celtic cross in the neighbourhood.

Farther north is **Efenechtyd Church,** remarkable for its font hewn out of a block of oak, and for a knocker on the door. The knocker is thought to be connected with the parable of the Ten Virgins and to have belonged to a nunnery that supposedly stood on the spot.

A walk or drive of about 6 miles along the Betws-y-Coed road or a journey for that distance in one of the buses that run between Corwen and Cerrig-y-Drudion, will enable the visitor to see the romantic **Pont-y-Glyn.** The *Geirw*, a tributary of the Alwen, here tumbles over a rocky slope, 200 feet deep, and rushes impetuously through a narrow glen, thickly clothed with foliage. High above, a branch road is carried across the ravine by a single arched bridge, of 50 feet span, to which the appropriate name of Pont-y-Glyn ("Bridge of the Glen") is given. It is sometimes known as *Pont Glyn Diphwys*. The road to it from Corwen runs past Rhûg.

Llangollen

Banks. *Barclays, Midland, National Provincial.*

Boating. Rowing-boats and canoes can be hired. Many charming canal trips are possible.

Bus services between Llangollen and Chester, Wrexham, Ruabon, Chirk, Glynceiriog, Corwen and Cefn.

Cricket. There is a good club of which visitors may become temporary members.

Distances. Bala, 22; Barmouth, 48; Berwyn, 1½; Birmingham, 73; Chester, 23; Corwen, 10; Dolgellau, 39; Liverpool, 39; London, 187; Manchester, 62½; Ruabon, 6; Shrewsbury (by road), 29.

Early Closing Day. Thursday.

Fishing. Above Chain Bridge is the Glyndwr Preserve. From Llangollen to Newbridge the Dee is preserved by the Llangollen Trout and Grayling Society and Llangollen Angling Association. Deep wading is necessary.

Golf. There is a 9-hole course about a mile from the town on the main A 5 Road.

Hotels. *Hand, Royal, Grapes, Bridge End, Tyn-y-Wern, Cambrian, Ponsonby Arms, Sun Trevor, Woodlands, Brynderwen, Clairbridge, Cheerio* (guest).

Market Day. Saturday.

Population. 3,275.

Post Office. Berwyn Street.

Tennis and Bowls. Off Victoria Promenade.

Llangollen stands in a sheltered valley, 7 miles in length, in the midst of the most beautiful of the hill districts of Wales.

The town is built on the Dee, the **Bridge** over which is regarded as one of the seven wonders of Wales. These, according to an old rhyme, are:

> "Pistyll Rhaiadr and Wrexham steeple,
> Snowdon's mountain without its people,
> Overton yew-trees, St. Winefride's Wells,
> Llangollen Bridge, and Gresford bells."

The bridge comprises four irregular arches. It is said to have been originally built in the reign of Henry I and to have been widened and added to in 1346, by Dr. John Trevor, Bishop

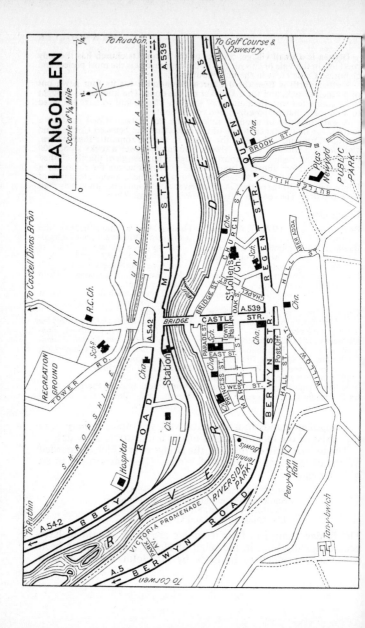

of St. Asaph and Chancellor of Chester. In later days an additional arch was erected, under which the railway passed, and the bridge was enlarged to double its former width. While widening the bridge in 1873, the workmen found, on a stone in one of the arches, the figures 1131, and the letters W.S. There is a fine view from the bridge.

The **Parish Church** is dedicated to St. Collen and from it the town derives its name. It is mainly a twelfth- and thirteenth-century structure and was considerably enlarged in 1861 by the then vicar, whose son, A. G. Edwards, became the first Archbishop of Wales. There is a splendid carved roof, said to have been brought from the neighbouring Abbey of Valle Crucis, and there are numerous marble monuments.

The town offers many facilities for sport and amusement, and is the centre of charming walks, drives and water excursions. These last are made by boats, comfortably fitted up, and drawn by ponies. The starting-point is the Canal Wharf, close to the bus terminus. Llangollen has become famous as the centre of the International Eisteddfod, held annually in July.

Excursions from Llangollen

Plas Newydd

Admission. Every day, 9 a.m. to dusk. On Sundays during the season, 11 a.m. to 4 p.m. (*Charge.*)

The Llangollen Urban District Council have acquired this mansion, which is regarded as one of the finest examples of black and white domestic architecture in all Britain, together with its magnificent natural glen. It stands about a quarter of a mile from the Bridge. Go up Castle Street, which continues the line of the bridge, and at the top of it, turn to the left. At the Grapes Hotel go to the right along Hill Street. From there the house can be reached by a path on the left (to which there are steps immediately beyond the line of houses), or preferably, by the drive which is gained by proceeding for another 170 yards.

Plas Newydd (New Hall) for many years was the residence of Lady Eleanor Butler and Miss Sarah Ponsonby, generally known as **The Ladies of Llangollen**. The two ladies, who came from Ireland in 1779, were as singular in their dress as in their mode of life. Their hair was short, un-curled and powdered. Each wore a man's hat and neck-cloth, and a blue riding-habit. Neither would sit for her portrait, but each wished for that of the other, and aided Lady Leighton in obtaining sketches, which were lithographed. Lady Eleanor died in 1829, aged ninety years, and Miss Ponsonby two years later, at the age of seventy-six. Both were interred in the churchyard of Llangollen, where a monument commemorates their virtues and those of an old and valued servant who lies under the same stone. They received visits from many celebrities, including Scott, Words-worth and the Duke of Wellington, as well as from persons of less note. Each visitor was expected to make a gift of a piece of carving or a curio, and the ladies employed a joiner in decorating the cottage and in searching for curiosities in the neighbourhood. Several of the articles which belonged

191

to them still remain in the house, which has changed hands more than once and has been enlarged, but both outside and inside it is still adorned with the vast amount of carving which they had had done for it.

In the grounds there is a stone circle, erected for the Gorsedd ritual of the National Eisteddfod of 1908.

Castell Dinas Bran

This is a ruin (wrongly called *Crow Castle*) on a conical hill, 1,062 feet high, facing the town, and opposite the end of the Bridge. The primitive character of the architecture indicates a very early date for the foundation of the structure. It is supposed to have been the stronghold of Eliseg, Prince of Powis, in the eighth century, and it was the seat of the lords of Vallé Crucis for centuries. In the reign of Henry III it afforded asylum from the fury of his justly enraged subjects to Gruffydd-ap-Madoc, who had sided with the English monarch and betrayed his country. The traitor was the son of the founder of Vallé Crucis Abbey, and there both father and son were buried.

Vallé Crucis Abbey

(Small charge for admission; ring for the attendant. Refreshments and teas available.)

Vallé Crucis Abbey, the Abbey of the Vale of the Cross, is a majestic ruin in a lovely sequestered valley on the right of the road towards Ruthin, about $1\frac{1}{2}$ miles from Llangollen. Most of the distance can be pleasantly traversed by following the towing path, a pretty tree-shaded walk, along the Canal, as far as **Pentre-felin** (where formerly there was a wharf for shipping slates), or by going to that spot by boat. The abbey lies on the Llangollen–Ruthin road, some 2 miles from Llangollen. This road goes over the celebrated and beautiful Horseshoe Pass.

The Abbey, founded in 1201 by Madoc-ap-Gruffydd-Maelor, Lord of Powis, for Cistercian monks, shared the general fate of monasteries in the reign of Henry VIII. The ruin consists of a nave with aisles, choir and two transepts, each of which had an aisle and two chapels. The west end has a central doorway with deeply recessed mouldings and dog-tooth ornaments. Above is a lofty six-light window, with eight trifoliated compartments. The choir is lighted by three lofty lancet windows and two smaller ones. To the south of the church are the remains of the cloister and monastic buildings, including the chapter-house.

By following the highroad for another quarter of a mile, there may be seen, in a field on the right, **Eliseg's Pillar,** one of the most remarkable memorial stones extant. It was erected on a tumulus in honour of Eliseg, a Lord of Powis, in the eighth century. It was originally 12 feet high.

Llantysilio Church is two miles to the north-west. It can easily be reached by following the Canal to its beginning at the **Horseshoe Falls,** by which the Dee feeds the canal, a little above the Chain Bridge, and then continuing

Pembroke Castle (*A. F. Kersting*)

Carew Castle (*A. F. Kersting*)

St. Govan's Head (*A. F. Kersting*)

Pembrokeshire Sands (*A. F. Kersti*

for two or three hundred yards along the footpath. The church (*Sunday services*—11, 6.30) stands on a very picturesque site, and is surrounded by a grove of old yew-trees and a few wych-elms. The foundation dates from the middle of the seventh century; the base of the building and part of the walls are dated about 1180, while the sanctuary roof and the font belong to the fourteenth century. The glass of the small window in the south wall is pre-Elizabethan. Portions of the interior were brought from Vallé Crucis Abbey, including two quaint glass panels now forming a narrow window. There are memorials of Robert Browning and of Sir Theodore and Lady Martin (Helen Faucit), who, as already mentioned, lived at Bryntysilio, almost overlooking the church.

In the neighbourhood is the fine **Llantysilio Hall.**

Moel (y) Gamelin (1,897 ft.) may be ascended by a path close to the tram-way which crosses the road near Vallé Crucis Abbey. A stiff incline and a winding path lead to the top. On Moel-y-Caer, the adjoining peak, are the remains of an ancient camp. The descent can be made past this camp, and over Moel Morfydd to Glyndyfrdwy, or past Llantysilio Church to Berwyn.

Moel (y) Geraint (Barber's Hill) (possibly "The Hill of the Kindred"), is 1,068 ft. high, and commands a most beautiful view of the Vale of Llangollen. From the main road (A5 Berwyn Street) turn left at the *Smithfield Inn* and immediately right; then bear left up Willow Lane. In about ½ mile turn left over a stile and follow the path through a field, across a lane, past some farm buildings on the left, and up through the woods till a wire fence is reached. A steep pull-up alongside the fence leads to the top, which is marked by a cairn. From here follow the path downwards till it reaches a gate; here turn right into a road. In about ¼ mile a signpost is reached. Turn right for Llangollen, or left for Berwyn. For the second alternative turn right again after about ½ mile, and rejoin the main road between Berwyn and Llangollen.

Chirk Castle and the Vale of Ceiriog

Chirk, a popular and rapidly growing place on the main line between Shrewsbury and Ruabon, is much visited on account of its castle and lovely scenery in its neighbourhood. From Llangollen, Chirk is reached by the London–Holyhead road (A5) 6 miles.

The **Castle** (*open 2–5 Easter week-end and each Sunday until end April; 2–5 Tuesday, Thursday, Saturday and Sunday, May to September; and 11–5 on Bank Holidays. Fee for castle and/or grounds. Refreshments*) is 1¼ miles west of Chirk Station. The Castle was built in 1310 and was an extremely strong fortification. The extent of the north side is about 240 feet. The west wall was considerably damaged by cannon during the siege by General Lambert commanding the Parliamentarian Forces under Richard Cromwell, August 1659. The magnificent gateway in front leads between two drum-towers into a quadrangle 150 feet by 100 feet. A curiosity in the collection of pictures is one by Richard Wilson, landscape and portrait painter of the first half of the eighteenth century, who misunderstood the comments of a Welsh shepherd, on his picture of the Water Falls at Pistyll Rhaiadr and painted in "ships" instead of a flock of "sheep." Running north-west from Castle Mill the remains of *Offa's Dyke* can be traced across the park. The Castle has been the home of the Myddleton family since 1595.

The Vale of Ceiriog, which runs westward from Chirk for some 15 miles, is considered by many to be even more picturesque than the lovely Vale of Llangollen. On a fine summer day few excursions are more enjoyable than travelling the $6\frac{1}{2}$ miles of it between Chirk and Glyncuriog on foot or by bus, and then walking over the hills to Llangollen, which is only 3 miles from Glyn.

By breaking the journey through the glen at Castle Mill, a visit to Chirk Castle can be very conveniently included in an excursion during April to September when the walk up to the Castle is open to the public.

Glynceiriog village is pleasantly situated, and has comfortable hotel accommodation. It used to be the centre of an important flannel industry. The village **Institute and Library** is a national memorial to *John Ceiriog Hughes*, a popular nineteenth-century lyric poet of Wales, to two other noted Welsh literary men, *Cynddelw* and *Huw Morus*, and to many other famous Welsh men and women. It is visited by thousands of people every year.

John Ceiriog Hughes was born in 1832 in nearby Llanarmon in the vale which gave him his bardic name of Ceiriog. When quite young he went to work on a farm. After following various occupations he became a stationmaster under the Cambrian Railway Company, and finally manager of the railway leading to the Van Mines. He died at Caersws in 1887. Fame came to him through his love poem, *Myfanwy*, at the National Eisteddfod at Llangollen in 1858. He has been aptly termed the "Robert Burns of Wales."

The Eglwyseg Rocks and the World's End

The **Eglwyseg Rocks** are enormous limestone cliffs running northward from the northern side of the Vale of Llangollen. The nearest point is 1 mile north-east of the town. A lane leading to the foot of the rocks is entered by crossing the Canal bridge and turning to the right. The general height is from 1,400 to 1,500 feet, but the loftiest point has an elevation of 1,648 feet. To the left is the **World's End,** a picturesque recess, 5 miles north-west of Llangollen, formed by the meeting of the heights of Craig-y-Gorwyn and Craig yr Adar. To approach it, cross the Canal bridge and turn to the left. The route lies along the base of the Eglwyseg Rocks, past the Eglwyseg Mission Church, through the farmyard of *Plas Eglwyseg* and thence by **Plas Uchaf,** or Eglwyseg Manor House, an Elizabethan mansion 2 miles beyond the farm, and a short distance from the termination of the valley. At World's End the mountains seem to make further progress impossible, but a path, which can be clearly followed, leads down the steep slope of the mountainside, from where a fine view of the Cheshire Plain can be obtained, and eventually to a road. Follow this, turning right at Onnen

Fawr farm, and shortly turning left for Rhosllannerchrugog. The distance is about 3½ miles from Eglwyseg to Rhos.

Ruabon (*Wynnstay Arms*) is some 6 miles from Llangollen. In the neighbourhood are coal mines and brickworks. The Church contains interesting monuments and a restored fresco of the fourteenth century. The Grammar School, pleasantly situated on the outskirts of the town, is of old foundation. Some 2 miles from Ruabon is the mining village of **Rhosllannerchrugog,** which has a population of over 10,000 and a most vigorous cultural life.

WELSHPOOL TO ABERYSTWYTH

The road is from Welshpool by Newtown, Llanidloes, Llan-gurig and Ponterwyd, and then by Llanbadarn Fawr, or alternatively by Devil's Bridge. A further alternative from Newtown is via Caersws, Carno and Machynlleth.

Welshpool (*Royal Oak*), population 6,500, is the assize town of Montgomeryshire, but is not particularly Welsh in appear-ance or sentiment. At one time it was a busy centre of the wool and flannel industry. For some miles beyond the town the road follows the broad valley of the Severn but if, after 2 miles, the left road is taken at a fork, **Montgomery** may be visited. Al-though nominally the county town it has less than a thousand inhabitants and is quaint and interesting.

The right fork leads directly to **Newtown** (*Elephant and Castle*), the birthplace of Robert Owen, the social reformer who died in 1858. His tomb is to be seen in the old churchyard of St. Mary's Church and he is also commemorated in the local museum bearing his name.

Llanidloes (*Lion, Humphrey's, Queen's Head*) is an ancient and picturesque town with an old half-timbered Market House, an interesting church partly dating from the thirteenth century, and a delightful waterfall.

At **Llangurig** (5 miles) the road from Builth Wells (p. 294) and Rhayader (p. 310) comes in from the left. The road then joins the infant Wye as it comes tumbling from the boggy slopes of Plynlimon Fawr, skirts that great hill mass and traverses a region once famous for its lead mines, traces of which are still visible in the dumps and in derelict waterwheels. Next comes **Ponterwyd** (*George Borrow Hotel*) with a good waterfall on the Rheidol, while the Eagle's Gorge is of great beauty. Two miles west of Ponterwyd the road begins to descend rather rapidly through Capel Bangor and Llanbadarn Fawr to the sea at Aberystwyth.

At Ponterwyd an alternative road to Aberystwyth runs off southward following the river past **Yspyty Cynfyn** to Devil's Bridge. The churchyard wall at Yspyty Cynfyn includes four stones which were thought to belong to a megalithic circle, but this is by no means certain; the largest, however, may be a menhir.

PLYNLIMON

Plynlimon (2,469 feet) is one of the three chief mountains of Wales, but since it rises quite gradually from a region that is already elevated, it has not the imposing appearance presented by many lesser hills. Indeed, the trip to Plynlimon is a walk over undulating and gradually rising moorland rather than a climb. Upon its dome-like slopes rise the rivers Severn, Wye, and Rheidol, and several streams of less note. It is one of the most watery and boggy mountains of Wales and, from the want of well-defined paths, one of the most difficult to ascend.

The road from Aberystwyth to the mountain runs through the villages of Llanbadarn Fawr, Capel Bangor and Goginan to **Ponterwyd** rising gradually to 1,358 feet at **Eisteddfa Gurig** which stands at the divide between the Wye head-waters flowing east and the Rheidol tributary, Afon Castell, flowing south-west. The mountain walk begins here, climbers following a mine road for about a mile. Then the track (about 1½ miles) is indicated by an irregular line of poles. On the summit is a cairn and about a mile to the north is **Llyn Llygad Rheidol**, from which Aberystwyth obtains its water.

The view from Plynlimon includes nearly the whole of Wales, together with parts of Shropshire and Herefordshire.

The descent can be made by following another line of poles along the ridge down *via* the *Dyffryn Castell Hotel* from whence it is two miles to Ponterwyd and the bus. At one point in this descent the succeeding poles are missing; here a path on the left must be avoided, and by going forward the poles will soon again be brought into view. Although the tracks are not well defined, it is best to keep to them, because much of the mountain slope is boggy, and in the event of a sudden mist there is a dearth of surface features that would assist the walker in finding his way. Dyffryn Castell Hotel (about 4 miles distant) is the nearest licensed house to the summit. The descent to the inn takes about 2 hours, and Dyffryn Castell is 16 miles from Aberystwyth *via* the Devil's Bridge, and 14 *via* Ponterwyd. On the whole it is less tiring to ascend from Dyffryn Castell, and to descend to Eisteddfa Gurig, the actual walking time being about 4 hours. It is possible to descend (NNW.) to Machynlleth, but the walk of over 10 miles is partly across moorland where the tracks are not always well defined. There are, however, some good views, and for the latter part of the journey the road is quite clear.

ABERYSTWYTH

Banks. *National Provincial, Midland, Barclays, Lloyds.*

Bathing. There are ample bathing facilities on two beaches, and the sea is seldom far from the Esplanade.

Boats. Maximum fares fixed by the local authorities, but private bargains can be made with the boatmen. All boats ply for hire on licence from the Corporation, who annually survey the craft and otherwise promote safety. In addition to *rowing-boats*, there are motor-launches, and *sailing-boats*.

Bus and Coach Services. Between Aberystwyth and all neighbouring towns. Services also to London and North and South Wales.

Distances. Aberayron, 16; Aberdovey, 28; Bala, 52; Barmouth (*via* Dolgellau), 44; Borth, 8; Corris, 23; Devil's Bridge, 12; Dolgellau, 34; Harlech, 55; Machynlleth, 18; Rhayader, 34; Rheidol Falls, 9; Strata Florida, 15; Towyn, 32.

Early Closing Day. Wednesday.

Entertainments. Municipal orchestra at the Marine Bandstand on the Promenade. Dancing and celebrity concerts at the King's Hall. Three Cinemas. College concerts weekly on Mondays in term-time. Annual Carnival.

Fishing. Excellent sea-fishing all year round. Various streams of the neighbourhood afford many facilities for freshwater fishing. Information regarding preserved waters from Aberystwyth Angling Association.

Golf. There is an upland 18-hole course at Bryn-y-Mor, a short distance north-east of the town.

Hotels. *Belle Vue Royal*, Marine Terrace; *Talbot*, Market Street; *Castle*, South Road; *Cambrian*, opposite station; *Marine*, Marine Parade; *Glanaber*, Union Street; *Central*, Terrace Road; *White Horse*, Terrace Road; and many others.

Parking-place. Corporation parking-place with waiting-room and cloak-room accommodation close to the railway station.

Population. Approximately 10,500.

Post Office. *General Post Office* in Great Darkgate Street, the principal thoroughfare, running east to west. Sub-offices in Bridge Street, at Llangawsai, and Penparcau.

Putting. Greens at Queen's Road and in the Castle Grounds.

Tennis, Bowls, Putting, etc.

Although the name indicates its situation at the mouth of the Ystwyth, it is the River Rheidol which has had the greater hand in excavating the break in the cliffs in which Aberystwyth is built. The Rheidol forms Aberystwyth harbour and is joined by the Ystwyth in the final few yards of its course to the sea. South of these rivers the ground rises again, and to the north the rise is almost precipitous. Between the Harbour and **Constitution Hill,** as this cliff is called, the sea front stretches in a

198

graceful curve, with the **Castle** ruins, the **University College** and the **Pier** towards the southern end and a long row of hotels, boarding houses and private residences throughout its length. The town itself has some wide, tree-lined streets, from which there are inviting glimpses of the hills on either hand.

Aberystwyth has been called the Brighton of Wales, and the name gives some indication of its character. It is the most important resort on Cardigan Bay, as well as the seat of one of the constituent colleges of the University of Wales and of the National Library of Wales.

Aberystwyth is situated on gravelly soil, almost in the centre of Cardigan Bay, which sends one arm northward for 50 miles to the Lleyn Peninsula in Caernarvonshire, while the other extends for an equal distance to the south-west, to Strumble Head in Pembrokeshire. Behind is the mountainous region o Plynlimon, so that the town is sheltered and affords a healthy combination of sea and mountain air, but although the high ground which affords protection from the easterly winds is not near enough to be oppressive, the climate is dry and bracing, and the amount of sunshine recorded is very high.

The **Beach** is composed of dark sand and pebbles. Near the Pier is a children's pool for sailing toy boats. At the north end of the Marine Terrace are **Craiglais Rocks** and **Cove**, a particularly attractive spot, when the tide is breaking over the reefs. The sandy shore of Clarach Bay, on the far side of Constitution Hill, is a popular place for the delights of paddling. Bathers, however, should exercise great care.

Aberystwyth Castle ruins are the property of the Corporation, and the surrounding grounds are pleasantly laid out as a public garden with a putting green. The remnants of the Castle indicate that it must have been of formidable dimensions. It was built in the reign of Edward I, and became one of the strongholds of West Wales. Captured by Owain Glyndŵr in 1404, it was lost four years later. During the Civil War it was held for the King till its surrender to Col. Rice Powell in April, 1646.

In the courtyard of the Castle is a stone circle erected for the National Eisteddfod of 1952. On the seaward extremity of the promontory is the **War Memorial,** surmounted by a figure of the Angel of Peace, while on the pediment is another figure embodying the idea of Humanity emerging from the entanglements of War.

University College

A great educational revival in Wales during the latter part of the last century reached its culminating point by the founding in 1893 of the **University of Wales** with the University Colleges of Aberystwyth, Bangor and Cardiff as constituents; another constituent college, at Swansea, was established in

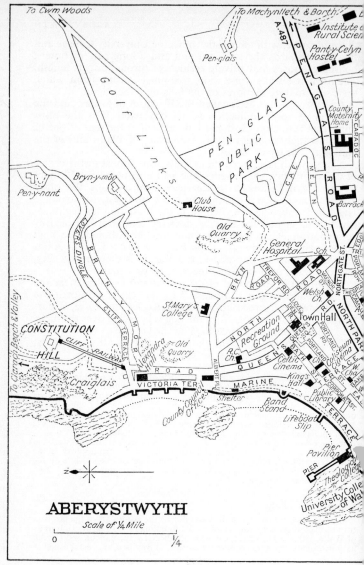

To Cwm Woods

To Machynlleth & Borth

A-487

Institute of Rural Science

Pen-glais

Pant-y-Celyn Hostel

PEN-GLAIS ROAD

County Maternity Home

CARADOC

Golf Links

PEN-GLAIS PUBLIC PARK

CAE MELYN

Bryn-y-môn

Pen-y-nant

Barrack

LOVERS' DINGLE

BRYN-Y-MOR CLIFF TERRACE

Club House

Old Quarry

General Hospital

Sch.

BRYN ROAD

TREFOR RD.

LOVE'S RD.

DINGLE RD.

Welsh Ch.

NORTHGATE ST.

NORTH PARADE

St. Mary College

NORTH ROAD

Town Hall

Recreation Ground

QUEEN'S RD.

PORTLAND RD.

Museum

Coliseum Cinema

THE

CONSTITUTION HILL

CLIFF RAILWAY

Alexandra Hall

Old Quarry

R.C. Ch.

QUEEN'S RD.

BATH

Celtic Cinema

PORTLAND ST.

CORPORATION ST.

CHALYBEATE ST.

Wm. Chy.

Craiglais

To Clarach Beach & Valley

ROAD

VICTORIA TER.

ALBERT PL.

MARINE

King's Hall

TERRACE

Public Library

County Council Offices

Shelter

Band Stand

Lifeboat Slip

Pier Pavilion

PIER

Theological College

University College of Wales

Z

ABERYSTWYTH

Scale of ¼ Mile

0   ¼

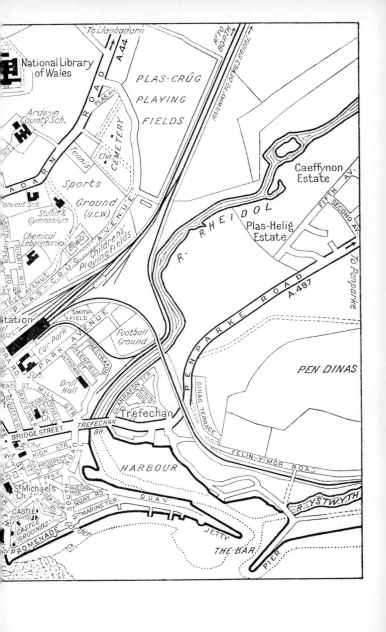

1920. In 1896, King Edward VII, then Prince of Wales, was installed as Chancellor of the University and on the same day the degree of Doctor of Music, the first degree bestowed by the University, was conferred on Queen Alexandra (then Princess of Wales).

The original college buildings on the Promenade were designed for use as an hotel but having been added to from time to time their architectural features are very mixed. The College now possess many large buildings which are landmarks in Aberystwyth. Overlooking the station is the Edward Davies Chemical Laboratory with its later and contrasting extension. At Penglais on the Machynlleth side considerable development has taken place with the erection of Departments of Geography, Geology and Social Studies; also recently built are a swimming bath, the Institute of Rural Science and a Biology Building. Opposite the latter the Physical Sciences building has venetian glass panels whose bright colours make a distinctive break with the Forest of Dean stone. There are various Halls of Residence throughout the town.

The National Library of Wales

Approached by Northgate Street and Penglais Road. Open free to holders of Readers' tickets. Visitors admitted to Central Hall and Gregynog Gallery.

In 1907 King Edward VII granted a charter for the establishment at Aberystwyth of the National Library of Wales, which opened two years later in a temporary home in the Old Assembly Rooms (now the Students' Union) in Great Darkgate Street. The present building was opened in 1937 and completed in 1955; it stands on a prominent site overlooking the town.

The Library's collection of Welsh printed books and manuscripts is the finest in the world. Among the many treasures may be mentioned the Black Book of Carmarthen, the oldest extant manuscript in the Welsh language, parts of which date from the end of the twelfth century; the Book of Taliesin (late thirteenth century); the White Book of Rhydderch (late thirteenth–fourteenth century) containing the earliest known complete text of the Mabinogion and the Arthurian romances; the "Hengwrt Chaucer" (*circa* 1420), which is considered to rank as the second in importance of all the existing texts of the *Canterbury Tales*; one of the only two copies printed in vellum of the Great Bible of 1539, which is possibly the copy presented to Henry VIII; the only known copies of the first book printed in Welsh (1546), the first book printed in Wales (1718), and the first Welsh book printed in America (1721); and about one hundred and twenty volumes of incunabula (i.e. books printed before 1500).

Under the Copyright Act of 1911 the Library is entitled to claim a copy of nearly all the books, periodicals, pamphlets, maps, volume and sheet music, etc., published within the British Isles, a privilege it enjoys in common with five other libraries in Great Britain and Ireland.

The contents of the Library now include nearly two million printed works, about 30,000 manuscript volumes, and many thousands of prints, drawings, and maps. It is also a repository for Welsh local records of all kinds, numbering approximately 3,500,000 at present. They include the older probate records, ecclesiastical, industrial, and educational records, estate deeds and documents, and other classes of archives, all contributing towards the complete picture of the history of Wales throughout the centuries.

As accessories to its main Departments the Library has its own private bindery, printing establishment, and photographic section.

Constitution Hill, at the north end of the Marine Promenade is 485 feet high, and affords extensive views along the coast and inland. For those who do not wish to climb, there is a *Funicular Railway*, which runs every few minutes during the season. Its gradient is 1 in 2.

Clarach Bay is a popular resort for picnics and bathing; it is reached by the path over Constitution Hill and along the cliff top. The **Clarach Valley** runs inland, a view up which gives a glimpse of the summit of Plynlimon. In the valley stands **Llangorwen Church** (*open daily*), containing a lectern presented by Keble, and a stone altar for a communion table. While staying at Cwm Cynfelyn, above the church, Keble wrote the latter part of *The Christian Year*. Cwm was the birthplace of Isaac Williams, the poet, a leader of the Oxford Movement.

Cwm Woods, reached by path past the Hospital and along the edge of the golf links, provide good walks, with a return by the Panorama Walk and Constitution Hill.

Llanbadarn Fawr

Llanbadarn is an old village on the main road about a mile east of Aberystwyth. The station is on the road leading from the church towards Plas Crug, which is associated with Owain Glyndŵr, who had possession of it when Henry of Monmouth, afterwards Henry V, was Master of Aberystwyth Castle.

Llanbadarn Church is said to have been founded by St. Padarn, a companion of St. Cadfan. For about 200 years it gave its name to a diocese of which St. Padarn was first bishop. Later, the see was incorporated with St. David's. The Church is almost entirely in the Early English style, but has been restored. There are some sculptures by Flaxman, and monuments of the Gogerddan and Nant Eos families. A flat slab in the chancel marks the grave of Lewis Morris, Welsh antiquary and poet (d. 1765). There are two ancient sculptured crosses in the south transept, together with three windows of good modern glass.

Some two miles south-east of Llanbadarn and four miles south-east of Aberystwyth, is **Nanteos** (*Open 2.30–5.30 Wednesday and Saturday in summer; Wednesday only in winter, Charge*). The name means "the Nightingale's Brook." At the mansion is kept the *Cup of Nant Eos*, which resembles the Holy Grail described by Tennyson in his *Idylls of the King*. It is said to have been a chalice made from the wood of the Cross, and to have come into the possession of the Nant Eos family from one of their ancestors, Stedman, the descendant of a duke of Arabia, who was brought by Coeur-de-Lion from the Holy Land.

Pen Dinas (413 feet), to the south of the town, is easily distinguished by the tall column upon it. This is in the form of a cannon on end and was erected in commemoration of the Battle of Waterloo by a local landowner who was present as an officer on the field. The hill is approached by way of Bridge Street and Trefechan, on the southern side of the town. Having passed under the railway bridge, keep left and then take a foot-path on the right near a cottage, opposite the Camping Ground entrance. The largest Iron Age Hill Fort in Cardiganshire occupies the summit of Pen Dinas, consisting of two adjacent fortified areas, each roughly oval in plan. The descent may be made on the seaward side where the path leads down to a lane; turn right here for the railway bridge mentioned above.

Allt-Wen (the white cliff) is 2½ miles south of the town. To reach its foot cross the river at the end of Bridge Street, and just short of the railway turn to the right, as for the stone pier. Presently cross the River Ystwyth by a wooden bridge, and follow the sea-bank which extends to the foot of the cliff.

The River Ystwyth may be followed to Llanychaiarn Church, on the left of the road after passing over the bridge.

Pont-Rhyd-y-Groes

This is a pretty village set among pleasantly wooded scenery. It can be conveniently visited in conjunction with Devil's Bridge.

Motorists take the second turning on the right at Piccadilly (Penparcau) about 1½ miles from Aberystwyth. The road thus follows the delightful **Ystwyth Valley** to Llanilar, three miles beyond which it passes near the estate of Crosswood where the National Agricultural Advisory Service for Wales and Monmouth have their centre. Two miles farther the road comes to Pont Llanafan, which strongly resembles the famous Pont Aberglaslyn, near Beddgelert. Thence through varied and charming scenery to **Pont Rhyd-y-Groes** (the Bridge of the Ford of the Cross), where the river runs through a deep gorge. Here one may enter the **Hafod** estate, the property of the Forestry Commission. Cars and cycles should keep to the road. The two routes rejoin near Hafod Church.

From the church it is about 3 miles by road to the Devil's Bridge, past an arch erected to commemorate the jubilee of George III. Just short of the arch the mountain road from Rhayader comes in on the right.

The Devil's Bridge

Road Route. The outward route is along a high ridge on the south side of the Rheidol Valley. The town is left by Bridge Street, which leads across the Rheidol. In about 400 yards bear left, under the railway with the road climbing steadily and giving increasingly good views across the town; the National Library stands prominently on the hill beyond. Keep straight on at the cross-roads about 1½ miles from Aberystwyth (the road to the right leads to Aberayron and Cardigan; left to Llanbadarn). Because of the greater height of this route, the views are more extensive and even more beautiful than those from the railway. The *Henffordd Arms* (7 m.), a road-side inn, is the only one on the route.

At nine miles the road is 970 feet above the sea, and from a spot close by there is an exceedingly fine view. Soon after this a sudden turn of the road brings in sight the wild scenery of the Devil's Bridge.

Return Route. It is usual to return to Aberystwyth by the main road from Llanidoloes, which is reached by continuing past the Hafod Arms Hotel and keeping to the left at the fork about 2 miles farther on. (The road to the right also joins the main road near Dyffryn Castell; turn left just after crossing a stream).

The **Railway** journey to the Devil's Bridge takes about an hour. The narrow-gauge line is 12 miles in length—*summer service only*. The *left*-hand side of the railway carriages affords the better view. The train moves slowly enough to allow every point—river, copse, rapid and rocky fall—to be seen and appreciated. As the line follows the contour of the mountains the curves enable the traveller to see not only the way he is going, but also the way he has come. This is especially the case at **Aberffrwd** ($7\frac{1}{2}$ m.), where the line passes first behind some houses and a chapel picturesquely situated on the side of the hill and presently in front of the same buildings.

A short distance beyond, and across the valley, an excellent view is obtained of the **Stag**, a curious scar formed by refuse produced by trials for lead in the mountain-side, which can also be seen from the road following the south side of the valley. Half a mile farther the **Rheidol Falls** can be seen, far below. The falls may be reached by road from Aberystwyth by the way of Capel Bangor and the lane past Glyn Rheidol. Soon after leaving **Rhiwfron**, 525 feet above sea-level, a glimpse is gained of the Swiss-like scenery for which the Devil's Bridge is famous. Away in the distance, but seemingly below, for the line is now higher than the Bridge itself, the hotel looks out from the forest of pines, the valley narrows to a point, and, far below, the river wends its way to the sea.

There are really three bridges, one above another. The lowest bridge, Devil's Bridge, is known to have been in existence in 1188 when Giraldus passed over it on his journey through Wales with Archbishop Baldwin. There does not seem any historical ground for the name Devil's Bridge; the Welsh name is Pont-ar-fynach (the Bridge over the Mynach).

For grandeur few places can compare with this spot, and to geologists the gorges make it one of the most interesting places in the Principality. Both the Rheidol and the Mynach, bounding from their lofty source, have scooped out great chasms, to a depth of about 800 feet, and at the bridge the waters of the Mynach leap wildly in a series of cataracts of a height altogether of over 300 feet. The great ravine, black with age, and in many parts covered with vegetation, is an impressive sight.

To get a full view of the falls (admission charge) cross the bridge from the hotel and first descend to the bottom of the ravine for a sight of the **Devil's Punch Bowl**, one of a number of huge cavities or "pot-holes" worn in the rocks by the dashing, seething waters of the *Mynach*, which, from the pot-hole, throws itself through a narrow perpendicular slit in the rock, 114 feet in depth, over which the bridges have been built. After climbing to the bridge again, descend through the woods on the other side to the actual junction of the Rheidol and the Mynach. It is a long descent by seemingly interminable steps, called Jacob's Ladder, but every yard reveals a new wonder. On the right is the fine fall of the **Rheidol**, while the Mynach, or **Devil's Bridge Falls**, are on the left. At the bottom of the glen, a picturesque bridge is crossed, and then there is a long climb of many steps to the top again. On the way are platforms from which to view the distinctive features of the five or six falls that make the Mynach cascade. This tour can be made comfortably in three-quarters of an hour, but it can be done in less time by those prepared to hurry.

Around the Devil's Bridge

Parson's Bridge (1½ miles). Cross the Devil's Bridge and follow the road to **Yspyty Cynfyn**, formerly a hospice for monks on their way to Strata Florida Abbey. In the churchyard walls are ancient stones. Take the by-road at the eastern end of the church, and follow it across a field. When the ravine comes in sight, leave the road for a steep path, leading through a grove of oak-trees, and the stream will soon be reached. Parson's Bridge was built by a clergyman who did duty in a neighbouring church as well as at Yspyty Cynfyn; hence its name. The scenery is remarkably fine. In the vicinity of the bridge is a small stone circle.

Tyncastell Roman Ruins (2 miles). Follow the main road towards Aberystwyth for about a mile and a half, then turn to the right and follow the by-road towards a farm in the distance. The return journey may be made to Devil's Bridge or to Rhiwfron station (½ mile), the way to which is along the by-road leading to the farm from the main road.

Tyn-llwyn Farm (½ mile). Cross Devil's Bridge and continue along the main road for about a quarter of a mile. Then take a footpath to the left of the main road, from which a beautiful view of the valley towards Aberystwyth is gained. Permission can be obtained at the farm to wander along the hills close by.

Over the hills to Rhayader. Walkers who want to get off the beaten track should follow the road which accompanies the Mynach for a mile or so above Devil's Bridge. In about 3 miles this reaches the upper valley of the Ystwyth, beside which a track leads eastward for several miles to a lonely chapel. From this point a track goes north-eastward to the main road near Llangurig and another goes south-east to the Elan Valley and so to Rhayader, both places connected by motor with Aberystwyth.

The moorland solitudes of the **Myherin Valley** and the **Rhyddnant Valley**, beautiful yet seldom visited, can be reached easily from Devil's Bridge by following the main road up alongside the Mynach for about half a mile and then branching to the left by a road that keeps close to the river; or the upper part of the Myherin Valley can be reached by taking a road that leaves the Ponterwyd-Devils Bridge Road near Yspyty Cynfyn.

Borth

Early Closing Day. Wednesday.
Distances. Aberystwyth, 7; London, 215.
Golf. 18-hole coast course.

Hotels. *Grand; Friendship; Victoria; Diana.*
Post Office near station.

Borth is a quiet but growing village on the coast 7 miles north of Aberystwyth. Its greatest attraction is its beach of firm dry sand extending for 4 miles, excellent for bathing and as a playground for children. The beach is bounded inland by a high bank of pebbles standing far above the level of the adjoining road. At the south end of the village rise cliffs which extend along the shore to Aberystwyth, and on this high ground are many new houses. Most of the older houses are built along the road leading from the station to the beach, and along the road parallel to the sea, but half the latter have their backs to the shore. Northward of the old village are many bungalows. On the flat lands north of Borth is a good 18-hole golf course. Along the beach may be seen at low tide the remains of a *Submerged Forest*, evidence of the encroachment of the sea that has, no doubt, been responsible for the legends relating to Cardigan Bay. Borth is noted for prawns, crabs and lobsters; bass-fishing near the rocks is good sport, and there is fresh-water angling.

The road northward from Borth leads to a ferry (pedestrians only) over the Dovey which saves a long detour round by Machynlleth and reduces the walking distance from Borth to **Aberdovey** (pp. 179–180) to less than 5 miles.

Bedd Taliesin, Cwm Einion, the Llyfnant Valley

These are places among the hills to the east of the Aberystwyth–Machynlleth road.

At the northern end of **Talybont** turn right past the church, and then keep to the left. The road leads up through trees and past a sharp double bend to open country at a height of some 500 feet. On reaching a T-shaped junction, take the road to the right and then pass through a gate, leaving a little chapel (Pensarn) on the right. The road turns left, and in about 200 yards a large stone slab is visible on the right. Close by is a narrow trough, which is the reputed grave of Taliesin. This was probably not the poet of the sixth century (a historical character) but Taliesin of the mediaeval tale, whose exploits are related in "Hades Taliesin" which Lady Charlotte Guest translated in her edition of the Mabinogion.

The view is extensive and varied. At the T-shaped junction turn left (or, if returning from the grave, keep straight on). Follow this road, which first turns right and then bears right, past the farm of Gwar-cwm-uchaf and down the slope, into the Cletwr valley and out to the village of **Tre'rddol**; which is just over nine miles from Aberystwyth.

The entrance to **Cwm Einion** (The Artists' Valley) is at **Furnace**, a further 3 miles along the Machynlleth road (1½ miles south of Glandyfi station).

The neighbourhood is favoured for picnics, and refreshments may be obtained near Furnace Fall. The **Llyfnant Valley** lies a mile or so north of Cwm Einion to which it is roughly parallel. The association of woodland and water, rippling brook and brawling cataract is seldom equalled. A walk of nearly 3 miles up the valley leads to the *Glaspwll Cascade* and a further two miles to the *Cwmrhaiadr Falls*. A mile and a half farther is *Pistyll-y-Llyn*, a waterfall that descends 300 feet, but there is seldom a great volume of water.

Strata Florida Abbey

Strata Florida lies about 15 miles by road south-east from Aberystwyth and is reached by crossing the Ystwyth at Pont Llanafan. Three miles farther is Ystrad Meurig, with Strata Florida railway station; the Abbey lies a good 3 miles east of this, by way of the hamlet of Pontrhydfendigaid (the name translated is "The Bridge of the Blessed Ford"). Here light refreshments can be obtained.

The **Abbey,** now in the hands of the Ministry of Public Building and Works (admission charge; keys, apply custodian), stands in a flat strip of meadow on the south bank of the *Teifi*. It is supposed to have been erected about 1164, for Cistercian monks, and to have been destroyed by Edward I, who later rebuilt it. Henry IV's troops then occupied it, and it was finally dissolved in the reign of Henry VIII. From the remnants, and from the stories told of it, the Abbey appears to have been a magnificent building. It has been described as the "Westminster Abbey of Wales," and is said to have been the burial place of Welsh princes, and of at least one celebrated bard—Dafydd ap Gwilym—who was laid to rest *circa* 1370.

Excavations have disclosed the outline of the Church, sacristy, Chapter House and cloisters together with the cloister garth. There are some interesting tombstones with Celtic designs in the angles between the Presbytery and the Chapels. The tile pavements are the finest to be seen in any ruined abbey in England or Wales, and the ornamentation of a Norman arch which formed the western entrance of the church is said to be unlike any other in Britain. A curious painting and a few relics may be seen in the farmhouse. Strata Florida is a latinized form of *Ystrad Fflur*, "the plain of the bloom."

Some 5 miles south of Strata Florida is the small and ancient town of **Tregaron,** which is at the side of a great peat bog, the largest in Wales, known as *Gors Goch Glan Teifi*.

Four miles west of Tregaron is *Llangeitho*, near the head of the Vale of Ayron, which was the scene of a great religious revival in the eighteenth century, under the influence of Daniel Rowland, who died in 1790, and to whose memory a statue has been erected in front of the chapel.

ABERYSTWYTH TO CARDIGAN

For the first few miles through Rhyd-y-felin and Llanfarian the road is inland and completely hidden from the sea, whilst for the succeeding portion it is wholly along the coast. It rises 500 or 600 feet, and commands extensive views, including Snowdon, Cader Idris and Plynlimon.

In 8 miles is the village of **Llanrhystyd,** a quiet little place with a stream bubbling down its main street. On the beach there is some good prawn fishing.

Aberayron (*Feathers Royal, Royal Oak, Prince of Wales, Harbour Masters Arms, Victoria*) a further 7 miles on, is situated at the mouth of the Ayron (or Aeron), a small stream containing salmon and sewin in their season and trout at all times. It is an unspoilt seaside village, dating from about 1807 when the two piers protecting the harbour were built. On the beach about 600 yards north of the harbour is a portion of a semi-circular fort called *Castell Cadwgan.*

New Quay (*Black Lion, New Quay, Brynarfor, Glyn,* etc.) with a population of only 950, is a delightful holiday resort in its own sheltered bay with pier and tidal harbour. It has fine sandy beaches from which there is excellent bathing. It is extremely popular as a sailing centre and has a flourishing yacht club. The Cardigan Bay Regatta is well-known as an annual event. Fishing is important and mackerel, herring and shellfish are caught for both local and inland markets.

Craig-yr-Adar—the Birds' Rock—to the west, is a haunt of many sea-birds, while in the nearby cliffs are many caves. The most remarkable is *Ogof-Deuben,* or the Two-head Cave, so called on account of its two openings. North-west of the town is **New Quay Head,** 300 feet high, which commands a fine view.

About a mile and a half from New Quay on the Aberayron side is **Llanina Church,** picturesquely situated in private grounds. It is one of the smallest churches in the county.

Llangranog, on the coast 7 miles south-west, is a curious little resort situated in a narrow glen with precipitous cliffs. On the north side is a singular cape called **Ynys Llochtyn.**

Cardigan

Boating. Up the river to Cilgerran or down to the estuary, according to the state of the tide.

Buses run daily between Cardigan and Carmarthen, *via* Newcastle Emlyn; Cardigan and Goodwick, *via* Eglwyswrw and Newport; Cardigan and Aberystwyth, *via* New Quay and Aberayron; Cardigan and Gwbert-on-Sea; Cardigan and Llangranog; Cardigan and St. Dogmaels; Cardigan and Whitland; and Cardigan and Narberth *via* Crymmych on Saturdays only.

Distances. Aberystwyth, 38; Cardiff, 93; Carmarthen, 28; Fishguard, 18; Haverfordwest, 26; Lampeter, 30; London, 235; New Quay, 20; Tenby, 33.

Early Closing Day. Wednesdays. Banks, etc., Saturdays.

Fishing. Cardigan is a good centre for fishing the Teifi, the Nevern and the Cych, and there is also sea-angling. In the tidal waters of the Teifi, below Cardigan Bridge, bass are caught. Full particulars from The South-West Wales River Board (Clerk, Mr. E. A. Griffiths, Solicitor, Penyfai House, Penyfai, near Llanelly). Salmon are taken with rod and line above Cenarth, 7 miles. Only a moderate rental is charged by the owners. Mackerel and rock pollock are plentiful off the coast.

Golf. *Cardigan Golf Club* at Gwbert-on-Sea, 3 miles, 9-hole course.

Hotels. *Black Lion; Grosvenor; Angel; Glanavon.*

Population. 3,780.

Post Office. Head Office in High Street.

Tennis. Hard courts in Gwbert Road (opposite Grammar School).

Cardigan (in Welsh *Aberteifi*—at the mouth of the Teifi) is a typical Welsh market town and is a convenient centre from which to visit places of interest. Boating on the river is quite popular, but a bar at the mouth of the river prevents the entrance of larger vessels. The ancient bridge is a good viewpoint. The **Castle** was founded in the time of Henry II by Rhys ap Gryffydd, Prince of South Wales. The Royalists vainly tried to hold it during the Civil War, and when it passed into the possession of the Parliamentarians it was rendered incapable of further defence. The ruins of the stronghold stand on a woody knoll. Not far from the castle is the **Parish Church** (services in Welsh and English), a very plain building (almost entirely rebuilt), devoid of any noticeable features other than the pinnacles and battlements of the chancel and the stepped buttresses of the tower. Beside it, on a site once occupied by a priory, is the Cardigan Memorial Hospital. It was in this building that Mrs. Katherine Philipps lived in the reign of Charles II, the "matchless Orinda", in inspiration, of Jeremy Taylor's *Discourse of Friendship*.

210

Walks and Excursions from Cardigan

To Gwbert, Aberporth and Traethsaith. Down the river from Cardigan, and on the right bank, is **Gwbert** (*goobert*)**-on-Sea,** consisting of some hotels (*Cliff, Glenafon*), a few houses, and good sands. It can be reached by a road along the estuary, or by the shore at low-water.

Gwbert has a sporting golf-course of 9 holes, the home of the Cardigan Golf Club and there is an active salmon fishery.

From Gwbert there is a fine walk on a grand line of basaltic cliffs on the Cardiganshire coast, past **Cardigan Island** to **Mount,** 4 miles. Another 4 miles ends at **Aberporth,** a secluded nook much in favour with artists by reason of its romantic scenery. This pretty spot can also be reached by the main road to Aberayron as far as Blaenanerch; having turned left here it is a further two miles.

A mile from Aberporth, and accessible by a beautiful walk along the cliffs, is **Traethsaith (Tresaith),** a residential place with a fine stretch of firm, level sand which at low-water extends to Penbryn, another mile.

St. Dogmael's, (*Webley Hotel*) is a picturesque fishing-village half a mile from Cardigan, and extending for about a mile and a half along the shore of the estuary of the *Teifi*.

St. Dogmael's contains the ruins of an Abbey founded about 1115 by Robert FitzMartin, Lord of Cemais, on the site of a monastic community of the old Welsh type. The remains are in the grounds of the vicarage and are in the charge of the Ministry of Public Building and Works. Behind the vicarage are the ruins of the refectory, with the western door still perfect.

To Cilgerran. Some 3 miles up the river on the left bank of the Teifi is **Cilgerran**, famed for the picturesque remnant of a **castle** said to date from about 1223. It can be reached by road, circuitous and uninteresting, or by rowing up the river.

A quarter of a mile from the castle is the **Church**, which has been rebuilt. It still has, however, a Norman tower. In the graveyard is a good Ogham stone.

Cardigan to Newcastle-Emlyn

This is a 10-mile journey (buses run every weekday; limited service, Sundays) along the valley of the Teifi that for charm of scenery is one of the best in all South Wales.

Soon after leaving Cardigan the road and river go rather far apart, through the stream making a great bend, but at **Llechryd**, 3 miles from the town, they come together again, opposite the beautiful park of **Castle Maelgwn**, and for the rest of the way, and for several miles beyond our goal, keep close company. Through a well-wooded glen we reach **Cenarth**, 7 miles from Cardigan, the site of a salmon leap Hereabouts coracles can be seen.

Newcastle-Emlyn (*Emlyn Arms*) is finely situated on the Teifi. It consists mainly of one large street, which runs at right angles to the high road, and is connected by a bridge with Adpar, on the north side of the river, in which good trout- and salmon-fishing can be enjoyed. Occupying a fine situation and commanding a delightful prospect are the ruins of a once famous **Castle,** built by Sir Rhys ap Thomas, who made it his frequent residence. A gateway 14 feet high, flanked on each side by an octagonal tower, acts as a frame to a grand landscape.

About 8 miles eastward of Newcastle-Emlyn (bus service) is the small town of **Llandyssul,** pleasantly situated on the Teifi and indeed a good fishing centre on that river.

Lampeter (*Black Lion Royal, Castle, Royal Oak*) or Llanbedr, signifies "the Church of St. Peter", but Lampeter Pont Stephen is the full name of the place, the addition being due to the presence of a bridge said to have been built during the reign of King Stephen. Lampeter is conveniently reached from either Cardigan or Aberayron. Its situation on a gentle hill beside the Teifi is delightful. A great attraction of this assize town is fine salmon and trout fishing. **St. David's College** was founded in 1822 and is now an open university college closely linked under its charter with Oxford and Cambridge and latterly, University College, Cardiff. Part of the buildings are open to visitors. Lampeter has several sporting facilities including a 9-hole golf course.

THE SOUTH-WEST COAST

Cardigan to Pembroke

The first place of any size on the road westward into Pembroke from Cardigan is **Newport** (*Llwyngwair Arms, Commercial, Llwyngwair Manor*), capital of the Norman Lordship Marcher of Cemaes. With a population of a little over a thousand it stands on the estuary of the River Nevern. Its Welsh name (Trefdraeth) signifies "Town on the Shore". It is a quiet but popular resort offering good boating and golf. Newport Castle (private) overlooks the town. **St Mary's Church**, in the Decorated style, is on the site of an earlier Norman structure and retains the original font.

Newport Cromlech stands in a field on the left of the road leading to the bridge and behind *Cromlech Farmhouse*. **Cerrig-y-Gôf**, in a field on the right 1¼ miles along the road to Fishguard, is one of the most interesting monuments in Wales; it consists of five cists in a circle, but these have been disturbed. There are cromlechs at Trellyffaint and Llech-y-Dribedd, both on Morfa Head, and Cromlechau Meibion Owen in a field adjoining Cilgwyn Farm near Cilgwyn Church, on the left of the road from Newport to Tafarnbwlch and the Presely Hills.

Within an easy walk of Newport is the **Pentre Evan Cromlech,** which is one of the finest of the ancient burial-chambers in Britain. The capstone is 16 feet long, by 8 feet wide and 2½ feet thick, and is supported by three uprights from 7 to 8 feet high.

Carningli Common. From the castle follow the road that runs towards the south-east into the Clydach Valley, and at the end of about a mile ascend the hills (Carningli Common) on the right. The highest ground affords a fine view of the Gwaun Valley and Presely Mountains and of the rugged coast-line. On the eastern summit are traces of a camp; on the western slope there are hut circles.

Nevern is 2 miles away, at the head of a wide horseshoe loop in the road from Newport to Cardigan.

The Church, for the most part Norman, stands on the site of one that was erected in the sixth century. Its tower extends across the full width, at the western end. Before the church porch stands the **Vitalianus Stone** of Romano-British times, bearing inscriptions in Latin and Ogham; another Ogham Stone is set in the window-sill inside the church—the **Maglocunos Stone.** Near the porch is a Celtic Cross, richly decorated and bearing an inscription that has not yet been deciphered. It is 12½ feet high. The church is dedicated to St. Brynach, an Irish saint and contemporary of St. David. To the north of the church, and adjoining the site of Nevern Castle, is the "Pilgrim's Cross"—a cross embossed on the cliff-face, with a kneeling-place at its foot—wayside shrine of pilgrims from Strata Florida to St. Davids.

Fishguard and Goodwick

Angling. Excellent trout-fishing can be had in the Gwaun near Fishguard, and both ground and mackerel fishing from boats provide good sport.

Bus Services. Between Fishguard and Cardigan *via* Newport, and Fishguard, St. Davids and Haverfordwest.

Distances. Fishguard to St. Davids, 16; Haverfordwest, 15; Newport, 8; Cardigan, 18; Rosslare (Ireland), 54 nautical miles.

Early Closing Day. Wednesdays.

Hotels. *Abergwaun; Cartref; Fishguard Bay.*

Population. 4,898.

Post and Telegraph Offices. At Fishguard and Goodwick.

Youth Hostel. Castell Mawr, Tref Asser, overlooking Pwll Deri Bay.

Fishguard consists of two parts, in addition to its fine bay. Those arriving by the Newport–St. Davids road first make acquaintance with the old village at the head of a creek—a medley of cottages and narrow lanes. A long, steep, winding hill takes one up to modern Fishguard. Here are shops, banks, etc., and from various points fascinating glimpses are gained across the Bay to Dinas Head.

On the northern side of Fishguard the road descends steeply, crosses the head of a wide valley to **Goodwick** (*goodick*), a prettily situated village in a sheltered spot on the west side of Fishguard Bay.

Fishguard Bay is sufficiently deep to float the largest Atlantic liners, is free from shoals and bars, and is well sheltered. It forms the port on the English side for the route to and from the Republic of Ireland.

The **Irish Quay,** alongside which lie the fine turbine steamers that ply to and from the corresponding harbour at Rosslare, and also the steamers to and from Waterford and Cork, is one-third of a mile in length.

The **Breakwater** runs out over half a mile across the bay from the Goodwick shore. It is a very massive structure, being a rubble mound with a concrete parapet, which is 90 feet above the bed of the sea. The base is over 350 feet wide.

February 22, 1797, is memorable for its hostile invasion of Great Britain when three French ships with 600 troops and 800 convicts under the command of Tate, an Irish-American, landed at Carreg Gwastad Point, 2½ miles west of Fishguard. They were ultimately captured by Lord Cawdar's motley army. Legend has it that the French were discouraged by the appearance on B'gny Hill of a large force, which was in fact a number of Welshwomen in national costume of red mantles and black beaver hats.

214

To Pen-caer. It is a good walk over Pen-caer, the peninsula on the west side of Fishguard Bay, and on by Mathry, whence buses run to Fishguard and Goodwick. The headland abounds in prehistoric remains. On the headland of Penanglas, in the immediate vicinity of Goodwick, is a ledge of rock displaying a stratum of basaltic columns, popularly called, on account of their appearance, *torthau ceiniogau* ("penny loaves"). Two miles north-west of Goodwick is **Llanwnda Church,** of which Giraldus Cambrensis was once rector. The sanctus bell-cote is still in position. Eastward of the Llanwnda Cove is **Carreg-gwastad Point,** the landing-place of the French invaders. At **Strumble Head,** the north-west corner of the peninsula, is grand cliff scenery. South of Strumble Head, about midway between that point and St. Nicholas, is **Carn Fawr** (Great Cairn), a rocky hill on which are the remains of an ancient fortress. The church at **St. Nicholas** exhibits an ancient stone inscribed TUNCCETA SORDAARIHIC CIT. Half a mile south of the church is a cromlech locally known as **Samson's Quoit.** On the coast west of this is **Abermawr,** a transatlantic cable station, while a little west of the peninsula is **Abercastle,** which must be mentioned because half a mile from it, on the coast road to St. Davids, is the **Long House Cromlech,** the finest of such relics in this part of Wales. It is 9 miles from Goodwick, *via* Manor Owen and Mathry.

Cilrhedyn Bridge, and the Presely Mountains. Cilrhedyn Bridge is 3½ miles from Fishguard, at a beautiful spot in the valley of the *Gwaun.* The valley is followed for a couple of miles and then a slight detour conducts to **Llanllawer Church.** Llanllawer's "Holy Well," built in the shape of a curved pyramid, is always a centre of attraction. The Field of the Dead (Parc-y-Meirw), but a short distance farther, contains eight monoliths, of which four are standing. They are 12–16 feet in height. The distance from them to Cilrhedyn Bridge is only a mile.

From Pont Faen a road leads to Rosebush, a small village from which begins the path to the summit of the Presely Mountains, Cwm Cerwin, or **Presely Top,** 1,760 feet. It is the source of most of the Pembrokeshire streams and a great landmark from every part of the county. Some of the stones of Stonehenge were obtained from Presely.

To Dinas and Dinas Head. From the lower town at Fishguard the road ascends, at first very abruptly and then more gradually, to a bare rocky tract that overlooks **Newport Bay,** with Dinas Head on the western side of it. Thence the route lies through the hamlet of **Bwlch Mawr** (traces of a camp on right-hand side of road) to **Rhos Dinas,** 4 miles. The headland is nearly all enclosed, but the highest ground at the northern extremity is unfenced and commands a view which more than repays one for the walk to the spot.

St. Davids

Approach. By bus from Haverford-west and Fishguard stations.

Distances. Haverfordwest, 16; Fishguard, 15; St. Davids Head, 2½.

Hotels. *City; Grove; Twr-y-Felyn;* *Old Cross; Warpool Court; Bee-hive (boarding).*

Golf. There is a 9-hole course on which visitors may play.

St. Davids ranks as a city through its possession of a cathedral. Otherwise it would be described as a village. It stands in a desolate situation a mile or so from the sea, and many visitors will be impelled to ask how a cathedral came to be built in so inhospitable a neighbourhood. The answer is that the cathedral originated in a monastic church, and that the monastic church was built here owing to the seclusion of the site. The locality is almost bare of foliage, with the exception of the valley of the River Alun, a small stream on the western side of St. Davids; but the golden blossom of the gorse, which is very abundant in the parish, relieves the monotony of the scene in spring and summer. The grandeur of the bold coast, the interest attached to the ancient Cathedral, the purity of the air, the bathing, fishing and shooting, make the village–city sufficiently attractive to secure constant occupation of the apartments offered to summer visitors.

The coast from St. David's Head to Jack Sound, i.e. the southernmost tip of St. Bride's Bay, is a splendid field for geologists. In the **City Hall** are a reading-room and library, and an Information Centre of the National Parks Commission.

The **Pebbles,** a thoroughfare lined with ancient houses, leads to the gateway of a thirteenth-century tower giving access to the Close, from which a stone staircase, called the Thirty-Nine Articles by reason of the number of steps, descends to the Cathedral.

St. Davids Cathedral

Admission. Daily.

Dimensions. The total length of the interior is 298 feet, of which 130 are contained in the nave. The breadth of the nave is 68 feet. The transepts measure 47 feet by 33. The tower is 124 feet high.

Services. Sundays, in English, 8, 11, 6; in Welsh, 9.30 a.m. Weekdays, Matins, 7.30; H.C., 8; Evensong, 6 summer, 4.15 winter.

The oldest part of the present building is the nave, dating from the last quarter of the twelfth century, when the Cathedral was rebuilt after having been burned down by the Danes in 1078. In 1220 the tower fell and destroyed the choir and transepts. They were almost immediately rebuilt as was also the lowest stage of the tower. The Lady Chapel was built about 1300, and sometime after 1328 Bishop Gower added to the height of the walls of the nave, inserted Decorated windows, added a stage to the tower, put up the rood screen, and built the south porch. The roof of the nave probably belongs to the first decade of the sixteenth century. Immediately afterwards Bishop Vaughan vaulted the chapel bearing his name to the east of the Presbytery.

It cannot be said that the bleak-looking exterior reflects the distinguished record of the see, but the interior generously compensates any sense of disappointment. From the south door one looks between the leaning piers of the nave arcade and can appreciate the great richness of the Norman ornamentation of the arches. From this point, too, can be seen the unusual

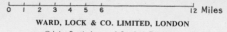

PEMBROKE, CARDIGAN, CARMARTHEN

0 1 2 3 4 5 6   12 Miles

WARD, LOCK & CO. LIMITED, LONDON

© John Bartholomew & Son Ltd, Edinburgh

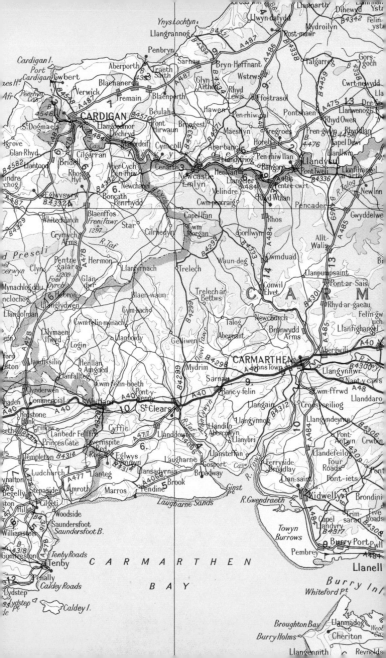

manner in which clerestory and triforium are combined. This richness of walls is matched by the very remarkable sixteenth-century roof of grey Irish oak. It comprises a number of pendant arches.

From the roof the eye falls to the magnificent fourteenth-century **Rood Screen**, the effect of which is increased by the gradual rise in the floor from west to east. The whole building has an unusual appearance owing to the colour of the stone. The purplish slate-coloured material came from Caerbwdy, and that which is redder from Caerfai. The style of the **Nave** is Transitional-Norman, and therefore this part architecturally goes back nearly half a century beyond the date of its erection. On the fourth and fifth piers on the south side are remains of ancient paintings. On the same side is the tomb of *Bishop Morgan* (d. 1504).

The rood screen has been carefully restored. Beyond it are the choir stalls of fifteenth-century work. The bishop's throne also dates from the fifteenth century, but portions of it are older, being parts of Bishop Gower's stalls. Its construction was due to Bishop Morgan, who was buried in front of it. A unique feature of St. Davids is that the reigning sovereign of Britain holds the first cursal prebendal stall. It is in the south-west corner of the choir, and is distinguished by a painted and carved wooden representation of the royal arms. This stall was occupied for the first time by a reigning Sovereign when the Queen visited the Cathedral on August 7th, 1955. Another unusual feature is the parclose screen separating the Choir from the Presbytery.

The large tomb in the centre of the Presbytery is that of Edmund Tudor (d. 1546), father of Henry VII. He was buried at the Grey Friars, Carmarthen, and on the dissolution of that religious house by his grandson his remains were brought to their present resting-place.

In the west bay on the north side of the Presbytery is **St. Davids Shrine.** Note the beautiful fifteenth-century oak sedilia on the south side of the Presbytery. In the bay eastward of these is the supposed tomb of *Giraldus Cambrensis*, the historian.

Eastward of the Presbytery is **Holy Trinity Chapel,** a somewhat unusual feature. Here is the altar of the Holy Trinity, and on either side of it are statues of Giraldus Cambrensis and Bishop Vaughan. Of great interest is the recess in the western wall, behind the High Altar. When first discovered, during modern restorations, this held certain bones, accepted as veritable relics of St. David, and these now lie within the casket in the recess.

Eastward of Holy Trinity Chapel is the Ambulatory, and eastward again the **Lady Chapel,** built by Bishop Martyn (d. 1328), whose tomb is on the south side. On the north side is the tomb of *Bishop Beck*, who died in 1293. Dean Howell restored the Lady Chapel and on the wall of its ante-chapel is a large bronze memorial of him. He was buried in the restored chapel of St. Nicholas.

In the south-east corner is **Edward the Confessor's Chapel,** the re-roofing of which completed the restoration of the cathedral. It has an altar and reredos of alabaster, a memorial to Viscountess Maidstone (d. 1923).

In the wall of the north transept is the shrine of St. Caradoc who died in 1124. Eastward of the transept is St. Thomas à Becket's Chapel, now refurnished in memory of Bishop Prosser (1927–50), third Archbishop of Wales. In the south transept is a portable altar stone said to have been brought by St. David from Jerusalem after his consecration as Bishop in the Holy City.

The Cathedral library contains many interesting volumes and other antiquities and will well repay a visit.

Next in point of interest to the Cathedral are the ruins of the **Bishop's Palace** (*open standard Ministry hours*), westward of the Cathedral, on the farther side of the Alun. The building was erected by Bishop Gower, about 1340, and was one of the finest edifices of its kind in the kingdom. Some two centuries after its foundation it was virtually destroyed by Bishop Barlow, who stripped off its leaden roof to provide dowries (according to local tradition) for his five daughters, each of whom became the wife of a bishop.

North of the Cathedral are the scanty ruins of **St. Mary's College**, founded by Bishop Houghton and John of Gaunt in 1365. The principal portion of the remains is part of the Chapel. Between the ruins and the Cathedral is the site of the Cloister.

The Cathedral, Palace and College were enclosed by a lofty embattled wall having four handsome gateways, of which the only one remaining is that to which the Pebbles path leads.

In **Parc-y-Castell**, south-west of the city, are the mounds of a camp traditionally assigned to St. David.

The Cliffs, Whitesand Bay and St. Davids Head

Caerbwdy Bay is about a mile south-east of St. Davids, but to reach it one must take the Haverfordwest road for little more than a mile to where, just after crossing a stream, there is a right turning leading to the bay. From the quarry at Caerbwdy much of the building stone for St. Davids Cathedral was obtained. It is of a pleasing reddish-purple colour.

The first part of the walk westward from Caerbwdy is round the promontory of **Pen-pleidiau**, separating Caerbwdy Bay from Caerfai Bay. At the extremity of the headland is a cliff castle, with four parallel embankments across the isthmus, and a fine view is afforded of the line of magnificent cliffs, on which immense numbers of sea-birds breed. Due east are the **Green** and **Black Scars**, at the entrance to Solva Harbour.

Caerfai Bay is a lovely and sheltered spot, and a delightful bathing-place. From Caerfai, also, was obtained some of the stone used in building St. Davids Cathedral. It is redder than that from Caerbwdy.

Following the coast westward for less than a mile, we reach the ruins of **St. Non's Chapel** and **St. Non's Well**, on the shore of **St. Non's Bay.** The saint was the mother of St. David, to whom she is said to have given birth on the spot where the chapel stands; from the slight remains, it appears as if the small edifice was built north and south, which is unusual. The spring, or well, as it is called, is about 40 yards north-east of the building. It is covered by a small vault.

Again going westward by the cliff-track, we arrive at **Chanters Sea,** the extremity of the headland on the west side of St. Non's Bay which commands a fine view of that inlet. Then a small bay is skirted and we come to **Porth Clais**, a narrow inlet, formerly a small coal and lime port at the mouth of the Alan river.

By following the cliffs for a couple of miles farther we reach the head of **Porth Lisky Bay.** Here, protected from mutilation by a strong iron cage, is a stone supposed to be a meteorite. Off the eastern horn of the bay is a chain of islets. The largest is **Careg Frân.** In the mouth of the bay are **Careg yr Esgob** (the Bishop's Rock) and other islets.

Porth Stinian, almost due west of St. Davids, is one of the finest lifeboat stations in the kingdom. It is also the site of **St. Justinian's Chapel** (Chapel Stinian) and **St. Justinian's Well**, both of which, with a tract of coast-land about 5 acres in extent, are protected by the National Trust. St. Justinian, hermit and martyr, who tradition says was the confessor of St. David, lived upon Ramsey until he was murdered. Then his body drifted to the mainland, and was buried near the spot where it reached the shore. A chapel also was erected there and became a place of pilgrimage. It was rebuilt by Bishop Vaughan (1509–1522) and the ruins are the remains of his building.

St. Davids Head forms the northern horn of the large inlet which the English call **Whitesand Bay**, and the Welsh Porthmawr, or the Great Bay. On its southern side is **Porth Sele**, a small cove at a point where we go down almost to the shore. A little beyond is **Ogof Golchfa**, where are caves accessible at low-water. On the shore of the bay are the **Burrows**, an undulating sandy tract that makes an ideal course for golfers. Near Whitesand Bay the ruins of an ancient chapel were unearthed a few years ago and several skeletons were found. Just south of the road from St. Davids is the site of the legendary Roman city of Menevia.

To reach **St. Davids Head** from this spot, one must follow the coast northward and westward for rather more than a mile, passing the little sandy cove of **Porth Melgan**. The head is a rugged promontory once defended by a double rampart of stones, now broken down. It is also the site

of several cromlechs and hut circles. The promontory affords a good view
of Whitesand Bay, of the rocky coast, of **Ramsey Island,** which is really an
isolated fragment of the St. Davids rock mass, and of the cluster of seven
isolated rocks called the **Bishop and his Clerks.**

The general flatness of the land in this western corner is relieved by
three or four rocky heights overlooking the coast near St. Davids Head.
Carn Llidi is the highest and the climb to the top is stiff enough to call
attention to the fact that actually the summit is less than 600 feet above sea-
level. A gully on the southern side should be used in making the descent.

St. Davids to Haverfordwest

"Sixteen miles and seventeen hills" is an old-time description
of the road between St. Davids and Haverfordwest. The hills,
however, are by no means formidable and certainly add interest
to the route. In 3 miles is **Solva** (*Bay, Cambrian, Ship Inn*)
with a romantic little cove reminiscent of Boscastle harbour.
On its east side is Gribin Point (National Trust). **Pen-y-Cwm** is
at the head of an inviting combe running down to the sea, and
then the road joins the shore at **Newgale** with a 2-mile stretch
of sand and a pebble embankment. The road now strikes inland
for Haverfordwest, passing on the left, perched on a high rock,
the tower of **Roch Castle** built in the reign of Henry III for the
protection of "Little England beyond Wales".

Haverfordwest

Airport. At Withybush, 2 miles
from town centre on Fishguard
road.

Angling. Trout and salmon fishing
in the Cleddau and its branches.

Buses to St. Davids, Milford Haven,
Fishguard, Broad Haven, Little
Haven, Tenby and Carmarthen.

Distances. London, 247; Carmarthen, 30; Cardigan, 26; Fishguard, 15; Milford Haven, 7;
Tenby, 21.

Early Closing Day. Thursdays.

Golf. A 9-hole course at Arnolds
Down, Narberth Road.

Hotels. *Mariners; County; Queens;
Castle.*

Population. 8,892.

Post Office. In Quay Street.

Haverfordwest is a prosperous and important inland market-
town. It is well built and climbs the slope of a steep hill beside
the Western Cleddau, which flows down to Milford Haven.
Upon a rocky eminence overhanging the river is the shell of a
Castle, built in the twelfth century by Gilbert de Clare, the first
Earl of Pembroke, as a protection to the English settlement.

The old town has four ancient churches, **St. Martin's, St.
Thomas's,** which has the tomb of Richard the Palmer, who in

220

the twelfth century accomplished a journey to Rome, **Prendergast** with its fourteenth-century tower, and **St. Mary's.**

St. Mary's Church, one of the finest in the county, was originally built in the middle of the thirteenth century but parts have been rebuilt or added since. Fantastic gargoyles are an interesting feature of the exterior. A remarkable feature of the nave and chancel is the clerestory, rarely seen in Welsh churches. It is Perpendicular, but the chancel itself is Early English. The nave and north aisle have carved roofs, that of the nave being very elaborate. At the west end of the nave is the much-defaced effigy of a pilgrim of the time of Henry VII. On the satchel are scallop shells, indicating that the shrine visited was that of St. James of Compostella in Spain.

Other public buildings include the **Shire Hall,** the **Masonic Hall,** the **Temperance Hall,** the **Market-house,** and two cinemas.

The **County War Memorial,** in Salutation Square, is a column, 20 feet high, constructed of Forest of Dean stone and surmounted by the Welsh dragon.

On the eastern side of the river is a very pleasant walk called **The Frolic,** a couple of miles in length. Along the western side of the stream is the **Parade,** which leads to a meadow containing the ruins of a Priory of the Augustines. The ruins can be seen from the bridge between the station and the main portion of the town.

Picton Castle (private) lies 2 miles east of Haverfordwest. It was built by William de Picton, in the reign of William II, and therefore is one of the most ancient residences in the kingdom. The park extends to the estuary of the *East Cleddau*, a noble sheet of water when the tide is in. The River Cleddau extends from Haverfordwest to the beautiful harbour of Milford Haven. Its scenery is exceptionally fine.

Adjoining Picton Park on the east are the grounds of **Slebech Hall,** a mansion built in 1780 by the last of the Barlow family on the site of a hospital of St. John of Jerusalem. The old church is a picturesque ruin. Close to the road stands a church erected by the late Baron de Rutzen; the spire is of very peculiar construction.

Broad Haven and Little Haven are on the western coast, 7 miles south-west of Haverfordwest (bus service). The road is uninteresting until near the end, when there comes into view the beautiful St. Bride's Bay. **Broad Haven** (*Royal, Broad Haven*), is a small hamlet, with extensive sands that afford good bathing. **Little Haven** (*St. Brides, Castle*), formerly an important harbour for the shipment of coal mined in the neighbourhood, is in a narrow combe immediately south of Broad Haven. There are good facilities for sea-fishing. The approach from Broad Haven or from Walton West involves negotiating a very steep hill.

Off the extreme west of South Pembrokeshire is **Skomer Island,** which in the nesting season is exceptionally rich in sea-birds; it is reached from

221

Marloes, but the birds are protected and permission to visit is necessary. Farther south is **Skokholm** with a level top and fine dark red cliffs and where a bird migration observatory has been set up. Farther east still is the islet of **Grassholm** with one of the largest gannetries in the British Isles.

Milford Haven

Milford, with its picturesque scenery, stirring historic associations, important fishing and transport interests and excellent recreational facilities, is at once one of the most popular holiday resorts and fishing ports in West Wales. It is rapidly becoming a yachting centre of note; situated on the north shore of the famous Haven, it enjoys a mild climate at all seasons, thanks to its southerly aspect and sheltered position, whilst its blue skies are unrivalled in the British Isles.

Milford Haven is the fourth largest fishing port in the United Kingdom. A fleet of steam trawlers is based at the port and a large number of East Coast and foreign vessels also make the Docks their headquarters during the greater part of the year. The harbour is one of the finest. It is about 11 miles long and covers about 20 square miles and is rapidly developing into one of the foremost oil ports of Europe. The British Petroleum Company has a crude oil terminal at Angle Bay which can accommodate tankers of 100,000 tons capacity, while the Regent Refining Company also have a terminal and refinery on the south shore. The Esso Petroleum Company have a large oil tanker terminal jetty and a refinery on the outskirts of the town.

Eastward of Milford is **Neyland** (bus service) where is a car ferry to **Hobb's Point** for Pembroke.

Pembroke

Early Closing Day. Wednesday.
Hotels. *King's Arms*, Main Street; *Lion*, Main Street; *Corston*, Castlemartin.
Population. 13,480.

Pembroke is built on a ridge which culminates in a great mass of limestone rock, the sides of which descend precipitously to the tidal waters of the Pembroke River, which flows into Milford Haven. On this rock, itself a great natural fortress, arose the **Castle,** formerly one of the largest and strongest fortresses in the kingdom and now a noble ruin. The building follows the natural shape of the rock and consists of curtain walls protected by towers (*admission charge*). Recently the fabric has been skilfully restored and the Henry VII Tower partly rebuilt.

The **Keep,** built about 1200, is one of our finest examples of a round keep. It is 75 feet high and 60 feet in diameter at the base, where the walls are nearly 20 feet thick. They are not less than 14 feet thick at the first storey. The summit is reached by a spiral staircase in the thickness of the wall. The buildings at the north-east corner date from the sixteenth century.

The first castle, "a slender fortress with stakes and turf," was built by Arnulph de Montgomery, in the time of William Rufus. His successor, Gerald de Windsor, was besieged in it by the Welsh. Other sieges followed, and the fortress was twice burned. Henry II sailed from Pembroke Castle to Ireland in 1172, his son John visited it, and Henry VII was born within it. On the outbreak of the war between Charles I and the Parliament, Poyer, Mayor of Pembroke, garrisoned the castle and held it for the Parliament, but when the war was practically over he changed sides and then held the fortress against his former friends. To put down this rebellion Cromwell laid siege to the castle in June, 1648. To prevent a recurrence of the trouble, the castle was dismantled. Three renegade leaders among the prisoners were sent to Army H.Q., at Windsor, and after trial were condemned to death. The Army Council resolved, however, to execute only one, and lots were drawn for the victim. On two papers was written: "Life given by God." The third, left blank, fell to Poyer, and he was shot.

On the hill beyond the castle are the remains of **Monkton Priory,** founded in 1098. To reach them, cross Monkton Bridge and turn to the right. Of the domestic buildings there are only some fragments among the farm buildings westward of the church, which originally was a double church, the long aisleless nave being used as the parish church, while the services of the monks were held in the chancel. After the dissolution the monastic church was allowed to fall into ruin. In recent years it has been restored.

Two miles from Pembroke is **Pembroke Dockyard,** which was founded nearly 150 years ago. Owing its existence to the establishment of the Royal Naval Dockyard, it has been the scene of building some famous ships for the Navy. It was here that the first steam man-of-war was built, as also the *Victoria and Albert*, the first of the line of Royal Yachts. Opposite the market is a Sunderland Flying Boat preserved as a memorial to the R.A.F. and their use of the base during the Second World War.

TENBY

Angling and Sea Fishing. The principal trout streams in the neighbourhood are at Lampeter Velfrey, 3 miles from Narberth Station; at Llawhaden, 3½ miles from Narberth, and at Ford, 7 miles from Haverfordwest. Tenby Bay abounds with fish, including bass, dabs, gurnards, mackerel, plaice, pollock, soles and whiting. Good sport is obtained from boats. Prawns are taken in the pools along the shore; crabs and lobsters near Giltar, Monkstone, and Waterwynch.

Annual Fixtures. Golf tournament. Bowling Week in August. St. Margaret's Fair held in July under a charter granted by Queen Elizabeth I. Sailing Regatta, takes place on August Bank Holiday Saturday and Sunday.

Banks. *National Provincial*, Tudor Square; *Barclays*, High Street; *Lloyds*, Tudor Square; *Midland*, Tudor Square.

Bathing. Excellent, especially from the South Sands, but swimmers must beware of a strong off-shore current on the south shore when the sea surrounds St. Catherine's Rock. There are no currents on the north shore. Tents may be hired.

Boating. Boats for hire. Motor-boat trips to Caldey Island, Saundersfoot, Lydstep, Pendine, and around the bay. Trips to the Stack Rocks by arrangement. Tenby Sailing Club. Messrs. P. and O. Campbell's Pleasure Steamers make trips to Ilfracombe and along the coast.

Bowling. In South Cliff Gardens.

Camping Sites. Innumerable camping and caravanning facilities. Apply Information Bureau, Guildhall.

Distances. Caldey (*boat*), 2½; Carew Castle, 6½; Freshwater East, 10; Giltar, 1½; Gumfreston, 2; Lamphey, 8; Llawhaden Castle, etc., 12; London, 239; Lydstep Caverns, 4½; Manorbier, 6; Milford Haven, 26½ (12 by Pembroke Dockyard Ferry); Narberth, 10½; Penally 2; Pembroke, 10; St. Issell's, 4; St. Florence, 4½; Saundersfoot, 3; Stack Rocks, 20; Waterwynch, 1.

Early Closing Day. Wednesdays.

Entertainments. Cinemas: *Royal Playhouse*, White Lion Street; *South Beach Pavilion* on South Side. Dancing at *De Valence Pavilion*, Upper Frog Street. Amusement arcade, Warren Street.

Golf. 18-hole course on the Burrows, to the west of the South Sands.

Hotels. Innumerable establishments of all types including: *Royal Gate House*, North Bay; *Esplanade*, *Atlantic*, *Imperial*, *Clarence*, *Cawdor*, *Belgrave*, *Buckingham*, all in Esplanade; and also *Cobourg*, High Street; *Hallsville*, Victoria Street; *Regent*, St. George Street; *White Hart*, *Royal Lion*, *Cliffe*, *Hilton*, *Croft*, *Giltar House*, on sea-front or near. Many others. Full list on application to Information Bureau, Civic Centre.

Information Bureau. Guildhall (Croft entrance). Tel. 2402.

Motor Racing at Lydstep. Speed hill-climbs.

Museum. In a portion of the Castle on Castle Hill.

224

Population. 4,500.
Postal. Head Office in Tudor Square.

Putting Course. South Cliff Gardens.
Tennis. Hard courts at St. John's Hill, and at South Cliff Gardens.

Tenby is situated on a narrow promontory on the western side of Carmarthen Bay. The site is wellnigh unique. The sides of the peninsula are limestone cliffs, in which are paths affording convenient passage between the Esplanade and the sands. At the seaward end of the peninsula is the Castle Hill, with St. Catherine's Isle as a kind of "annexe". On one side of the headland are the Harbour and the North Sands, on the other side are the South Sands, so that a sheltered spot on the margin of the sea can be found whatever wind is blowing; and while one bay attracts by its agreeable coolness in the height of summer, the other has a genial air that is welcome when a low temperature is general.

Tenby is a bright, clean-looking town. The buildings are mostly of stone, and many have received a wash of colour. Viewed from a distance the patches of colour fronting the North Sands and the Harbour, and the old-world air that hangs about the latter, give the place quite a foreign appearance.

The railway station is on the west side of the town. Almost due east is the Castle Hill, and about midway between the two are the business portions and the principal hotels.

Along the eastern side of the parades is a portion of the **Town Walls** which enclosed the old town.

In earlier days there were probably nearly twenty towers and five gateways. The walls may have been first built by William de Valence, Earl of Pembroke, who died in 1296, and was half-brother to Henry III, but there is reason to believe that they were not erected until later, as the earliest known historical reference to them relates to the grant made to the town in 1328 by Edward III of certain dues for seven years to help the inhabitants to enclose their town and build a quay. The walls ran from a small watchtower still standing on the cliffs above the South Sands to a similar tower that was above the North Bay.

At the opening into St. George's Street, about midway between Warren Street and the Esplanade, is the South Gate, locally known as the **Five Arches.** Of these openings, three are modern. The Gateway shows two distinct periods of building. The northern archway was the original portcullis gateway, and it still has the grooves through which the gate was raised or lowered.

Close to the Five Arches is the local War Memorial, and opposite them is the **Roman Catholic Church** of the Holy Rood and St. Teilo. The crucifix in the vestry is of pre-Reformation date.

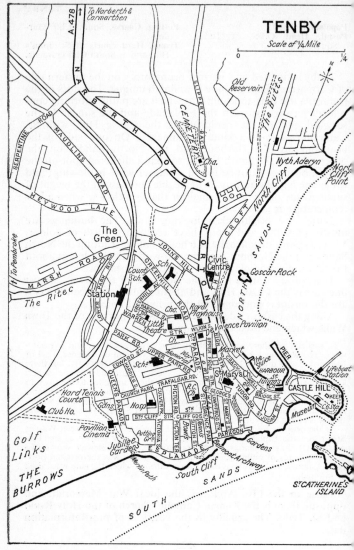

TENBY

Scale of ¼ Mile

0   ¼

To Narberth &
Carmarthen

A.478

NARBERTH ROAD

SERPENTINE ROAD

MAUDLINS ROAD

HEYWOOD LANE

To Pembroke

MARSH ROAD

The Ritec

The Green

CEMETERY

SLIPPERY BACK

Cha.

Old
Reservoir

The Butts

Nyth Aderyn

North
Cliff
Point

North Cliff

CROFT

NORTON

North Sands

Goscar Rock

St. John's Hill

Civic
Centre

GREENHILL AV.

Sch.

County
Sch.

Station

GREENHILL RD.

GREENHILL RD.

Cha.

HARDING ST.

WARREN ST.

Little
Theatre

Co.

Royal
Playhouse

De Valence Pavilion

W.JON'S.

UPPER FROG

Market

The
Norton

The
Juice

Harbour

St. Julian's

PIER

Lifeboat
Station

CASTLE HILL

Museum

QUARRY

LOWER PARK RD.

PARK RD.

EDWARD ST.

WARREN ST.

UPPER PARK RD.

Sch.

HARRIES ST.

TRAFALGAR RD.

CHURCH PARK

CULVER PK.

VICTORIA ST.

Hosp.

Sth
CLIFF

STR. CLIFF GDS.

PICTON RD.

PICTON TER.

Bowls

R.C.

Memorial

Cha.

St. Mary's Ch.

ST. FLORENCE

CROSS ST.

ST. GEORGE'S ST.

WHITE ROSE

WARR HOUSE ST.

ST. MARY'S ST.

TUDOR SQ.

BRIDGE ST.

ST. JULIAN ST.

PARAGON

Belmont Archway

Gardens

QUAY

Castle

St. CATHERINE'S ISLAND

Hard Tennis
Courts

Club Ho.

Golf
Links

THE
BURROWS

Pavilion
Cinema

Jubilee
Gardens

QUEEN'S PARADE

Putting
Grn.

ESPLANADE

Merlin's Path

South Cliff

SOUTH SANDS

TOWN

HIGH ST.

UPPER FROG ST.

© Ward, Lock & Co., Limited

St. Mary's Church, in the centre of the town, is the parish church and, with the exception of St. David's Cathedral, the largest church in Pembrokeshire. The extreme length is 145 feet; the greatest breadth, 80 feet, and it has seating for 1,500. The building is of the Early English and Perpendicular styles. The latter predominates. The building consists of a nave, chancel, wide north and south aisles, and a lofty embattled tower, containing a peal of eight bells and surmounted by an octagonal spire, 152 feet high, forming a landmark for mariners. The only external feature of note is the west doorway, the remnant of a great cruciform porch built in 1490.

An effective feature of the interior is a flight of eleven steps at the eastern end. The west windows are instanced by Freeman as particularly fine examples of the most beautiful form of Perpendicular work, and the choir roof is described by him as "a grand specimen of the cradle form." When it was being repaired in 1842, a cannon ball, probably fired during the siege of Tenby by Cromwell's troops was found in one of the beams.

The holy table contains the slab of the ancient high altar.

The eastern end of the north aisle is **St. Nicholas' Chapel,** with a remarkably designed reredos, and the corresponding part of the south aisle is the **Chapel of St. Anne.** The organ, font, and several windows are memorials to more recent residents.

Of the various tombs and monuments, the most beautiful are those of father and son, *Thomas and John White*, in St. Anne's Chapel, the eastern end of the south aisle. They were members of a family that gave Tenby great merchants and served as mayors of the town. The oldest monument is on the east side of the north entrance. It displays the effigy of a woman (a widow or a nun) under a cinque-foiled canopy, and dates from not later than the early years of the fourteenth century.

Westward of the church are two arches thought to be remains of a Carmelite nunnery, called St. Mary's College, founded in 1399, and still farther west is the Church House. In St. George's Street, on the south side of the church, is an ancient entrance to the churchyard, Town Hall and gaol.

The **Harbour,** protected by a long stone pier, provides good shelter for many small boats and a few trawlers. **St. Julian's Chapel,** at the head, is patronised by fishermen and their families. Beyond the harbour is the lifeboat house and slipway.

Castle Hill is a nearby insular knoll—now a recreation ground—providing good views. The castle remains consist of a watch-tower, part of the main entrance and fragments of the walls. The date of its construction is thought to have been twelfth–thirteenth century. A section of the building now contains a **Museum** (*admission charges*), which contains collections of shells, cave implements, geological specimens and items of local interest.

Elsewhere upon the hill are several ancient cannon. They have been remounted by the School of Artillery, Manorbier, and consist of early seventeenth-century Culverins (weighing about 4,000 lbs. and capable of firing a 15-lb. shot about 2,000 feet) and seventeenth-century Sacres (weighing 2,500 lbs. and firing a 5½-lb. shot about 1,500 feet). The conspicuous monument on the hill is the *Welsh Memorial of the Prince Consort*.

St. Catherine's Rock is a precipitous mass accessible on foot at low water. On it is an impressive fort, constructed to guard the approaches to Pembroke Dockyard (it is now dismantled and converted to a residence (*admission charge*)). In the pools and crannies may be found many zoophytes, seaweeds and anemones that elsewhere on the British coast can usually be obtained only by dredging.

The South Sands extend from Castle Hill to **Giltar Point** a distance of nearly 2 miles. Beyond the Point is **Proud Giltar,** a limestone mass rising 120 feet out of the water. On the Burrows behind South Sands are the golf links. The North Sands stretch for 2 miles to **Monkstone Point,** the headland separating Tenby Roads from Saundersfoot Bay. About the middle of the beach is a great sandstone rock called **Goscar.**

A mile and a half north of Tenby is **Waterwynch,** a pretty little bay backed by fine cliffs. In the next inlet are the **Raven Cliff** and the **Fern Rock.**

Excursions from Tenby

Saundersfoot (*St. Brides, Hean Castle, Cambrian, The Gower*) is a seaside village 3 miles north of Tenby, with a population of about 1,000. It offers safe bathing on a sandy beach, backed by cliffs crowned with trees. To the south of the village is a small harbour the piers enclosing which are pleasant resting-places. The north cliff is occupied by **Hên** (*hayne*) **Castle** and its well-wooded park. "Hên" is Welsh for "old". The local spelling is usually "Hean", an erroneous form of the word.

For an enjoyable ramble from Saundersfoot, follow the cliff-path for 1 mile to **Wiseman's Bridge**, a good spot for a bathe, and there turn inland by a road skirting the grounds of Hên Castle. At the end of about a mile it joins the road from Saundersfoot Station, near **St. Issell's Church** with its distinctive narrow tower.

Pendine, now the site of an experimental rocket station, is a small village on the coast, 8 miles from Saundersfoot, with fine cliff scenery, firm sands and rich in shells. Proceed to Amroth and then follow the main road to **Marros** village. There cross the high land near the church and descend to the shore. Pendine sands are famed in motor-racing circles as the scene of earlier record speeds.

Penally (*Penally House Hotel*) is a picturesque village south-west of Tenby on the slope of the eastern end of the Ridgeway from which it overlooks the Burrows and the sea. The ancient **Church** has a thirteenth-century altar-tomb of William de Naunton and his wife, a Norman font, and two hagioscopes, or squints, at the angles between the chancel and the transepts. Penally is one of the three places in which St. Teilo, the co-founder of Llandaff Cathedral, is said to have been buried. The others are Llandeilo and Llandaff.

Hoyle's Mouth. The name is applied to a cave in the side of a wooded limestone cliff, $1\frac{1}{2}$ miles south-west of Tenby. It is of great geological and archaeological interest. A light is required to explore the cave.

Caldey Island

Passage to and from the island can be made by motor-boat belonging to the monastery, or by private boat. A regular service operates from Tenby harbour.

The Island is private property, but landing is permitted on certain conditions.

Caldey has been called "the Island of the Saints." As early as the sixth century, if not before, it was the site of a monastery. From the twelfth century to the sixteenth Caldey belonged to Benedictines of the Congregation of Tiron. Upon the Dissolution of Monasteries in the reign of Henry VIII it passed into secular hands; in 1906 it became the property of an Anglican Benedictine community which was received into the Church of Rome in 1913, and in 1928 it was sold to Cistercian monks from Chimay, Belgium.

About $2\frac{1}{2}$ miles from Tenby harbour, the island is the natural breakwater of Tenby on the south side. The length is about $1\frac{1}{2}$

miles; the breadth, two-thirds of a mile. About 556 acres consist of highly-productive land.

The **Monastery** (the Abbey of St. Samson) is the principal building on the island. The monks are about forty in number. The village church is a small and very plain building, possibly of Celtic foundation. A lane, overshadowed by a fuchsia hedge of many years' growth, leads to the old monastic buildings dating from the thirteenth century, and the **Priory Church.**

At the south-west corner of Caldey, the highest portion of the island, is a lighthouse. Off the western point a reef of rocks, bare at low tide, connects the island with **St. Margaret's Isle** famed for its cliffs and caves. A watch-tower, thought to date from the eleventh century, overlooks the Priory Bay.

To Gumfreston and St. Florence

Leave Tenby by Greenhill Road and Heywood Lane. About a mile from the railway, bear to the right. On the right are the ruins of Scotsborough House, the residence, early in the seventeenth century, of Thomas ap Rees, whose monument is in Tenby Church.

Gumfreston Church stands almost isolated in a beautifully wooded glen. The tower, the body of the church, and the font are thought to date from about the year 1300. The tower, 65 feet high, is divided into five chambers. In the north wall of the nave is a curious Baptistery. A bronze sanctus bell and some sixteenth-century pewter communion vessels are preserved in a recess behind the pulpit. The chancel arch is exceptionally low. Between the north transept and the chancel is a squint or hagioscope. In the south wall of the chancel is a Decorated piscina. At the lower end of the church-yard are mineral springs, with water said to be similar to that which made Tunbridge Wells famous.

St. Florence is a village some 4½ miles west of Tenby, in a valley of great charm and beauty. From Gumfreston the road ascends to the quaintly-named farm of *Wedlock* and then comes to a mansion called **Ivy Tower.** Just past the gates a lane on the left leads to **St. Florence.** Most of the houses are clustered round the church, one of the oldest in South Pembrokeshire, certainly dark, but well worth a visit. Great chimneys form a striking feature of some of the dwellings.

The return to Tenby can be made by continuing southwards for about a mile to the Ridgeway, or by the popular **Devonshire Drive,** a winding lane in great part arched by noble trees. It is entered against Ivy Tower gates and leads to the Narberth Road.

The **Lydstep Caverns** are about 5½ miles from Tenby by way of the coast and a mile less by the road. The road route lies through Penally and thence to the village of **Lydstep.** From the Post Office a lane leads to Lydstep Haven and a path (right) runs down to Lydstep Caverns. The famous caverns are on the farther side of Lydstep Point, a precipitous, flat-topped limestone mass now cared for by the National Trust. The inlet west of Lydstep Point is **Skrinkle Haven.** It is one of the most striking portions of the coast, for two large masses of rock extend like walls into the sea, and divide the haven into three beautiful coves. On the east the cliffs are composed of grey lime-stone and on the west of green and red sandstone.

Manorbier is an interesting village 5½ miles by road south-west of Tenby.

The **Castle**, the chief attraction, is one of the finest in South Wales. It is a private residence but *is open for viewing daily, including Sundays, from 10.30 to 7 p.m. between* 1 *April and* 30 *September. Admission charges of* 1s. (*children*, 6d.). In the words of Fenton, it is "the most perfect model of an old Norman baron's residence, with all its appendages, church, mill, dove-house, ponds, park and grove, still to be seen and traced." It was originally built in the reign of Henry I by Gerald de Windsor, Constable of Pembroke and husband of the beautiful Nest, a Welsh princess who had been Henry's mistress. Giraldus Cambrensis, the ecclesiastic, topographer, and historian, was their grandson. He was born in Manorbier Castle about 1146.

Below the castle the valley falls to the little bay, a good spot for picnics. The little stream watering the valley flows through marshy land, once occupied by beautiful ponds stocked with fish. Beyond is a round tower, formerly the Columbarium or dove-house. Very few such structures are now standing.

On the opposite side of the valley is the **Church**, an extremely interesting building. It was originally Norman and was erected at the same time as the oldest parts of the castle. The tower dates from about 1270. The north transept was originally Early English. In the fourteenth century the de Barry Chapel was built and the north aisle was added to the nave. The chancel, south transept and south aisle belong to the fifteenth century. The Early English architect formed arches in the Norman walls.

Lamphey Palace is 8 miles west of Tenby and accessible by rail or road. The direct road route is along the **Ridgeway,** with fine views on either hand. There is also the lower road, running through **Lydstep,** near Manorbier, and by **Hodgeston** (*hodson*), where there is a church with a beautiful Decorated chancel and remains of a piscina and sedilia richly ornamented with the "ball-flower". This church also possesses one of the oldest chalices of the church in Wales—an Elizabethan, dated 1569.

Lamphey is 2 miles west of Hodgeston and is a small village consisting of a few quaint old cottages.

The **Palace** (*open Ministry of Public Building and Works standard hours; charge*) was one of the country residences of the Bishops of St. Davids and is now a picturesque ruin. It is commonly said to have been built by Bishop Gower, who held the see from 1328 to 1347, but it was erected partly before and partly after his time, as it is an Early English shell with Perpendicular insertions and additions. The Chapel is a detached building with a fine Perpendicular east window.

Two miles due south of Lamphey is **Freshwater East** with a good expanse of sandy shore good for bathing and yachting. On the right-hand side is Trewent Point, from which there is a fine view. Farther to the west is Greenala Point, on which there is an ancient earthwork.

St. Govan's Head and the Stack Rocks

Note.—The area is now used as a tank-training ground and visitors must be prepared for roads and paths being closed at short notice. Notices of firing days are inserted in local weekly newspapers and displayed in Bosherston Post Office.

St. Govan's Head is the most southerly point of Pembroke and is a favourite resort of motorists and picnic parties. The cliff scenery is wild and grand, and the turf at the top is ideal for an invigorating walk. The wind blows powerfully at times, and strangers are warned of the danger then of approaching too near the cliff edge.

Either going or returning, advantage should be taken of the opportunity of passing through the Stackpole estate. The former beauty of this estate was lost when the trees were felled, but young trees have been planted.

A short drive east from Stackpole village brings one down to **Stackpole Quay,** a charming spot, said to be the smallest quay in Britain. Nearby is **Barafundle Bay** which is reached by a short walk from the quay along a cliff path, which discloses fine scenery. The well-sheltered bay is popular for picnics. Crabs and lobsters are caught locally.

Charmingly placed among the woods about a mile north of Stackpole is **Cheriton, or Stackpole Elidor Church,** a fourteenth-century building restored under the direction of Sir Gilbert Scott. It contains several ancient monuments of the Stackpole family and others and a chantry altar-slab with the inscription CAMU . . . ORIS—FILI FANNVE, which is assigned to the seventh century.

Two miles beyond Stackpole village is the village of **Bosherston.** In the burial-ground is a cross with a carving of the head of Christ, in low relief, at the inter-section of the limbs. Between Bosherston and the sea at Broadhaven (not to be confused with the Broadhaven on St. Bride's Bay) is a series of lakes, probably a drowned river estuary known as the **Lily Ponds** (Angling tickets locally).

In another mile and a half the lane comes to an end on the wind-swept cliffs above **St. Govan's Head.** Just below that point of the cliffs nearest to the lane-end is —

St. Govan's Chapel, a hermitage built across a ravine forming the only approach to the sea for several miles on either side, so that the path actually passes through the building. Tradition and legend have gathered round the building, but there is no historical record. It probably dates from the end of the thirteenth century. The chapel is a small, plain building with a ridge roof and bell-cote. The interior measures 18 feet by 12 feet. The roof is a plain stone vault. On each side of the chapel is a stone seat. Just within are a well and an aumbry. Still in position is a stone altar, said to be the tomb of St. Govan. To the right of the altar are a piscina and an aumbry.

St. Govan's Head stands boldly out to sea about three-quarters of a mile east of the Chapel. This is a grand spot from which to watch the waves crashing on the rocks during a south-westerly gale. Westward from the Chapel the cliff-path in a third of a mile brings us tot he **Huntsman's Leap,** the second ravine westward of that containing the chapel. It owes its name

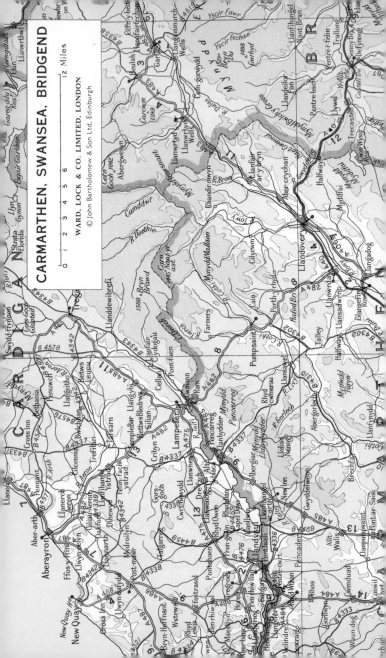

CARMARTHEN, SWANSEA, BRIDGEND

WARD, LOCK & CO. LIMITED, LONDON

© John Bartholomew & Son Ltd, Edinburgh

0 1 2 3 4 5 6   12 Miles

to the tradition that it was cleared by a sportsmen in full career, who afterwards died of fright inspired by reflecting upon his feat.

A little farther is **Bosherston Mere,** a small circular opening near the edge of the cliff. It is the top of a natural funnel that comes up from a large cave. When the sea dashes into the cave, the air is driven out through the funnel and carries with it clouds of foam.

Half a mile farther is a small cliff castle on the left and in another mile and a half a small bush-like patch generally called the **Sunken Forest.**

From the shore of **Bullslaughter Bay** there is a good view of the Stack Rocks and of a fine natural arch, "The Green Bridge".

A short mile from the "forest" is a cliff camp enclosing the **Devil's Punch Bowl,** a magnificent cauldron which the sea enters through an arch. The sides go down perpendicularly to a depth of some 150 feet. The crannies are the nesting-places of sea-gulls. The best view is obtained from the seaward side. The edge can be approached with safety if care is taken to avoid the narrow fissures in the surrounding rock. The scene is one to which no description could do justice, or convey any idea of its sublimity and grandeur.

Just beyond the cauldron are the far-famed **Stacks,** two lofty columns of limestone, which from April to the first week in August are the haunt of innumerable seabirds, principally guillemots and razor-bills. The eggs are laid on the bare rock.

From a point a little westward of the Stack Rocks three fine natural arches may be seen in a line. Half a mile beyond this viewpoint is an inlet called the **Wash,** containing a huge slab of limestone, rich in fossil corals and having a curiously rippled and fissured surface.

A visit to Pembroke from Stack Rocks may be made by way of **Warren,** which has a church with a fine tower and steeple, and through **Monkton,** or *via* Castlemartin and Freshwater West with its fine beach.

Carew (pronounced *Carey*), 6½ miles west of Tenby, via Gumfreston, is the site of some fine castle remains, a church, and an ancient stone cross.

The **Church** (at Carew Cheriton, on the south side of the main road) is a cruciform building mainly in the Decorated style, but it has a Perpendicular embattled tower. The main part of the structure is assigned to Bishop Gower (d. 1347) whose favourite four-leaved flower will be noticed on the pier arches. In the chancel are effigies of a knight-crusader (thought to be Sir N. Carew [d. 1311]) and a priest. In the north transept, formerly the mortuary chapel of the Carew family, is an altar-tomb with effigies of Sir John Carew (d. 1637) and Elizabeth his wife. In the churchyard is a small disused ossuary chapel.

About half a mile north of the church is **Carew Castle** (*admission charge*, 10–4 or 7: *Sundays during August only*, 2.30–5.30) on a slight hill overlooking a creek of Milford Haven (one of the best views is from the far end of the bridge). During the Civil War it was garrisoned for the King, but when Tenby Castle fell Carew surrendered also.

Much of the work remaining was done under the direction of Sir Rhys ap Thomas, the chief Welsh supporter of Henry VII, and Sir John Perrott, supposed to be a natural son of Henry VIII. The plan of the building is rectangular, with a round-fronted tower at each angle and a gate-house on the east front. The chapel, in a tower on the east side, has a groined roof and probably dates from the time of Edward II. On the east side of the first floor is a fireplace with the arms of Spain. North and east of the quadrangle are the State apartments, and other rooms partly built by Sir John Perrott. At various points flights of steps lead to the battlements.

Overlooking the road is a **Celtic Cross,** of the ninth or tenth century, 14 feet high and richly decorated with the characteristic Celtic interwoven scrolls. In a small panel on the back is an inscription, in Latin minuscles, often translated "Meredith of Rheged. f. x." Rheged was an ancient district of South Wales. A cast of the cross can be seen in the National Museum of Wales.

Llawhaden is 14 miles north of Tenby. It is best reached by road or by rail to Narberth, from which it is 4 miles distant.

Narberth is a market town with over 1,000 inhabitants. South of the town amidst grazing land are the fragments of a **Castle,** probably Edwardian. For a time Narberth Castle was held by Roger Mortimer, the favourite of Isabella, the consort of the unfortunate Edward II.

For Llawhaden go to the right from Narberth Station. Cross the top of the town to the vicarage and go straight on to Robeston Wathen, crowned by a venerable-looking church. Walkers are allowed to pass through the gate of Robeston Wathen house and along the drive. Pass through the gate at the end of the drive, take the lane in front and descend the hill, or cross the fields about half a mile down the lane.

Llawhaden Church is prettily situated by the side of the East Cleddau. Built into the east wall is an ancient cross. A chapel contains the mutilated effigy of Bishop Houghton of St. Davids (d. 1389). A steep lane opposite the churchyard gates leads to the **Castle,** a former residence of the Bishops of St. Davids and for many years an uncared-for ruin. In 1930, however, the Ministry of Public Building and Works became the guardians of the castle and much-needed renovation and other work was put in hand. It can be visited at any reasonable time (*small admission charge*).

THE VALLEY OF THE TOWY
Carmarthen—Llandeilo—Llandovery

The Valley of the Towy is a fertile tract some 30 miles long and 2 miles wide in a wild and rugged region. It crosses Carmarthenshire from north-east to south-west, and is the largest valley in the county. The hills that rise on either side are beautifully wooded or richly grassed. The valley contains the market towns of Llandeilo and Llandovery, while the port of Carmarthen commands all the traffic through the fertile land round the head of the estuary.

The Vale of Towy has been called "the heart of South Wales". It is famous in Welsh life, Welsh history, and Welsh song. In the days of the Welsh Princes it was the political centre of the southern kingdom, and, save Glamorgan, was the most distinguished strip of South Wales.

The river that runs through the valley has been "celebrated for all time for the sewin that begin to run in the first July floods." As in the Usk and Teifi, fish run up it freely, travelling far into the mountain gorges. It is partly preserved, but permission to fish is readily obtained.

Carmarthen

Buses. Carmarthen is connected with Cardigan, Newcastle Emlyn, Pontyberem, New Quay, Llanelly and Ammanford, Brecon, Pendine, Tenby, Haverfordwest, Aberystwyth, Laugharne and Aberayron. There are daily road services to Cardiff and London.

Cinemas. *Capitol,* John Street; *Lyric,* King Street.

Early Closing Day. Thursdays. *Market Days.* Wednesdays and Saturdays.

Distances. Cardigan, 28; Fishguard, 40; Haverfordwest, 30; London, 212; Tenby, 27; Newcastle Emlyn, 20; Llandeilo, 15; Kidwelly, 9; St. Clears, 9; Swansea, 27.

Hotels. *Boar's Head; Ivy Bush Royal; Park; Golden Lion; Red Lion; Nelson; Jeremy's Commercial.*

Museum. County Museum in Quay Street.

Population. 12,910.

Post Office. King Street.

Though Carmarthen has no notable building to appeal to the general visitor, apart from its Parish Church, there is very much to interest the stranger in the life of the town, which is a busy, old-fashioned place. A number of the streets are narrow, irregular and steep. The assizes for three counties are held in the town, as are also various shows, races, and meetings of more than local interest. Carmarthen stands on rising ground on the north side of the Towy. The site was occupied by the Roman settlement of Maridunum, the "sea fort", of which the word Carmarthen (Welsh *Caerfyrddin*) is the Celtic equivalent. It presents a striking appearance when viewed from the bridge over the river, as the buildings extend from the edge of the stream to the summit of the ridge which is backed by the higher ground of Penlan Hill, while away to the right are the Hills of Merlin (3 miles) and Llangunnor. A splendid wide bridge spans the Towy.

The Roman occupation of the site extended beyond the later boundary of the town, as marked by the wall which once defended it. Relics of Roman times are to be seen in the County Museum in Quay Street.

The **Castle** occupied one point of the ridge on which Carmarthen stands. Two towers, gatehouse and outer walls remain intact, but they are so obscured by buildings that little can be seen of them from the town side, while the ramparts are blocked with houses built against them. At one period Carmarthen was the residence of the Princes of South Wales, and town and castle were then frequently attacked either by the English, or by the Welsh who sought to recover them from the English. During the Civil War the castle more than once changed hands. It was finally dismantled by the Parliamentarians. Castle Hill is now the site of County Hall and most of the county council offices.

St. Peter's Church at the east end of Spilman Street is an old building on the highest ground in the older portion of the town. The date of its erection is unknown. The earliest reference to the building is in a document of the time of Henry I (1100–1135). The south aisle and its chancel were built about 400 years ago. The east end of the south aisle is the Consistory Court of the Bishop of St. Davids.

In Priory Street is the carefully-guarded stump of an **Oak Tree**, the palladium of Carmarthen, according to one of the legends connected with it. The English rendering is—

> "When this oak shall tumble down,
> So will fall Carmarthen town."

King Street terminates in **Nott Square,** the site of a monument to the memory of General Sir William Nott. Within the railings enclosing the monument is a tablet commemorating the martyrdom of Dr. Robert Ferrar, Bishop of St. Davids, who was burned here during the Marian persecution of the Protestants in 1555.

The **Bulwark,** a popular promenade, runs for about a mile on the south side of the river. There is a similar walk on the north side. Boating is popular, and in the fishing season several coracles are still to be seen.

Penlan Hill to the north of Carmarthen is the highest point in the immediate vicinity. From the summit an almost bird's-eye view of the town is obtained, as well as a wide prospect over the surrounding country. On the hills in the middle distance is **Nelson's Tower,** or Paxton's Tower as it is locally called, because it was erected by Sir William Paxton.

Abergwili, a small village 2 miles from Carmarthen, near the confluence of the Gwili and the Towy, may be reached by following the main road to which Priory Street leads, or by the Parade, by turning left there, and proceeding by Pond Side (the path alongside the little stream) to the high road. It is the site of the palace of the Bishop of St. Davids. Bishop Richard Davies, the translator of the Bible into Welsh, was buried at Abergwili, and the pretty little church contains a monument to his memory.

Merlin's Hill is a wooded height about a mile beyond Abergwili.

Llangunnor Hill is a beautiful hill on the south side of the Towy, 1½ miles from the town. In the church near the top is a monument to Sir Richard Steele, the essayist, who lived for a time near the foot of the hill.

Llangyndeyrn Lime Rocks are a mile south-east of the village from which they take their name. The village is on the *Gwendraeth Fach,* one of the best trout streams in the county. It is 6 miles from Carmarthen by the upper Llanelly road, which passes within a quarter of a mile of the summit of the neighbouring limestone ridge. Upon the ridge are two ancient stone circles. At Capel Dyddgen, on the right-hand side of the road, are the ruins of an ecclesiastical building, and near it is a large cave.

Llanstephan (*Union Hall, Castle*) may be reached by bus from Carmarthen (8 miles). On the summit of a precipitous hill, of which the base is washed by the sea, is the shell of a castle. The parish church dates from the twelfth century. There is a pretty cliff walk around the hill to **St. Anthony's Well.**

Laugharne is an old borough teeming with interest for those with antiquarian tastes. It is situated on the coast between Llanstephan and Pendine (p. 229), about 12 miles from Carmarthen, from which it can be approached *via* **St. Clears,** on the main road between Carmarthen and Pembroke. It has a castle of which the keep and a gate named after Henry II are in a good state of preservation.

Kidwelly

The borough of Kidwelly lies due south of Carmarthen, from which it is 9 miles by road and 12 by rail. It is at the confluence and combined mouth of the *Gwendraeth Fawr* and *Gwendraeth Fach,* whence it derives its name in Welsh of *Cydweli.* The borough is one of the oldest in the Principality having received its first charter under Henry I.

The town is chiefly noteworthy for a noble old **Castle,** the remains of which have been carefully strengthened so that the relic is the best preserved of the nine castles in Carmarthenshire. It was originally founded during the times of Henry I, the earthwork defence being of this period.

237

Later additions were made in the time of Edward II. (*Ministry of Works Standard Hours; charge.*) The four round towers enclosing the courtyard can be climbed. Two other towers flank the gateway, which is nearly perfect ; another is on the outer side, and from the east face of the castle the chapel tower projects.

The **Church** dedicated to St. Mary the Virgin during the Norman period, belonged to a former Benedictine Priory founded by Roger, Bishop of Salisbury (1107–39) as a cell of Sherborne Abbey. It is one of the few monastic churches which were preserved at the suppression of the monasteries, and permitted to remain as the church of the parish.

North-west of Kidwelly on the Towy estuary is the village of **Ferryside** from which there is good bathing.

Llandeilo

Angling. In the Towy. Particulars from Hon. Sec., Llandeilo Angling Association.

Early Closing Day. Thursdays.

Golf. 9-hole course.

Hotels. *Cawdor Arms; Angel; Castle; King's Head; Salutation; Waverley.*

Markets Provision market on Saturday; cattle, alternative Mondays.

Population 1,906

Situated on a high bluff in the heart of the Towy valley, the historic little market town of Llandeilo has many attractions to offer the visitor who seeks the quiet rest of a rural scene. Charming from a distance, it does not disappoint at close quarters. Those with a taste for country sports—golfing, fishing, shooting, tennis, bowls, walking, etc.—will find ample provision for their inclinations. The town derives its name from its **Church,** which is dedicated to St. Teilo. The church was rebuilt in 1848 in the Decorated style, but the tower is Perpendicular. On the wooded height called Penlanfawr is **Penlan Park,** presented to the town by the sixth Lord Dynevor.

Dynevor Park, a large and very beautiful tract, adjoins the town. Visitors accompanied by permanent residents may enter from the lodge on the Carmarthen road, just beyond the market, or by a broad pathway which leads from the bridge and passes the pretty little church of **Llandyfeisant.** Above the church the two roads meet and lead towards **Dynevor Castle,** the home of the Dynevor family since the fifteenth century (*written application to visit*).

Llyn Llech Owen, or the lake of Owen's Stone, is a lovely beauty-spot some six miles out on the Llanelly road. The yellow water-lily grows here.

Carreg Cennen Castle, a ruined fortress south-east of Llandeilo, is with its surroundings one of the most striking sights in this part of Wales. It is 4¾ or 7 miles from Llandeilo, according to the route taken. Motorists take the road alongside the *Cennen* river, or a south-easterly course (steeper) over the Trichrûg ridge past Caeglas and up Penstorom Hill. The former means a journey of 7 miles, the latter one of 4½ miles.

The **castle** (*charge. Ministry hours*) stands on a 300-foot high rock on three sides of which are precipitous crags. On the only accessible side the approach is commanded by two towers. On the south side, near a short flight of steps, is an iron gate guarding a passage, partly built and partly bored through the solid rock for 150 feet. The castle consists of an outer ward, an elaborate ramped entrance, heavily defended, and an inner ward defended by corner towers and a fine gatehouse. The domestic quarters occupy the east side of the inner ward.

Dryslwyn Castle lies about 5 miles west of Llandeilo, on the north side of the Towy. Portions only of the hall and chapel remain. While it was being besieged in the reign of Edward I, unskilful mining brought down one of its towers upon a party of the besiegers, causing the death of many, including Lord Stafford and other persons of note.

Llandovery

Buses. Between Llandovery and Brecon, Ammanford and Lampeter, etc.

Distances. Carmarthen, 27; Llandeilo, 12; Swansea, 34; Lampeter, 21; London 185; Brecon, 21; Builth, 23.

Early Closing Day. Thursdays.

Hotels. *Castle, Royston, North Western, Dyfri, Picton Court.*

Market Day. Friday.

Population. 1,950.

Llandovery, a busy trading centre of a large agricultural district is an attractive town. Its College is one of the principal public schools of Wales.

The word "Llandovery" is a corruption of the Welsh Llan-ym-ddyfri, meaning the "Church among the Waters", an appropriate name, as the town is situated between the Towy and its feeder, the Bran, while the Gwydderig and other streams are in the immediate vicinity. On a knoll, approached through the yard of the Castle Hotel, is a small fragment of the **Castle,** which once dominated the district. It is said to have been erected by the Normans about the year 1100, and almost immediately to have been taken by the Welsh, who retained possession until the time of Edward I.

Llanfair Church at the north end of the town contains the grave of William Williams, the greatest writer of hymns Wales has ever produced.

In the burial-ground of **Llandingat Church** at the opposite end of the town is the grave of the celebrated *Rhys Prichard* who became vicar in 1602 and gained fame by his preaching powers and as the author of the metrical stanzas forming the contents of *Canwyll y Cymry*, or *The Welshman's Candle*, a book that is said to have done more good in Wales than any other except the Bible.

Trecastle, a quiet little village, is 9 miles east of Llandovery on the bank of the Usk, and on the Llandovery–Brecon road at a point where it is met by the Trecastle Old Road and other roads. The road runs in the valley of Afon Gwydderig, which in parts is a deep wooded glen. The old road between Trecastle and Llandovery runs over high ground, and affords lovely views. It passes by the ancient camp on Y Pigwn, a conspicuous hill between the Gwydderig River and the head-waters of the Usk. At Trecastle is the Cwm Wysg reservoir of Swansea Corporation.

Ascent of the Carmarthen Van. The only mountains of South Wales which have a greater height than the **Carmarthen Van** or Beacon (2,632 feet) are the Brecon Beacons. A few hundred feet below the summit are lakes famed for their trout. Enthusiastic anglers occasionally camp on the mountain-side. The nearest inn, *The Cross Inn*, is 1½ miles from the church on the Llangadock-Trecastle mountain road.

The **Shortest Route from Llandovery** is *via* **Myddfai** (*muthva*), 4 miles, and Llanddeusant, 8 miles, to Blaenau Farm, 9 miles. The road as far as Myddfai is very fair, but the remainder of the route is mainly along winding lanes with steep pitches, and is very rough for cars. Alternatively Blaenau Farm may be reached *via* **Llangadock** mid way between Llandovery and Llandeilo. At Bleanau Farm a steep climb begins. The lake seen on the side of the mountain must be kept on the left, and 2 miles from Blaneau the ridge will be gained at a point 2 miles to the west of the highest peak.

Caio is on the Lampeter road about 8 miles from Llandovery. The route lies through the pretty village of **Llanwrda,** and along the winding glen of Cwmdwr, the Dulas stream being crossed and recrossed several times. Caio and its neighbourhood are full of historic interest. At **Maes-llan-wrthwl** a great battle is said to have been fought between the Romans and Britons. The Roman commander fell. His two monumental stones, mentioned in Gibson's *Camden*, are now to be seen at Pant-y-polion. The neighbourhood contains several tumuli, and Roman bricks are frequently discovered in turning the soil.

For **Llanwrtyd Wells** and the continuation of the road through the Irfon Valley, see p. 296.

The Towy at Llandeilo (*G. D. Bolton*)

The Teifi at Cenarth (*G. D. Bolton*)

Langland Bay, Gower (*G. D. Bolton*)

The Sugarloaf, near Abergavenny (*Woolverto*

SWANSEA, GOWER AND DISTRICT

Swansea

Airport. Scheduled services to London, Midlands, Channel Islands, Ireland and the Continent.

Bathing. Sea-bathing on the foreshore at Trafalgar Arch, near Swansea Bay Station, Brynmill, and at the various bays around the Gower peninsula. Fresh water baths close to the sands.

Buses, etc. Buses cover the principal streets and serve the suburbs. Also services to Neath, Aberavon, Port Talbot, Margam, Blackpill, Oystermouth, Parkmill, Oxwich, Reynoldston and other places in Gower as well as long-distance services to Carmarthen, Cardiff, etc.

Distances. Cardiff, 40; Brecon, 39; Bridgend, 21; Carmarthen, 27; Llanelly, 11; London, 192; Neath, 8; Mumbles, 5.

Early Closing Day. Thursdays, excepting grocers (Mumbles — Wednesdays).

Entertainments. There is a theatre and several cinemas. In the parks there are concerts during the summer.

Fishing. Soles, cod, gurnet, ling, whiting, and other fish are caught near the shore.

Golf. *Swansea Bay Golf Club*, Jersey Marine, Neath. Bus services from Swansea to Neath. *Clyne Golf Club*, overlooking bay, 3 miles from Swansea (18 holes). *Langland Bay* course of 18 holes, 6 miles from Swansea High Street. *Pennard Golf Club*, (18 holes), 8 miles from Swansea High Street. Close to sea. Also at Morriston Golf Club, 18 holes, 3 miles. There is a small municipal course at Blackpill.

Hotels. *Grand; Mackworth; Dragon; Dolphin*, etc.

Market. Oxford Street. The largest in Wales.

Population. 171,000. The second largest town in Wales.

Post Office. In Wind Street.

Tennis and Bowls. In the public parks.

Swansea (in Welsh *Abertawe*) has for long been a favourite resort of holiday-makers by reason of its sea-bathing and the natural beauty of its surroundings. In addition it has almost a monopoly in the exportation of anthracite, the valley, of which the town is the natural outlet, being very rich in this fuel.

Swansea is exceedingly fortunate in its situation, and so contrives to combine the stern duties of an oil-port with the pleasures of a holiday resort. From the mouth of the River Tawe there stretches westward a magnificently curved bay. Although the eastern end is concealed by the shore line railway, from Blackpill to Mumbles magnificent panoramic views may be enjoyed from the road.

Among the notable dates in Swansea's history is 1306, when it received a charter conferring the privilege of building and repairing ships. In 1791 it obtained its first Harbour Act.

The first dock was opened in 1852. In 1850 the former Great Western Railway arrived at Swansea and in 1923 its docks, which now number five and cover an area of 270 acres, were transferred to that Company; in 1924 a new dry dock was opened. A further dry dock, 675 feet long, serving ships of 32,000 tons deadweight has been constructed.

The chief exports are oil, coal, coke, tin-plate and iron and steel; and the chief imports oil (very much more than half the total), iron and steel (including scrap) building and road-making materials, grain, timber and general merchandise.

Swansea acquired a new industry when it was selected by the Anglo-Iranian Oil Company as their port in Great Britain. Their tankers enter the Queen's Dock, and from the tankers' holds the oil is pumped, through an underground pipe track 4 miles long, into refineries at **Llandarcy**, near **Skewen**, where has sprung up a complete miniature township consisting of shops, churches, chapels, a railway station, a hospital, schools and hundreds of houses. After treatment the oil is pumped back for distribution. Llandarcy is linked by an oil pipe line to the oil port at Milford Haven. The town is named after Mr. D'Arcy, who discovered the Persian Oilfields in 1903.

As Cardiff is the general name of the eastern section of the South Wales ports, so Swansea is the general name for the western section, comprising Port Talbot, Neath (including Briton Ferry), Llanelly and Burry Port, each with its own individuality. The area has a radius of about 16 miles, and within it, besides the modern mammoth steel and tinplate works at Margam, Velindre and Trostre, there are many other works and a large number of collieries. Swansea town is the cradle and nursery of Siemens steel.

Swansea is seen to best advantage by those who approach by sea. The bay is a broad and beautiful crescent comprising nearly half the coast-line of Glamorgan. Long piers mark the harbour entrance, and as the town is built in terraces along the hill-side, it produces a striking and pleasant impression when viewed from the water.

The docks are at the eastern end of the town, and the whole of the industries are enclosed in the valleys extending northward and eastward. The beauties of the town lie westward of its High Street.

Although Swansea appears to be very irregularly built, a few words will convey an idea of its general plan. The River Tawe runs north to south through the town, which is chiefly situated on the western side of the stream. Running almost parallel with the river are High Street, Castle Street and Wind Street, forming one long curved thoroughfare extending from the railway station to dockland. From this thoroughfare branch off to the west three principal thoroughfares, each quite a mile long. The northernmost is the Alexandra Road–Walter Road, which goes off opposite the Western Region station. On one side of Alexandra Road is the building containing

242

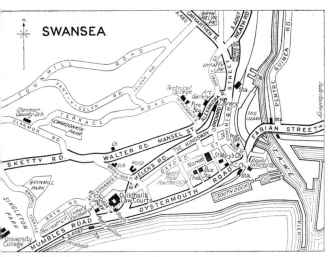

© Ward, Lock & Co., Limited

the **Public Library** and the **College of Art.** On the opposite side of the road is the **Glynn Vivian Art Gallery,** containing a fine collection of old and modern masters, and other works of art. **Walter Road** is a broad boulevard with some of the finest residences in the town; it leads to the picturesque suburb of Sketty. Parallel to Walter Road is the fine new **Kingsway** with dual carriageway divided by strip flower gardens and lined by modern shops almost continental in aspect. At the eastern end of this thoroughfare is a large island of shrubs and flowers from which leads **Princess Way** to join **Oxford Street.** In Oxford Street is the **Market,** the largest in Wales.

St. Helens Road and Oxford Street merge together near the fine **Guildhall and Law Courts** which occupies much of the site of the former Victoria Park. The buildings are modern with a conspicuous tower. Adjoining is an indoor swimming bath and the Brangwyn Hall with its art gallery. Behind the buildings are tennis courts and bowling greens, and the **Patti Pavilion,** used for concerts, dancing, etc. Close by is the **St. Helen's Football Ground.**

The **Castle,** which gives its name to the central portion of the long thoroughfare running north and south, is said to have been built after 1106 by an Earl of Warwick. It was rebuilt by Bishop Gower, of St. Davids, about 1330. The remains have been incorporated into modern buildings used as offices by the *South Wales Evening Post.*

In Victoria Road, near the Docks terminus of railways and Victoria Station, stands the **Royal Institution of South Wales,** founded in 1835. It comprises the **Swansea Museum** (*daily* 10–5; *admission* 6d.), containing a collection of Welsh "bygones," with a Welsh kitchen and prehistoric relics from the caves of Gower. The library and reading-room are open to members only.

A short distance from the Royal Institution is the newly built **St. Mary's Church.** In Singleton Park on the Mumbles road is **Swansea University College,** built in 1920, and since greatly enlarged. Adjoining is the mammoth Swansea Hospital.

This railway and the public road skirt Swansea Bay. About half-way to Mumbles is *Black Pill*, with its single-arched bridge, wrongly attributed to the Romans. Hereabouts is the Clyne Castle estate, formerly the home of Admiral Vivian but now acquired by the Swansea University College. The renowned rhododendron gardens are open to the public. Further developments at Blackpill include a boating lake and children's pleasure gardens known as Blackpill Lido. A pleasant garden walk along the sea-front has now been made at Lilliput, between Blackpill and West Cross.

MUMBLES, OR OYSTERMOUTH

Mumbles, or Oystermouth (*Mermaid, George, Antelope*), long the favourite resort of Swansea people, extends along the curve of the bay which it fronts, and climbs the high ridge of the western horn of the inlet. Boating, bathing, sea-fishing, tennis and bowls are popular pastimes. There is a good motor road round the head, with parking-places and refreshment facilities. **Mumbles Pier** is well-equipped with all kinds of modern amusements. Adjoining the *Mumbles Pier Hotel* is a fine dance hall.

244

Perched on high ground, some 200 yards inland from the shore, is ivy-clad **Oystermouth Castle,** the successor of a castle burnt in 1257. The chapel and some of the apartments are in fairly good preservation. Upper rooms can be reached by staircase, and there is a path along the top of the outer wall.

The **Parish Church,** of Norman origin, contains a font dated 1251, and the grave of Thomas Bowdler, of Bath, the expurgator of Shakespeare and Gibbon.

Mumbles Head, made famous by the heroic action of its "Grace Darlings", the sisters Ace, daughters of the lighthouse-keeper, is the outer of two islets off Mumbles Point. The islets can be reached on foot at the lowest tides. Under the lighthouse is a small cavern known as **Bob's Cave.** About half a mile to the west are the **Mixon Sands,** marked by a bell-buoy. Between the village and the Head are the Lifeboat and Coastguard stations.

On the southern side of the Head is **Bracelet Bay,** a favourite picnic ground. The name is a corruption of Broadslade, while "slade" is the equivalent of "slide" and has reference to a landslip. The cliffs here present lovely views across to the Devon and Somerset coasts and eastward to the hills behind Swansea.

Gower

Accommodation. There are hotels at Oystermouth (The Mumbles), Langland Bay, Caswell Bay, Bishopston, Parkmill and Reynoldston. There is fairly good accommodation at Port Eynon, and there are some houses where a bed can possibly be obtained at Pwll-du Bay and Llanrhidian. Accommodation can also be obtained in Rhossili.

Road Routes. The Gower road leaves Swansea at Alexandra Road, Sketty Road, etc., and runs more or less through the centre of the peninsula. For Oystermouth, the Mumbles and neighbouring bays take St. Helens road and follow the shore past the University College; but for Bishopston, Pennard, Oxwich, Port Eynon, etc., turn inland at Black Pill.

Gower, the "land of the setting sun", the wild peninsula, forms an ideal playground westward of Swansea. It is some 14 miles in length from the Mumbles in the east to Worms Head on the west, and is from 4 to 6 miles broad. For the walker there is no more inviting district in the whole country. It is an area of agricultural or common land, with a picturesque coast of limestone cliffs on its southern side. Inland it is traversed by good roads and footpaths, and all along the coast there is a most interesting cliff route. The bays have beaches of smooth sand; some are noted for the beauty and peculiarity of their shells, and at most of them fishing and boating can be enjoyed. Running inland from the coast are picturesque glens and valleys. For anglers there are the Burry, Parkmill and Bishopston streams holding small trout, and in the season a few sea-trout; there is a lake at Penllergaer, near Morriston, holding fine trout, large tench, carp, perch and roach. For both the rivers and the lake permission to fish must be obtained.

The South Coast of Gower

From Oystermouth to Worms Head the coast presents a succession of interesting features. A road in continuation of the Parade leads through a cutting in the limestone cliff to Bracelet Bay, whence the coast can be followed to **Limeslade Bay** and **Rotherslade Bay,** with bungalows and refreshment booths, which indicate a popularity with day visitors. Rotherslade Bay is but a miniature opening, and is really a part of—

Langland Bay, about 1½ miles from Mumbles Head (*Langland Bay, Osborne, Brynfield, Eastbourne*). This is a beautiful inlet with a fine stretch of level sand, a belt of shingle, another of rocks, a few green meadows, then a series of villa-dotted inclines. Here, as elsewhere, the rocks are worn into grotesque shapes by the waves.

Caswell Bay .(*Caswell Bay, Caswell Cottage*) is reached by a road which winds down through a bracken-covered valley, in some respects more beautiful than Langland. It has even better sands, and the outer rocks on both sides are remarkable for the number of caves.

Brandy Cove, at the western end of Caswell Bay is a wild little inlet with traditions of the contraband trade in brandy.

Pwll-du (black-pool) **Bay,** about a mile to the west, with a pebbly ridge along its front, is shut in on its western side by a great headland of red limestone. (Bus to Pyle Corner, a mile from the coast.) It lies at the outlet of—

Bishopston Valley, one of the prime beauty-spots of Gower (National Trust). It is a narrow, tortuous gorge through the limestone, running inland for about three miles. Through the gorge flows a river which, for over a mile, has an underground course. At the head is the village of **Bishopston,** some 2 miles from Caswell.

To the west of Pwll-du Head is more National Trust land, including—

Bacon Hole, a hollow in the cliff, in which the bones of ancient animals and prehistoric wall paintings were discovered in 1850. A little farther westward is **Minchin Hole,** another cave that proved to be rich in bones.

About a mile beyond Minchin Hole is—

Three Cliffs Bay, so called from three huge cliffs prominent in the view from the sea. It is a pretty spot. There are bold masses of rock, glittering sands, a background of wooded hills and a tiny stream, the *Pennard Pill,* which flows from the valley called Cwm Ilston. On the east side of the bay is **Pennard Castle,** an uninteresting ruin, and westward is a huge mass of limestone known as **Great Tor.** A good road runs from Pennard Church, across the Common to the turf-covered cliffs. At low-water the sands can be crossed to Oxwich, 2 miles away. Less than a mile from Pennard Castle is *Gower Inn,* at **Parkmill,** a pretty spot reminiscent of Devonshire, on the main road from Swansea.

The walk across the sands of—

Oxwich Bay, very popular with visitors, opens up views of richly wooded cliffs and other fine scenery. The place from which the bay takes its name is but a hamlet, with guest house accommodation at the Rectory and houses and farms at **Horton,** between Oxwich and Port Eynon. Oxwich Church is built on a rocky ledge in a grove of trees at the extreme end of the bay. The building seen standing above the hamlet during the walk across the sands is **Penrice Church,** prettily situated and on a fine view-point. Within view also are the modern **Penrice Castle,** occasionally open to view, and the ivied ruin of the ancient building which it has replaced. Oxwich also has the remnant of a Castle now used as a farmhouse. It is about 1½ miles from the hamlet, from which it is approached by a beautifully wooded but steep lane. The principal portions are a six-storeyed tower and a gateway bearing the arms of Sir Rice Mansel, who built it in 1541.

Port Eynon Bay has over a mile of excellent sands which stretch from Horton near the eastern end to **Port Eynon** on the west. The latter is a quaint village with two old thatched cottages and an old lifeboat house which now serves as a popular Youth Hostel. The sea fishing is good and the small craft sailing popular. The descent by car to the village is down a steep hill with some very sharp turns.

The coast from Port Eynon Point to Overton Mere and on to Overton Cliff has been purchased for public use. This part, well-known for its lobster and crab fishing, includes just west of the Point—

Culver Hole, a curious cave not easy to find without a guide. The natural entrance has been nearly closed with masonry. Within are upper floors which were reached by a staircase and each of which has a window opening.

There is a cliff walk most of the way from Overton to Rhossili, about 2 miles along which are the **Paviland Caves,** two in number, about a hundred yards apart, at a point called Yellow Top by reason of the golden patches of lichen upon it. The caves are accessible by land only at dead low-water.

About a mile westward of Yellow Top and reached by a lane from Middleton (on bus route) is—

Mewslade Bay, generally considered the most picturesque inlet in all Gower. Around it are stupendous cliffs, carved by the water into every variety of fantastic form.

Thurba Head, east of Mewslade Bay, the adjoining Pitton Cliffs and much of Paviland Cliffs are National Trust property.

At Middleton the road turns sharply to the right and climbs the hill-side to give magnificent views westward as it goes on to **Rhossili,** a quiet little village on a fine cliff overlooking Rhossili Bay, with its 3 miles long beach. (Hotel: *Wormshead Cottage.*) The church has a good Norman doorway and a quaint little tower, and there is a tablet to Evans who died with Scott on his fatal polar adventure. Evans was born in Rhossili. The sands are magnificent and from the top of the Down, 633 feet high, on the north side of the village, there is an extensive view. On the summit are chambered tombs and a few cairns.

Worms Head, at the western extremity of the south coast, and reached by a breezy walk over the turf from Rhossili, is a noble promontory broken up into cliff and chasm. It is a mile from the mainland to the extreme point and the Head is the outer of two islets. Between the two islets is the **Devil's Bridge,** a narrow but not dangerous track over the neck of rocks. The Head rises about 200 feet above high-water. In one of the rocks is a blow-hole.

Reynoldston (*King Arthur Hotel*) is a small, pleasant village standing around a green and possessing one of the few hotels that are to be found in Gower away from the Mumbles and neighbouring resorts. The village (buses to and from Swansea, 12 miles) is at the western end of Cefn-y-Bryn and is a good centre for walks over the neighbouring commons, with their keen air and fine views, as well as to the various coves, bays and villages around the Gower coast.

About a mile from the village is the cromlech known as **Arthur's Stone,** a block 14 feet long, 6 feet wide and 8 feet thick, resting on smaller stones. The way to it from the hotel is across the green and then to the right up the hill-side. At the top the moor is crossed near a diminutive tarn, and from the opposite slope the stone is seen standing in a hollow.

Weobley Castle, an interesting ruin, stands about a mile and a quarter west of Llanrhidian. It was a medieval fortified manor house, the hall and kitchen wing dating from the late thirteenth century, the solar, gate-house range and chapel of slightly later date. Admission 3*d.*

Near **Llanrhidian Church** are some stone stocks.

Penclawdd on the coast is well-known for its cockles.

Llangennith is between 4 and 5 miles north-west of Reynoldston (bus service). It held a priory founded in the reign of Henry I. Burial slabs of three of the priors may be seen in the church, the largest in Gower. It is in the Early English style, but has been restored. It contains a mutilated fourteenth-century effigy of one of the Delameres, a Norman family that held the manor of West Town. In the churchyard is the grave of Phil Tanner the famous folk-song singer of Gower. Llangennith lies between Rhossili Down and **Llanmadoc Hill,** the summit of which shows traces of an ancient camp, and affords an extensive view.

248

Llanelly

(*Stepney Hotel*: population 30,000), lies across the Loughor estuary to the north of Gower. It is the largest town and port (the port has been closed for trading purposes since 1951) in Carmarthenshire. Having in the immediate vicinity vast stores of the finest anthracite coal, it is ideally placed for a booming trade. Through the generosity of Sir Stafford and Lady Howard the inhabitants are in possession of Bryncaerau Castle and park of about $24\frac{1}{2}$ acres, formerly a seat of the Buckley family. The park, now *Parc Howard*, has been laid out for games, with a children's paddling pool, while the mansion has been converted into a picture gallery, museum and refreshment rooms. It may interest some readers to recall that the *Friendship*, the first seaplane to be flown across the Atlantic, came down off Burry Point after flying non-stop from Trepassey, Newfoundland, in about 22 hours, June, 1928. A modern tin-plate works has been opened at Trostre, as part of the Steel Company of Wales.

NEATH

Bus Services. Between Neath and Swansea, Port Talbot, Margam, Pontardawe, Ammanford, Glyn-Neath, Dulais Valleys, etc.

Early Closing Day. Thursdays. **Market Days.** Wednesdays and Saturdays.

Golf. *Neath Golf Club*, above Cadoxton-juxta-Neath, and *The Swansea Bay Golf Club* is within easy reach. Bus service.

Hotels. *Castle; Cambrian; King Edward VII; Dorothy.*

Population. About 30,884.

Neath is an important place on the main railway line between Cardiff and Swansea. The natural beauty of the town's immediate vicinity is marred by collieries and works, and the town itself has not much attraction for the tourist.

Neath Abbey though violated by a railway line, has lost its former forlorn appearance, thanks to the Ministry of Public Building and Works who are carrying out restoration work. The Abbey was founded for Benedictine monks in 1129 by Richard de Granville of Bideford. At its dissolution it was granted to Sir Richard Cromwell, nephew of Thomas Cromwell, the minister of Henry VIII.

Little remains of its former glory but the ground plan of the church can be traced, and there are considerable portions of the two towers which formed part of the west front. South of the church are the domestic buildings, in which great alterations were made in the middle of the seventeenth century. The most interesting portion is a refectory or workshop with an alcove on its eastern side. In the latter are windows of a later date than the building. On the south-west is a fragment of a building with fine lancet windows.

On the west side of the town, at the east end of Castle Street, are the remains of the **Castle,** said to have been founded by the Richard de Granville mentioned in connection with the abbey. The chief feature is the main gateway, which is flanked by towers and probably dates from about 1300.

On June 2, 1949, in the course of excavations on a new housing site at Neath Abbey Road, the site of the Roman fort of **Nidum** was discovered. This Fort on the main Roman road from Caerleon through South Wales is referred to in the Antonine Itinerary. The foundations of two gateways have been preserved and are scheduled as ancient monuments.

In 1922 the borough was so far extended as to bring within its bounds **Briton Ferry,** at that time an independent industrial town some 3 miles south of the centre of Neath. Here are several large steel, iron and tin-plate works.

The distance between Cardiff and Swansea has been considerably eased and shortened by the new bridge built, at a cost of a million and a half pounds, over the **Neath** at Briton Ferry. The bridge links with the direct Swansea road at **Jersey Marine** on the opposite bank, thus saving the long crawl through the congested streets of Neath.

On the coast a little south of Briton Ferry is **Port Talbot**, a docks town busy with tin-plates and patent fuel, and adjoining again to the south is the once rural locality, with an ancient monastery, known as **Margam**, now transformed into the world's greatest undertaking in steel manufacture, the £70 million Abbey Works of The Steel Company of Wales. There are seven miles of roads within its perimeter. **Aberavon** is the residential part of Port Talbot and its vast areas of sand-dunes are very popular in the summer months.

The Vale of Neath

Bus Service from end to end of the Valley.

Few districts contain more features of natural interest than the Vale of Neath, but owing to the depth of the gorges in which the streams run it is by no means easy to find the waterfalls in summer when the trees are in full leaf. One has to be guided by the sound of falling water: an illustrated booklet dealing with the waterfalls and the underground rivers has been issued by the National Museum of Wales.

Although the charm of the Vale begins to manifest itself as soon as one gets clear of the busy townships at its foot, the most beautiful part of the district begins near Pont Neath Vaughan about 12 miles to the north-east, and covers many square miles around Ystradfellte. It is a tract of sylvan scenery, of ferny dales, high waterfalls, wooded hills, and romantic gorges, with the rivers making their tortuous ways towards the south, and it is this section to which the average country-lover alludes as "The Vale of Neath"; the lower part of the Vale is less remarkable, although it is by no means without special attractions.

Six miles from Neath, for instance, a turning on the right leads to a bridge and to the village of **Resolven.** Pass through the village, bear to the right at the War Memorial, and follow the road southwards for about half a mile. Cross the Melincourt brook by the bridge just short of mine-workings and go up the ravine for a short distance to **Melincourt Fall,** which has a height of 80 feet.

Pont Neath Vaughan may be said to mark the beginning of the "holiday" Vale of Neath. The hamlet lies in the midst of wooded hills at the confluence of the Nedd and the Mellte. About a mile to the north the Nedd is joined by the Pyrddin, and about 2 miles to the north-east the Mellte joins the Hepste. The ravines through which those streams and others near them flow are exceptionally beautiful.

About 1¼ miles from Pont Neath Vaughan (and in the valley of the Pyrddin, which comes in from the left) is the **Lower Pyrrdin Fall,** known also as the Lady Fall—Ysgwd (*us-goo-id*) Gwladys. It is 30 feet high and its aspect varies greatly according to the amount of water in the river. In dry weather there may be hardly a trickle, but after heavy rain the water falls with a noise like thunder and the gorge is filled with spray. Half an hour's rough scrambling will lead to **Ysgŵd Einon Gam** which is about 80 feet in height, and situated at the end of a deep narrow ravine beyond which further progress is impossible.

The Nedd or Little Neath also has its falls. A track that begins near the *Angel Inn*, close to the stream, leads past the confluence of the Pyrrddin and the Neath, crosses the footbridge, and gives access to the Lower Fall, a much finer spectacle than the Upper Fall. The path from the lower to the upper fall is quite easy to follow, as it keeps close beside the stream, finally coming out at Pont Felin Fach, whence a lane crosses the river and leads back to the Ystradfellte–Pont Neath Vaughan road.

One of the best of the falls in the district is **Ysgŵd-yr-Eira**, "the Spout of Snow," locally known as the **Upper Cilhepste Fall**. Situated on the river *Hepste*, it is a sheet of water between 50 and 60 feet high, precipitated so far from the cliff that one may walk behind it, and except in time of flood, the passage is a dry one.

Those who pass behind the Upper Cilhepste Fall may go on to a series of cascades known as the **Lower Cilhepste Fall**. The route from the Upper Fall follows a track through a wood for about 100 yards, and then goes down to the bed of the stream, which marks the rest of the course to the fall.

On the Mellte, about 4 miles from Pont Neath Vaughan, are the **Clyngwyn-Falls**, three in number, of which the middle, or Horseshoe, fall is generally considered to be the finest fall in the Vale.

The falls may be visited in the course of a delightful tramp over the hills—

From Pont Neath Vaughan to Brecon, 20 miles. Follow the Brecon road for about 2½ miles; look out for Hermon Chapel in the distance, and then, just before Clyngwyn Farm appears on the right, there may be seen on that side a track leading to the **Middle Clyn-gwyn Fall**; this is in two portions, a straight fall of water being succeeded by a cataract. It is well worth seeing, but strangers should ask local directions as it is difficult to reach.

The **Upper Clyn-gwyn Fall** is reached by going up to the top of the hill and then descending to rejoin the road. In about 2 miles one arrives at the Church and the *New Inn* of **Ystradfellte**, standing amidst trees. Here the walker does well to remember that this is the only place of refreshment between here and Brecon, a distance of about 14 miles. From Ystradfellte the road climbs a wild upland country for several miles, and then after falling towards Heol Senni is crossed by another that rises again to join the Merthyr road at an altitude of 800 feet, from which there is a fine view of **Brecon**, still 4½ miles distant.

More than a mile of rough going lies between the Middle Clyn-gwyn Fall and **Porth-yr-Ogof**, Cavern Gate, an arch 43 feet wide and 20 feet high, forming the mouth of a natural tunnel, over 200 yards in length, through which the Mellte flows. By the aid of artificial light the cavity can be penetrated for nearly half its length, and by following side passages (on the right) one meets the stream in its underground course. The lower mouth is only a small orifice. Porth-yr-Ogof is about 4 miles from Pont Neath Vaughan. The cave can be reached by car from Penderyn, by following the Brecon road to its junction with the Ystradfellte road, taking the left hand fork, and bearing to the left again at the next fork, after about a mile.

THE CARDIFF DISTRICT

Cardiff - Barry - Bridgend - Porthcawl

Cardiff

Airport. Cardiff (Rhoose) Airport is near the coast some 10 miles south-west of the city. There are scheduled services to and from various towns throughout the country, the Channel Islands, and many overseas destinations.

Angling. Corporation Waters at Llanishen and Lisvane; season and day tickets. Coarse fishing at Roath Park lake.

Baths. Hot and cold, swimming and Turkish baths, Wales Empire Pool, Wood Street.

Boating. At Roath Park and on the Taff at Llandaff.

Bowls. In Cardiff Arms Park, Roath Park, and most of the suburban parks.

Bus Services to all parts of the city and to and from all neighbouring places of any importance—e.g. Porthcawl, Cowbridge, Merthyr, Barry, Newport, and practically all parts of the coalfield. Long-distance buses to Swansea and Carmarthen and *via* Gloucester to London. The Central Bus Station, from which start all the city services as well as many inner city routes, is situated immediately in front of the General Railway Station.

Distances. Barry, 8; Birmingham, 119; Bristol, 90; Caerphilly, 7; Castle Coch, 4; Clevedon (*water*), 17; Liverpool, 140; London, 160; Llandaff, 2½; Newcastle, 310; Newport, 11½; Penarth, 4; Porthcawl, 30; Swansea, 45; Tenby,

104; Weston-super-Mare (*water*), 11.

Early Closing Day. Wednesdays.

Entertainments. *Theatres: New Theatre*, Park place. *Cinemas: Capitol; Olympia; Odeon; Gala; Park Hall; Prince of Wales;* and others in the suburbs. *Concerts, etc.;* Sophia Gardens Pavilion. *Dancing:* City Hall; Victoria, Cowbridge Road; Kennard Rooms, Richmond Road; Capitol Theatre; Sophia Gardens Pavilion; Top Rank Suite, Queen Street.

Golf. *Cardiff Golf Club*, at Sherborne Avenue, Cyncoed, 2 miles. *Radyr (Cardiff) Golf Club*, 18-hole course at Radyr, 5 miles. *The Glamorganshire Golf Club* has an 18-hole course at Penarth, 4 miles (*see* p. 265), and there are links at Creigiau, St. Mellons, Wenvoe, Llanishen, Whitchurch, and Dinas Powis.

Hotels. *Angel*, Westgate Street; *Park;* Park Place; *Royal, Queen's, Central, Sandringham, Philharmonic,* all in St. Mary Street; *Alexandra*, Queen Street; *Windsor*, Stuart Street; *Bristol*, Panarth Road; *Grand*, Westgate Street. Many private hotels and guest houses.

Information Bureau. Municipal Offices, Greyfriars Road (Tel. 31033, Ext. 296.)

Population. 260,164.

Post Office. In Westgate Street.

Principal Sights. The City Hall and

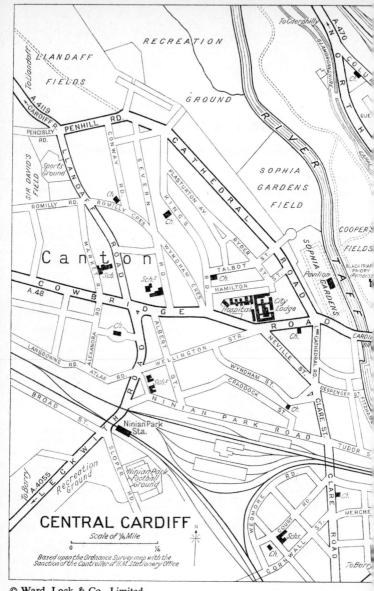

CENTRAL CARDIFF

Scale of ¼ Mile

0   ¼

Based upon the Ordnance Survey map with the
Sanction of the Controller of H.M. Stationery Office

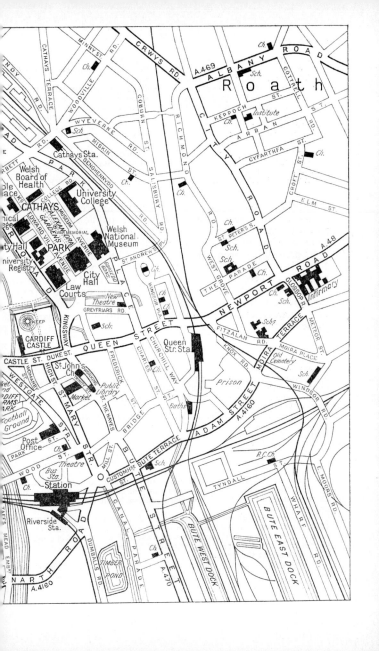

Law Courts, National Museum of Wales, Temple of Peace, and other public buildings in Cathays Park; the Castle, the Docks, with the mechanical devices for loading and unloading; Roath Park; Bute Park (Castle grounds); St. Fagans Welsh Folk Museum.

Sporting Events. *Cardiff Arms Park:* Rugby Football, County Cricket, Tennis and Bowls. *Ninian Park:* Association Football. *Maindy Stadium:* Athletics, Cycle racing. *Pontcanna Fields:* Horse Shows, Horticultural events. Indoor Bowling Stadium, Rhyd-y-Pennau Road.

Steamers. From the Pier Head to Penarth, Bristol, Weston-super-Mare, Ilfracombe, etc. Full details from P. & A. Campbell, Ltd., Pier Head, Cardiff (Tel: 32621.)

Tennis in Roath Park, Cardiff Arms Park, Cathays Park, and most suburban parks.

Y.M.C.A. Station Terrace, Queen Street.

Y.W.C.A. 126 Newport Road.

Cardiff (in Welsh *Caerdydd*) has much to interest the visitor in its broad streets, particularly fine public buildings, its pleasant parks and public gardens, and its close proximity to areas of beautiful and varying scenery.

Its growth has been phenomenal. In 1801 the population was 1,018. It is now 260,164. The city owes its rapid rise and prosperity to its geographical position as the natural outlet for the steam-coal area of the South Wales coalfield and the entrepôt for foodstuffs for a very large population, to the mineral wealth in its vicinity, and to the enterprise of individuals interested in its development.

Although Cardiff, as we see it, is so modern, its history dates back to ancient times. The Romans established themselves here, and when their legions were withdrawn the place became part of the great kingdom of Morgannwg, and, from the fifth to the end of the eleventh century, was under the sway of Welsh princes, the last of whom was dispossessed by a Norman baron, Robert Fitzhamon, who seated himself at Cardiff as Lord of Glamorgan.

By the marriage of Fitzhamon's only daughter and heiress, the lordship passed to the Earls of Gloucester. In the reign of Henry I Cardiff Castle became the prison of the King's eldest brother, Robert, Duke of Normandy, the captive having been committed to the care of the Earl of Gloucester. In the year 1158, nearly a quarter of a century after the Duke of Normandy's death, the Welsh made a successful attack upon Cardiff. The castle was well garrisoned, and the paid retainers of the lord filled the town, but the Welsh gained possession of the stronghold, and carried off the Earl, the Countess, and their only son. The captives were retained until the grievances of the Welsh had been redressed and valuable concessions granted to them.

The town and castle were almost entirely destroyed by Owain Glyndŵr in 1404, during the insurrection of the Welsh in the reign of Henry IV. It is said that the only part of the town which escaped was the street containing the Grey Friars' Convent, and that owed its immunity solely to the love Glyndŵr had for the fraternity.

From the Earls of Gloucester the castle passed to the le Despensers;

...ck Mountain Country near Abergavenny (*A. F. Kersting*)

The Honddu Valley (*A. F. Kersting*)

The Wye at Builth Wells

Elan meets Wye near Rhayader (*A. F. Kers*

from them to the Warwick family; and finally to the Crown by the marriage of Richard III with the Lady Ann of Warwick. After various other changes of possession it was sold by Edward VI to Sir William Herbert, afterwards Earl of Pembroke, from whom it passed to the Earls of Windsor, and from them by marriage to the House of Bute. It was finally transferred to the City Council in 1947.

During the Civil War the town and castle were at first held for the King. They changed hands more than once, and then the Royalists were finally defeated at St. Fagan's, between 3 and 4 miles from the town.

Cardiff Castle

Open. May to September weekdays, 10–12, 2–8, Sundays 2–5; March, April, and October weekdays 10–12, 2–4. Admission, 2s. Handbooks on sale at the entrance. Conducted tours.

Formerly the residence of the Marquis of Bute, the Castle is now in the charge of the City Council. The site has been in constant occupation since the Romans established a camp upon it in the first century. Their camp covered an area of about 7½ acres, and was surrounded by a wall varying in thickness from 9 feet 9 inches to 10 feet 3 inches. Portions have been laid bare by excavations and can still be examined from the public thoroughfares. When the Normans took possession of the site, they erected a keep on an artificial mound about 40 feet high and surrounded by a moat, near the north-west angle of the Roman Camp. That keep was their castle from the eleventh century to the fifteenth. In the thirteenth century the position was strengthened by the erection of the Black Tower, erroneously called Duke Robert's Tower, at the south entrance, and by various walls which had to be passed before the entrance to the keep could be attacked. That Duke Robert was held prisoner at Cardiff Castle there is no doubt, but the tower to which his name has been given was not the place of his confinement, as it was not built until long after his time. In the Black Tower is a dungeon without apertures for light or ventilation and to which the only access was by a trap-door in the floor of the chamber above it.

The great octagonal tower, which forms such a fine feature of the present castle, was built between 1425 and 1439. Its spire was added about 1875 The domestic buildings which have been constructed around this tower display various styles from fifteenth-century to that of the present day. They are built against the Norman west wall, which is on remains of the Roman wall. In the kitchen Roman work can be seen.

The central portion of the Castle was erected soon after the completion of the octagonal tower. It contains the Banqueting Hall and Library. The north wing, built towards the end of the eighteenth century, contains the Drawing-room. To the south of the central portion is the guest tower, erected in the last quarter of the nineteenth century. On the extreme south is the **Clock Tower**, built to improve the appearance of the town and to provide a public clock and a set of private apartments for the lord of the Castle. One of the apartments is the Winter Smoking-room. The upper parts of the windows are filled with glass, displaying the gods from whom our Saxon ancestors named the days of the week. The central boss of the vaulting is carved into a representation of the sun. On the spandrels of the vaulting and in circles on the walls are the twelve signs of the zodiac. Also on the walls are delineated the occupations of the four seasons. The frieze of the chimney-piece shows the amusements of lovers during the winter, and bears the motto "Omnia vincit amor et nos cedamus amori" (Love conquers all; let us also yield to love).

Over the motto stands the figure of Diana the Huntress with bow and arrow. The apartment above is the Bachelor's Bedroom. The next apartment contains the clock; above that is the kitchen, and at the top of the tower is the Summer Smoking-room.

From the entrance hall of the Castle a door leads to the **Library,** a magnificent apartment measuring 75 feet by 23 feet, occupying the whole area of the fifteenth-century Castle.

Of the several doorways leading from the library, one communicates with the **Drawing-room.** Among its many objects of interest is a Louis XIII clock, invented by the fourth Earl of Bute, who was Prime Minister.

The **Grand Staircase** leads from the Entrance Hall to the **Great Hall,** and from it entrance is also obtained to the **Banqueting Hall,** the most notable apartment in the Castle. It is lined with walnut wainscoting surmounted by frescoes representing incidents in the life of Robert, Earl of Gloucester, the second Norman lord of Cardiff. In the octagonal tower is the **Chaucer Room,** one of the gems of the Castle. It is approached by a stair constructed in the thickness of the wall. The **Private Chapel** is one of the richest portions of the Castle. It is lined with marble diapered with enamelled shields, and on both walls and ceiling are beautiful illustrations of sacred subjects.

The Castle walls which face upon Duke Street and Cathays Park have been built upon the fragments of the Roman wall that survived, and considerable stretches of the latter are to be seen at the base of the new wall.

Cathays Park lies north of the Castle, and was once part of the Castle grounds. It covers 60 acres, and is the site of Cardiff's Civic Centre, consisting of a remarkable group of public buildings. The central building as one approaches from Queen Street is—

The **City Hall,** a very fine building in Renaissance style (1901–6). The main frontage extends over 265 feet. Above the Council Chamber a huge dome is surmounted by an immense Welsh Dragon. The west frontage extends for 325 feet; above rises a lofty clock tower (200 feet high). The interior of the building is well worth seeing, and contains many paintings and statues of Welsh national heroes.

Across King Edward VII Avenue, on the west side of the City Hall, are the **Law Courts,** an equally imposing construction. Eastward of the City Hall, across Museum Avenue, is the—

National Museum of Wales (*Weekdays*, 10–5, *Thursdays* (*summer*) *until* 8 *p.m.*, *free*; *Sundays*, 2.30–5, 6d.). The Museum was formally opened by King George V in 1927, and has since been enlarged. The exterior, like that of the other buildings in the Civic Centre, is of Portland Stone. Of special interest are the models of Welsh countryside and those of plants, the series of birds, the finds from the many recent archaeological excavations in Wales, works by Welsh artists and a notable collection of French nineteenth-century paintings. There are some fine working models illustrating Welsh industry. Catalogues and handbooks describing the collections or dealing with the subjects to which they relate are on sale at the entrance.

University College of South Wales and Monmouthshire is entered from Museum Avenue. The College, founded in 1883 and since 1893 a constituent College of the University of Wales, accommodates in its main building in Cathays Park the departments of Pure and Applied Mathematics, Physics, Chemistry, Botany, Zoology, Geology, Archaeology, Music and Education. To the north of this site the new Faculty of Arts building houses twelve departments of the Faculty and the Faculty of Economic and Social Studies. On the same enclosure is new accommodation for the pre-clinical departments of Anatomy, Physiology and Biochemistry and a new library. The Applied Science departments—Civil, Electrical and Mechanical Engineering, Metallurgy and Mining—are located on the original site of the College in Newport Road.

There are three Halls of Residence for students of the College; two for women—Aberdare Hall in Cathays Park, and Llandaff House at Penarth, and one for men—University Hall at Penylan. The College playing fields at Llanrumney cover 33 acres.

The College overlooks Alexandra Gardens, where is the **Welsh National Memorial** of the First World War, a striking double circular colonnade enclosing the Cenotaph.

On the western side of the Gardens is another group of public buildings, including, from south to north, the **Law Courts,** the **University Registry,** the **Glamorgan County Hall,** with its façade in classic style and striking groups of statuary, the **Welsh College of Advanced Technology,** and the **Hall of Nations.**

In part of Cathays Park to the south of the group of civic

buildings are a number of memorials, and in front of the Museum is a group of monoliths forming the Gorsedd Circle in connection with the Welsh National Eisteddfod of 1899. In the south-eastern corner of the Park are the carefully preserved ruins of the Herbert Mansion and the Grey and Black Friars' Convents.

From the National Museum pass into Park Place, on the east, and turn right. Beyond the *New Theatre* is Queen Street; turn right again, and at the crossing just short of the Castle turn to the left down St. John Street for—

St John's Church (*Sunday services*, 8, 11 *and* 6.30.) Built of grey lias limestone in the Somerset tradition, the style is mainly Perpendicular, though many of its original characteristics have been lost during successive "restorations." The tower, built in 1483, is the finest in South Wales, but it is so closely surrounded by other buildings that much of the effect of its graceful proportions is lost. It contains a peal of ten bells and a clock, and is surmounted by four open stone lanterns richly ornamented with pinnacles and vanes.

The Central Library is a few yards south of St. John's Church. It is the headquarters of a large branch, school and hospital-library system, comprising reading-rooms, a lending library, research room, commercial and technical library and a reference library which contains many rare and valuable books and manuscripts.

A turning opposite the Library entrance leads to **St. Mary Street,** one of the busiest streets in the city. At one end is the Castle; and at the other the commencement of the huge Dock System. Here are banks, shops, offices and cinemas, and a few yards westward, in Westgate Street, is the **Chief Post Office**. Also in Westgate Street is the entrance to **Cardiff Arms Park**, the scene of important Rugby football matches, and with provision for cricket, tennis and bowls.

The Docks are a notable feature. They are remarkable for their size—165 acres of deep water—and for their appliances for loading and unloading vessels. In 1794 the Glamorganshire Canal was opened, permitting an effective method of tapping the vast mineral wealth of the adjacent valleys and when, four years later the canal was extended to the sea an era of prosperity commenced with the flow of coal direct to the ships loading in its lower reaches. The first docks were constructed by the second Marquis of Bute, who in 1839 opened the West Dock. As the local railways expanded the need for further docks arose, and the East Dock was opened in 1859 followed by the Roath Dock in 1887. Trade continued to increase and the construction of a further Dock of 52 acres was undertaken, which was opened by King Edward VII in 1907 and named Queen Alexandra Dock. There is today excellent warehouse accommodation, a cold store, well equipped transit sheds, and a flour mill and granary at Cardiff Docks.

Besides Cathays Park open spaces in Cardiff include the Castle Grounds **(Bute Park)** on the east side of the Taff and stretching 2½ miles from the city centre to Western Avenue. **Roath Park** (102 acres) extends north-eastward from the centre, and includes the **Botanical Gardens**. A 32-acre lake is available for boating and there are facilities for various sports.

The **Garth** is a hill near Taff's Well, five miles or so from Cardiff (train or bus) that is worth a visit. It is over 1,000 feet in height and affords excellent views across the Bristol Channel in one direction and into the coalfield in the other. Good views of the Cardiff plain and the Channel are also to be had from the hills south of Caerphilly (reached by road from Cardiff *via* Llanishen). The view northward from Caerphilly mountains includes the hills that form the northern rim of the coalfield, 18 miles to the north, and can be made the feature of an interesting drive from Cardiff to Newport, *via* Llanishen, Rudry and Machen, or Llanishen, Caerphilly, Bedwas and Machen.

Llandaff

This ancient city (*Black Lion, Mitre*), of which the name signifies "the sacred enclosure on the river Taff", is about 2 miles north-west of Cardiff and forms part of the County Borough. It is a favourite residential quarter with a parish population of just over 1,300. At Llandaff is the well-known Howell's Glamorgan School for Girls.

Llandaff Cathedral

Admission. Daily, dawn to dusk.
Dimensions. Length, including Lady Chapel, 245 feet; width, 70 feet; height, 65 feet; north-west tower, 105 feet high; south-west tower, 195 feet 7 inches.
Services (in English), on Sundays, 8, 9, 11, 3.30 and 6.30; weekdays 7.30 (Tuesdays and Fridays, 7) and 6.

The Cathedral, badly damaged during the war but now restored, is one of the earliest ecclesiastical foundations in Britain. As is well known, the introduction of Christianity into Wales long preceded the mission of Augustine and the foundation of the province of Canterbury. Teilo, the first Bishop of Llandaff of whom we hear, probably founded the first church in the sixth century, as well as a school for priests. Urban (1107–34) was the first Bishop appointed under Norman influence, instead of by the Welsh princes, and in 1120 he began the construction of a new cathedral. Of his work little more is left than the massive Norman arch above the reredos and the window openings south of the presbytery. The present building is partly Early English and partly Decorated and was mostly completed by 1287. Reconstruction of the nave, west front and the towers however took place in the mid-nineteenth century.

The central part of the **West Front** is pure and beautiful Early English.

261

The **North-Western** (or Jasper) **Tower** is a Perpendicular structure resting on the arches of its Early English predecessor and crowned with an open-worked parapet. The **South-Western Tower** is modern, designed by Prichard to replace an Early English tower of which scarcely anything remained. Under canopies, in which massive buttresses terminate, are statues of St. Peter and St. Paul, to whom the Cathedral was dedicated in the later Middle Ages, and a statue of Bishop Ollivant, in whose time the restoration was completed. Above the aisle roof is an arcade of four arches, including seated figures of the Evangelists. The lancet windows of the belfry stage are flanked by niches containing figures representing the various nations of the world. Above the arches of the windows project heads of the great mission apostles and preachers.

The Interior

Both the north door and the south have fine Transitional work.

From the west end, the graceful arcades, the east window, the truly remarkable Norman arch above the High Altar, and the stone roof and east window of the Lady Chapel, combine in a dignified and beautiful view. The capitals of the main arches are beautifully sculptured. There is no triforium, the clerestory immediately surmounting the string-course and having a passage cut through it. At the west end of the nave the three great lancets with their mouldings occupy the entire width. A group of shafts from the windows is brought to the ground on either side of the portal, which descends several steps to the floor, thus greatly enhancing the general effect of the west end. The new pulpit commemorates the fourth Archbishop of Wales. The new font is the work of Alan Durst, A.R.A. The aisles, re-built in the Decorated period, need only be mentioned for their windows with ogee heads and reticulated tracery.

Principal restoration work in the nave has been the replacement of the high-pointed ceiling of the last century by a flat wooden ceiling, as was evidently intended by the original builders. The timber, very hard and of red and yellow colour, came from Malaya and Africa. The eastern end is spanned by a new parabolic concrete arch which supports the barrel-shaped organ case in front of which is suspended a large figure of Christ in Majesty, the work of Sir Jacob Epstein.

Most of the glass in the nave is the work of the Pre-Raphaelites, Morris and Marshall. The window above the altar is by John Piper.

The small chapel under the north-west tower was given by the 53rd Welsh (Infantry) Division in 1958. The Division also paid for the recasting of the bells and the repairs of the clock and carillon. The famous *Rossetti* triptych of the "Seed of David" forms the reredos of this chapel.

The **Presbytery** was rebuilt in the Decorated period, but the Norman arch at the east end, the Norman south wall, and parts of Norman windows were retained. The richly moulded Norman arch which stands at the east end has four orders, characteristically ornamented. The exterior one has a series of small circles, each studded with points and having eight leaves within—a most uncommon feature.

The presbytery aisles lead into the **Lady Chapel,** with a fine vaulted ceiling. The glass here is modern and the work of the late Geoffrey Webb. The East window, installed in 1951, is a Jesse window. The **Chapter House,** of Early English date, is peculiar in being square, with a central round pillar.

To the north-west of the Cathedral and connected to the nearby Prebendal House by a processional way flanked by vestries is the Welch Regiment Memorial Chapel, built in 1956. This ranks as one of the most significant of modern, ecclesiastical buildings.

Bishop's Palace. The remnant of an ancient Episcopal Castle forms the garden entrance to the old Bishop's Palace built in 1751. It is now used as the Cathedral Choir School, the only one of its kind in Wales.

St. Fagans. Rather more than 4 miles west of Cardiff, by the side of the *Ely*, and near the site of a fierce battle between Cromwell's soldiers and the Welsh Royalists is St. Fagans, a picturesque village with thatched cottages. (32 bus from the Western Region Station.)

It is dominated by the Castle, a many-gabled Tudor mansion, built within a thirteenth-century curtain wall. After being in the possession of the Windsor family since 1730, the Castle, with its gardens and grounds, was presented by the Earl of Plymouth to the National Museum of Wales for development as a national folk museum. In addition there are 98 acres of land on which have been erected buildings from different parts of Wales. The principal exhibits are St. Fagans Castle, sixteenth-century house with its garden; a barn (1500–1600) removed from Flintshire; a woollen mill (c. 1760) complete with machinery, from Brecknockshire; a timber-framed house (1600) removed from Montgomeryshire; a stone-built farmhouse (1630–1730) removed from Gower, Glamorgan; a Unitarian Chapel (1777) from the Teifi Valley, West Wales; a long-house (1730) from Radnorshire; a farmhouse (1470) from Denbighshire; a cottage (1762) from Caernarvonshire; a wood-turner's shop; basketmaker's shop. Textiles, wood-turnery and baskets are for sale. *Open daily (except Mondays), 11–7; Sundays, 2.30–7 and Bank Holidays. In winter until 5 p.m. Small charge. School parties free. Restaurant.*

St. Nicholas. About half a mile south of St. Nicholas, 6 miles from Cardiff along the Cowbridge road, is a chambered tomb (cromlech or dolmen) of the New Stone Age, one of the largest and best preserved in the whole of the country. The capstone, 22 feet by 15 feet and over 3 feet thick, is estimated to weigh over 40 tons. The remains of another burial chamber can be seen from the roadside near St. Lythans about a mile and a quarter south-west of St. Nicholas.

Caerphilly

(*Clive Arms, Boar's Head*. 9-hole golf course). The town, famous as the home of the celebrated cheese, is well-known also for its magnificent castle and the exquisite Nantgarw Porcelain. Caerphilly is rich in Eisteddfodic tradition and has been the birthplace of many famous poets, harpists and musicians including Ieuan-ap-Iago, author of the words of the Welsh National Anthem. Today it is a bustling, progressive place with many new light industrial activities.

Caerphilly Castle

Admission charge. May–September, 9.30–7; Sundays, 9.30–7. March–April, 9.30–5.30 and 2–5.30. October, 9.30–5.30 and 2–5.30. November–February, 9.30–4 and 2–4.

The ruins, popularly said to be the largest in the kingdom, cover 30 acres, but of their history little is known. The castle was begun about 1268 by Gilbert de Clare, Earl of Gloucester and Lord of Glamorgan and later enlarged by the younger Hugh Despenser, unworthy favourite of Edward II. No one can say with certainty when or by whom it was wrecked.

The most singular feature of the castle now is its leaning tower. It is a massive piece of masonry 50 feet high, and 9 feet out of the perpendicular, as the result of an explosion some time during the seventeenth century that demolished half of one of the towers, and displaced the remaining half.

The castle was given by Edward VI to William, Earl of Pembroke, and from his family it passed by marriage to ancestors of the Marquis of Bute, who now holds it.

Castell Coch (*charge; Ministry Standard hours*) is about 3 miles south-west of Caerphilly near the Pontypridd road. The "Red Castle" as it is called from the colour of its stone, is on the site of an ancient fortress. It is picturesquely situated on a wooded height in a region that still has much natural beauty, in spite of the dismantled iron-works in the valley below. The small medieval castle is a triangular structure originally built about 1260. After having been long a ruin, Castell Coch was restored in 1875 by William Burgess for the third Marquis of Bute, and is now Ministry property.

Nantgarw, on the Pontypridd road, is the place where nearly 150 years ago the famous porcelain bearing that name was made; with its contemporary, Swansea China, these pieces of classic and artistic porcelain are eagerly sought after by collectors.

Pontypridd (*New Inn*), 6 miles north-west of Castell Coch, with a population of 35,000, is famed for its picturesque single-arched bridge, designed and built in 1756 by a native self-taught stonemason, William Edwards. The town is situated at the southern apex of the Rhondda Valley, long renowned for the best steam-coal in the world. Badly hit by the depression in pre-war years the town now enjoys a good measure of prosperity. Many new light industries have been established in recent years at the Treforest Industrial Estate—the largest industrial estate in Wales. There are cinemas, a theatre and some fine shops. In the town centre is the particularly fine Ynysangharad Park. The town stands at the confluence of the *Rhondda* with the *Taff*. The latter comes down from **Merthyr Tydfil,** and the Rhondda has a more westerly course, while between the two lies the valley of the *Cynon*, which flows past **Aberdare,** another centre of the coal and iron industries, and joins the Taff at Abercynon. A few miles to the west of Aberdare is the Hirwaun Trading Estate.

CHEPSTOW, CARDIFF, NEATH

0 1 2 3 4 5 6   12 Miles

WARD, LOCK & CO. LIMITED, LONDON

© John Bartholomew & Son Ltd, Edinburgh

Cardiff to Merthyr Tydfil. The present road from Cardiff to Merthyr Tydfil runs along by the eastern side of the valley of the Taff past Pontypridd and Quaker's Yard, but the old road followed the crest of the neighbouring hill ridge: the Roman road to Brecon followed the next ridge to the east and went past **Gelligaer,** where the site of an important Roman encampment has been excavated.

Merthyr was once one of the most important industrial centres in the country, and in the eighteenth century and the early part of the nineteenth produced enormous quantities of iron. Today it is the centre of a great many light industries.

Cyfarthfa Castle is a beautifullly situated building on the road to Brecon that now houses the local Secondary School and Museum. The latter is well worth a visit. The Castle, although in the medieval style, was built in 1825 by Crawshay, the "Iron King."

The first steam-propelled locomotive to run on lines in this country went from Merthyr to near Abercynon, in 1804, drawing trucks laden with coal and iron. It was made by Richard Trevithick, and portions of the route he used can still be seen. A memorial to Trevithick was unveiled in 1934 at Gwalia Place, in Merthyr. It faced the former ironworks where Trevithick built his locomotive. The memorial is built largely of the "chair stones" on which the lines of the old tramway were laid, and includes sections of the lines.

Penarth

Road Route from Cardiff. At foot of St. Mary Street take turning in front of *Central Hotel* (on right), keep to left and pass under railway. Cross river and keep straight ahead. Alternative *via* Leckwith.

Bus Services. To Barry, Dinas Powis and Cardiff; Bridgend, Porthcawl, Cowbridge, Llantwit-Major, etc.

Early Closing Day. Wednesday.

Population. 20,897.

Entertainments. A cinema, pier attractions, ballroom, art gallery, etc.

Golf. *Glamorganshire Golf Club Links* (18 holes), adjoining Lower Penarth Station. *Dinas Powis Golf Club* (18-hole course adjoining Cwrtyrala Woods).

Hotels. *Esplanade*, Esplanade; and numerous guest houses.

Post Office. Albert Road.

Sports. Bathing, bowls, putting, tennis, in addition to golf, as above.

Steamer Trips. To Weston-super-Mare, and other Bristol Channel resorts.

Penarth is situated on a bold headland on the west side of the Taff estuary, 4 miles from Cardiff. The early growth of the town, from a former fishing village, was due to great development of the shipping trade and coal export boom in which Penarth shared as one of the customs ports of Cardiff.

Being on a headland, Penarth has two shores—north and south. Along the latter runs the wide **Esplanade**, with extensive views across the Bristol Channel. Here are sea-water **Baths** and the local Yacht Club. From the pier in summer steamers ply to and from numerous places of interest in the Channel. Running for about half a mile along the cliff are the pretty **Windsor Gardens. Alexandra Park** has a bandstand and shelters, and is a grand view-point, as is also **Penarth Head.** The **Church of St. Augustine** was rebuilt in 1866. In the churchyard are the remains of a preaching cross. Facing the station is the **Turner House Gallery,** founded in 1888 and since 1921 incorporated in the National Museum of Wales. Open daily, except Mondays, 2–6 p.m. (Winter, 2–5 p.m.).

Walks from Penarth

To Lavernock, 2½ miles to the south, by way of the cliff. Lavernock is the site of a very small church on an ancient site. A plaque on churchyard wall commemorates the first transmission of a radio message over water by Marconi in 1901—from Lavernock to the Flat Holm. The sandy St. Mary's Well Bay is popular for bathing.

To Sully, about a mile and a half west of Lavernock, the site of an ancient church and a fragment of a castle. On Sully Island, accessible by foot at low tide, is an ancient promontory fort.

To Cwrt-yr-Ala, in the course of a circular walk of about 6 miles *via* Michaelston and Dinas Powis. Much of the route is over fields and through woods.

To Dinas Powis, about 3 miles, mainly by field-paths. (*Golf Links.*) Half a mile farther is the hamlet of **St. Andrews.** Just short of it is a rocky height on the right, called from the arrangement of the rocks the **Bishop's Seat.**

To Llandough and Upper Reservoir, or the walk may be continued through Leckwith to Cardiff. At Llandough there is a large modern hospital.

Barry

Road Route from Cardiff. Cross bridge beside Castle and follow Cowbridge road to Culverhouse Cross, and then along A 4050 road through Wenvoe; or *via* Dinas Powis and Cadoxton to Barry.

Bathing. Good and safe at all states of the tide.

Boating. In Whitmore Bay.

Bowls. Public greens in Central Park, Romilly Park, and Victoria Park. The Athletic Club is open to visitors.

Bus Services. To Penarth, Llantwit-Major and Bridgend, Dinas Powis, Cardiff, etc.

Early Closing Day. Wednesdays.

Fishing. Excellent sea fishing along coast.

Golf. The *Brynhill (Barry) Club* has an 18-hole course 1½ miles from Barry Dock or Barry Station. There is a miniature golf course on Nell's Point. *The Wenvoe Golf Club*, about 3½ miles from Barry, has an 18-hole course.

Hotels. *Barry*, Broad Street; *Knap*, The Knap; *Ship; Marine*, Barry Island; *Brain's Barry Dock*, Barry Dock; *Waters Edge*, The Knap.

Population. 42,059.

Steamer excursions in summer.

Tennis. Public courts on Barry Island, in Romilly Park, Central Park, Victoria Park, Alexandra Gardens, and Gladstone Gardens.

Yachting. The Barry Yacht Club at Pier Head.

266

Barry, of quite modern growth, is one of the three ports comprised in the Customs port of Cardiff. About 1880 those interested in securing increased accommodation at Cardiff, being unable to come to terms with the Marquis of Bute, determined to construct a dock at Barry, which was then a tiny village with only seventeen inhabited houses and a total population of eighty-five. It is now a municipal borough with a population of over 42,000. The first dock was opened in 1889, after an expenditure of more than two million pounds. The dock covered 73 acres, and was then largest in the world, but almost immediately a second dock was needed, and Barry now possesses three docks with a total deep-water area of 114 acres. Splendidly situated about 9 miles south-west of Cardiff, they offer great advantages in having the entrances close to deep water.

The town itself is well situated on a slope rising from the docks to a point about 300 feet above sea-level. Barry Island, the Knap Beach and Porth-kerry Bay are the chief attractions. Of interest, too, is the ancient church of Cadoxton, dedicated to the local saint, Cadoc, from whom the parish takes its name. The church contains several features of archaeological interest, including medieval wall paintings and a font claimed to be Saxon.

The Town Hall and Public Library constitute the finest group of public buildings in Barry. Behind them is the Central Park. South-westward, Holton Road and its continuation lead to Romilly Park, a charming, well-timbered spot, near the western extremity of Barry, having bowling greens and tennis courts, cricket and football pitches; it is a very popular resort. A short distance north of the park are the ivy-clad remains of a manorial residence, commonly called Barry Castle, an authentic relic of Norman days.

Barry Island is an island only in name, there being the width of dock between it and the mainland portion of the town. Its seaward side is curved to form two wide bays, separated by Friars Point, where there are pre-historic burial mounds. The associations suggested by the name of the Point are centred in the remains of the ancient Abbey, near the station, where there is also a Roman Well. Near Nells Point on the eastern side of the island are a few stones of the supposed shrine of St. Barrock, or Baruc, from which the island takes its name, and which in turn is said to have become the cognomen of the family known as de Barri, and including among its members Gerald de Barri or Barry—Giraldus Cambrensis.

The bay eastward of the Point is lined by a fine promenade, with roomy shelters. There are tennis courts, a miniature golf course and bowling greens. The clean, gently-shelving sands provide safe bathing.

The Council have spent considerable sums upon improving the amenities of Whitmore Bay and The Knap, with the result that these two centres attract something like a million visitors annually. There is an amusement park at Whitmore Bay. It extends from Nell's Point to Friars Point, at the west end of which is the inlet called Barry Harbour. Beyond this stands Knap Point, a fine rocky promontory. Extending farther westward for more than a mile is Porthkerry Bay, having a fine line of cliffs for a background. On the inner side of the bay is a fine promenade, and behind that are a series of recreation grounds, including a large modern swimming pool (350 feet by 90 feet) a boating lake, and tennis and bowling greens, etc.

At the western extremity of Porthkerry Bay are the **Bullcliff Rocks,** which rise a hundred feet above the sea. Beyond them is a picturesque spot called the **Golden Stairs,** and just beyond that is the entrance to **Porthkerry Park,** one of the chief attractions of the immediate vicinity of Barry. From the park there is a steep climb to Porthkerry church.

Barry is a convenient centre from which to visit the Vale of Glamorgan, remarkable as much for its natural beauty as for its picturesque villages and its antiquarian remains. Among the latter is the cromlech near the village of **St. Nicholas,** which can be reached by way of Colcot or Wenvoe.

From Barry it is an easy run westward by road to—

Llantwit-Major, or Llanilltyd-fawr, so named after St. Illtyd, the founder of a monastery here in the fifth century, and one of the earliest Christian centres in Britain. It rapidly became a famous school from which saints and scholars went out along the Roman roads, and even across the sea to Brittany. The only remains of those early days are the eighth-century carved stone crosses and pillars now in the church. There are several remains of the later medieval monastery. The parish church consists of the older **West Church,** and the newer **East Church.** The West Church has a fine carved roof and many interesting relics including a restored medieval altar. The East Church is Early English and is notable for its series of frescoes not long uncovered. The font is said to be a thousand years old.

The *Old Town Hall* and nearby inns are picturesque. They belong to the thirteenth century.

A few miles north-east from Llantwit-Major is **Old Beaupré,** where there is a magnificent porchway, the only relic of a once beautiful mansion of the sixteenth century.

St. Donat's Castle, romantically placed among woods overlooking the coast is 2 miles west of Llantwit. Founded according to tradition by Guillaume le Esterling, reputed ancestor of the Stradling family, it has been described as "unquestionably one of the most perfect of the ancient baronial halls of Wales." A characteristic feature is the curtain wall which rises from the moat and surrounds the principal buildings, gatehouse, guard-room and baileys. The castle has never been uninhabited and is now occupied by the Atlantic College. The park comprises 120 acres.

Cowbridge is an ancient borough, amongst the smallest in the country, 5 miles north-east of Llantwit-Major. It lies on the main Cardiff–Swansea road some 12 miles west of Cardiff and 7 miles east of Bridgend. It is the centre of the beautiful Vale of Glamorgan and retains the Edwardian south gate of the former walled town. The church has many points of interest and the Grammar School adjoining was founded in the sixteenth century. Nearby is the ruined Gate-house of St. Quintin's Castle. To the east is **Stalling Down,** an open heath very popular in summer months, and within easy reach is **St. Hilary,** a hamlet with houses of charm overlooking open country and with an interesting and ancient church.

Bridgend

Bridgend (*Wyndham Arms, Castle, York, Dunraven Arms*)

is a market and industrial town and centre of South Wales with a population of some 15,110. It lies on the northern edge of the beautiful Vale of Glamorgan between the hills and the sea and not far distant from the large centres of Cardiff and Swansea. It is on the main London to Fishguard railway line and transport from the bus station connects with all parts of the country. The town is in easy distance of the seaside resorts of the Bristol Channel and the well-known valleys of Rhondda, Llynfi, Ogmore and Garw. The river *Ogmore* runs through the town and with its tributary the *Ewenny*, which joins it near the sea, there is good fishing.

Coity Castle, some 2 miles north-east of Bridgend, is a picturesque ruin, consisting of a large outer ward and a circular inner ward. The Keep was probably built in the latter part of the twelfth century, and when entire was of four storeys. The great Gate-house on the east belongs to the early fourteenth century, but the present windows were inserted at a later date. To the south of the inner ward was the Hall. Against its side is the thirteenth-century round tower of the castle. The curtain wall on this side of the stronghold dates from the opening years of the fourteenth century. (*Open daily 9–8 summer, 9.30–4 winter, 6d.; guide pamphlet, 3d.*)

Coity Church (*c.* 1324) is a cruciform building in the Decorated style. The interior is attractively unusual by reason of the rib vaulting at the crossing. In the chancel stands a pre-Reformation oak chest. The carving on the panels depicts the emblems (or instruments) of the Passion. The chest is reputed to be a reliquary. There is a fine west window of the nave. The quaint gargoyles on the tower are worthy of note.

Ewenny Priory, Ogmore and Southerndown

Ewenny Priory (*admission to Church and to Wall Walk Defences*) is 2 miles almost due south of Bridgend. Follow the Southerndown road to the point where, after crossing the by-pass, it descends to the *Ewenny* river. Immediately beyond the bridge turn to the left and follow the lane beside the stream.

Ewenny is of interest as a fine example of an ecclesiastical fortified building. Even today the wall it presents to the Ewenny stream has a business-like appearance quite at variance with one's usual impressions of monastic walls; and the church tower has more than a passing likeness to a castle keep.

The Priory was founded in the early part of the twelfth century by William de Londres and his son Maurice for a community of Benedictine monks from Gloucester. Many of its original features are uninjured. The preserved portions comprise the main gateway, much of the exterior embattled wall, and the **Church.** The principal external feature of the church is a massive fortified tower. Internally it has some of the purest Norman work in Britain. The massive piers and arches of the aisle arcading are most impressive, and the transepts and the presbytery are very fine. The reredos is below the western tower arch; across the eastern arch is a very fine fourteenth-century wooden screen.

Ogmore Castle (*Key at farmhouse opposite*) is an interesting ruin of twelfth-century work which has probably one of the earliest stone keeps of the county, a rectangular building of three storeys. In the bailey is a fragment of a fifteenth-century court-house.

Near the castle stepping stones provide a crossing of the river for **Candleston Castle,** the ruins of a fifteenth-century fortified mansion, once the residence of the Cantelupes. Nearer Bridgend is **Merthyr Mawr** a pretty village of thatched cottages protected by sand-dunes.

Ogmore-by-Sea (*Craig-yr-Eos; Brig-y-Don*) lies on the southern side of the estuary where there is a sandy beach at the base of low cliffs. The region eastward from here is becoming increasingly popular with visitors.

Southerndown (*Buses to Bridgend: fine 18-hole golf course*), on the top of a steep cliff overlooking the Bristol Channel, is a quiet, healthy village which might well develop into a better known resort, but for the fact that there is no sand when the tide is in. The coast-line, magnificently rugged, is in places over 300 feet high.

Some 5 miles farther along the coast (9 miles from Bridgend) is **St. Donat's Castle** (*see* p. 268). The road passes, at Marcross, a pretty lane running down to the coast at **Nash Point.** This is a popular place for picnics, the lower part of the combe and the cliff-tops being covered with springy turf.

Porthcawl

Amusements. The town has cinemas, and plays, concerts, dances, etc., are held at the Pavilion, a fine building on the Esplanade. At Coney Beach, eastwards of the Harbour, is an amusement park providing a wonderful variety of entertainments.

Angling. Freshwater fishing for sewin and trout in the rivers Ogmore, Ewenny, and Kenfig. The Ewenny is the best river in the county for large trout, and grayling are sometimes landed.

Bathing. There is good bathing at Sandy Bay, east of the Harbour, and at the far western end of the front at Rest Bay. Due regard should be paid to the warning notices before attempting to bathe from other parts of the shore.

Bowls. There are eight greens at Griffin Park, New Road. Annual tournaments.

Buses connect Porthcawl with Bridgend, Cardiff, Aberavon, Neath, etc.

Caravan Sites. Several large and well-equipped sites in the area under the control of the Council. Modern caravan camp at Happy Valley.

Distances. Cardiff, 26; Bridgend, 7; London, 186.

Early Closing Day. Wednesdays.

Golf. An excellent 18-hole course belonging to the *Royal Porthcawl Golf Club*, on the shore. The *Kenfig and Pyle Golf Club* has a fine 18-hole course within easy reach.

Hotels. *Seabank; Esplanade; Pier; Sandville; Westward Ho; Porthcawl; Marine;* Private: *Fairways; Atlantic; Bryn-y-Mor; Gwalia;* and numerous others. *Trecco Bay Holiday Camp.*

Information. Grand Pavilion.

Population. 12,210.

Tennis. There are public courts at Griffin Park, and at the Council's Playing Fields, Locks Lane.

Porthcawl is a popular holiday resort situated on a low, rocky promontory on the northern shore of the Bristol Channel, midway between Cardiff and Swansea. While sheltered from north and east winds by the neighbouring range of hills, it is open to the warmer westerly breezes of the Atlantic. Fog and snow are rare, and for a west coast town the rainfall is moderate.

The town is well kept and has attractive shops; it has numerous hotels and boarding-houses, including many that will give satisfaction to the most fastidious.

Porthcawl is justly proud of its **Sea Front** or Fronts, for there are at least two. Eastward of the Harbour mouth and Porthcawl Point, and facing south, is **Sandy Bay**—a favourite bathing-place —and the splendid roadway, the Eastern Promenade, extends to **Coney Beach**, taking its pattern as well as its name from the world-famous Coney Island, New York. Next comes a small inlet called **Trecco Bay**, its name being taken from a vessel wrecked there many years ago. Its eastern horn is the western horn of **Newton Bay**, an expansive inlet which receives the *Ogmore* River, and has before it the **Tusker Rock**, from which project skers—dangerous ledges of submerged rocks.

At the Harbour mouth is a small stone **Pier**. Nearby is a small public garden with a putting course.

Westward of the Point the general aspect of the sea front is south-westerly. The **Esplanade** is a gay and popular rendezvous of holiday-makers. Centrally placed is the handsome **Grand Pavilion** where is staged first-class entertainment throughout the year. A feature is the large area of covered seating accommodation in front. A pleasant underwalk below road-level is popular and there is a paddling pool for children among the rocks. The views seaward are very fine.

Apart from the Grand Pavilion, the largest and perhaps most interesting building in the town is **All Saints' Church**, reached by a short walk along Mary Street off the Esplanade. The Church, a handsome Chapel of Ease, was built before the First World War and lacks a tower.

The Esplanade is continued by West Drive for nearly two miles from the harbour mouth across the 73 acres of **Lock's Common**, above the low cliffs leading to **Rest Bay**, another popular and safe bathing-place. Here are car parks, the *Rest Convalescent Home* and the **Golf Links** and beyond stretch the long range of sand-dunes which to many people are not the least attractive feature of a Porthcawl holiday.

Now incorporated in the town is the interesting village of

Newton, which part is approached by the New Road, which goes off from the northern end of John Street at the level-crossing.

The object of special interest here is the **Parish Church.** The massive tower is believed to date from the thirteenth century. Like others of its time situated in spots similarly exposed to hostile attacks, it was intended to serve as a fort in case of need. Below the parapet, on its eastern side, there are still to be seen the supports of the platform from which missiles could be discharged at the enemy. The south porch shows work of the thirteenth, fourteenth, and fifteenth centuries. The plain font is of late-Norman date. In the churchyard is buried the Rev. John Blackmore, father of the novelist.

A hundred yards south of the church is a curious well of clear spring water, which rises as the tide ebbs and falls as the tide comes in. It is known as **St. John's Well.** Stone steps lead down to it. A Latin verse, with English translation, is engraved on a slab fastened to the wall.

A number of Bronze Age burial mounds have been found in the fields and on Newton Down. Under one of these, at Mount Pleasant Farm, one of the only two Neolithic house foundations so far found in Wales was discovered and Neolithic stone axes have also been turned up by the plough. The first early Iron Age (500 B.C.) occupation site found in South Wales was in the sandhills between Newton and Candleston.

To the west is **Nottage,** a former walled village now incorporated in the town of Porthcawl.

Nottage Court, or Ty Mawr, the Great House, now designated as of special architectural and historic interest, was awarded after the Reformation 1545 to an ancestor of the present family (who married a Lougher of Sker) and largely rebuilt about 1570, in the style then popular as a compliment to Queen Elizabeth I, whose mother, Anne Boleyn, had been created Countess of Pembroke and was also Lady of the Pembroke Manor of Newton Nottage; she is linked, traditionally, with the earlier house, formerly the Noche Court Grange of Margam Abbey. Since 1545 it has descended through different generations of the present family, except for about 70 years in the eighteenth century, when it was mortgaged and passed temporarily out of the family's possession. On its recovery in 1780, it was restored and later added to in Victorian times. During the foundation work for the latter addition, certain Roman objects were unearthed.

It contains fine late-Tudor stone fireplaces and pointed doorways, some pannelled rooms and beautiful tapestries of fifteenth and seventeenth centuries.

Embedded here and there in the walls, which are a distinctive feature of the village, are some few fragmentary remains of a Chapel-of-Ease (probably attached to the Abbey Grange) which fell into disuse and ruin after the building at Newton of the Parish Church of St. John, notably a simple fleur-de-lys cross-slab, and part of the chapel doorway in a cottage opposite the back entrance to the Court.

Sker House, to which reference has indirectly been made, may be reached by road *via* Nottage, from where it is some 2½ miles towards the north-west, or by a pleasant walk, in the same direction, along the coast, from the Esplanade, *via* Rest Bay and the Golf Links. Interest in it mainly arises from its association with Blackmore's *Maid of Sker.* The house, a gabled pre-Reformation structure, standing amid the sandhills, was originally a grange of Margam Abbey, later held by the monks of Neath, and is now a farmhouse.

In the immediate vicinity of the house are the *Pyle and Kenfig Golf*

Links, and a mile due north, in the midst of the sandy waste, is a natural lake, **Kenfig Pool.** The pool is the haunt in winter and autumn of many interesting bird species while the marsh around it has a rich and varied flora.

Less than half a mile above the northern point of the lake, is the site of the **Buried City of Kenfig,** once one of the ancient boroughs of Glamorgan. The present hamlet clusters round the road and the church of St. Mary the Magdalene. An old inn has a large room which served in later years as the "town hall." From the thirteenth century onward the ancient borough suffered by the encroachment of the sand from the neighbouring dunes, and by the sixteenth century only slight vestiges of the castle remained.

The sand of Kenfig is extensively transported for constructional purposes, but without diminishing the supply, for as fast as it is removed, the loss is made good.

From Kenfig, a road running northward meets, at the end of some 2 miles, the main Cardiff–Swansea road. About a mile from the junction of the roads, with a lovely background of woods and hills, is—

Margam Abbey. Those going westward by road see first Margam Castle, formerly the seat of the Talbots, on the right about 3 miles after passing Pyle. Margam Abbey may be reached by taking the first turning on the right after passing the Castle. The Cistercian Abbey was founded by Robert, Earl of Gloucester, in 1147. The original nave of the Abbey Church is the parish church of Margam and has been so used since the dissolution. Due to the friendship of Father Stanton of Holborn with Theodore Talbot, Margam Abbey became the centre of the Tracterian movement in South Wales. The church and its setting make a very lovely scene. In a separate building in the churchyard is an interesting collection of stone crosses from the fourth century onwards (open Wednesdays, Saturdays and Sundays, 2.30–5), while in the church are tombs of the Mansel family.

Close to the main road are the mighty Abbey Works of the Steel Company of Wales, the largest steel works in Europe.

NEWPORT TO BRECON—THE USK VALLEY

The River Usk is one of the most beautiful rivers of Great Britain and for 57 miles winds its course from the Carmarthen Van through delightful and interesting country to the Bristol Channel a few miles below Newport. Almost from end to end there is good trout fishing while there are many pools where visitors may fish for salmon.

Newport

Angling. Newport is a good centre for sea-angling and river-fishing. For the latter application should be made to the Secretary of the Newport Angling Association, or to the Secretary of the Gwent Anglers Ltd. Salmon, trout, roach and dace are caught. Fishing is also permitted in the Corporation reservoirs.

Baths. At Stow Hill and Maindee.

Bus Services. Principal local services start from the Bus Centre in Dock Street. London and the Midlands from Clarence Place.

Distances. Cardiff, 12; Swansea, 57½; London, 149; Gloucester, 44; Abergavenny, 19; Monmouth, 24; Pontypridd, 19.

Early Closing Day. Thursdays. *Market Days.* Wednesdays and Saturdays.

Golf. *Newport Golf Club*, Great Oak, Rogerstone, 3 miles from the town (18 holes). *Tredegar Park*, ¼ mile from Bassaleg station (18-holes). The Newport and Machen buses pass the course. *Llanwern Golf Club*, about 4 miles from the town (18 holes).

Hotels. *Kings Head*, High Street; *Westgate*, Commercial Street; *Queen's*, Queen's Square; *Tredegar Arms*.

Places of Interest near Newport. Caerleon, 3 miles; Caerwent, 8; Raglan Castle, 16; Usk, 11; Caerphilly Castle, 12; Chepstow, 16; Tintern Abbey, 21½; Monmouth, 24. For a description of places not included in this book, see our *Guide to the Wye Valley.*

Population. 108,000.

Post Office. High Street.

The busy town of Newport owes to two factors the position which it occupies today as one of the leading distributing centres for the importers and exporters of South Wales and the Midlands, and also as an important sea-board manufacturing centre. One, its favourable geographical situation on the Bristol Channel, at the mouth of the tidal river Usk, with close proximity to the South Wales and Monmouthshire coalfield; the other, the far-sighted commercial and industrial enterprise which has utilised and improved the natural advantages of the

274

port. As a result, the docks at Newport are among the most up-to-date in Britain. Its **Alexandra Docks** form a huge single sheet of deep water. An outstanding feature is the deep-sea lock, one of the largest in the world, being 1,000 feet long and 100 feet wide, and affording direct access from the Bristol Channel to the Alexandra South Dock for the biggest liners afloat.

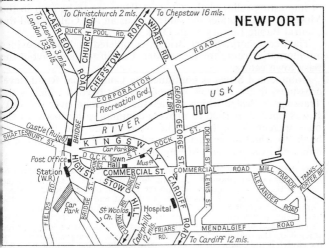

In spite of the name "Newport", the town has ancient origins. That it was a place of importance in the twelfth century is evident by its castle and church, and its origin probably dates back at least to Roman times. Since 1939 it has been an Assize town. The modern Civic Centre, westward of the Station dates from 1938.

The remains of **Newport Castle,** founded about 1130, rebuilt in 1448, and finally battered into ruins by Cromwell's troops, are on the river bank at the eastern end of High Street. On condition that the remains should be preserved and the historic portion restored, Lord Tredegar presented them to the town, and the restoration has since been undertaken by the Ministry of Works. The greater part of the Castle was purchased by his uncle, the late Viscount Tredegar, from the Duke of Beaufort.

The bridge over the River Usk, 60 feet wide, forms the main

275

gateway for road traffic from London to South Wales. At the farther end of the Bridge, in Clarence Place, is the **Cenotaph** Followed in the other direction (towards Cardiff), High Street ends at a fork: the left branch is Commercial Street, the right Stow Hill. In the former is the *Westgate Hotel*, which contains carefully-preserved wooden pillars bearing marks of bullets discharged during an attack made in 1839 by Chartists. A number of interesting relics of the Chartist Riots are to be seen in the **Museum,** which, under the same roof as an Art Gallery and the Central Public Library, is in Dock Street.

The new George Street Bridge, completed in 1964, provides an alternative route for Gloucester–Cardiff traffic to avoid the busy town centre.

Commercial Street is continued by Commercial Road (level crossings) to the railway, some 600 yards beyond which is the **Transporter Bridge** which carries the high road over the Usk. It was opened in 1906 to provide communication between the busy mercantile centres of the western side and the eastern bank, to which huge factories and iron and steel works have migrated from all parts of England.

At the top of Stow Hill, mentioned above, is the old **Parish Church of St. Woolos** (a corruption of the Latin form of the Welsh Gwynllyw, the name of the patron saint), which, on the creation of the diocese of Monmouth, in 1921, was chosen as the Pro-Cathedral, and in 1930 was made the *Cathedral Church*. It has been so carefully restored that its Norman features have been preserved. The tower was built by Jasper Tudor, Earl of Pembroke and uncle to Henry VII, who died in 1495, and whose mutilated effigy is on the western front. Separating the tower from the main body of the church is the Chapel of St. Mary; between the chapel and the nave is a Norman arch, thought to be the most remarkable example of its class in the whole kingdom.

The church is about half a mile from the station and a little beyond it is **Belle Vue Park,** an exceedingly pretty park which is well laid out and generally boasts a fine display of flowers. Music is provided in the park during the summer months and there are bowling greens and tennis courts.

Beechwood Park at Maindee occupies the top of a hill from which some striking views may be obtained; it is approached from the main Newport–Chepstow Road. This park is also well laid out with facilities for games such as bowling and tennis.

The Cathedral Church and Belle Vue Park are on the route to **Little Switzerland,** the best of the beauty-spots on the outskirts of the town. The prospect comprises the hills and valleys of Monmouthshire on the one side and the Bristol Channel on the other. Quite close to the Canal, and by walking alongside one can go right up into the hills and through beautiful valleys.

Whilst the town is not directly on the coast, bathers and swimmers are catered for at the town's well-equipped public baths at Maindee Square and Stow Hill. There are also two open-air lidos in private ownership, one at Bulmoor near Caerleon and the other at Allt-yr-yn.

The long narrow valleys leading from Newport to the north of the county are not entirely devoid of their natural beauty despite the great strides of industrialism. In one valley is **Cwmbran,** one of the places being developed under the New Towns Act 1946; higher is **Pontypool,** near which town is the immense factory of British Nylon Spinners, and the road continues to Abergavenny. The next valley to the west contains a huge aluminium works at **Rogerstone** and above are **Abercarn, Crumlin** and other industrial towns leading up to **Ebbw Vale** with its celebrated steelworks. In other valleys are **Tredegar** and **Rhymney,** busy townships of coal and heavy industries.

Three miles north-eastward of Newport is—

Caerleon-on-Usk, the Roman *Isca,* now a small town with narrow streets that have an air of quaintness and antiquity. It was, as its modern name implies, "the fortress of the legion", actually of the 2nd Augustan Legion. As such, it ranked among the most important military stations in the Roman Empire. Most of the modern town lies within the *enceinte* of the Roman fortress.

The fortress was first established about A.D. 75. It comprised a rectangular enclosure, 540 yards long by 450 yards broad, defended by a ditch, a stone rampart equipped with look-out turrets, and a clay bank. The stone rampart is still preserved in places to a height of about 12 feet. The fortress was entered by four symmetrically placed gateways. The interior was occupied by administrative buildings and barracks, the former aligned across the centre of the fortress in two rows defined by streets, the latter across the areas in front of and behind the principal buildings. Outside the fortress to the south and west were the non-military buildings, including shops, houses, temples, bath-buildings and an elaborately constructed amphitheatre. In addition there were the tileries of the legion and the cemeteries. The amphitheatre, the only one in this country that has been fully excavated, was erected during the last twenty years of the first century A.D. The site, together with that of barrack buildings near the west corner, is now in the care of the Ministry of Public Building and Works. Important collections of Roman material found in and about the fortress are preserved in the **Legionary Museum** (now a branch of the National Museum of Wales) near St. Cadoc's Church.

Other subjects of interest on the site are the Norman motte at the eastern angle of the fortress, the fifteenth-century church, and the *Hanbury Arms* (visited by Tennyson) overlooking the river.

Usk is a small town and famous angling station, charmingly situated on the river of the same name. It lies NNE of Newport, from which it is 11 miles distant by road. Usk contains the shell of a castle destroyed during the Civil War, and a church which belonged to a Benedictine nunnery.

The Church at **Bettws Newydd** 4 miles from Usk, on the Abergavenny road via Clytha, has its rood-loft intact, and a very elegant, although small, rood screen.

The Church of **Llangwm Uchaf,** 4 miles to the east of Usk on the Chepstow road, also has a rood-loft and screen of remarkable beauty.

Abergavenny

Situation. On the Usk, at the confluence of the Gavenny, at the feet of three mountains, the Sugar Loaf, Blorenge and Skirrid.

Angling. Tickets for trout and salmon fishing can be obtained at the offices of the Abergavenny Corporation, Town Hall.

Banks. *Barclays; Lloyds; Midland; National Provincial.*

Boating. On the canal at Llanfoist, rather more than a mile from the town.

Bowls. Corporation bowling green in Bailey Park, and at the *Abergavenny Bowling Club* in Avenue Road.

Bus Services. Between Abergavenny, Crickhowell and Brecon; also between Abergavenny, Pontypool, Brynmawr, Usk, Llanover, Hereford and Newport, Raglan and Monmouth.

Distances. Birmingham, 74; Gloucester, 39; Hereford, 24; London, 144; Monmouth, 15;

Newport, 20; Ross, 23; Swansea, 50; Worcester, 49.

Early Closing. Thursday. *Market Days*—Tuesdays and Fridays.

Entertainment. Cinemas. Dances and plays at Town Hall.

Golf. The *Monmouthshire Golf Club* has an 18-hole course on the right bank of the Usk, 2 miles.

Hotels. *Angel*, Cross Street; *Llansantffraed Court*, Raglan Road; *Swan*, Cross Street; *Victoria*, High Street; *Station*, *London*, Monk Street; *Rothesay*, Monmouth Road.

Hunting. The Monmouthshire Hounds hunt the district, and some of the meets of the Llangibby Hounds are within easy access of Abergavenny.

Population. 9,625.

Post Office. Frogmore Street.

Tennis. In the Castle grounds, on the cricket ground, and in Bailey Park.

Abergavenny is a clean, healthy, flourishing market town, charmingly situated. It is protected from north-easterly winds, and by reason of the site being in a hollow, the air is rather relaxing, though on the high ground it is bracing enough. It is advertised as the "Gateway of Wales" and the description is very apt when the town is seen from the Monmouth road, the Sugar Loaf on one side and Blorenge on the other forming lofty portals between which is spread Abergavenny, and beyond which is seen the lovely country on towards Crickhowell. The town shares with Crickhowell the advantage of being one of the best starting-points for excursions into the Black Mountains.

278

It is also the centre of many delightful walks, and offers visitors and residents many sports and pastimes.

The main thoroughfare is almost parallel to the Usk in this part of its course. It is known at various portions as Frogmore Street, High Street, and Cross Street. In and near this thoroughfare are some of the principal hotels, and the **Town Hall,** which contains the Corporation Offices. Here, too, is the **Market Place.** There is a **Public Library** in Baker Street.

St. Mary's Church, at the east end of the town, was originally the church of a Benedictine Priory, founded at the end of the eleventh century. It was much enlarged during the fourteenth century. The tower contains ten bells.

The chancel contains twenty-four stalls of carved oak which bear the name of Wynchestre, the prior in the fifteenth century. Adjoining the chancel on the south is the **Herbert Chapel,** containing an ancient recumbent figure in oak, believed to be the effigy of George de Cantelupe, Lord of Abergavenny, who died in 1273. The **Lewis Chapel,** on the north side of the chancel, has a huge recumbent figure in oak representing Jesse, the father of David; it was once the base of a genealogical tree of our Lord.

Adjoining the south transept stands the east wall of the ancient Priory which was demolished in 1952. The wall is left standing because of its historic features.

Holy Trinity Church (*daily Eucharist*) is the centre of an interesting group of buildings standing on the Grofield in Baker Street, westward of Frogmore Street. On either side are four almshouses for church-women, and on the south side is the vicarage. The church, founded in 1840, has a pleasing interior. The illuminated screen is modern.

Abergavenny Castle (*open daily. Museum open certain afternoons in summer*). The ruins are situated at the south-east end of the town, on rising ground where the *Gavenny* joins the *Usk.* The grounds are pleasantly laid out and include tennis courts and putting green.

The Castle was founded soon after the Norman Conquest, but the principal remains belong to the fourteenth century. In the year 1177 it

witnessed the massacre of the most renowned chieftains of Powis, who had been invited here by William de Braose, under pretext of celebrating Christmas. The deed was done to revenge the death of Henry of Hereford, uncle of William de Braose. The friends of the slaughtered chieftains retaliated by assaulting the Castle. Having obtained possession, they burnt it to the ground and carried off the governor and his wife and all the garrison as prisoners. The barony of Abergavenny is attached to the possession of the Castle, and is thus enjoyed not by creation but by tenure, like the earldom of Arundel. The Castle is now scheduled as an Ancient Monument.

Walks and Excursions from Abergavenny

Along the Riverside. To the right of the Castle entrance is a path which leads to the River Usk, and thence goes westward (upstream) to the bridge, beyond which the path is continued to **Llanwenarth Church**, about 1¼ miles farther. The return to Abergavenny can be made by a road which passes the Church.

Alongside the Brecon and Newport Canal. The nearest point of the canal to Abergavenny is at Llanfoist. Proceed to the south side of the bridge and beyond the *Bridge Inn* turn to the right. Immediately beyond the brewery turn to the left, up a narrow lane which is continued by a footpath that leads to a tunnel under the canal. A stile on the right near the tunnel gives access to the towpath at a point nearly a mile from the bridge.

(1) *In a south-easterly direction.* Continue along the path for nearly 2 miles, and just before reaching the third bridge, turn into a lane which soon meets the Llanelen road. There turn to the right for the village of **Llanelen**, a quarter of a mile from the foot of the lane. It has a fine stone bridge over the Usk, erected in 1821 by John Upton of Gloucester, the engineer of the fortifications of Sebastopol. It is about 2 miles by the high road from Abergavenny.

(2) *Towards the north-west.* The village of **Govilon** is 1½ miles from Llanfoist, and from it the return to Abergavenny can be made by bus, by high road, or the riverside (*see* the first walk). From Govilon the walk alongside the canal can be continued to **Gilwern**, a village prettily situated at the entrance to the Clydach Valley, and much frequented for boating on the canal. Gilwern is interesting on account of the manner in which roads and waterways seem to proceed at all levels and in all directions. It is a good 1½ miles beyond Govilon. The return can be made by bus from Gilwern.

The walk alongside the canal can be extended to **Llangattock** (Llangattwg), a charming stretch of about 5 miles, and then the return could be made from Crickhowell (on the opposite side of the river) by bus. Llangattock is near the south end of Crickhowell Bridge.

Ascent of Skirrid Fach (Little Skirrid). The hill forms part of Coldbrook Park. The summit (886 feet), under a mile from the station, commands a fine view of the town and of a portion of the valley of the Usk. The route is over the footbridge at the station, then south for 160 yards, and then alongside a hedge and watercourse. The latter has to be crossed at a point where a path bounded by wire fences leads from it towards the summit.

Ascent of Skirrid Fawr (Holy Mountain). The summit (1,601 feet) is 4 miles from the town. Follow the Ross road to a point rather more than 2¼ miles from Abergavenny, and there take a stile on the left. Keep near the hedge on the right and ascend to the wood about midway up the second field. Follow the path winding through the wood to a gate in a wall. There turn to the right, proceed to another gate in the same boundary and turn sharp left. Keep to the left of a hillock standing in front and make for a gap in the hill ahead. The route lies along the gap until boggy ground is reached, and there it winds round to the right to a path which leads to the ridge. This is nearly a mile long, very narrow, and rises in a series of humps to the summit, where there are a deep fissure and a precipice caused by a great landslip, which tradition says occurred on the night of the Crucifixion —hence the name "Holy Mountain." Two upright stones on the summit are the only remains of an ancient chapel here. The view from the summit is very extensive on every side.

Ascent of the Blorenge. This is a massive-looking hill, really part of the rim of the South Wales Coalfield, on the south side of the Usk. Its name ignifies the Blue Ridge. The ascent is more difficult than that of the Great Skirrid for the route goes over much soft ground. Follow the Merthyr road over the Usk, and a little beyond the first milestone bear to the left. In less than half a mile are a lane on the left and a footpath on the opposite side of the road. Follow the footpath to a bridge over the canal. Cross the bridge and then ascend the lane leading from it. Take the first turn to the right. Just beyond a cottage a field-path leads to the open mountains, up which the climber can strike across to the summit (1,832 feet).

The view in almost every direction is rich and varied, but is particularly charming over the valley of the Usk.

Ascent of the Sugar Loaf. This height (1,955 feet) owes its name to its conical shape. The ascent is a favourite excursion from Abergavenny, and with the exception of the last 500 feet the climb is not difficult. Indeed, it is possible to drive a long way towards the top by way of Triley, and from Abergavenny there is a zigzag path for ponies. From the town to the summit by the usual route is about $3\frac{1}{2}$ miles.

Proceed to Brecon Road station and pass under the right-hand arch. Follow Chapel Road for rather more than half a mile to a wicket-gate adjacent to a drive-gate on the left. Pass through the wicket-gate and follow the footpath from it into a lane. Go up the lane for a few hundred yards and then, when faced by a white cottage, turn sharp right. A steep climb leads to the open hill-side of the *Rholben*, a shoulder of the mountain. Thence the ascent may be continued by a steep green path or by the more gently sloping pony-path. The summit is a narrow ridge some 300 yards or more in length.

The Sugar Loaf is National Trust property. It commands a charming view extending from the Bristol Channel to the Malvern Hills.

Through the Fairy Glen. The **Fairy Glen** is the local and appropriate name of the lovely gorge of the *Clydach*, beautifully wooded, filled with ferns and through which the stream goes rushing and tumbling.

It is about 6 miles from Abergavenny, but it may be included in a circular excursion of which the walking distance may be reduced to some $3\frac{1}{2}$ miles, thus: Take the bus to Brynmawr at the head of the valley striking up from Gilwern. Below the roadway the Clydach rattles down its well-wooded gorge. The Fairy Glen is about half a mile below Brynmawr. At Blackrock village turn to the right, and follow a fenced path leading to a bridge over Pwll-y-Cwm Waterfall. From Clydach the bus can be taken to Abergavenny, but it is a good walk down the valley to Gilwern, an obvious alternative to the main road appearing on the left at the foot of the hill.

To Llanthony Priory and Capel-y-ffyn Monastery. The former is 11 miles from Abergavenny, the latter 15 miles. From the *Skirrid Mountain Hotel*, which claims to have been built in 1100, it is an increasingly attractive walk of 7 or 8 miles to **Llanthony** a hamlet situated in the sequestered valley of Ewyas, in the heart of the Black Mountains. Its name is an abbreviation of *Llandewi Nant Honddu*, "the Church of St. David on the Honddu brook."

The **Priory,** often called the Abbey, was an Augustinian monastery founded in the opening years of the twelfth century. It is now a venerable ruin. The greater part is in the Transitional style, but portions are as late as the fourteenth century. Much of the church remains. Adjoining the south transept is the Sacristy, still perfect, and next to it is a good part of the Chapter House. The Prior's Lodge and the south-west Tower have been converted into the *Abbey Hotel.* Next is a farmhouse called the Court. Across a field to the south-west of the farmhouse is the gate-house of the Priory, now used as a barn. A few yards south of the ruined Priory is the little **Parish Church,** a restored Norman structure with a very good roof and an ancient font. It is dedicated to St. David, as the full name of the hamlet indicates. (*Key at Abbey Hotel.*)

Capel-y-ffyn Monastery, 4 miles higher up the valley, and beside Nant-y-bwch, a tributary of the Honddu, was a conventual institution founded in 1870 by the late Father Ignatius, an Anglican clergyman. After the founders' death in 1908, the small community ceased to exist and the church fell into disrepair.

To White Castle. This Castle, one of the best-preserved fortresses of the Marches, is situated about 5½ miles ENE of Abergavenny, and is reached by way of Llanthewy Skirrid and Llanvetherine, and turning to the right about a mile and a half beyond the last-named village. It lies about a mile from the main road. It was one of three castles built to hold the Welsh in check, the others being Grosmont and Skenfrith. It is supposed to owe its name to the white plaster with which it was covered and of which portions are still visible. Its early history is obscure, but it was re-fortified about 1184, and was altered and extended by Hubert de Burgh in the thirteenth century. (*Standard hours, charge.*)

To Raglan Castle. A road excursion of 9 miles, south-east of Abergavenny, *via* Llanvihangel-nigh-Usk, and north of the main road at Raglan. The Castle has been well described as "the most perfect Decorated stronghold of which this country can boast—a romance in stone and lime." The ruins (*charge*) mainly belong to the fifteenth century, but a fortress probably occupied the site in the time of Henry II. For fuller details, *see* the *Red Guide to the Wye Valley.*

To Grosmont. Grosmont, a quaint little old-world village and a popular glianng station, is situated on the Monnow, 11 miles north-east of Abergavenny, in the midst of beautiful scenery. The importance Grosmont once had was due to its **Castle,** one of those built for the protection of the western frontier of England against the Welsh. The remains include two round towers, and an exquisite octagonal chimney dating from about 1300. They are now under the care of the Ministry of Public Building and Works, which has carefully carried out necessary repairs. (*Standard hours, charge.*)

Grosmont **Church,** dedicated to St. Nicholas, is a cruciform structure of stone in the Transitional and Early English styles.

Crickhowell

Situation. On the north side of the Usk, and on the high road between Brecon and Abergavenny.

Buses to Brecon, Talgarth. Abergavenny, etc.

Distances. London, 150; Abergavenny, 6; Brecon, 14; Builth, 27.

Early Closing Day. Wednesdays. *Market Day*—Thursday.

Fishing. In the Usk for salmon and trout, and in the Grwyne-fawr and Grwyne-fechan rivers.

Golf. Penmyarth Golf Club with 9-hole course in Glanusk Park, beside the main road to Brecon —2 miles from Crickhowell. Teas at Clubhouse.

Hotels. *Bear; Beaufort; Gliffaes,* etc.

Population. About 1,400.

Post Office on Abergavenny road.

Pony trekking and **Caving.**

Youth Hostel. High Street.

Crickhowell (in Welsh *Crug-hywel*—Howell's rock) is an ideal spot for a quiet holiday amid pleasant scenery and within easy reach of a larger centre. It is 14 miles from Brecon and about 6 from Abergavenny, the site of the nearest railway station, with which Crickhowell is connected by bus. Crickhowell is a pretty little town—hardly more than a village—picturesquely grouped on and around the hill crowned by its church. There are the fragments of a castle, a notable many-arched bridge over the Usk, two public halls, and several places of interest in the neighbourhood.

The **Church** (Sunday services, 8.30, 11, 6) was dedicated in 1303. It has been restored, and has modern aisles. Recumbent figures in niches in the chancel represent Sir Grimbald Pauncefoot and his lady. The latter became a widow and then founded the church.

The ivied fragments of the **Castle** are reached by a path from the Abergavenny road opposite the Post Office. The Castle was built in the thirteenth century, but an artificial mound and an entrenched base court indicate that the site was a stronghold before the Norman invasion.

At the west end of the town is the fourteenth-century gatehouse of **Porth Mawr** (Great Gate). It forms the entrance of a private residence, and frames a lovely aspect of the valley of the Usk. (The gatehouse may be inspected on appointment.)

Walks and Excursions from Crickhowell

To the Vale of Grwyney. Follow the Abergavenny road to Glangrwyney village (2 miles). There take the first turn to the left and go up the vale as far as Llangenny Bridge; there take the lane also to the left that leads to Crickhowell and commands fine views of the Usk valley.

Ascent of the Sugar Loaf. From Llangenny Bridge a lane (on the right) leads to the shoulder of the mountain, and thence the ascent is up a grassy slope.

To Partrishow Partrishow is 6 miles to the north-east of Crickhowell. Follow the road to **Llanbedr,** a beautifully situated little village, and from its church go almost due east to *Croes-fach* (1¼ miles); keep to the left of the stream, the *Grwyne Fawr*, and at the next fork (about ¼ mile) again

283

take the left branch, and then keep straight on for about 1¾ miles. The road is on the rise all the way. **Partrishow Church** was rebuilt at the latter part of the fifteenth century. It has a beautiful carved-oak screen. On the road, some 50 yards below the church, is a stone inscribed with two crosses directing the pilgrim of olden days to the **Holy Well of St. Mary**, about 200 yards up the brook, and once in great repute.

To Tretower. Leave Crickhowell by the Brecon road, and at the end of half a mile you are abreast of the **Gwern Vale Cromlech**, a poor specimen of such ancient burial-places. A mile and a half beyond fork to the right to **Tretower** (3¼ miles), where, on the left, overlooking the Rhiangoll stream, are the fragments of a Castle which was once defended by Sir James Berkeley against Owain Glyndwr. The sole remaining tower has two fine chimney-pieces. **Tretower Court**, the seat of the Vaughan family, is a very fine specimen of a fourteenth-century fortified manor house. (*Charge; standard hours.*)

To Puck's Dale. On the south side of the Usk take the first turn to the left. The road, which at first runs quite close to the river, forms part of the route to the village of Gilwern and so to Abergavenny, and for a great part of the way to Gilwern it is very lovely. The return from Gilwern (where the roads wind and climb over river and canal in a remarkable manner) may be made *via* the village of **Llanelly** (south of the Canal), the birthplace of Sir Bartle Frere. A short walk from it is the romantic dingle called **Puck's Dale**—Nant-y-Pwcca—the reputed scene of Shakespeare's *Midsummer Night's Dream*. In the stream in the dingle are small waterfalls.

Brecon

Situation. Near the foot of the Beacons, by the confluence of the Tarell and the Honddu (*hon-thee*), the "Black Water," with the Usk.

Angling. In the Usk. At Llangorse Lake (p. 288) free fishing for pike, roach, perch, and eels.

Boating. On the Usk. Sailing on Llangorse Lake.

Bus Services. Between Brecon, Crickhowell, Abergavenny, Devynock, Trecastle, Llandovery, Lampeter, etc. Also to Merthyr, Aberdare, Swansea and Cardiff, and to Builth Wells, Rhayader and Aberystwyth.

Distances. London *via* Monmouth and Abergavenny, 167; London *via* Hereford, 170; Builth, 16; Abergavenny, 20; Crickhowell, 14; Worcester, 60; Gloucester, 60.

Early Closing Day. Wednesdays. *Market Day*—Friday.

Golf. The Brecon Golf Club has a 9-hole course on Newton Farm, within easy distance of the town.

Hotels. *Castle of Brecon; George; Wellington; Gremlin; Markets Tavern.*

Population. 5,870.

Post Office. St. Mary Street.

Sports Club. The Brecon Sports Club is open to visitors for tennis and cricket.

Although Brecon (also called Brecknock) has but a small population, it is, as a touring centre, one of the principal inland towns of South Wales. The greater part is on the northern bank of the *Usk* and on both sides of the River *Honddu*. From its position at the meeting-place of the latter stream with the Usk it obtained its Welsh name of *Aber-Honddu*. The site of the town is one of considerable charm, the valley being fertile and bounded on either side by hills, pleasantly wooded or clothed with grass.

The centre of the town, known as the Bulwark, is marked by the imposing **Shire Hall,** from which the ground falls to the river, with fine views across to the Beacons. Here is the **Captain's Walk,** a short, pleasant, shaded promenade, ending on the bank of the Usk, at the sole remaining fragment of the old town wall.

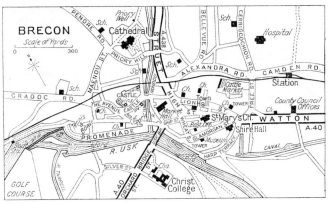

© Ward, Lock & Co., Limited

St. Mary's Church, or the Town Church, as it is commonly called, is at the far end of the Bulwark. It dates from the twelfth century, but restorers have robbed it of much of its interest. The Norman pillars, the fourteenth-century stoup used for 300 years as a font (Mrs. Siddons was baptised in it), and the very fine sixteenth-century tower deserve mention.

The **Brecknock Museum** (*weekdays* 10–12 *and* 1–4) is reached by a narrow passage south of the church leading to Glamorgan Street. It has an interesting collection illustrating the natural history and archaeology of the county. Also in Glamorgan Street is the Roman Catholic Church.

At the far end of Glamorgan Street turn to the right into Wheat Street. In High Street are the **Guild Hall** and the **Siddons Wine Vaults.** The Assembly Rooms at the former are used for concerts and the like. The house now known as the Siddons Wine Vaults, and much modernised, was formerly the *Shoulder of Mutton Inn*, and while it bore that name was the birthplace of Sarah Siddons (1775).

Follow High Street northward to Castle Street, the left-hand turning just past the Market Hall. This leads to a bridge over a ravine, down which the waters of the Honddu come rushing into the Usk.

Brecon Castle (*apply Castle Hotel*). The ruins, on the farther side of the ravine now mainly consist of embattled walls and restored towers and are nearly all in the garden of the *Castle Hotel*. One remnant, the *Ely Tower*, is on a lofty mound in the garden of the *Bishop's Palace*, opposite the hotel. The tower owes its name to having been the prison of Morton, Bishop of Ely, when Richard III was on the throne and a Duke of Buckingham was lord of Brecon. The fortress was built about the eleventh century by Bernard de Newmarch, who obtained some of the materials from the old Roman station of **Caer Bannau**, 3 miles off, the capital of the Welsh kingdom of Brycheiniog, overthrown by him.

Brecon Cathedral

Open daily until 7.30 *p.m. in Summer.* 6 *p.m. in Winter. Sunday Services at* 8, 11, 3.30.

The Cathedral (until 1923 the parish church of Brecon) is the glory of Brecon, for of the churches of Wales it is second only to St. Davids Cathedral. It is the third church which has occupied the site. Bernard de Newmarch found one here and removed it that he might erect a nobler building, and that in its turn gave place to the present structure. Built of old red sandstone of a beautiful colour from a local quarry, it was begun in the early part of the thirteenth century by the construction of the chancel, transepts, and tower. In the fourteenth century, the nave, which was that of de Newmarch's church, lost its Norman character by being gradually transformed into a Decorated building. The only remains of the Norman nave are the north and south walls and the font.

The ground plan consists of a nave with aisles, a north porch, a central tower or choir, with transepts, and an eastern limb forming a large Presbytery without regular aisles, but with a remarkable arrangement of chapels on each side. The total length exceeds 200 feet, the width is 60 feet. The building was restored by Sir Gilbert Scott.

Within the Cathedral, at the west end, is the very fine Norman font; here too may be seen various sepulchral slabs, incised with crosses and trade emblems.

The nave is grand, harmonious, and spacious. Note that the position of clerestory windows is unusual, as they are placed over the pillars instead of over the arches.

At the east of the north aisle is the **Chapel of the Corvizors** (shoemakers), where in a fine decorated recess is the recumbent effigy of a layman (about 1350) who may have been the builder of the nave.

The **Tower** contains five bells. In its arches the Early English work begins.

The **North Transept**, or Battle Chapel, is so called because, until comparatively recent years, it was the burial-place of the inhabitants of the hamlet of Battle, three miles from Brecon, probably attached to the priory and named after the parent house, the celebrated Battle Abbey in Sussex.

The **Chancel** is the finest part of the Church. Its builder intended it to be vaulted and erected the vaulting shafts and springers, but their design was not further carried out until 650 years later, when the vaulted ceiling, so long delayed, was constructed by Sir Gilbert Scott.

Within the sanctuary are triple piscinae and sedilae, remarkable for their size and beauty.

North of the chancel is the Havard Chapel, the burial-place of a Norman family of that name. Originally, this chapel was one of two which opened out of the north transept. In the fourteenth century they were combined and extended eastward to form the Lady Chapel. This has now been restored as the Regimental Chapel of the South Wales Borderers (24th Regiment).

The south transept, or the **Chapel of the Red-Haired Men**—the Normans —was probably the burial-place of the garrison of Brecon Castle.

In St. Lawrence's Chapel, on the south side of the chancel, is a bronze effigy, designed by Sir W. Goscombe John, R.A., in memory of Bishop Bevan.

From the west side of the transept we pass through an Early English arch into the South Aisle, where is the door through which the monks passed between the cloisters and the church. Through it we look into the Cloister Garth, and up to the private grounds of the **Deanery**. On the west side of the Cathedral are an ancient tithe barn and Almonry.

On the southern side of the Usk, in a line with the Cathedral and the Castle, is **Christ College,** the well-known Welsh Public School. It was founded by Henry VIII, and is housed in picturesque buildings that include portions of a Dominican Friary. The dining-hall, library, and chapel belong to the thirteenth century. The Chapel, indeed, is the restored choir of the ancient Church. Several bishops of St. Davids of the sixteenth century were buried within, and it contains some interesting effigies. The Sunday services are open to visitors.

On the same line of thoroughfare, but farther from the town, is **St. David's Church,** the representative of an ancient building which collapsed in 1852.

At the east end of the town are the **Barracks** together with the Headquarters and museum of the South Wales Borderers.

Walks and Excursions from Brecon

The Priory Grove and Llanddew. A shady walk beginning near the Cathedral. It is best approached by way of an iron bridge from the Struet, a thoroughfare that continues northward the line of High Street. For three-quarters of a mile the Honddu flows on the right. Then the path drops to a stone footbridge over the stream. From a disused forge on the farther side a footpath leads to the Hay road and on to **Penlan Park,** commanding a very fine view of the Beacons.

Llanddew is about 2 miles north-east of Brecon. Of the churches in the county of Brecknock, that of Llanddew is probably the most ancient, and it stands next in point of interest to the Cathedral at Brecon. In the precincts stood an ancient residence of the Bishops of St. Davids including Giraldus Cambrensis.

To Pen-y-Crug. A hill about 2 miles north-west of the town. It is crowned by an ancient British camp with well-preserved trenches and high embankments, and commanding a magnificent panoramic view. Leave from the Avenue, near the Castle Hotel, *via* Maendu Street and left into Pendre Road. In half a mile turn left into lane from which a further steep lane, left, carries past a farmhouse. A forward gate gives access to the hill.

To Llanfrynach. Llanfrynach is a pretty village with a charming little church about 3½ miles south-east of Brecon, from which it may be reached by a variety of routes. Perhaps the most pleasant is that which at first lies along Dinas Road, entered from the western end of the Usk Bridge, against Christ's College. Follow the road through the lodge gates of the grounds of Dinas House and as far as the second iron gate beyond it; then take the footpath on the left and proceed alongside the stream.

To the Rhyd-goch Falls. These are south-west of the town in one of the tributaries of the Afon Tarell, a feeder of the Usk. They are only small, but the glen is exceedingly pretty. From the western end of the Usk (Llanfaes) Bridge, follow the Llandovery road to a point some two or three hundred yards past St. David's Church, and there turn to the left. Having passed Ffrwdgrêch Lodge, about three-quarters of a mile from the main road, cross a stream and then take the middle of the three roads beyond it. It leads in three-quarters of a mile to a bridge (Pont Rhyd-goch) just above the larger of the two falls, to which a path runs from the near side of the bridge. To reach the other fall, cross the bridge and walk towards the source of the stream. (The falls are on one of the routes to the Beacons.)

To Slwch Hill. This hill—a favourite view-point, one mile east of the town—is reached by way of Free Street and Cerrig Cochion Road and then by the lane on the right at the Intermediate School. The hill is crowned by a British encampment and a clump of firs.

To the Gaer (Y Gaer), or Caer Bannau. The site of the Roman *Bannium*, on the north side of the Usk, nearly 3 miles west of Brecon, and near to Battle village. It is one of a chain of fortresses constructed in Wales during the Roman invasion. Proceed from the Castle Hotel along the Avenue, and then turn to the left about 200 yards short of the Cemetery. The camp can be visited by permission. Excavated relics of the Roman period may be seen at the adjacent Gaer Farm.

To Sennybridge. This little village, 10 miles west of Brecon, may be reached by road *via* Aberyscir. It is an excellent fishing centre, and details can be obtained from Sennybridge Fishing Association. On the way to Sennybridge, and about 2½ miles from Brecon, is the little village of **Llanspyddid,** in the churchyard of which are some of the finest yews in Britain.

Llangorse Lake

Llangorse Lake (Llyn Safaddan), some 5 or 6 miles east of Brecon, is the largest natural lake in South Wales. It is about 2½ miles in length and about half a mile wide, but the depth is not great. The water is popular with anglers, who have free fishing for pike, roach, perch, and eels. Boats can be hired, and sailing is a favourite amusement. Accommodation can be found at boarding-houses near the lake, and at two small inns in the village. The vicinity is a pastoral region backed by mountains. At the lower end is the **Allt** (Allt yr Esgair) (1,287 feet), standing alone and overlooking the Usk valley. On the south side of the lake stands the beautiful little church of **Llangasty-Tal-y-llyn.** Its tower is a favourite view-point. The village of **Llangorse** is half a mile from north side of lake. In Llangorse Church is a very ancient inscribed stone.

Talgarth

Talgarth (*Ashburnham Arms Inn*), meaning "The foot of the hill", is an appropriate name for this little town at the foot of the Black Mountains. It is about 8 miles north-eastward of Brecon and is an admirable centre for the tourist in search of rural beauty.

In the neighbourhood are **Cwm-trappe,** a wooded dell, the Pwll-y-wrâch Falls on the River Enig and the **Parc Woods,** which afford fine views of the hills of Brecknockshire and Radnorshire.

The Beacons

The ascent of the Beacons is one of the chief excursions from Brecon. The main points (from east to west, over a distance of about 10 miles) are Pen-y-Fan, Fan Fawr, Fan Llia, Fan Nedd, and Fan Gihirych. **Pen-y-Fan** (2,907 feet) is the loftiest peak in South Wales. The view from it is uninteresting towards the south, where the principal feature is moorland, though when the air is clear the Bristol Channel can be distinguished. Towards the east the Black Mountains are the most prominent objects; in the west are mountains stretching away to the Carmarthen Van, but towards the north the prospect is varied and most lovely. It looks across the valley of the Usk and Llangorse Lake, and in clear weather the view includes distant heights like Plynlimon and Cader Idris.

The favourite routes from Brecon to the Beacons are—

1. *Via* **Ffrwdgrech.** The first portion of this route is identical with that to the Rhyd-goch Falls (*see* p. 288) as far as the bridge beyond the lodge. Having crossed the bridge, take the left-hand road. It follows the Gwdi stream to Blaen Gwdi Farm. There turn to the right, and at the end of a quarter of a mile turn to the left, and the way to the top of Pen-y-Fan is plain.

2. By the bus service which runs over the Beacons to Merthyr. A good point at which to alight is at the Café and Youth Hostel, 8 miles from Brecon, only 1,600 feet below the summit of Pen-y-Fan, and about 2 miles from it. The ascent is easy and the summit lies on the far side of a valley in which flow the headwaters of the River Taff.

3. *Via* **Torpantau** near the Pen-twyn reservoir. Torpantau is 1,400 feet above sea-level. About 2 miles due north is Gwaen cerig-llwydion and half a mile farther, to the left, is Cwm Oergwm, and thence the route follows the ridge towards the west. Brecon can be reached from the summit by way of Ffrwdgrêch in about two hours. (No inn at Torpantau.)

A road, passable for cars in good weather, leads from Torpantau in a north-westerly direction past Neuadd Reservoir to a col at the head of Cwm Cynwyn, from which one can follow the ridge westward to Pen-y-Fan, or continue to Brecon, about 5 miles due north.

About ¼ mile from Pen-y-Fan is the peak called **Corn-du** (2,863 feet). To reach it from Pen-y-Fan involves making a slight descent of about 100 feet and a rather steeper climb.

The Bwlch Pass

Bwlch Pass is a narrow valley by the Buckland Mountain, at an elevation of 732 feet, on the road between Brecon and Abergavenny, about 8 miles from the former town. At the pass a fine view suddenly meets the eye. The Brecon and Abergavenny buses go through the pass. A walker who delights in fine scenery and is returning to Brecon should go on from Bwlch to Tal-y-llyn, 5 miles by direct road, or 6½ miles via Llangorse. The road from Brecon to Abergavenny is one of the most beautiful in South Wales, and those who can only go from Brecon to Bwlch Pass will see the best part of it. Five miles from Brecon the road passes **Cwm Gelanedd,** the 'Valley of Slaughter'', and there, nearly opposite the milestone, is an inscribed stone, said to have been erected in memory of a Roman officer who was killed in a battle against the Welsh.

Craig-y-nôs Castle. Travellers on the road from Brecon to Neath or Swansea, *via* Penwyllt, 18½ miles from Brecon, may obtain a good view of Craig-nôs Castle, the "Rock of Night," for many years the home of Madame Patti. It stands on the right of the road and is now known as the Adelina Patti Hospital. A fine stalactic cave (*Dan-yr-Ogof*) is situated near Craig-y-nôs.

Owing to the heavy rainfall on the southern slopes of the Beacons and the sparsely populated character of the country, the region constitutes an excellent gathering ground for water. In the two valleys (Taff Fawr and Taff Fechan) that unite near Merthyr to form the Taff there have been made large reservoirs to supply Cardiff and Newport respectively, while Neath draws its water from a reservoir on the river Dringarth near Ystradfellte and Swansea from one near Craig-y-nôs. The Cardiff reservoirs in Taff Fawr are especially beautiful, and are seen from the road between Brecon and Merthyr. There is also a large reservoir near Tal-y-bont in Brecknockshire for the supply of Newport.

HAY-ON-WYE TO BUILTH WELLS

Hay-on-Wye

Distances. London, 164; Hereford, 21½; Brecon, 15½; Glasbury, 4; Builth, 18; Three Cocks, 5½; Talgarth, 8; Crickhowell, 20.
Bathing Pool. The Warren.
Early Closing Day. Tuesday.

Entertainments. *Plaza Cinema.* Tennis courts and putting green.
Hotels. *Crown; Swan.*
Market Day. Thursday.
Population. 1,310.

Hay-on-Wye, sometimes known as "Welsh Hay", is built on a hill rising from the bank of the Wye, and is a good centre for climbing the Black Mountains and exploring the upper reaches of the Wye. The older part of the town is a tangle of rather narrow and winding streets. The name is said to be derived from the Norman–French *haie* or German *haga* ("an enclosed place"). The Welsh name of the town is Tregelli, which has been rendered "the town in the forest".

In the town are the remains of a **Castle** which was built about 1090. It was burnt in 1216 by King John, and again in the fifteenth century by Owen Glendower. The Norman gateway and tower have remained and adjoining the stronghold are the residential quarters built in the reign of Queen Elizabeth I and now privately owned.

The **Chapel of St. John** in Lion Street was probably founded about 1254. Since 1550 it has been used for various purposes, but is now restored for use of the parish.

The **Parish Church,** dedicated to St. Mary, stands west of the town. The lower part of the square embattled tower is dated about 1200; the south entrance door is a good example of Early English architecture, but the present church dates mainly from 1834, when it was rebuilt and enlarged. The registers go back to about 1680. The chalice, dated 1576, bears the inscription "Oure Lady Paris of the Haia," the meaning of which has been given as "Our Lady (St. Mary), parish of Hay."

Near the Church are the **Bailey Walk,** a popular promenade, which takes its name from the earthwork remains of the old motte and bailey castle next to the church. The **Steeple Pool** is a deep and dangerous part of the river. According to local tradition, it contains a peal of bells that once hung in St. Mary's Tower.

Followed westward the Bailey Walk leads to the **Warren,** a picturesque spot commanding fine views.

Mouse Castle is the name given to an ancient camp, a Norman motte and bailey, about a mile east of Hay-on-Wye. From the tree-covered hill, the site of the earthworks, are beautiful views.

Craswall Priory is about 5 miles south-east from Hay-on-Wye. From the town the route is *via* the Forest Farm, and keeps the road to the left all the way. It passes the Birches Farm and runs along the Parks, where it turns sharply to the left across the moorland which formed the grazing park of the Priory. We pass the **Holy Well**, which is one of the headsprings of the river Monnow, and then arrive at the *Abbey Farm*, near which are the almost buried ruins of the Priory. This is said to have been founded in 1222. The remains contain some beautiful work of the thirteenth and fourteenth centuries.

Clyro is a little more than a mile north-west of Hay-on-Wye, and may be reached either by a footpath through the fields or by the road. Approaching, we pass near the site of **Clyro Castle** of which the only remains are a portion of the moat and a small mound.

Painscastle is 3 miles north-west of Clyro. The **Castle** was built by Matilda de Breos and repaired and adorned in 1231, when Henry III held his court in it. The only traces of the fortress are the mound on which it stood and the surrounding moat.

Hay-on-Wye to Builth Wells

This is a run of 18 miles. For the whole distance the road and river are close companions, and the scenery is delightful, especially from the road on the southern bank of the river, which gives fine views of the Aberedw Rocks and for miles runs beneath trees and within a few yards of the rushing river. An alternative road runs north of the river via Clyro; turn sharp left there for **Llowes**. In the church here is the *Great Cross of St. Meilig* dating from the seventh century and weighing some 3½ tons. Between Llowes and Glasbury is **Maesllwch Castle** which occupies a beautiful site north of the Wye. The remaining section of this comparatively recent building (1829) is privately occupied. **Glasbury-on-Wye** is a pretty village on both sides of the river.

About a mile beyond Glasbury we reach *Three Cocks Junction*, giving its name to the famous old angling and coaching hostelry—the *Three Cocks Hotel*. Near by is *Gwernyfed*, an Elizabethan house in which Charles I was once a guest, and which is now a school.

From Three Cocks we pass through very beautiful scenery. The hills and rocks close in, and though at times stretches of deep and still water are passed, there frequently appear rapids, which now form the chief feature of the river scenery. **Llyswen,** where the river makes an extraordinary bend, is said to have held the residence of the early Welsh princes. Beyond Llyswen are the castle and beautiful woods of **Llangoed.** On the north side of the river comes **Boughrood** (*bockroad*) (*Boat Inn*), also with a castle. The village is beautifully situated on the left bank of the Wye, which is here crossed by a stone bridge.

The scenery here is particularly charming, and there are delightful walks. One is up a pretty glen to **Llanerchoeddlan Wells;** another is to **Llanstephan Church.**

Four miles farther upstream is **Erwood** (*errood*). Its name is properly *Y Rhyd*, "the ford". The passage was near the spot where the river is crossed by a bridge. The village post office is pointed out as having been the lodging-place of Henry Mayhew, the founder of *Punch*, when hiding from his creditors in the early years of last century, and the parlour of the inn as the spot where the great idea of founding that journal occurred to him.

It is but a short walk from the village to the stream called *Bachwy*, or Bachowy, and the **Falls of Craig-pwll-du,** in English the "Rock of the Black pool." The water falls some 40 feet among wild and romantic rocks, which makes the ravine intensely gloomy.

Aberedw village stands at the spot where the Wye receives the Edw brook, which comes rushing to it through a rocky gorge. Aberedw Rocks consist of a series of piled slabs and blocks of rock resembling gigantic masonry. They extend along the Radnorshire bank of the Wye in perpendicular form, rising to a height of several hundred feet for a distance of nearly a mile. They are alternated with patches of greensward, and are partially concealed by hanging woods. Aberedw Church can be reached by a footpath that runs from the bridge over the Edw. The church has been much restored, but possesses a fourteenth-century screen.

About a mile from the village, high up on the bank of a ravine, is **Llewelyn's Cave,** cut out of the solid rock, and measuring nearly 6 feet square. Its position is indicated by a pole near the entrance. To reach it, follow the road which passes through the village and across the stream. Take the right branch at the fork beyond the stream, and make your way upward through the trees. On reaching open ground bear left to a stile. The cave is only a short distance farther. It was from this cave, according to tradition, that Llewelyn rode to Builth to seek shelter from the English, but the townspeople would not admit him.

Builth Wells

Banks. *Barclays; National Provincial; Midland.*

Cinema in Market Hall Buildings.

Dancing in the Strand Hall.

Distances. London, 173; Brecon, 17; Hay-on-Wye, 19; Llandrindod Wells, 7; Llangammarch Wells, 9; Llanwrtyd Wells, 12; Newbridge-on-Wye, 5½; Rhayader, 13; Three Cocks, 14.

Early Closing Day. Wednesday.

Golf. There is a 9-hole course at the west end of the town.

Hotels. *Lion; Swan; Plough; Greyhound; Llanelwedd.*

Market Day. Monday.

Population. 1,570.

Post Office in Strand near Bridge.

Sports. Bowls, tennis, fishing, golf, putting, cricket, motor-cycle racing. Every year the *Hawkstone Otter Hounds* hunt the Wye and its main feeders, and for a fortnight in July Builth Wells is usually the headquarters of the hunt. Pony-trekking holidays are arranged throughout the season.

Builth, or Builth Wells, the *Bullorum* of the Romans, is picturesquely situated on the Breconshire bank of the Wye, 413 feet above sea-level. Seen from a distance, the town, the bridges, the winding river and the background of lofty hills on the south and west make a charming picture. The town commands the trade for many miles around and is a busy little place with much in its daily life to interest strangers. The Wells commemorated in the name are about a mile from the town.

The **Parish Church,** which stands at the west end of the town, has a squat massive tower of the fourteenth century, but the rest is modern, having been rebuilt in 1870. The only notable monument is a recumbent effigy of John Lloid of Towey, of the sixteenth century.

Alongside the Wye and overlooked from the stone bridge of six arches, built in 1760, is the **Groe,** a flat, grassy area of 15 acres, forming a public recreation ground and a favourite promenade. Here is the principal **Car Park** (charge).

Of the former *castle* which once stood at the east end of the town nothing now remains but the earth mound.

The **Death of Llewellyn.** Special interest attached to Builth Castle owing to its intimate connection with the death of Llewelyn ap Griffith, the last native Prince of Wales. Llewelyn, being engaged in his great struggle with Edward I, was led to believe that the newly restored castle at Builth would be surrendered to him by its governor, John Giffard, who had fought with him under De Montfort against Henry III, and was related to him by marriage. In the supposed furtherance of the plot, the Prince was induced to pay a secret visit to Aberedw. With one squire and a bodyguard of eighteen men he rode to Llechryd and forded the river, and then leaving his men to hold the ford, he and the squire rode on to Aberedw, where the Prince was to meet one who would conduct him to a secret meeting of the local chiefs. Tradition says that while he waited he engaged a smith to reverse the horses' shoes, as snow was on the ground, and anyone finding his tracks would

294

suppose he was going in the opposite direction to that which he had taken. The expected messenger did not arrive, and the Prince learned that a band of his foes led by Edmund and Roger Mortimer and Roger L'Estrange was trying to surround him. With his squire he stole away to a cave which may still be seen at Aberedw. At dawn they went stealthily to Llechryd, but the river was swollen and the ford impassable. The nearest bridge was at Builth and to that the Prince led his men. The smith had been terrified into confessing the trick of the horseshoes, and the Prince's foes had followed him so closely that they were in sight as he crossed Builth Bridge. It was of wood, and Llewelyn and his men broke it down behind them. The pursuing band turned back and galloped down the valley to cross at Y Rhyd (Erwood), 8 miles below. Contrary to his expectation, Llewelyn was refused admission to Builth Castle. To gain a place of safety, he led his little band to Pont y Coed, a wooden bridge over the Irfon near Llanynis Church. Then, the Prince left his men at the bridge while he went on to Llanvair farmstead, near Cefyn-y-bedd. During his absence his foes reached the bridge, and every man was killed. Freed from opposition, the Prince's pursuers dashed off in search of the little force Llewelyn had left on the neighbouring high ground when he went on his ill-starred ride to Aberedw. On their way they came upon two men hurrying in the same direction. These they struck down without recognizing them as the Prince and his squire. Later the Prince's assailant returned and having identified his victim cut off his head. The trophy was sent to the King at Rhuddlan and thence to London. There being current an old prophecy that the Prince of Wales would wear his crown in London when the English money became round, which had actually happened that year, the head was in mockery crowned with ivy. Then, having been exposed to the jeers of the population in the streets, it was fixed on the Tower after the barbarous practice of the age.

John Giffard and his companions became known among the Welsh as the "traitors of Builth," and for long feeling ran high between them and the townspeople, but by the King they were generously rewarded with grants of land.

Between two and three miles from Builth Wells, on the Llangammarch road, is **Cefn-y-Bedd**, "the ridge of the grave," a name formerly believed to refer to the grave of Llewelyn, but it is now known that Cefn-y-Bedd was the name of the spot before Llewelyn's death. The spot where Llewelyn was killed is near a cottage on the left-hand side of the road going towards Llangammarch, and is marked by an obelisk.

Just over a mile south of Builth the Brecon road crosses the river *Duhonw* at the White Bridge, **Llanddewi'r-cwm**, in the midst of fine scenery and half a mile short of the church. The original church was built in the seventh century. A little above the bridge is the **Fairies' Glen.** A few yards short of the bridge a turning on the left leads to a mountain lake, **Pant-y-llyn,** $1\frac{1}{2}$ miles distant. The hill affords magnificent views and upon it is an abundance of red heather.

North-east of Builth is **Llanelwedd,** where the church was restored and enlarged in 1877. The tower, nave and chancel belong to the early part of the fourteenth century. **Llanelwedd Hall** dates from Elizabeth I's time and now serves as headquarters of the Royal Welsh Agricultural Society. The adjoining land is the permanent site for the annual Royal Welsh Show.

A little eastward of Llanelwedd Church are the paths over the **Llanelwedd Rocks.** One, running almost due north, leads to *Carneddau Farm*; the other, having a north-easterly direction, runs to Maen-Cowyn, above which are two British camps.

THE IRFON VALLEY

The Irfon comes down to the Wye at Builth Wells from the same prolific group of mountains which gives birth to the *Towy*, the *Teifi*, and many a smaller stream. From its source to its junction with the Wye it is perhaps 30 miles long, and for half that distance it is accompanied by a good road through striking scenery.

Llangammarch Wells (*Cammarch, Lake*) is a small village near the confluence of the *Cammarch* with the Irfon. It is about 560 feet above sea-level and is overlooked by the Eppynt Hills, which rise a thousand feet higher.

The **Church** stands on a knoll overlooking the station; the village is beautifully situated and before the railway embankment intruded, the view from across the river must have been worth halting for.

The water for which Llangammarch became famed contained barium chloride, a rare constituent. It was recommended for certain heart diseases, chronic rheumatism and gout. The barium chloride well and pump house, now disused, are in the grounds of the Lake Hotel.

As a restful centre for a relaxing holiday in unspoiled country. Llangammarch has a good deal to offer; good fishing (trout and salmon in the Irfon), rough shooting and pony–trekking, The district is the haunt of the lapwing, curlew, buzzard and, on occasion, kites.

Strong walkers have plenty of scope and the **Eppynt Mountain** (1,560 feet), which is close at hand, is worth climbing for the sake of the view and the exhilarating mountain air.

Llanwrtyd Wells (*Abernant Lake, Dol-y-Coed*) is a pleasant, small Breconshire town, straggling along both banks of the Irfon, in a sheltered valley 750 feet above sea-level, surrounded by lofty mountains, a fact partly accounting for its rather high rainfall. There are a number of holiday pursuits available, including shooting, both hotels having rights over a considerable area of countryside.

A short distance up the valley are the sites of the two groups of springs which at one time were used for therapeutic uses. Just below the station is a large artificial lake with boats and canoes, and on its shore are refreshment rooms and a concert pavilion.

One of the charms of Llanwrtyd Wells is the easy access to the delightful countryside surrounding it. Routes lead across

ABERYSTWYTH, RHAYADER, BRECON

0 1 2 3 4 5 6   12 Miles

WARD, LOCK & CO. LIMITED, LONDON

© John Bartholomew & Son Ltd, Edinburgh

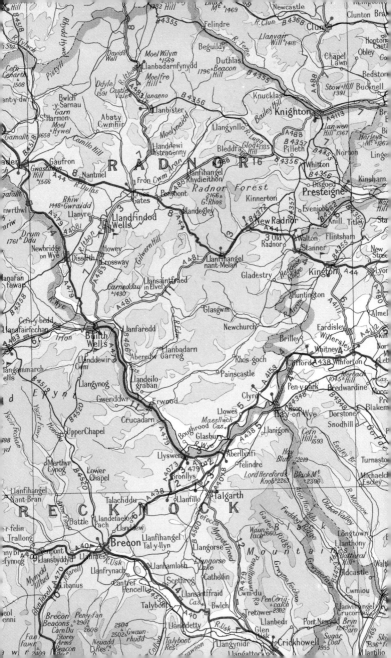

hills, streams and through forests. It is therefore not surprising that **pony-trekking** has become firmly established.

Half a mile out of the village along the Beulah road is the flourishing British Legion factory for making attractive woollens and tweeds. Visitors are welcome to watch the manufacture.

For **Llandovery**, south-east from Llanwrtyd Wells, see p. 239.

The Irfon Valley road strikes north-westward from Llanwrtyd Wells, closely following the wood-fringed stream and though narrow is a pleasant motor road. On the left, about 1½ miles from the town, stands **the Old Church** of Llanwrtyd. It is of little intrinsic interest, but its situation is delightful. The house called *Dinas*, standing near the Church, is interesting to Welshmen through having been the home of John Lloyd, a descendant of a Welsh chieftain known as Elystan Glodrydd. Another John Lloyd, a later member of the family, was a distinguished scholar and poet.

Abergwesyn is 5 miles farther up the valley. It is a lonely hamlet consisting of a small chapel and a few scattered cottages. It stands on a plateau 1,100 feet above sea level, at the confluence of the *Gwesyn* with the Irfon, and surrounded by lofty hills. The half-hour's labour of climbing to the summit of the height opposite the inn is well repaid by the glorious view obtained.

At Abergwesyn the road divides. The left branch follows the Irfon, which above the hamlet is a mountain torrent, raging in the narrow confining channel it has cut in the slate rock, and whirling and foaming in the huge cauldrons it has scooped out. A mile or so up it is the **Wolf's Leap**, a deep and rugged gorge in a spot of such striking and solitary grandeur that the spectator is almost as much impressed with the prospect as a whole as with even the most awesome of its details. This road, one of the wildest and loneliest in Wales, and with gradients of 1 in 4, continues with tarred surface, to Tregaron, 14 miles away in Cardiganshire.

The right-hand branch of the road at Abergwesyn offers an alternative route back to Llanwrtyd, but it is double the length of that along the valley. The country through which it winds is less wild than the upper valley of the Irfon, but is very beautiful. The road, at one time rather rough, has now been tarred. It passes the delightful seat of Llwynmadoc and the village of **Beulah**. From the latter it runs almost due south to the main road between Llangammarch and Llanwrtyd.

Garn. This hill rises 1,464 feet above sea-level and opens up a magnificent prospect. It can readily be ascended from Llanwrtyd by following the road up the valley beyond the farther gates of Dolecoed Park. A few hundred yards beyond the Park, the road turns to the left over a stone bridge, and at this point a gate on the right gives access to a mountain road which leads up Garn by an easy gradient.

Beyond Glen View, the road leads to a ledge, from which there is a short and easy climb to the summit. From this vantage point one looks upon miles and miles of the beautiful country spread all round.

Pen Twyn, a companion pillar to Garn, stands on the western side of the Irfon and commands a similar view. A zigzag path has been constructed to a resting-place called *Spion Kop*, about half-way up. The view even from this spot is delightful and more than compensates the labour of mounting to it, although it is, of course, less extensive than the prospect from the summit. To reach the highest point, the climber strikes up the slope above Spion Kop at will, there being no defined track.

LLANDRINDOD WELLS

Banks. *Lloyds; Barclays; Midland.*

Baths. Of various kinds at the Park Baths. There is a Swimming Pool at the *Metropole Hotel.*

Boating. On the lake on the Common.

Bowls. 4 Greens in Rock Park and 1 in the Recreation Ground. Tournament in August, and occasional international and other championships.

Cinema. *Grand Pavilion.*

Coaches run trips during the season to a large number of places of interest, including the Elan Valley and Birmingham Waterworks; Abbey-cwm-hir; Newbridge-on-Wye; Builth Wells; Aberystwyth; the *Forest Inn*, Radnor Forest, for Water-Break-its-Neck; the Alpine Bridge, etc. Connections with provincial centres and daily service to and from London.

Distances. Abbey - cwm - hir, 10; Builth Wells, 8; Cardiff, 66; Doldowlod, 7; Elan Valley, 18; Hereford, 41; Leominster, 35; Llanbadarn, 5; Llangammarch Wells, 16; Llanwrtyd Wells, 19; Llanyre, 2; London, 173; Rhayader, 12.

Early Closing Day. Wednesday.

Entertainments. Dancing at *Winter Gardens* and in several hotels. Sunday concerts during the season.

Fishing. Fishing licences for the Ithon and all information can be obtained from Anglers' Depôt, Park Crescent (and *see* p. 296). Coarse fishing in Lake. (Details from the Surveyor, Town Hall).

Golf. The *Llandrindod Wells' Club* has an 18-hole course. *Tel.:* 2010.

Hotels. *Barcourt; Metropole; Rock Park; Glen Usk; Beaufort; Rose Hill; Mostyn; Commodore; Old County Club.*

Hours for taking the Waters. Weekdays: 7 a.m. to 9 a.m.; 11 a.m. to 12.30 p.m.; 3 p.m. to 4.30 p.m. Sundays: 7 a.m. to 9 a.m.; 11 a.m. to 1 p.m. The Chalybeate Spring is free; for other waters a charge is made.

Information Bureau. Adjoining Town Hall in Temple Street.

Population. 3,300.

Post Office. Station Crescent.

Putting. Prince's Avenue.

Tennis. Recreation Ground, on Common and at various hotels.

Llandrindod Wells stands pre-eminent among the inland health and pleasure resorts of Wales. It is situated on a plateau 700 feet above sea-level, overlooking the charming valley of the **Ithon,** a tributary of the Wye, and around it rise the green Cambrian Hills, not mighty peaks like Snowdon and Cader Idris, but gentle hills and glens.

As a resort, it was first brought into notice by its healing waters, and these continue to attract large numbers of visitors; but in recent years the town has grown in popularity as a holiday centre for those who appreciate a place that is up to date and yet restful, with facilities for outdoor recreations of all kinds and adequate provision for indoor entertainment. For motorists the town is most conveniently placed. The excellent hotel accommodation and number of conference halls available have made Llandrindod Wells a favourite meeting place for conferences of all kinds.

The modern name of the town signifies "the Church of the Trinity" and refers to the old Parish Church near the lake.

Llandrindod Wells lies on the east side of the Ithon valley, about six miles above the junction of that river with the Wye. It is divided into two sections by the railway running north and south, and a little to the east of the railway **Temple Street** runs approximately parallel with it.

Temple Street is the road by which most visitors will enter the town. Midway is **Temple Square,** a junction of five ways by the Methodist Church. To the north of this is the **Library** and the **Town Hall,** with the pleasant **Temple Gardens** opposite.

From the Methodist Church, one of the "five ways" is **Princes Avenue,** a wide road across the 50-acre **Common,** with its putting greens, to the **Lake**—14 acres in area, nearly a mile in circumference, and with an island in the middle. The lake provides safe boating, and is stocked with chub, tench, carp and other coarse fish.

Crowning a knoll not far from the southern end of the lake is the **Parish Church,** locally known as the "old church", which was restored and re-opened in 1895. Above the lake and the church is the 18-hole **Golf Course** of the Llandrindod Wells Golf Club. **Little Hill,** 1,165 feet, the highest ground in the immediate vicinity of Llandrindod rise behind the course. A fairly steep road goes up to the summit (*Cairn Tea Room*).

From Temple Square a short walk along **Spa Road** brings one to **Holy Trinity Church** (the Town Church) on the left. Behind this is the **Recreation Ground,** with tennis courts and bowling green, and the **Grand Pavilion,** which houses a cinema, and can accommodate an audience of 1,200. The path along the southern boundary of the Recreation Ground leads in one direction to Temple Street and at the other end passes under the railway into **Rock Park.** The park occupies a picturesque glen and contains the Springs for which Llandrindod Wells became famous. Trees, shrubs and flowers, and the little brook that tumbles through the glen, make this a most attractive spot in which to linger. In Rock Park are the **Pump Room,** the present **Medicinal Baths,** and the **Winter Garden** in which concerts and

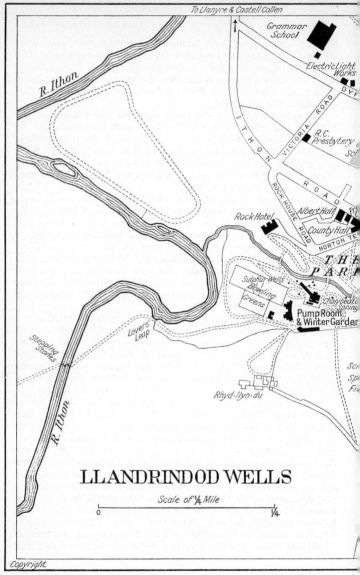

To Llanyre & Castell Collen

Grammar School

Electric Light Works

R. Ithon

DYF

ITHON

VICTORIA ROAD

R.C. Presbytery

Sch

ROAD

ROCK HOUSE ROAD

Rock Hotel

Albert Hall

County Hall

PO

NORTON TE

THE
PARK

Sulphur Wells

Bowling Greens

Chalybeate Spring

Pump Room & Winter Garden

Lovers Leap

Stepping Stones

R. Ithon

Rhyd-llyn-du

Sc
Sp
Fi

LLANDRINDOD WELLS

Scale of ¼ Mile

0   ¼

Copyright

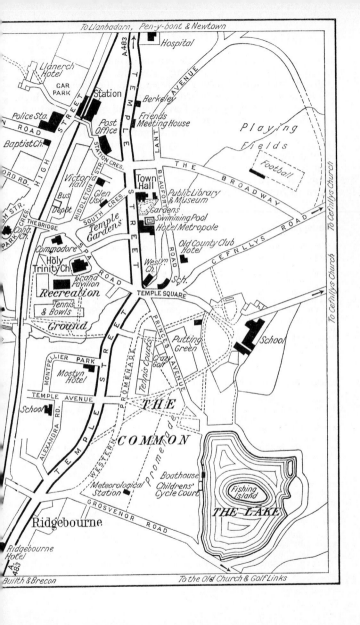

dances are held. Beyond these are the famous bowling greens on which so many championships are held.

From the Pump Room a path leads to the *Ithon* at a spot known as *Lovers' Leap*, a projecting rock about 30 feet high.

Leaving the Park by **Park Terrace** instead of returning under the railway, one comes to **County Hall;** opposite this, on an island site, is **Christ Church** (Congregational), a former pastor of which was the eccentric Kilsby-Jones. In the **High Street** just beyond the church may be seen the site of the former Baths, destroyed by fire and now temporarily transferred to the Park. From Christ Church one may cross the railway bridge and return by Spa Road to Temple Square.

The Springs

The Pump Room is open daily at the following hours: 8–9 *a.m.;* 11 *a.m.–* 1 *p.m.;* 3–4.30 *p.m.*

The Romans searched for mineral waters in the neighbourhood and gave the name *Balnea Silures* (Silurian Baths) to one place in the locality. But the comparatively modern record of the medicinal use of the waters goes back to the days of Charles II. Even at that time the place was known as "Ye Wells." It was not, however, until the late nineteenth century that real growth of the spa developed. From time to time additional springs were discovered and developed but the only springs in use today are those in Rock Park. These include no fewer than eight springs, furnishing lithia, saline, radium sulphur, magnesium, chalybeate, Roman and other waters.

Excursions from Llandrindod Wells

Disserth, Newbridge-on-Wye. Just under 2 miles south of Llandrindod the Builth road passes **Gaer Ddu** (Black Fortress) an ancient camp beyond which is **Howey** a little village on the banks of a tributary of the Ithon, which at times assumes torrential proportions. At one time all locally-grown corn was ground at Howey Mill. South-east of Howey and over-hanging the Builth road are the **Carneddau Hills,** a high range of rocks running almost parallel for several miles. The loftiest summit is 1,430 feet.

Beyond the village, a road goes right at Crossway for **Disserth** where the plain but interesting church is beautifully situated. The box pews, some with dates as remote as 1666 and the rough-hewn roof-timbers are of varnished pitch-pine. In the churchyard are some particularly fine box trees while some of the memorial stones bear quaint inscriptions.

Over the bridge at Disserth the road leads (left in ½ mile), or field paths immediately left of the bridge, to **Newbridge-on-Wye,** a pretty village.

To Cefnllys. Cefnllys lies two miles east of Llandrindod and can be reached by road or paths past Bach-y-graig.

On the opposite bank of the river rises a precipitous hill, surmounted by the entrenchments of the ancient **Cefnllys Castle,** which was built about

1242 by Ralph Mortimer, Earl of Wigmore and Lord of Maelienydd (the Yellow Hills), but the site is said to have been previously occupied by the Princes of South Wales, and a silver thumb-ring, dug up in what has been called the Castle Garden, may have been the signet ring of one of the princes.

The plain and simple **Church,** close to the Ithon, is dedicated to St. Michael. The registers date from 1679. The pulpit bears the date 1663, and there is a well-preserved Perpendicular screen. The key is kept at the Rectory (Spa Road, Llandrindod Wells).

It is difficult to realize that there was a time when Cefnllys was so important that it was made a borough, and that it formed one of a group which returned a Member of Parliament from the reign of Henry VIII until the Redistribution Act of 1885. Courts Leet were held, under the presidency of the steward or deputy steward, at the farmhouse called the Neuadd, when the jury made presentment as to persons to be chosen as burgesses. Those burgesses formed the electorate of the constituency. The number dwindled to six or eight, but a polling station had to be provided for them in case of a contested election. The electorate was increased by the Reform Act of 1832, and the contributory boroughs then were New Radnor, Knighton, Presteigne, Rhayader, Knucklas and Cefnllys, but even in the middle of that century and while still a borough, Cefnllys contained only three houses of the value of ten pounds a year.

The **Alpine Bridge,** or *Pont-y-graig*, spans the Ithon about a mile north of Cefnllys where there is charming river scenery. The bridge is of wood, reinforced with steel girders and quite simple, but the environment has great natural beauty. The deep banks of the rocky river are covered with mosses, ferns and flowers to the water's edge, and shaded by overhanging trees in great variety, while the waters of the Ithon rush through the defile.

Llanyre and Castell Collen. Llanyre is a small village a few miles north-westward of Llandrindod Wells. Near by is the site of **Castell Collen** (Castle of the Hazel Tree), in the parish of Llanfihangel-Fach-or-Helygan, a one-time rectangular Roman camp, possibly known as *Magos*. It was defended by stone walls, 8 feet thick and a fosse. On the west side is outer work. The buildings inside were all of stone. Various finds made during excavations may be seen at the museum in the Library in Llandrindod Wells.

To Abbey-Cwm-Hir

Buses connect with Rhayader and Llanidloes.
Distance. 9 miles.

Inn. Teas available.
Admission. The Abbey is open all the week. Free.

The charm of this excursion lies at least as much in the pleasant scenery through which the road passes as in the scanty ruins themselves.

The route lies northward from Llandrindod Wells, along the main road to Newtown, Montgomeryshire, passing **Llanbadarn Fawr Church** and **Crossgates,** where the road intersects at right-angles the main highway from London to Aberystwyth. Half a mile farther, the pipe track of the Birmingham Waterworks is crossed at **Fron,** where the aqueduct tunnels through a hill near the Rock Baptist Chapel (to the right). Less than a mile farther the road leading to Abbey-cwm-hir goes off on the left and in a few minutes the valley of the *Clwedog* is reached. The road from this point is almost level, but winds through the hills, which rise sharply right and left, with delightful views.

As Abbey-cwm-hir is approached more closely, the valley becomes narrower. At the entrance to the valley the highway crosses the brook, and the valley broadens. Between the river and the higher ground along which the road goes are the scanty ruins of the once celebrated Abbey, reputed to have been the second largest religious house of the Cistercian order.

Abbey-cwm-hir is generally said to have been founded in 1143, by Cadwallon ap Madoc, Lord of Moelynaidd, but this has been challenged on the ground that as the Welsh were then in revolt against the Normans, a Welsh prince would not be likely to apply to a Norman bishop for Norman monks. In 1231, Henry III, enraged by alleged treachery on the part of the monks, caused considerable damage to be done to the structure, and in 1401 it was practically destroyed by Owen Glendower in his conflict with the English king. The building was only partially restored, and on the dissolution of monastic bodies by Henry VIII, the manors and lands belonging to the Abbey—valued at £28 17s. 4d.—were granted to Sir Thomas Williams, one of the Lords Marchers.

The area of the ruins is very extensive—255 ft. by 73 ft.—but the nature of the superstructure can only be imagined, for there remains but the solid foundations of the chapel and cloisters, the massive stonework that formed the steps of the high altar, and here and there the broken base of an Early English clustered column. Six pointed arches belonging to the Abbey, with ornamented piers and carved figures, are said to have been taken to Llanidloes, where they form part of the Parish Church. The screen appears to have been taken to Newtown, Montgomeryshire; much of the beautiful carved stone was used for the erection of an Elizabethan house in the neighbourhood, and a quantity of the stone walls was carted to Llanbister for the construction of the church in that village. The monastery was strongly entrenched by earthworks thrown across the valley eastward and westward, and stood in an enclosure of ten acres. The fishponds still remain, and with the other grounds form part of the demesne of the present Abbey—a handsome mansion.

It is strongly maintained by many antiquaries that the remains of the last native Prince of Wales (Llewelyn) were interred in the Abbey, and not in a field at Cefn-y-bedd. There is much ground for the assumption that the prince died in the Roman Catholic faith, and that the excommunication pronounced against him was withdrawn. Therefore, it is argued, the prince would be interred with full honours, and the only suitable place in the locality at the time was this Abbey.

Modern religious life in the village is represented by a beautiful little church and a Baptist chapel.

A short distance to the north-west, in a narrow defile called **Bwlch-y-sarnau** ("the defile of the causeway"), can be traced the remains of the Roman road running from Castell Collen into Montgomeryshire. On a neighbouring hill named **Garn** is a British cairn.

LLANDRINDOD WELLS TO PRESTEIGNE

Distances. From Llandrindod Wells: Penybont, 5; Llandegley, 6½; Water-Break-its-Neck, 12; New Radnor, 15; Presteigne, 22½.

The main Newtown, Montgomeryshire, road out of Llandrindod leads northward to **Llanbadarn Fawr** (3¾ miles). Here the church is dedicated to St. Padarn who founded the first church on the site in A.D. 520. In the porch, left, is a small inscribed Roman Centurial stone marked Valflavini (Century of Valerius Flavinus) which is probably about 1,500 years old. The inner doorway consists of a fine Norman arch and carved typanum, the only specimen of its kind in South Wales.

At the Cross Gates crossing turn right for Penybont, a small hamlet which at one time, owing to its central position, was quite an important place. Being on the main road between London and Aberystwyth, a constant stream of traffic passed through the village in the old coaching days, especially during the summer months—a feature which has to some extent been revived by the long-distance motor coaches. The periodical fairs for the sale of cattle and horses are usually well attended.

Passing over a picturesque and breezy common, we reach about a mile and a half beyond Penybont the little village of—

Llandegley

6½ miles from Llandrindod. It has a series of mineral springs— saline, sulphur and chalybeate. The **Well House** is situated in a meadow, approached by a broad path from the centre of the village; the chalybeate spring is a little way off.

The waters of Llandegley were formerly believed to be a remedy for the St. Tegla's disease, or the "falling sickness," and it is said that very curious customs were observed in monastic times by sufferers who used the water.

Of the **Church,** dedicated to St. Tegla, the most interesting feature is the ancient screen.

South-west of the village are the **Llandegley Rocks,** a favourite resort which affords a fine view.

Five miles from Penybont is the *Forest Inn* where cars may halt for the walk to Water-Break-its-Neck.

Water-Break-its-Neck lies on the southern slopes of the extensive upland of Radnor Forest. On a fine summer day it is a most enjoyable walk over the upland to the **Warren Plantation,** which contains the fall. At the highest points magnificent views are obtained. The track is easy to follow. It begins opposite the inn, to the left of *Tomen Castle,* another fortified mound, and runs past a farm and up the hill to a stile. Still on the rise, the track leads to a gate, and then almost at once comes to a fence, where it inclines to the right, and a short distance farther enters a dell through which it passes to a stile. Thence it runs straight on to a cart-track, which goes to the right of a wood that must be entered by a stile. A few yards from this stile is the glen in which the fall graphically known as Water-Break-its-Neck will be found, except after a long period of dry weather. The cataract is 70 to 80 feet high, and falls precipitously into a deep and dark chasm. The bottom of the glen into which the water falls can be reached by a path to the right.

Radnor Forest is not the tree-clad area its name would imply, but a bare uncultivated mountain 2,186 feet high. The scenery as one crosses the various tracks is of supreme grandeur.

From the *Forest Inn* the main road bears away to the left through uncultivated country, and in less than a mile passes, left, the church of **Llanfihangel Nant Melan.** In another 3 miles is **New Radnor** (*Eagle Hotel*) at the head of a fertile valley. In Norman times it was a place of importance, and was strongly fortified. The scanty ruins of a once almost impregnable *Castle* stand on a commanding eminence above what is now practically a country village. The Castle was built in the latter half of the eleventh century. It was demolished by King John, rebuilt by his son Henry III, and finally destroyed by Owen Glendower.

In the reign of Henry VIII, Radnorshire received its present name and New Radnor was made the county town. The shire or county court was held alternately at New Radnor and Rhayader. In the course of time Presteigne superseded Rhayader and ultimately became the county town and the site of the present county buildings. The assizes are still held in the Shirehall at Presteigne, but all the other administrative work of the county is carried out at Llandrindod Wells, on account of its central position. Until 1885 New Radnor was the chief of the group of Radnor boroughs which returned a member to Parliament. The Acts passed for the reform of municipal corporations swept away all its ancient privileges of local government, and the borough is now merged for all purposes in the county.

Harpton Court is about 1½ miles south-east of New Radnor. A mile farther in the same direction is **Old Radnor,** or *Pen-y-graig*, which possesses a fine old church with a rich screen, an organ case of the time of Henry VIII, and what is probably the largest and oldest font in Britain. A mile eastward are the **Stanner Rocks** and extensive limekilns which produce a fertiliser, widely celebrated as the "Old Radnor Lime".

Harley Valley, running towards the north-west, is a beautiful ravine. At its head is Shepherd's Well, and beyond are peat beds, from which the townsfolk used to get their fuel before the railway was made.

During July and August numbers of "pickers" frequent the hills to harvest the whinberries, which grow on what are locally known as "wires".

East of New Radnor the road continues 3 miles to **Walton** and past **Burva Bank,** crowned by its ancient camp and the point at which **Offas' Dyke** crosses into Herefordshire.

Presteigne

Hotels. *Radnorshire Arms; Bull; Duke's Arms; Castle; Oxford Arms.*

is pleasantly situated on the Lugg, one of the largest feeders of the Wye. The population numbers about twelve hundred. There are facilities for fishing, shooting, golf, bowls and tennis and a Floral and Agricultural Show is held each year in August.

The **Church,** re-dedicated to St. Andrew by the Normans, is a handsome building, comprising nave, tower, chancel, north and south aisles and

Lady Chapel. Part of the north wall of the present church is Norman and there are other traces of Norman work. Two pillars in the walls of the north aisle are Norman. On the north wall is a Flemish tapestry of the early-sixteenth century depicting the triumphal entry of Christ into Jerusalem. The window over the communion table in the Lady Chapel contains all that remains of the old painted glass. In the tower is a fine peal of eight bells (tenor 14 cwt.) on which the curfew is still rung. Indeed, the curfew has been rung for nearly 400 years and Presteigne is one of the few towns where this practice continues. The registers date from 1561 and are the earliest in Radnorshire.

The *Radnorshire Arms*, a picturesque black-and-white hotel in High Street, bears the date 1616 over its porch. It is said to have been for a time the residence of Sir Charles Hatton, who had been Queen Elizabeth I's secretary. It was first opened as an inn in 1792, and here the coaches to and from Aberystwyth stopped for many years.

A wooded eminence, called the **Warden,** on the west of the town, is a public recreation ground and affords beautiful views. It was the site of a Norman castle, the mound and courtyard foundations of which may still be seen.

About a mile from Presteigne are the picturesque ruins of **Stapleton Castle.** From the summit of **Wapley Hill,** $2\frac{1}{2}$ miles, eight or nine counties may be seen. The top of the hill is the site of an exceptionally fine ancient British camp, which is an excellent specimen of early earthwork fortification. Tradition says that it was the last home of Caractacus, before his final defeat by the Romans.

Knighton

Road Route (19 *miles*) passes through Llanbadarn Fawr, Crossgates, Penybont, Llanfihangel Rhydithon, the sequestered village of Bleddfa, and Pilleth.

Hotels. *Norton Arms; Swan; Chandos.*
Market Day. Thursday.
Early Closing Day. Friday.

Knighton, a market town of about 1,850 inhabitants, on the north-eastern border of Radnorshire, is called by the Welsh *Tref-y-clawdd*, "The Town-on-the-Dyke", because it is built on **Offa's Dyke.** The rampart may be traced for several miles north and south of the town and is seen at several points in the Wye Valley, and a short distance beyond **Frydd Hill** is a portion but little injured by time or man, the Dyke being still about 30 feet high and the trench some 15 feet deep.

Knighton stands on a hill about 700 feet above sea-level, and is surrounded by high hills clad with wood and pasture. From its site proceed three valleys, two broad and park-like, the other winding between overhanging woods. Through one of the broad vales flows the Teme, here dividing Radnorshire from Shropshire. Some of the houses were built in long-bygone days, but there are also many modern villas, for Knighton is an attractive place either for permanent or temporary residence, especially for those who find pleasure in angling—the Teme affording some excellent fishing. Tennis, cricket, golf and bowls are available and there is a modern cinema and a public library.

The lower portion of the Church dates from the early twelfth century; the upper portion has been restored at various periods and the whole heightened in modern times. The old Church was taken down in 1876 and the present nave and chancel built between 1876 and 1897.

Knighton once possessed a castle, of which there are now but the scantiest traces on Castle Bank, at the upper end of the town. In the public recreation grounds called Bryn-y-Castell, on the eastern outskirts of the town, is a large tumulus, of which, however, nothing appears to be known.

Craig-y-Don is a wooded dingle 1½ miles from Knighton.

Caer Caradoc, or Gaer Ditches, an ancient camp on a hill some 3 miles north-east of the town, and east of the Clun road, is supposed to have been the scene of the final defeat of that brave British chief, Caradoc, or Caractacus.

Three miles west of Knighton is **Knucklas,** a very tiny place, but one of the Radnor Boroughs until that constituency was abolished by the Reform Act of 1885. Its Welsh name, *Y Cnwclas*, signifies "The Green Hillock." This rises above the Teme, and was once crowned by a castle of which scarcely anything remains. On one side of its site is a cliff 300 feet high.

Knucklas Castle was long held by the Mortimers. Tradition connects the site still earlier with King Arthur, and claims that here he married Guinevere.

Near **Stowe,** two miles east of Knighton, remains of a Roman villa were discovered in 1925.

Near the village of **Bucknell,** which has a station about 4 miles beyond Knighton, is another ancient camp also connected with the British chief Caradoc. It is known as **Coxwall Knoll,** and some antiquarians consider that this and not Caer Caradoc was the scene of his last stand.

At **Pilleth,** 5 miles south-west of Knighton and about the same distance from Llangunllo station, Owen Glendower took Sir Edmund Mortimer prisoner in 1402. According to tradition, eleven hundred of Mortimer's army were slain while being driven down Pilleth Hill, or Bryn Glas, westward of the church. Colour was given to the story by the uncovering of a mass of bones by a plough, after which agricultural operations on the spot, which was probably the common burial-place of the slain, were discontinued and the ground was planted with trees.

RHAYADER AND THE ELAN VALLEY

(*Llandrindod to Rhayader*, 12 *miles. From Rhayader to the bridge between the two lower Reservoirs*, 7½ *miles.*)

The shorter route between Llandrindod Wells and Rhayader runs through Llanyre to the Wye Valley and then up the latter. It is a very pretty road, much of it being bordered by trees, and is less busy than the longer route, via Llanbadarn Fawr and Cross Gates. This, the main road, leaves Llandrindod by Temple Street and turns sharp to left ¼ mile beyond Llanbadarn Church along the Aberystwyth highway. From Cross Gates the course of the aqueduct of the Birmingham Waterworks can sometimes be seen to the right of the road. As the road proceeds westward, it opens up a fine view of Llandrindod Wells and an ever-changing panorama of the Radnorshire mountains. From the summit of Dolau Chapel Pitch, there is a beautiful view of Nantmel Valley. Then the valve-houses of the aqueduct are passed, and Dafarn Eithen Pitch, with its summit 811 feet above sea-level, has to be ascended. About a mile beyond this hill the aqueduct crosses the road, a white gate at each side marking the spot.

Rhayader

Bus Services. Daily to and from Llandrindod Wells, Cardiff, Aberystwyth, etc. Several times weekly from other centres. On Fair days and market days in summer to Llanidloes and Garreg Ddu.
Early Closing Day. Thursday.
Market Day. Wednesday.

Hotels. *Lion Royal; Royal Oak; Castle; Elan Valley; Warwick; Claremont; Elan.*
Sport. Bowls, tennis, putting, billiards, fishing, pony-trekking.
Caravan Park and Camping Site. Municipal site adjoins A 44 and the Wye.

Rhayader or *Rhaiadr-Gwy*, "the Waterfall on the Wye", is a clean, healthy little market town which is said to have existed since the sixth century. It owes its name to a series of small falls that were practically destroyed in 1780 by the erection of the stone bridge which carries the high-road over the river.

The town is finely situated among bold and high hills, the sides of which are pierced with deep ravines and gorges. Four streets radiate from the War Memorial, and are named after the cardinal points of the compass. Between North Street and the Wye is Church Street, ranking as one of the principal thoroughfares.

310

For several centuries the town was dominated by a **Castle** on a hill by the side of the Wye. Only a trace of it remains. The stronghold is said to have been built about 1178 by Rhys ap Gruffydd, Prince of South Wales.

The Park and Recreation Ground, opened in 1951 and known as **Waun Capel,** lies in a setting of natural beauty on both banks of the Wye, and offers various sports facilties.

The **Church,** dedicated to St. Clement, Bishop of Rome, A.D. 67–76, is thought to stand on the site of the castle chapel. It was rebuilt in 1733, the tower is 1783, and a thorough restoration was concluded in 1898.

On the opposite side of the Wye and south of the bridge is **Cwmdeuddwr Church,** of probably older foundation than Rhayader Parish Church. Near its churchyard gate is a tumulus.

Birmingham Corporation Reservoirs

There is excellent fishing in the reservoirs. Tickets from Elan Estate Office, Rhayader.

West of Rhayader are the high and far-extending **Cwmdeuddwr Hills,** and through the valleys run the rivers *Elan* and *Claerwen*, which have been impounded to provide a water supply for the city of Birmingham.

The land in the Elan and Claerwen district being very poor, with few inhabitants, but having a large volume of pure water running in its streams, was admirably adapted for the gathering ground of the water required by a great city. The area purchased by Birmingham is 45,562 acres, or about 71 square miles, and its highest point is 2,115 feet above the level of the sea.

The original scheme provided for the construction of three Reservoirs in the Elan Valley and three in the valley of the Claerwen. All the former were completed and brought into use by 1904. The Claerwen valley plan, however, was revised and a new dam constructed on the river between 1946 and 1952 in place of the proposed three dams authorized in 1892. Thereby the gross storage was increased to 21,800 million gallons.

The drive through the valley is very delightful, good roads having been constructed alongside the Reservoirs. Even before the formation of the great artificial lakes, the romantic valley of Elan was one of the attractions of Mid-Wales, and had been described as one of the wonders of Radnorshire. Shelley wrote of the scenery as "divine." A thousand acres of the hillsides have been planted by the Birmingham Corporation, and the increased surface of the water also adds to the former charms of the district.

The nearest point of the Reservoirs to Rhayader is but 4 miles distant. Only a short distance farther is the **Caban Côch Dam,** 556 feet in length, 122½ feet thick at its base, rising 122 feet above the river bed, below which its foundations go down 25 feet. Over its summit, in time of flood, there is a magnificent waterfall that dashes into the river bed so far below. The

Caban Côch Reservoir extends 3½ miles up the Elan, 2 miles up the Claerwen, and has a surface area of 500 acres.

Under the deep water are the sites of a Baptist chapel and the old chapel-of-ease for the parish of Nantgwyllt. Submerged also are the sites of Cwm Elan and Nantgwyllt House, each a residence of the poet Shelley.

This great lake is bisected by a submerged dam at **Carreg Ddu.** This is regarded as one of the most remarkable features of the stupendous works, for it is a unique engineering expedient adopted for the purpose of obtaining a sufficient height of water above Frankley Reservoir, near Birmingham.

The submerged dam is 40 feet lower than the dam at Caban Côch. Over it is a viaduct, from which a road, about 2¼ miles long, goes to the Dol-y-Mynach Dam in the Claerwen valley. Near the submerged dam is a tower, in which the flow of water to the filter beds is regulated. The route of the aqueduct to Birmingham lies to the south of Rhayader, to the north of Four Crosses, near Knighton, Ludlow and Cleobury Mortimer, through Wyre Forest, and by Kidderminster, Stourbridge and Hagley to Frankley, where the water is stored. The water crosses the Wye, the Ithon, the Teme three times, the Severn and the Stour, besides numerous smaller streams.

Cars take the road along the east side of the Caban Côch Reservoir to the head of the great lake, where a bridge carries the road over the bed of the Elan. Motorists should proceed with caution at this point, however, for the bridge over the stream connecting the reservoirs is very narrow, and on the succeeding hill is a very sharp hairpin bend.

Above the bridge is the **Pen-y-gareg Dam,** 417½ feet long, holding up the water of a lake with a surface of 124 acres. A good road on the west side of the valley skirts the lake, which stretches northward for about 1½ miles. There we come to the **Craig Goch Reservoir,** 217 acres in area and some 2½ miles in length. Above its dam, which is 120 feet high and 390 feet long, a road is carried on arches through which the overflowing water pours, making a very fine sight.

The road over the submerged dam at Carreg Ddu leads to the Claerwen valley. In this valley at Llanerch-y-cawr is an old Welsh longhouse, no longer habitable but on which a preservation order has been made because of its historical interest. A further sample of this type of farmhouse was dismantled a few years ago at Cilverwynt, a mile or so farther up the valley, and was subsequently re-erected at the Welsh Folk Museum at St. Fagan's. Immediately upstream of the confluence of the rivers Claerwen and Arban is the **Claerwen Reservoir** 184 feet high and with a curved dam 1,166 feet in length (almost twice as long as the Caban Dam) which is a wonderful sight in times of flood. The water conserved forms a reservoir nearly 4 miles long with a capacity of 10,625 million gallons. A 12-feet carriageway with footpaths either side across the dam and two raised dais on either side of the roadway over the central main spillway section offer very fine viewpoints.

INDEX

313

315

316

317